Ruth & Esther

Other Focus on the Bible Commentaries

Old Testament

Deuteronomy Allan Harman ISBN 1 85792 665 X
Judges Dale Ralph Davis ISBN 1 85792 578 5
Judges & Ruth Stephen Dray ISBN 1 85792 323 5
Ruth and Esther Boyd A. Luter and Barry C. Davis ISBN 1 85792 805 9
1 Samuel Dale Ralph Davis ISBN 1 85792 516 5
2 Samuel Dale Ralph Davis ISBN 1 85792 335 9
Job Bill Cotton ISBN 1 85792 515 7
Proverbs Eric Lane ISBN 1 85792 451 7
Song of Songs Richard Brooks ISBN 1 85792 486 X
Daniel Robert Fyall ISBN 1 85792 249 2
Hosea Michael Eaton ISBN 1 85792 277 8
Jonah, Micah, Nahum, Habakkuk & Zephaniah John L. Mackay ISBN 1 85792 392 8
Haggai, Zechariah & Malachi John L Mackay ISBN 1 85792 067 8

New Testament

Matthew Matthew Price ISBN 1 85792 285 9
Mark Geoffrey Grogan ISBN 1 85792 114 3
1 Corinthians Paul Barnett ISBN 1 85792 598 X
2 Corinthians Geoffrey Grogan ISBN 1 85792 220 4
1 & 2 Thessalonians Richard Mayhue ISBN 1 85792 452 5
1 & 2 Timothy & Titus Douglas Milne ISBN 1 85792 169 0
Hebrews Walter Riggans ISBN 1 85792 328 6
1 Peter Derek Cleave ISBN 1 85792 337 5
2 Peter & Jude Paul Gardner ISBN 1 85792 338 3
1, 2 & 3 John Michael Eaton ISBN 1 85792 152 6
Revelation Paul Gardner ISBN 1 85792 329 4

Ruth & Esther

God behind the Seen

A. Boyd Luter
& Barry C. Davis

Christian Focus

ISBN 1 85792 805 9

This edition published in 2003
by
Christian Focus Publications,
Geanies House, Fearn, Ross-shire,
IV20 1TW, Scotland

www.christianfocus.com

Previously published in 1995 by
Baker Book House, Grand Rapids, USA

Cover design by Alister MacInnes

Printed and bound by
Mackays of Chatham

Contents

Preface

Tragedy and triumph—the books of Ruth and Esther portray the stories of two women who achieve success against all odds. One woman overcomes a personal tragedy, the other a nationwide crisis. The roads they take to succeed, however, are quite different.

Ruth, a woman living in the country of Moab, marries into a Jewish refugee family only to see her husband, father-in-law, and brother-in-law die. Her sister-in-law deserts her and even her mother-in-law, in grief, tries to send her away—back to her own family, away from the people of God. Ruth, however, determines both to stay with her mother-in-law, Naomi, who desperately needs Ruth's help, and to serve the one true God, the God of Israel. Despite devastating losses, Ruth stands true to her word, willingly cares for her mother-in-law, and acts righteously before God and before her newly adopted countrymen, the Jews. Because of Ruth's faithfulness, God, in his providence, blesses her (and subsequently all of humanity) beyond anything she (or we) could ever have imagined. Ruth honors God; God, in turn, wonderfully cares for her as one of his own.

By contrast, Esther, a Jewish orphan living in exile in the Medo-Persian empire, marries into royalty—Gentile royalty—and becomes queen. Yet in order to do so (and at the instructions of her cousin who is also her adoptive father), she conceals her Jewish faith from all who are in the palace and even from her husband, the king. Furthermore, when her people are condemned to death by the prime minister, Esther at first tries to avoid her responsibility to speak out on behalf of her people, preferring rather to hide in what she believes to be the security of the palace. When her adoptive father exposes the foolishness of her plan, however, Esther relents and determines to win her husband, the king, over to her side (and hence to the side of her people). Esther is successful, the prime minister is deposed, and Esther's adoptive father becomes prime minister. With the crisis averted and their enemies defeated, the Jews establish the holiday of Purim to commemorate their actions in delivering themselves from their enemies.

The books of Ruth and Esther, quite obviously, are more than merely stories of the struggles of two women. These books picture the struggles of two groups of people (Jews at different times in history) attempting to manage their day-to-day existence, one (in the Book of Ruth) desiring to honor God at a time when those around them are committed to godless self-gratification, the other (in the Book of Esther) seeking to overcome a life-shattering crisis when they themselves are far from their expected place of blessing. The Jews in each story, however, take significantly different approaches to secure their goals. The former resort to spiritual and moral measures to achieve their ends; the latter lean toward a political solution.

This joint volume on the books of Ruth and Esther highlights the different actions taken in the respective stories. In doing so, the two commentaries themselves take somewhat different approaches in their individual presentations of the materials at hand. Although both present the flow and structure of each of the main sections of their books, the commentary on Ruth (by Luter) takes a more pastoral approach than does the commentary on Esther (by Davis), which tends to interweave more technical details together with an application component. (The commentators have intentionally chosen these different tactics in order to fill significant gaps that exist among already published evangelical commentaries on Ruth and Esther.) Neither commentary, however, addresses to any great extent higher critical issues, preferring rather to focus its attention on the exegesis of the texts at hand.

Despite their methodological differences, both commentaries recognize a similar theme that flows through each of their respective books—the providential care by the unseen God for His people. Though the sovereign and loving actions of the Lord are, at most, subtle in Ruth and no more than "peeking between the cracks" of the text of Esther, God's guiding hand is nevertheless always present and powerful on behalf of his people, even when painful loss (Ruth 1:3–5) and unjust schemes (Esther 3–4) seem to have the upper hand. God's actions demonstrate that seemingly out-of-control crises, whether those described at the individual level in the Book of Ruth or those portrayed at the national level in the Book of Esther (or at any level of the believer's experience today), are under the watchful care of the one true God who faithfully carries out his all-wise plan for all of history and (most comfortingly) for all of his people.

These two commentaries have not been developed in a vacuum. They have been directed by the technical skills and personal encouragement of Allan Fisher, Jim Weaver, and Paul Engle, all of Baker Book House. Their various efforts in extending the invitation to write this volume and in patiently seeing the project through to its conclusion are greatly appreciated. In addition, Ralph Davis (no relation), the lead writer of the *Expositor's Guide to the Historical Books* series, deserves much recognition and thanks for having reviewed the early chapters of both of the present commentaries and for having offered valuable comments that have been beneficial in the development of the entire volume. His excellent work in authoring previous volumes in the series has set lofty standards of quality toward which the writers of this work have set their sights.

At the beginning of this project, the authors were both teaching in California, living in the same neighborhood, and even attending the same church. In the passage of time, however, the providential leadership of the Lord has put more than two thousand miles between them. From the human perspective, the writing of *God behind the Seen* might have been easier to complete had the authors been able to maintain eyeball-to-eyeball interaction and accountability. Yet, there is no doubt that the unseen God who guided Ruth into Boaz's field (Ruth 2:3) and gave King Ahasuerus insomnia (Esther 6:1) knows precisely what he is doing in these matters. The fact that this collaborative venture could be completed, despite the distance, is a tribute to our ever-present God. So too is the harmonious duet that the books of Ruth and Esther offer, despite the distance in miles and centuries that separated the events (and composition) of each.

Soli Deo gloria! (To God alone be glory!)

Easter 1994

Part 1

Expositions of the Book of Ruth

A. Boyd Luter

Introduction to Ruth

Suppose you walked out the door of your home tomorrow morning and found an unmarked parcel on your doorstep. Inside the package you find only an anonymous manuscript for a short story. Your curiosity is aroused, so you pore over what proves to be a delightful narrative.

Would you then put the short story aside and say, "That's the end of that!"? I doubt it. As a curious person I would be driven to know who had written this marvelous piece, when and why it was done, who were its intended readers, and the like.

Admittedly, not everyone is so curious. For some, just the pleasure of taking in the story of unknown origin is enough. But, since John Bunyan is not Erma Bombeck, it does make a difference to consider who wrote what, when, why, and for whom.

Perhaps you've heard it said of the interpretation of Scripture, "A text without a context is a pretext." Such a truism is first intended to prevent Bible students from misinterpreting Scripture by ripping a phrase or verse out of its literary setting or context. Careful consideration of the surrounding verses is often highly enlightening as to the meaning and significance of the passage in question.

It is equally valid, though, to speak of the historical context of a book of the Bible. It is not too much to say that it is a "pretext" to think that a book can be fully, even adequately, understood without some serious consideration of such background factors as authorship, date and occasion of writing, and the original audience as its wider context.

So, whether from natural curiosity or interpretive logic (take your pick), it should be concluded that the pursuit of such introductory questions is not boring prologue, unnecessary filler, or scholarly overkill. Exactly the opposite: such inquiries probe the living, breathing situation out of which a book like Ruth emerged to take its place in the canon of God-breathed Scripture (2 Tim. 3:16).

For the purposes of the average reader or expositor, it is helpful to parallel these questions to the opening night of a Broadway play. There, out of sight backstage is the beaming author of the story being played out before that first audience. The why and wherefore of his literary effort makes contact in that initial setting. Though nothing important is lost in content or the grandeur of a long-running play like "The Phantom of the Opera," the author and his thought processes are the circumstances of its literary birth.

What are the roots of the Book of Ruth? Who is the guiding authorial genius of this marvelous short story?[1] When and why was it written, and who were the first to hear this timeless narrative? How did Ruth fit into the Hebrew Scripture—what Christians call the Old Testament—for its long-running engagement? No pretense of a full-scale treatment will be made here.[2] But what follows will be helpful in seeing Ruth against its historical and canonical backdrop.

Who wrote Ruth and when? According to the Babylonian Talmud (Baba Bathra 14b–15a) and traditional Jewish thinking, it was Samuel. If that identification is correct, Ruth would have to date from before Samuel's death, recorded in 1 Samuel 25:1.

1. See E. F. Campbell, Jr., "The Hebrew Short Story: Its Form, Style and Provenance," in *A Light Unto Your Path,* ed. H. N. Bream, R. D. Heim, and Carey A. Moore (Philadelphia: Temple University Press, 1974), 83–101.

2. For somewhat different recent evangelical introductory discussions, see Richard I. McNeely, "Ruth," in *Baker Encyclopedia of the Bible,* ed. Walter A. Elwell (Grand Rapids: Baker, 1988), 2:1871; R. K. Harrison, "Ruth," in *Evangelical Commentary on the Bible,* ed. Walter A. Elwell (Grand Rapids: Baker, 1989), 179–80; or F. B. Huey, Jr., "Ruth," in *Expositor's Bible Commentary,* ed. Frank E. Gaebelein (Grand Rapids: Zondervan, 1992), 3:509–15. The most comprehensive conservative treatment of this generation is Robert L. Hubbard, Jr., *The Book of Ruth,* New International Commentary on the Old Testament (Grand Rapids: Eerdmans, 1988), 23–46.

Three points of tension concerning this possibility appear from the evidence of the book: reference to the period of "the Judges" in Ruth 1:1 sounds like that period is now in the past, while it can be safely said that Samuel is the link between the Judges and the Jewish monarchy, beginning with Saul; explanation of the custom in Ruth 4:7 also makes it seem that Ruth's readers are long removed in time from this occurrence; and the book climaxes with two references to "David" (4:17, 22). Of course, David did not become king in any sense until 2 Samuel 2:4, some years after Samuel's death.

These considerations make it obvious why many scholars opt for an anonymous writer for Ruth during the reign of David (Ruth 4:17, 22) or, possibly, Solomon. However, it is possible to explain all three factors, allowing for Ruth to have been penned by Samuel. First, technically, the era of the Judges ended when Saul came to the throne (1 Sam. 10:1; 11:14–15); thus the reference in Ruth 1:1 is not decisive. Second, since the transaction and custom in 4:7 happened at least in the generation of David's great-grandparents (i.e., Boaz and Ruth),[3] enough time has passed to account for the need for such an explanation. Finally, the references to David could just as easily have occurred because of Samuel's early anointing of David to succeed Saul (1 Sam. 16:13), David's rising popularity in Saul's court and army (18:5–8), or the apparent awareness of David's claim to the throne by others (20:31; 23:17).

If Samuel wrote Ruth, it could have been as early as about 1020 b.c. If it originated as late as Solomon's reign, it may be dated down to about 950 B.C. Ultimately, of course, the Lord is the overseeing divine author of Scripture (2 Tim. 3:16; 2 Peter 1:21). Thus, no matter what the precise date was, because the Lord never changes (Mal. 3:6), this Scripture will never be "dated."

Who were Ruth's original readers, and why was it written? The preceding discussion strongly implies that it had to do with David's claim to the throne, or, if later, the ongoing claim of the Davidic line through Solomon. Perhaps much of Israel came to

3. It is quite possible that there are "gaps" in the family tree (i.e., generations left out) in Ruth 4:18–22, for the purpose of styling it to an ideal ten-generation length. See the discussion in chapter 7.

know that David had Gentile blood in his veins, by virtue of having a Moabitess great-grandmother, Ruth (Ruth 1:4). If so, the Book of Ruth would likely have been widely read in Israel as a crucial defense for David's kingship. This was especially necessary since David was assuming the place that was expected to be occupied by one from the house of Saul.

This would seem to offer the most plausible explanation why "all the tribes of Israel came to David at Hebron," and said to that aspiring king of mixed bloodline, "Behold, we are your bone and flesh" (2 Sam. 5:1 NASB).[4] Having drawn this conclusion, the people proclaimed him "shepherd" and "ruler over Israel," then "anointed David king" (5:2–3). It is plausible that the narrative of Ruth played a large part in this recognition of the Lord's sovereign preparation of the greatest king of Israel.[5]

Finally, what is Ruth's placement in the Bible? In English Bibles, Ruth is nestled between Judges and 1 Samuel in what is commonly known as the Historical Books. It occupies the same location in the Septuagint (LXX), the Greek translation of the Old Testament, but there the section is called the Former Prophets.[6] Some consider this to be its original position in the Hebrew Bible, also.

However, the Hebrew Bible places Ruth in the Writings (Kethubim), its third major section, between Proverbs and the Song of Songs. There is even some evidence that Ruth once headed the Writings section, a position usually considered to be that of the Book of Psalms (see Luke 24:44).

Either way, the wonderful story of Ruth occupies a special additional role. It is read annually by the Jewish people at the

4. Note the striking similarity in wording and the ironic parallel to 2 Sam. 5:1 in Abimelech's appeal to the people of Shechem to become "king" in Judg. 9:2. His point in stating "I am your bone and your flesh" (9:2) was that he was their close relative (9:3; lit., "brother"), even though the circumstances of his birth and lineage were far less than spotless (8:31).

5. Further backing for this approach to the date and purpose of Ruth is found in A. Boyd Luter and Richard O. Rigsby, "An Alternative Symmetrical Structuring of Ruth, with Implications for the Dating and Purpose Questions," forthcoming in the *Journal of the Evangelical Theological Society,* 1995.

6. For the significance of the designation *Former Prophets,* see D. Ralph Davis, *No Falling Words: Expositions of the Book of Joshua,* Expositors Guide to the Historical Books (Grand Rapids: Baker, 1988), 11–12.

Feast of Pentecost, celebrating the harvest and first fruits (see Ruth 1:22; chap. 2–3), taking its honored place among the Feast Scrolls in the Writings.

Strikingly, that means Ruth may have been read in proximity to Peter's sermon at Pentecost, in which the apostle repeatedly referred to David and his words (Acts 2:25–31, 34–35) in making his defense for the ultimate Son of David, Jesus Christ (2:22–24, 32–33, 36). That would make Ruth an indirect, but still important, apologetic for Jesus' right to rule on David's throne (see Luke 1:31–32), as rightful King and Messiah (Matt. 1:1, 5).

In taking the time to turn up the lights and address these questions, you will never view our story, the Book of Ruth, in the same way again. Its compact elegant narrative remains a literary gem in its own right. But it shines all the brighter against its illuminating historical background!

1

Scene 1: A Dead-End Shortcut
(1:1–5)

If Julie Andrews had asked me to list "a few of my favorite things," shortcuts would have been included. I dearly love to try shortcuts, especially when driving. Unfortunately, not all my shortcuts work out. Quite a few of my sincere attempts to save time or distance turn out to be longer scenic routes . . . even dead ends.

Some of my failed shortcuts are quite laughable, but others are not funny at all. They're irritating and wasteful of time and fuel. Needless to say, I've become famous (perhaps "infamous" is more accurate) among family and friends for these impromptu voyages where, seemingly, no (sane) man has gone before (apologies to *Star Trek* fans).

Recently, however, I've begun to see the error of my ways. A significant moment of realization came when, hurriedly ferrying my children from one scheduled activity to the next, I turned a corner a bit faster than was entirely safe. From the back seat one of my daughters yelled, "Oh, no! Dad, is this one of your shortcuts? We'll never get there!"

As starkly candid as those words were, I needed to hear them. Shortcuts do frequently lead to dead ends, not just on the highway. Many of life's crucial decisions are made with the shortsighted choice being to take a shortcut or the easy way out. Many who make such decisions live to regret such choices when the longer-term consequences become clear. Sometimes, unfortunately, that is too late.

When you approach the opening paragraph of the beautiful narrative of Ruth, you rapidly notice that the family of Elimelech (into which Ruth marries) plows into just such a disastrous dead end. Their choice to attempt what appeared to be a logical shortcut ended in tragedy. The supposed ticket out of difficult circumstances in their hometown of Bethlehem (Ruth 1:1–2) carried them only as far as a graveyard in Moab (1:3–5).

This painful reality in the experience of Naomi and Ruth demonstrates a timeless scriptural principle that could have a timely influence in your life. Ruth 1:1–5 teaches that a decision to take a spiritual shortcut could bring you to a disastrous dead end before the Lord.

The Forest and the Trees

Before considering the details and movement of the initial portion of Ruth, it is helpful to understand how it fits into, and functions within, the whole book. To grasp anything more than just the beauty or grandeur of individual trees, you need a map of the forest. Similarly, the overall map of Ruth sheds considerable light on the role of 1:1–5 within the wider narrative of Ruth.

Ruth is an exquisitely crafted short story[1] with six scenes[2] and a unique concluding family tree serving as an epilogue (4:18–22). Both the introductory scene before us (1:1–5) and the concluding one (4:13–17) contain about seventy words in Hebrew and also balance each other perfectly as thematic book-

1. See the compact, but definitive, discussion of this literary genre in E. F. Campbell, Jr., "The Hebrew Short Story: Its Form, Style and Provenance," in *A Light Unto My Path,* ed. H. N. Bream, R. D. Heim, and Carey A. Moore (Philadelphia: Temple University Press, 1974), 83–101, esp. 90–92.

2. Recently Walter C. Kaiser, Jr. and Moises Silva, *An Introduction to Biblical Hermeneutics: The Search for Meaning* (Grand Rapids: Zondervan, 1994), 71, have stated in regard to narrative literature like Ruth, "The most important feature of the narrative is the scene. . . . The author uses scenes to focus attention on one particular set of acts or words. . . ."

ends for the whole narratvie.[3] It is also exceedingly likely that 1:6-22 and 4:1-12 mirror each other even more extensively, as do chapters 2 and 3.[4] Further, the movement of the story of Ruth hinges on a middle pivot point: the realization that Boaz is a legitimate kinsman-redeemer (goel) for the imperiled heroines, Ruth and Naomi (2:18-23; 3:1-5). This center-facing (chiastic) effect cinches the overall symmetrical design of Ruth:[5]

The Mirroring Structure of Ruth[6]

Scene 1 (1:1-5): Emptied of hope for the family's future, through death

Scene 2 (1:6-22): First steps toward hope through commitment and honesty

Scene 3 (2:1-23): Immediate provision and protection by a gracious goel

Scene 4 (3:1-18): Ongoing provision and protection "proposed" to a willing goel

Scene 5 (4:1-12): Final steps toward a hopeful future through shrewdness and commitment

Scene 6 (4:13-17): Refilled with joy at the family's future, through birth

Epilogue (4:18-22): A family's past, present, and future fit for a king

This sturctural diagram will be assumed throughout the exposition of Ruth in order to keep in balance the telescopic and microscopic perspectives on its marvelous contents. Keepin the big picture of Ruth in mind also helps the reader to see the unseen

3. See the chart highlighting these extensive conceptual parallels in chapter 6.

4. See the chart detailed structural diagrams in chapters 2 through 5.

5. For discussions dealing with the general symmetrical design of Ruth, see Stephen Bertman, "The Symmetrical Structure of Ruth," *Journal of Biblical Literature* (1965): 265-68; John W. Reed, "Ruth," in *Bible Knowledge Commentary: Old Testament*, ed. John F. Walvoord and Roy B. Zuck (Wheaton: Victor, 1985), 417-18; and Phyllis Trible, "Ruth, Book of," *Anchor Bible Dictionary*, ed. David Noel Freedman (New York: Doubleday, 1992), 5:844.

6. The following is adapted from the overall diagram of Ruth in A. Boyd Luter and Richard O. Rigsby, "An Alternative Symmetrical Structuring of Ruth, with Implications for the Dating and Purpose Questions, "forthcoming in the *Journal of the Evangelical Theological Society*, 1995.

providence of God at every bend and turn of the narrative. The divine Name is mentioned directly in the text thirteen times (1:6, 8, 13, 16, 17, 20, 21; 2:12, 20; 3:10, 13; 4:11, 13), but many other factors also point to the Lord's powerful, but caring, activity.

Going Where the Grass Is Greener (1:1–2)

The initial scene of Ruth (1:1–5) subdivides into two parts. In 1:1–2 Elimelech's family relocates from Bethlehem to keep from bottoming out in a famine. But in 1:3–5 the bottom drops out anyway while the family is living in Moab. Sadly, 1:1–5 is the only scene in the narrative in which the Lord's name is not found.

While Ruth 1:3–5 makes the journey undertaken in 1:1–2 look like a bad move, we do well not to judge harshly without putting ourselves in the shoes of Elimelech, Naomi, and their sons. They may have decided to go where the grass is greener for plausible reasons.

For example, there may have been major political considerations. These events took place "in the days when the judges governed" (Ruth 1:1 NASB).[7] That entire era of Israel's history was notably unstable politically. Israel as yet had no king and, as a result, almost everyone did as they pleased (Judg. 17:6; 18:1; 19:1; 21:25).

In Judges 2:11–19 a cycle of instability that occurred over and over throughout the period of the judges is described. First, Israel's sin, which provoked the Lord, is discussed (2:11–13). Second, Israel is defeated by one of its enemies and placed in servitude (2:14–15). Third, the people of Israel "groan" in their oppression and affliction (2:18), and cry out in supplication to the Lord (e.g., 3:9, 15; 4:3). God then hears and grants his people salvation from their captors through one of the various judges he raises up (2:16, 18). Soon the cycle would begin again, for the people of Israel "did not listen to their judges" (2:17).[8]

In the midst of such ongoing political uncertainty, it is difficult at best to know what to do. A contemporary parallel may be

7. For a perceptive, and highly readable, recent treatment of the Book of Judges, see D. Ralph Davis, *Such a Great Salvation: Expositions of the Book of Judges,* Expositors Guide to the Historical Books (Grand Rapids: Baker, 1990).

8. This pattern is developed helpfully and concisely by F. Duane Lindsey, "Judges," in *Bible Knowledge Commentary: Old Testament,* 382–84.

seen in Hong Kong. In 1997 that great city will cease to be a British crown colony and will be under the control of communist China. Far-reaching assurances have been made by the Chinese that they will not disturb the general state of affairs in Hong Kong. However, in the bloody wake of the tragedy in Tienanmen Square and other restrictions, it is difficult for residents of Hong Kong to view the future with other than alarm and uncertainty. As a result, many are leaving, or preparing to leave, while that is still possible. And, with no clear sense of what the future holds, can they be blamed for going where the grass is greener?

Attempting to determine where the story of Ruth fits into the narrative of the Book of Judges is, at best, guesswork.[9] But, wherever it fits into the wider period, the lack of central leadership in Israel (Judg. 21:25) made for foundational instability from a political standpoint. Could the family of Elimelech be blamed for considering a move under such shaky circumstances?

There also were highly plausible economic considerations for relocating. At that time, "there was a famine in the land" (Ruth 1:1 nasb). In an agriculturally based economy, obviously, a famine is devastating. Also, it is not known if this particular famine was a curse from God (Deut. 28:18, 24), in keeping with a defeat by one of Israel's surrounding enemies (Deut. 28:25). In earlier times, several famines are recorded in which there is no indication of God's hand of judgment (e.g., Gen. 12, 26, and 46). For the purposes of the Book of Ruth, only the fact of economic hardship, not the why behind the scene, is in play.

In making the choice to move, Elimelech finds himself in good company. In similar straits, Abraham had gone to Egypt (Gen. 12). Isaac chose to go to Philistia (Gen. 26). Then, a generation later, Jacob and his family are clearly led by God to go down to Egypt (Gen. 46:2–4). With the extensive precedent of such choices by the patriarchs of Israel, cutting your losses economically by temporarily relocating to where the grass is greener could not be ruled out.

Regional and national economic downturns in recent years also caused many families to relocate across the United States.

9. Though John W. Reed, "Ruth," in *Bible Knowledge Commentary: Old Testament,* 415–16, concludes that the characters in Ruth may well have been contemporaries of Gideon (Judg. 6–8).

Perhaps they preferred not to, but the reality was that they had to migrate where job opportunities provided a means for them to support their families.

Some of the more extreme stories of economic famine happened in connection with the oil industry in the mid-1980s. One of the saddest of these instances took place in Bartlesville, Oklahoma, home base of Phillips Petroleum Corporation. A friend of mine was pastoring a church in Bartlesville during the oil boom, and things were developing well. Then came the unforeseen bust, called Black Wednesday in Bartlesville. Almost overnight the vast majority of people in the church who worked for Phillips, or related industries, were laid off. So, with all those workers scurrying for any kind of jobs they could find anywhere, the church suddenly became a ghost town and the pastor also was forced to leave in a short time.

Suffice it to say that economic deprivation can make what would otherwise be a highly undesirable move look much more attractive. But there is also a touch of irony in the statement that "there was a famine in the land" (Ruth 1:1).[10] Elimelech and his family lived in Bethlehem-Judah (1:1), and Bethlehem means "house of bread" in Hebrew. In other words, the bread basket of Judah was empty, and Bethlehem's residents were looking elsewhere for sustenance.

The writer's play on words on the meaning of Bethlehem might be better understood by some puns on the name of cities closer to home. Think about these: gang warfare in Philadelphia, the City of Brotherly Love, or demonic activity in Los Angeles, the City of Angels. Granted, neither Philadelphia nor Los Angeles lives up to its name in any full sense, and probably Bethlehem didn't either. However, the force of the pun still stands, and the Jewish reader chuckled under his breath even as he read of Elimelech and his loved ones packing to avoid the long-term effects of the famine.

Additionally, there were significant social considerations in such a choice. Elimelech and his family were "Ephrathites of Bethlehem in Judah" (Ruth 1:2). While this may merely speak of a clan that settled in Bethlehem, there is good reason to think that the Ephrathites were the aristocracy of Bethlehem.[11]

10. Robert L. Hubbard, Jr., *The Book of Ruth,* New International Commentary on the Old Testament (Grand Rapids: Eerdmans, 1988), 85.

11. Ibid., 91.

In the television miniseries "The Kennedys of Massachusetts," empire-builder Joseph Kennedy Sr. was portrayed as hating the bluebloods, the old-money families of the Boston social register, because he grew up on the wrong side of the tracks and was an Irish Catholic. In Bethlehem, it is likely that Ephrathites were the bluebloods, and the name *Elimelech,* meaning "God is my King" in Hebrew, may also indicate the upper-class background of his family, since the name's ending was associated with power.

In times of reversal, "when you've got nothin', you've got nothin' to lose." But when you're on top of the heap, it's a long way down to hit bottom. Apparently, Elimelech, Naomi, and their sons came to feel that there was more risk to their social status in standing pat in Bethlehem than in chancing an adventure in Moab.

Finally, there was a basic practical aspect of such a decision to go where the grass is greener. On a clear day, "the fields of Moab" (Ruth 1:1) could be seen from the ridges outside of Bethlehem. In this case, the green fields of Moab seen in the distance across the Dead Sea would have been a marked contrast to the brown and dusty fields of Bethlehem and its surrounding area. Day after day, that fertile, watered environment beckoned to Elimelech and became more and more of a plausible getaway option. Less than fifty miles away by the shortest available route,[12] it made perfectly good sense to spell relief M-O-A-B.

We often reason that the best route is the shortest one between two points. It would appear that Elimelech was thinking the same way: the shortest trip equals the best choice. Such a deal! The quickest, easiest plausible option also gets you where the grass is greener.

But beware of making decisions strictly from the consideration of such factors! As Erma Bombeck has sagely (and hilariously) observed, "the grass is always greener over the septic tank."[13] The green grass, which is attractive at a distance, may turn out to be loco weed. Even shortcut decisions made for plau-

12. Cyril J. Barber, *Ruth: A Story of God's Grace,* rev. ed. (Neptune, N.J.: Loizeaux, 1989), 28, 29.

13. Erma Bombeck, *The Grass Is Always Greener over the Septic Tank* (New York: McGraw-Hill, 1976).

sible, logical reasons can run into dead ends. Those reasons often do not tell the whole story.

The deafening silence in regard to the name of God in Ruth 1:1–2 may well hold the key to understanding what happens in 1:3–5. The failure to consult the Lord (i.e., there is no evidence that Elimelech's family did so) appears to be the missing link in their decision.

Getting Comfortable Without God's Go-Ahead (1:3–5)

Ruth 1:3–5 shows the outworking of Naomi's family decision to flee the forbidding circumstances in Bethlehem. They begin to get more comfortable in Moab, only to be made incredibly uncomfortable in the ensuing tragedies. Here we see the principle that deciding to get comfortable without God granting permission can have deadly consequences. These consequences can be both immediate (1:3–4a) and long-term (1:4b–5).

The most immediate problem that arose after the trek from Bethlehem to Moab was the death of Elimelech (1:3a). Surely this was a great shock! Had Elimelech been having any significant physical problems, undoubtedly he would not have undertaken such a trip and the stress of relocation, learning a new culture, and the like. Perhaps there were few, if any, warning signs . . . and then he was dead. The head of the clan, the father in that patriarchal society, was gone!

How often as a pastor I was called to deal with individuals who had taken the vocational shortcut: early retirement in order to live it up while they were still young enough to enjoy it. For six years I pastored a church in a where-the-grass-is-greener locale in the central Texas hill country, and watched the retirees come and go, often with deadly rapidity. It was incredible how often a seemingly healthy, even vigorous, person in his or her mid–fifties to early sixties would die within a few years, even a few months, after retirement.

Well, Elimelech obviously had not retired in the modern sense. But he had taken the easy way out of the famine back in Bethlehem and headed for where the grass at least looked greener. What did he accomplish? He crashed into a literal dead end. His attempted shortcut proved to be his last round-up.

After such relatively immediate grief (1:3b), the remaining family members might normally be expected to quickly move back to Bethlehem. After all, the thought of burying Elimelech on foreign soil would not have been a congenial idea. But, for whatever reasons, that move did not transpire. Perhaps Elimelech's and Naomi's sons, Mahlon and Chilion (1:2), were even more comfortable after such a short period of time than might be normally suspected. They both marry quickly (1:4a); perhaps the marriages were arranged by their father before his death.

It is quite well known that Jews considered all Gentiles to be dogs. However, if anything, Moabites occupied an even lower position in Jewish thinking. Going back to the way that Moab treated Israel on the way to the Promised Land (Deut. 23:4), Moabites, along with the Ammonites, were relegated to an ongoing religious outcast status, if they lived among Israel. They could forget participation in "the assembly of the Lord" (23:3) until the tenth generation.

Admittedly, this stipulation is not an out-and-out forbidding of Jews to marry Moabites. But, it is asking to be looked down on by other Israelites, and to be prohibited from participating in Jewish worship and fellowship as a family. The Moabite spouse and the children were not welcome (Deut. 23:3). This was a big and painful price to pay for such a mixed marriage.

Even today mixed marriages, whether racial or religious, often result in a lack of acceptance by either race or group. That can be painful, especially to a couple whose love is color-blind. Yet, there are still many instances of open bigotry against such couples, and especially toward their children. Not infrequently, partners in mixed marriages feel more comfortable living in certain parts of the country than others because of the degree of acceptance in an area.

Probably Mahlon and Chilion would have felt more at home in Moab after marrying Moabite wives (1:4a). But such a short-term decision proves to have terrible long-term consequences. They were fighting the losing battle of old roots versus new roots. Their historic family roots back in Israel, specifically Bethlehem (1:2), were insistently beckoning them to return home. But the longer they stayed, especially now that they had married into Moabite society, the deeper their roots were going down into Moabite soil.

This progressive rooting into Moab is seen in the subtle wording in several places in this paragraph. In Ruth 1:1 they went to "sojourn" (stay only temporarily) in Moab. In 1:2 they "entered . . . Moab and remained there." In 1:4 we are astounded to read that these refugees "lived there about ten years."

What happened? How did the short stay of 1:1 become the long-term lease of 1:4? Perhaps something that frequently happens to me can serve to illustrate the progression in this case. When I'm studying or writing at home, sometimes I'll take a break and walk into the room where our television is and sit down to watch for a moment. I'll start out on the edge of the couch. But, if I'm not careful, I'll stay and start to get comfortable. A lot of times I'll wake up some time later, having fallen asleep on the couch, even though all I initially intended to do was to sit down for a minute and relax.

I wonder if the family started off to sit on the edge of the couch ("sojourn") in Moab, if you will. But they got more and more comfortable ("remained"). Then, they finally fell asleep ("lived there about ten years") and, in a real sense, never woke up until it was too late.

That's the next, and most devastating, long-term consequence. In rapid succession Mahlon and Chilion also both died (1:5). The women who mourned the tragic loss of sons and husbands were in a hopeless situation. Naomi was now left without husband, children, descendants, or provision for her basic needs. Her daughters-in-law, Ruth and Orpah (1:4), were little better off. Yes, they were younger, still of marriageable age. But they had been barren for many years (1:4). Since ten years of childless marriage were considered grounds for divorce under rabbinic law,[14] it is doubtful how many takers there would be in the remarriage market.

What a rude awakening! It looked like the plausible shortcut that became a painful dead end had no way out. Could the end be far away?

Similar emotions are evident as you read the dialogue of Gerald Healy's play, *The Black Stranger*. During the Irish potato famine of the mid-nineteenth century, the government put starving men

14. Hubbard, *Ruth,* 95.

to work digging roads. Though it is back-breaking labor, there is some dignity in such an occupation. However, it is not long before a character named Michael finds out that the roadwork has no ultimate purpose or destination. In poignant wonder he states the obvious, "They're makin' roads that lead to nowhere."[15]

The trip that Naomi, her husband, and sons had begun ten years before (1:1–2), that Ruth had joined for the ride (1:4), led nowhere. It wasn't just that it was a wild goose chase. It was much worse: their goose was cooked!

Dead End or Doorway?

Was it really all over but the crying? That's definitely the hopeless impression left by Ruth 1:5: two funerals and no visible means of support.

But, it was not time to give up! When circumstances are hopeless, God specializes in turning dead ends into doorways to glorify himself. That's what the remainder of the beautiful story of Ruth is about: the comeback from the depths of despair through the door of the Lord's providential guidance and provision.

Naomi and Ruth perhaps could have wept over the graves of their loved ones indefinitely. But it wasn't a realistic option in their destitute circumstances. So, they quit traveling the road to nowhere, that road to where the grass looks greener but which exacts such a terrible toll. As will be seen in the next chapter, they started on the long road back. Every step would bring them closer to God's blessing and hope for the continuance of their seemingly "as good as dead" family name.

Before Continuing, Get the Inside-Out Perspective

The 1994 National Football League playoffs saw big-name quarterbacks Joe Montana and Troy Aikman both go down with serious concussions. Interestingly, a person with a concussion may look fine on the outside, but have scrambled eggs between his or her ears. If there is any possibility that their understanding is fuzzy, they should not be allowed to go on to the next phase of what they are involved in.

15. Cited by Joe E. Trull, *The Seven Last Words of the Risen Christ* (Grand Rapids: Baker, 1985), 26.

Before continuing on through the Book of Ruth, this complementary inside-out (i.e., chiastic or center-facing)[16] look at Ruth 1:1–5 will make sure that there is no mental fuzziness in getting the point of this foundational passage and how it parallels material in the second half of the narrative.

The Focus of Ruth's Introduction[17]

A Famine in Bethlehem: Discomfort (1:1a)
  BShort stay in Moab planned by Naomi's family (1:b)
    C Names of Naomi's immediate family entering Moab (1:2)
      D Naomi widowed (with two sons) (1:3)[18]
    C′ Names of Naomi's Moabite daughters-in-law (1:4a)
  B′Long stay in Moab and death of Naomi's sons (1:4b–5a)
A′ Bereavement in Moab: Devastation (1:5b)

Naomi's life has been traumatically emptied through the devastating deaths of her husband and two sons. It will not be joyfully refilled until the last scene of the narrative in Ruth 4:13–17.

16. Kaiser and Silva, *Hermeneutics,* 75, make the key point that "chiasms may involve the inversion of anything from words or clauses in two parallel lines of poetry to a series of dialogues or even a series of chapters of narration."

17. Luter and Rigsby, "Alternate Symmetrical Structuring."

18. As will be seen in chapter 6, this central point becomes even more significant in the light of the "point" of the inverted structure of Ruth 4:13–17: Ruth is better to Naomi than *seven sons* (4:15b).

2

Scene 2: The Long Road Back
(1:6–22)

In September 1990, I contracted viral pneumonia and had to be hospitalized for four days. It was a nightmare to undergo the endless tests and be awakened to be given medication in the middle of the night while in the hospital. But, frankly, that wasn't the most difficult part of my illness.

For me it was much tougher to have to lie in bed at home and rest for most of the next three weeks, regaining my strength, before I was finally allowed to go back to work in any limited sense. But, that was the normal necessary physical "comeback" process from the ravages of a potent disease like viral pneumonia.[1] I was not an exception to that rule.

Neither was Naomi an exception to the rule that there is a grief process to work through in an emotional and spiritual comeback from devastating loss. If anything, that kind of comeback is generally more difficult and unpredictable than a physical recovery process. It will not necessarily proceed at a well-known rate, even if you do all the right things. Grief frequently

1. This incident also led to considerable personal insight and growth emotionally and spiritually, which has been discussed in depth in Boyd Luter, *Looking Back, Moving On: Applying Biblical Principles of Freedom to Your Life* (Colorado Springs: NavPress, 1993).

varies greatly, not only from person to person, but even from one specific loss in a person's life to another.

In Naomi's case, she was dealing with a cumulative triple whammy. Losing your spouse (Ruth 1:3) would be enough grief to last most people for quite some time (in not a few cases, for the rest of their lives). But, it was only a matter of time (1:4) before Naomi would also suffer the equally painful double-barreled loss of her only beloved sons: Mahlon and Chilion (1:5).

Yes, Naomi was not just at the bottom of the barrel in trying to sustain her existence without the financial support of husband or sons. The barrel had fallen on her with the overwhelming emotional force of finality and despair. What could she do now, even just to *survive* physically? Her apparent options at the desperate point were extremely limited, as will be seen. She also initially perceived that, in the dire circumstances in which they found themselves, she and her widowed Moabite daughters-in-law (1:4) were actually more of a hindrance to each other than a help (1:8–13).

That perception, however, proved to be completely mistaken. As Naomi was about to learn, and as many need to relearn in our modern society: *Your comeback process will be limited considerably unless there is recommitment to each other and the Lord.*

The Heart of the Matter

That the preceding principle is intended by the biblical author as the central thrust of Ruth 1:6–22 is clearly seen when the chiastic internal structure of the passage is observed. D. Ralph Davis has helpfully likened chiastic (i.e., inverted or center-facing) literary structure to a sandwich.[2] The main point of making such a sandwich is, of course, not the bread or the condiments you use, although they may enhance the overall flavor considerably. The heart of the sandwich is the meat or whatever alternative you put in the middle.

The following brief structural display indicates how this sandwich effect works in Ruth 1:6–22.[3] It is as simple as A, B, C and C′, B′, A′ in the last half of the outline. A and A' are the outer

2. D. Ralph Davis, *No Falling Words: Expositions of the Book of Joshua*, Expositor's Guide to the Historical Books (Grand Rapids: Baker, 1988), 25.

layer of the inverted structure. B and B′ are the middle layer. C and C′ get to the heart of the matter of what 1:6–22 is seeking to communicate to its readers.

- A Leaving Moab to return to Bethlehem for food (1:6–7)
  - B Describing an impossible situation, blamed on God (1:8–13)
    - C Leaving: the natural response to adversity (1:14a)
    - C′ Recommitment: the supernatural road to a comeback (1:14b–18)
  - B′ Admitting a bitter attitude, focused on God (1:19–21)
- A′ Arriving in Bethlehem with a Moabitess at harvest-time (1:22)

The rest of this chapter (and the remaining chapters on Ruth) will move through this kind of structure, homing in from the outer (i.e., A, A′) to the inner (i.e., C, C′) layer. That sequence will most effectively demonstrate how the twin elements in each literary layer work together hand in hand (i.e., in complement or contrast) to present the overall unified message of the passage.

Those Excruciating First Steps (1:6–7)

It is a challenging task for a toddler to learn to walk for the first time. But, it is even more frustrating, if not more difficult, for a person who has been either severely injured or paralyzed to begin to try to walk again. They remember what it was like before: then it was so easy and second-nature; now, it is painful and exhausting, or at the very least, awkward.

It has only been a few years since Los Angeles Dodgers pitcher Orel Herschiser suffered what was then thought to be a career-ending rotator cup injury. Herschiser has spoken candidly about that dark and painful period of his life, only months after he had set the major league baseball record for consecutive

3. This diagram is adapted from A. Boyd Luter and Richard O. Rigsby, "An Adjusted Symmetrical Structuring of Ruth, with Implications for the Dating and Purpose Questions," forthcoming in the *Journal of the Evangelical Theological Society,* 1995.

scoreless innings pitched. After the necessary surgery, there was a period of time in which the desire to rehabilitate the shoulder was almost overwhelmed by the pain, fear, and discouragement. But, he did endure those excruciating early steps to come back and pitch well for a team that came within a game of winning the National League West Division in 1991.

When people sustain tremendously difficult losses, or go through intense trauma (especially if it is prolonged), they may well have to virtually learn to walk again emotionally and spiritually. Ruth 1:6–7 records the hesitant, but absolutely necessary, beginning of that healing process for Naomi.

After ten years in Moab (1:4), where the family had initially gone to dodge the effects of a severe famine in Judah, the tribal area that included Bethlehem (1:1), the situation was ironically reversed. Now, Naomi was destitute in Moab and making the only reasonable decision to escape her desperate situation: "to return to the land of Judah" (1:7 NASB) as rapidly as possible![4] It is at this point that the initial reference to God in the Book of Ruth is found. The author states that, after the devastating period of famine, the Lord again "had graciously looked after his people"[5] by providing them food (1:6).

This positive reflection of God's good hand extended to his people is in stark contrast with Naomi's later repeated expression of her affliction at the hands of the Lord (1:13, 20–21). The pain of loss she felt so intensely blinded her to ways in which the Lord was already at work in her life, providing the needed resources to sustain her life in the uncertain time ahead.

Unrecognized Resources (1:22)

That Naomi's comeback trail is the central theme of this section of Ruth (1:6–22) is verified by the purposeful repetition of the term *return* at its beginning (1:6, 7) and end (1:22).[6] This

4. Leon Morris, "Ruth," in Arthur Cundall and Leon Morris, *Judges, Ruth,* Tyndale Old Testament Commentaries (Grand Rapids: Eerdmans, 1968), 253.

5. The translation is that of Robert L. Hubbard, Jr., *The Book of Ruth,* New International Commentary on the Old Testament (Grand Rapids: Eerdmans, 1988), 97. It better communicates the inherent sense of covenant loyalty in the Hebrew *phaqad* than the more common translation, "visit" (KJV, RSV, NASB).

6. Ibid., 99–100.

bracketing effect serves to both introduce and underscore the ongoing importance of her painful comeback.

It probably seemed initially to Naomi that not much had been accomplished in terms of progress as she arrived back in Bethlehem (1:22). All that she had to show for her ten years of living in Moab (1:4), beyond the clothes on her back, was a Gentile daughter-in-law who determined that she would tag along through thick and thin (1:16–18). Even that loyalty may well have seemed more of an albatross (hanging heavily around her neck) than an asset (that would soon pay significant dividends).

Yet, her resources at that dark point were considerably greater than she imagined. Not only was Ruth, who turns out to be the heroine of this story (see 4:11, 13, 15), by Naomi's side. They also arrived just in time for the beginning of the barley harvest (1:22).

Now, Moabites most definitely did not possess most favored nation status with Israel (Deut. 23:3). Still, under the stipulation of the Mosaic law, they, along with other aliens living among the Jews, were given the right to gather the grain in the corners of the fields, as well as whatever else was overlooked by the reapers (Deut. 24:19; Lev. 19:9). So, in a very real sense, the Lord had scripturally (and providentially) preplanned to meet the pressing physical needs of Ruth and Naomi.[7]

My wife and I had a somewhat similar experience (at a different level of need) not long ago. Because of some large unexpected expenses, stacked on top of the already outrageously high cost of living in Southern California, we were left wondering what assets we had available to help in that financial crunch time.

As it turned out, because of prayerful decisions made, in some cases over ten years earlier, the resources were available. Borrowing some of our own money from an annuity and cashing in a universal life insurance policy, replacing it with a much more reasonable term life policy, made a sizeable difference at a point where we felt like our backs were against the wall. Don't tell me

7. As will be noted consistently throughout this exposition, it is much more than mere coincidence that the specific provisions of the Scriptures and the personal guidance of the Lord combine over and over in the Book of Ruth to meet the various needs of the characters as they become clear. The Lord of providence can be trusted to provide both the believer's "daily bread" (Matt. 6:11) and the range of other needs (Phil. 4:19).

that the same hand of the Lord that had Ruth's and Naomi's needs completely under control is not still at work in similar situations today!

The Impossible Dream—No Thanks to God (1:8–13)

In this section Naomi summons up all her persuasive ability to attempt to convince her two Moabitess daughters-in-law that accompanying her back to Bethlehem would be a futile—if not virtually suicidal—decision. In the face of their display of persevering loyalty (Ruth 1:10), Naomi only intensifies her efforts to push them away by painting a grim verbal picture of her impossible situation (1:11–13a) brought on, in her painfully nearsighted perception, by the bullying hand of the Lord (1:13b).

In Naomi's defense, it should be observed that she appreciated Ruth and Orpah a great deal because of their kindness to her and her sons, their deceased husbands (1:8b). She only wanted the best for these younger women, who were still of a marriageable age (1:9). But, at this point she simply could not fathom that it would be the best thing for them to remain with her.

So, with increasing force (1:8, 11, 12, 15), she urges Ruth and Orpah to return to their family homes (1:8), even though such a decision would mean great pressure to worship the Moabite god, Chemosh (1:15).[8] In her Job-like grief and agony, Naomi could not see any light at the end of the tunnel. Immediate survival was as much as she dared hope for—and that was not guaranteed.

It is yet another touch of literary irony that Naomi's argument for parting ways with Ruth and Orpah is based on the Levirate marriage[9] statute in the law (Deut. 25:5–10). Thus, the scriptural background for the climactic scenes in Ruth 3–4 is initially raised, then cast aside as totally implausible in this set of circumstances. Naomi, however, only conceives that the Levirate legislation can

8. Hubbard, *Ruth,* 116.

9. Hubbard, *Ruth,* 48ff., 109, argues his opinion that Levirate marriage is not in view in Ruth. However, Hubbard's arguments are not only against the overwhelming scholarly consensus, but he failed to convince his editor in the New International Commentary on the Old Testament series, R. K. Harrison, whose later commentary on this passage champions the Levirate marriage position (Harrison, "Ruth," in the *Evangelical Commentary on the Bible,* ed. Walter A. Elwell (Grand Rapids: Baker, 1989), 182–83.

benefit her daughters-in-law through her physical offspring (1:11–13). It apparently never occurred to her at this stage that there was a related, legally viable avenue by which the younger women could be remarried within Israelite society (4:5–10).

In essence, Naomi viewed herself as being jinxed. But, in her mind, this was not just some impersonal streak of bad luck. She was totally convinced that the Lord had it in for her. Robert L. Hubbard graphically renders the last part of 1:13: *"Indeed, Yahweh's own hand has attacked me."*[10] And, as will be seen momentarily (1:20–21), she was becoming increasingly embittered toward the Lord because of that conclusion.

Bitter Disappointment with God (1:19–21)

It's too bad that Naomi didn't either live in our era or that Philip Yancey didn't live in hers. She would have been a classic subject for his realistic, but unsettling, book, *Disappointment with God.*[11] If Naomi would respond the way that she did to the women of Bethlehem (i.e., asking to be called by the nickname *Bitter* [One];[12] 1:19–21) that she hadn't seen in ten years (1:4), imagine what might have come out in the presence of an interviewer skilled at drawing out a person's deepest feelings!

However, as wrong as we might argue that Naomi's ongoing bitterness was (Eph. 4:26, 31), it was still there, riding just below the depressed surface of her personality. And, there is one up-side to be noted: she was at least honest about her perspective and attitude toward God.

There is a personal reason why I can admire Naomi's honesty about her bitterness, at the same time that I do not condone it. Candidly, I have not always been so honest—even with myself. On two separate occasions in my nearly twenty years in ministry I have allowed unfair things that were done to me to lodge in my heart and produce in me a "root of bitterness" (Heb. 12:15).

I'm now ashamed of how I handled (or, did not handle) those situations. In the first incident, it was nearly two years before I

10. Hubbard, *Ruth,* 107.

11. Philip Yancey, *Disappointment with God: Three Questions Nobody Asks Out Loud* (Grand Rapids: Zondervan, 1989).

12. The Hebrew *mara* means "bitter" (*BDB,* 600). See also Harrison, "Ruth," 183; Morris, *Judges and Ruth,* 262, for helpful compact explanations.

could own up to my bitterness toward the person that had wronged me. In the second, it was over six months. (That, I hope, could be charted as some progress!) In both cases, when I finally admitted my bitterness—first to myself, then to my wife and others—I took a giant step in the right direction. That proved to be the turning point in uprooting the bitterness!

There is good reason to conclude that the same thing was true for Naomi. In replying to the wondering inquiry of the women of Bethlehem (1:19)[13] she emphatically[14] claims that it is the Lord that has left her "empty." Admitting her bitterness toward God is *the end of the beginning*, at least emotionally, for Naomi.

How can that be ascertained? By Ruth 2:20, certainly no more than a few days (or perhaps less than a day) later,[15] Naomi begins to exhibit a much more positive attitude toward the Lord. As she is emptied of the bitterness with which she had been filled during her extended period of grief (1:3–5, 13), she is being readied for the fullness of joy that she will experience at the climax of the narrative (4:14–17).

Bailing Out Before the Bitter End (1:14a)

When it looks like an airplane is going to crash soon, the smart thing to do is obviously to don your parachute, then get out while the getting's good. Unfortunately, this "bail out when things look bad" mentality has been frequently transferred to human relationships.

Going your separate way when things are going bad is not only the natural thing to do, it is today often viewed as the only logical thing to do. There may, of course, be incredibly painful,

13. Note the complementary role to this passage in the overall chiastically structured narrative of the people of Bethlehem rejoicing because of Boaz's and Ruth's "fullness" in 4:11–12, then Naomi's refilling (beautifully balancing her emptying in 1:3–5) in 4:14–17.

14. Hubbard, *Ruth,* 125–27, not only notes the emphatic positioning of "full" versus "empty," but also faces off the Lord as Naomi's legal opponent through the use of the strong phraseology *has witnessed against me.* See also E. F. Campbell, Jr., *Ruth,* The Anchor Bible (Garden City, N.Y.: Doubleday, 1975), 83.

15. Hubbard, *Ruth,* 136, sagely observes that the "abruptness" of 2:2 "suggests that virtually no time has passed since the arrival of Naomi and Ruth" (1:19–22).

even dangerous, legitimate reasons in some cases. However, the decision too frequently boils down to taking the easy way out.

As we move to the focal central layer (1:14–18) of the styled chiastic arrangement of Ruth 1:6–22, we note initially that Orpah bails out. Not that she didn't attempt short-term to continue on with Naomi (1:10), or that she wasn't emotionally upset by the prospect of leaving (1:14a). Ultimately, though, she was persuaded by Naomi's mounting emotional-logical appeal (1:11–13), and she soon left to go back "to her people and her gods" (1:15 NASB).[16]

It is, of course, impossible to know where along the road back to Judah (1:7) that the conversation between Naomi and her daughters-in-law took place. However, whatever the location, it is not too much to call it a crossroads in both their horizontal (i.e., human-to-human) and vertical (i.e., human-to-divine) relationships. Orpah, for all her tears (1:9, 14), still was disengaging from both her existing relationship with Naomi, as well as whatever level of realization and loyalty she might have developed (i.e., through marrying into the family) to Israel's God (1:15).

Committing for the Comeback Trail (1:14b–18)

As Orpah disappeared over the horizon behind them (1:14a), Ruth firmly "clung" (1:14b NASB) to Naomi.[17] This is the same term used in Genesis 2:24 to describe the commitment between Adam and Eve, the first husband and wife.[18]

That the idea of a deeper recommitment (i.e., presumably some degree of loyalty by Ruth toward both Naomi and the God of the family she had married into already existed) is the intended sense is strongly supported by Ruth's following solemn

16. The withdrawal of Orpah (1:14) is paralleled in the Book of Ruth's overall inverted structure by the withdrawal of the unnamed kinsman in 4:6–8.

17. Louise Pettibone Smith, "Ruth," in *The Interpreter's Bible,* ed. George A. Buttrick (Nashville: Abingdon, 1953), 2:836, astutely observes of Ruth 1:14, "Nowhere is the quality of Hebrew style (with its exclusion of all unnecessary comment) better exemplified than in this verse. Action, emotion, and contrasting character are expressed in six Hebrew words."

18. E. S. Kalland, *"dabaq," Theological Wordbook of the Old Testament,* ed. R. L. Harris, Gleason L. Archer, and Bruce K. Waltke (Chicago: Moody, 1980), 1:177–78, develops this idea of commitment in terms of affection and loyalty.

life-and-death vows to both Naomi and her God (1:16–17).[19] At this point Ruth moves center stage[20] in the narrative[21] alongside Naomi. It is also noteworthy that Naomi did nothing further to attempt to dissuade Ruth (1:18).

Of the roughly 140 marriages I've performed over the course of my ministry, about one-quarter have requested during premarital counseling that Ruth 1:16–17 be used in their wedding services. For my first few years as a pastor I was quite hesitant to comply with their wishes. It seemed inappropriate to me for a bride and groom to repeat the words of a recently bereaved (1:5) daughter-in-law to her previously widowed (1:3) mother-in-law.

With time and reflection, however, I have changed my mind. These verses are a classic biblical statement of the kind of commitment to each other and, particularly, to the Lord that is necessary for the relationship between a Christian husband and wife to endure and grow throughout life (and even beyond). Now, whenever I'm asked to do a wedding, I almost beg the couple to include Ruth 1:16–17!

Be Prepared to Hit the (Comeback) Trail

Ruth's two-pronged deeper commitment (1:14b, 16–17) to Naomi and the Lord is the literary pivot point of this wider section (1:6–22), what I called earlier the heart of the matter. It is through God's providential guidance, as will be seen in the next chapter, and the growing insight that accompanies such recommitment as you face life's reversals and failures, that it is possible to rebuild beyond the shattered pieces of your previous personal world.[22]

Let's face it! It may be the rebuilding of homes from hurricanes in Florida, from flooding up and down the Mississippi Valley or

19. Hubbard, *Ruth,* 114, renders the latter part of Ruth 1:17 this way: "if even death itself separates me from you" (so also Campbell, *Ruth,* 174–75; Morris, *Judges and Ruth,* 261; and the RSV). If this understanding is correct—and the construction and context both support it—then 1:17 strongly implies a hope of mutual life beyond death related to a shared trust in Israel's God.

20. Hubbard, *Ruth,* 115.

21. For a related discussion of the significance and character of Ruth, see A. Boyd Luter, "Ruth," *The Complete Who's Who of the Bible,* ed. Paul Gardner (Grand Rapids: Zondervan, 1995).

22. A humble, heartfelt recent example is Gordon MacDonald, *Rebuilding Your Broken World* (Nashville: Nelson, 1988).

earthquakes in California. It may be more personal setbacks, ranging from severe diseases, injuries, or grief to robbery or bankruptcy. But, lumped together, there are as many people in need of comebacks as ever today. If tragedy hasn't hit close to home with you, it could well be just a matter of time. The smart thing to do is combine the Boy Scout motto with the central truth of Ruth 1:6–22: Be prepared and *be committed* (1:16–17)!

3

Scene 3: Feeling Lucky?
(2:1–23)

On our last summer vacation, it seemed that almost everywhere we drove was lottery land. Signs along the interstate highways reported the multimillion dollar pots for the next drawings. In some states, the number of options available left the gnawing impression of a lottery of choice for budding compulsive gamblers (not totally unlike a drug of choice for chemical addicts who don't realize how close to the bottom they have already slipped).

Given the incredible odds against winning any sum of consequence, the only rationale for entering a lottery, or engaging in any kind of gambling, for that matter, is "luck." To listen to common statements like "I feel lucky!" or "I've got a few bucks to spare, so I'll take a chance on Lady Luck" or "I'm due for a stretch of good luck about now," luck is a great deal like an epidemic, a traveling tent show or a long-awaited cool front or rainfall.

Of course, there's the other side of the luck aisle. Many superstitious types believe they are cursed with bad luck. And, a lot of people feel "If I didn't have bad luck, I wouldn't have any luck at all."

If Naomi and Ruth had been superstitious, they might well have blamed bad luck, *very* bad luck indeed! Their compounded misfortune (Ruth 1:3, 5) had forced them into a hand-to-mouth existence

(1:6). It also caused Naomi a great deal of embarrassment before her former neighbors when she returned to Bethlehem (1:19–21).

Interestingly, although Naomi does not try to explain her difficulties by the concept of luck (1:13, 20–21), the writer of Ruth initially appears to do so at the beginning of Ruth 2. In 2:3 the awkwardly literal rendering, "her chance chanced upon," serves to convey the striking assertion that is veiled by such common translations as "she happened" (NASB) and "As it turned out" (NIV). Hubbard's paraphrase, *"As luck would have it, she happened upon,"*[1] better captures the force of this strange statement.

At this point it would seem that the author of Ruth has laid out two conflicting explanations for why events take place: God's personal, if perhaps hard-edged, providence (1:6, 13, 20–21) and impersonal blind luck (2:3). However, in the next verse after the reference to chance (2:4), as well as at the centerpoint of the scene (2:12), it becomes clear that the Lord God is the source of blessing.

When the dust from the field (2:2–3) in this scene settles, the realization emerges that Ruth 2, rather than calling into question divine providence, actually strengthens it, even by its ironic mention of luck (2:3). You can almost visualize the author with tongue in that bearded Jewish cheek pulling for his readers to get this main point of the chapter: *As a believer, you get lucky because of the grace you're receiving from God who favors you.*

Mapping the Terrain In and Out of Boaz's Field

Because of the sense of abrupt urgency in Ruth's statement and action in 2:2–3,[2] it is a strong possibility that she went out to glean in the fields early the very morning after arriving in Bethlehem (1:19, 22). If that is so, there would have been no opportunity to get the lay of the land. Yet, even though she did not know her way around in that new place, she ended up in Boaz's field (2:3) as surely as if she had a map with an X that marked the spot.

Of course, she had no map. Ruth was guided sovereignly by the Lord. But, there is a kind of map in regard to this scene that

1. Robert L. Hubbard, Jr., *The Book of Ruth,* New International Commentary on the Old Testament (Grand Rapids: Eerdmans, 1988), 140.
2. Ibid., 136.

is available to the reader. It is the careful literary structuring of the chapter.[3] The amazing crafting is very similar to, but even more elaborate than, that seen in Ruth 1:1–5 or 1:6–22. Those passages contain three layers in their inverted construction, compared to four in chapter 2.

"Lucky" Favoritism and Faithfulness

- A Looking ahead to "finding favor" from someone through gleaning (2:1–3)
  - B Morning declaration of the Lord's blessing (2:4)
    - C Ruth's extraordinary request for provision (2:5–7)
      - D Boaz's graciousness prompts Ruth to *ask*: "Why have I found favor?" (2:8–10)
      - D′ Boaz *answers*: Ruth's faithfulness and faith are the basis for human and divine favor (2:11–13)
    - C′ Boaz's extraordinary invitation and provision (2:14–16)
  - B′ Evening realization of abundant blessing (2:17)
- A′ Looking back on favor found from Boaz through gleaning (2:18–23)

The outer layer of the chiasm introduces and cements the role of Boaz, the kinsman, as the one who shows favor to Ruth (2:1–3, 18–23). The second layer highlights how blessing took place in Boaz's field between the morning and evening of the work day (2:4, 17). The third layer parallels Ruth's startling request and Boaz's equally unexpected provision (2:5–7, 14–16). The emphasized middle layer asks and answers the key question, "Why are you showing favor toward me?"

If It Looks Like Luck . . . (2:1–3)

As the saying goes, "If it looks like a duck, and it quacks like a duck, it probably is a duck." That perspective initially sounds relatively foolproof, but there is at least one glaring exception.

3. Much of the following schematization is based on A. Boyd Luter and Richard O. Rigsby, "The Chiastic Structure of Ruth 2," *Bulletin for Biblical Research* 3 (1993): 49–58.

Consider the case of the decoy that is put out by hunters to attract other ducks. It looks like a duck (to the ducks flying by), and duck calls are clearly heard in the vicinity. But, to conclude this is sufficient proof of true duckhood would doom you to soon begin ducking for cover.

Similarly, the surface appearance that Ruth 2:1–3 is describing a merely chance meeting (2:3) between Ruth, the desperate, destitute alien (2:2), and Boaz, the influential landowner (2:1, 3), has no more substance than a thin layer of facial makeup. The unfolding of details of the rest of the passage and the following narratives clearly indicate that it is scheduled: "at the right place, at the right time," orchestrated by the Lord, who has prepared an appointment book for all of us (Ps. 139:16).

This section introduces the reader to the person who would provide for the immediate (and long-term) needs of Ruth and Naomi. Clearly he was previously known to Naomi (2:1), but it is more difficult to determine how. He was certainly a "relative" (NIV) by Naomi's marriage to Elimelech (2:1, 3), and Naomi's response to Ruth in the corresponding member of the outer chiastic layer indicates that he was apparently a close relative (2:20). Hubbard goes beyond the understanding of family relationship (2:1, 3), though, and views Boaz as a "friend"[4] of Naomi. That would explain Naomi's seemingly personal insight into, and preference for, Boaz.[5]

Two other juicy tidbits of information emerge from these verses. First, Boaz is specifically said to be from Elimelech's "clan" (2:1, 3 NIV), "the link between the family and the larger unit, the tribe."[6] This is likely the first clear-cut clue in the book as to the royal destiny of the descent of the Perezite clan of the tribe of Judah (4:12, 18), of which Boaz and Elimelech were both members.[7]

4. Hubbard, *Ruth,* 132–33.

5. But, it does *not* explain Naomi's apparent distance from Boaz until after he is married to Ruth (4:13–17), though embarrassment at her poverty or some physical condition that also kept her from gleaning might be involved.

6. F. B. Huey, Jr., "Ruth," in *Expositor's Bible Commentary,* ed. Frank E. Gaebelein (Grand Rapids: Zondervan, 1992), 3:527.

7. Huey, "Ruth," 519, is an example of scholars that understand "Ephrathites" (1:2) as the inhabitants of Bethlehem, whether of the tribe of Judah or Ephraim. However, Hubbard suggests that not only did the term have "aristocratic" overtones (91), it was "probably an ethnic way of specifying the clan

Secondly, Boaz is described in Ruth 2:1 as "a man of standing" (NIV). Though he may well have been a "man of great wealth" (2:1 NASB), given his land holdings and other resources (e.g., 4:9–10) evident in the book, the phraseology employed here was most likely at least partially a reflection of his twofold "nobility": both his high social class and his exemplary noble character.[8]

In particular, the character aspect is probably being highlighted because all the further mentions of Boaz in the narrative portion of the book display his godly character and integrity more directly than the social-financial angle.[9] Also, and decisively, virtually counterpart wording is seemingly purposefully used to describe Ruth in 3:11, where it is usually rendered "woman of excellence" (NASB; cf. Prov. 31:10) or "woman of noble character" (NIV), with no possible implication of wealth or social position.

Ruth had politely requested[10] Naomi's "permission" to go forth and glean in 2:2. She had that legal right as both an "alien" and a "widow," according to Deuteronomy 24:19. Still, the reality was that "the owners of the fields were not always cooperative."[11] And, it is likely that the description *Moabitess* is again used here (Ruth 2:2; cf. 1:22) to underscore the other strike Ruth had against her in that culture and time: being a detested Moabite (Deut. 23:3) woman.

Thus, is it any wonder that Ruth is specifically concerned about finding a landowner "in whose sight I may find favor" (2:2 NASB)? In the elegant structuring of this chapter, that parting-concern to "find favor"[12] would have been what echoed through

---

within the tribe of Judah to which the family belonged" (90). If Hubbard is correct, the theme of the lineage of the royal Judahite line (cf. Gen. 49:10) is being subtly emphasized from the beginning of Ruth.

8. J. N. Oswalt, *"gabar,"* in *Theological Wordbook of the Old Testament* ed. Richard L. Harris, Gleason L Archer, and Bruce K. Waltke (Chicago: Moody, 1980), 1:148.

9. For further development of this perspective on Boaz, see A. Boyd Luter, "Boaz," in *The Complete Who's Who of the Bible,* ed. Paul Gardner (Grand Rapids: Zondervan, 1995).

10. Hubbard, *Ruth,* 136, may be correct in understanding the force of a declaration in Ruth's words in 2:2a. Still, the nature of Naomi's immediate response (2:2c), as well as Ruth's later deference to Naomi (3:5), implies at least an element of request in 2:2a.

11. Huey, "Ruth," 527.

12. The term used in 2:2, 10, 13 is also a significant secondary Hebrew term for "grace." See Edwin Yamauchi, *"chanan," TWOT,* 1:303.

Naomi's anxious mind throughout the day to be answered upon Ruth's return (2:18–23). It also frames Ruth's question to Boaz at the midpoint of the chapter (2:10).

It May Be the Lord (2:18–23)

To say the least, it would have been interesting to watch the sequence of Naomi's responses when Ruth arrived back from the field that first day. She would have been prepared to ask Ruth whether she had found favor with a landowner before anything else. But, 2:18 implies that the initial shock at Ruth's exceeding abundant (Eph. 3:20) payload of grain (2:17) left Naomi speechless. Then, she hungrily devoured the leftovers from Ruth's lunch with Boaz (2:14).

So, it might have been a while before Naomi got around to asking the big question (2:19). By that time, she cannot contain her thankfulness. The one who wanted to be renamed "Bitter"—perhaps only hours before (cf. 1:20)—now pronounces a doubled blessing on the gracious landowner, who proves to be Boaz (2:19–20). More significantly, she also refers positively to the name of the Lord (2:20), so recently the resented villain in her personal story (1:20–21).

Naomi's response to Ruth's answer at this point seems to indicate that the first glimmer of the plan hatched in Ruth 3 was already forming. When Ruth told Naomi that Boaz was "the man" (2:19) under whom she gleaned, it set in motion a chain reaction—a domino effect of well-positioned uses of "the man" through the end of chapter 3 (2:19, 20; 3:3, 8, 16, 18). As will be seen in chapter 3 any hope that Ruth and Naomi have for the future will be riding on "the man," and that echoed wording points back to 2:19, 20.[13]

In addition, Boaz is described as a "kinsman-redeemer" in 2:20, hard on the heels of speaking of his familial "kindness to the living (i.e., Ruth and Naomi) and the dead (i.e., the deceased husbands)." Both pieces of evidence "probably hinted that Boaz was a potential husband for Ruth."[14]

13. The repeated definite article ("*the* man") characteristically draws attention to the initial antecedent usage of the term.

14. Hubbard, *Ruth,* 187.

If Naomi was indeed beginning to brainstorm, she would have plenty of time to think creatively. Boaz had invited Ruth to work exclusively in his field—and thus in his guaranteed safety (2:21)—until the end of the grain harvests (2:23). That would be seven weeks (cf. Deut. 16:9), "normally from late April to early June."[15]

Of course, in all this the One who is the ultimate source of Ruth's and Naomi's good fortune is the Lord (2:12). His role, though not as immediately apparent as Boaz's, is just as real and even more foundational. Even at this point in the story, God's artistry as producer and director of this beautiful narrative is spectacular!

The Source of Blessing (2:4)

The second layer of the chapter's structure continues to develop the same subject. Such a perspective on the Lord's blessing would have been standard fare for the God-fearing Jew of that day. Yet, the exchange between Boaz and the reapers in his field still went well beyond the norm. Whereas the average greeting was "Peace *(shalom)* be with you," Boaz offered "The Lord be with you!" (2:4 NIV). This prompted the reapers to respond with "The Lord bless you!"[16]

Boaz's words accomplish two purposes at this early juncture in Ruth 2. They are the initial behavioral evidence that Boaz truly is a "noble" (i.e., godly) person (2:1). Further, after the implications of the wording in 2:3, his greeting clinched the presence of the Lord in this scene.[17] The initial "behold" (2:4) quite possibly calls attention both to Boaz's timely arrival *and* his striking words.

Beyond What You Ask or Think (2:17)

Interestingly, the corresponding verse in the second layer of the chiasm in chapter 2 does not mention the Lord directly.

15. Huey, "Ruth," 533.

16. In the Hebrew, the order of the greeting and response is reversed, indicating that the two form a "micro-chiasm," emphasizing the Lord's presence and blessing.

17. Hubbard, *Ruth,* 144.

What it does focus on, though, is the Lord's blessing—in this case the phenomenal amount of grain that Ruth brought home from her first day of gleaning (2:17).

An "ephah" has been variously estimated as from twenty-nine to fifty pounds.[18] The exact weight is not as important as the realization that it is *many* times what the average gleaner could expect to bring home. It would be enough to feed Ruth and Naomi for at least two weeks. And, with more grain coming in from Ruth's daily gleaning over the ensuing weeks (2:21–23), perhaps there was even enough to sell and meet other basic needs.

Certainly Boaz's generosity and favoritism toward Ruth (2:14–16) and her own hard work "in the field until evening" (2:17) were key factors in her extraordinary success. However, to reason back from the *effect* of the ephah of grain only to the (intermediate) *human* cause is to stop short of a full explanation. The *ultimate* cause is the unseen sovereign God who undergirds and blesses (2:4) the responsible choices and efforts of his people.

Surprising Curiosity and Boldness (2:5–7)

The third layer of the chapter's inverted structure hastens to explain how Boaz becomes aware of Ruth and her amazing request (2:5–7), then deals with the request in an even more amazing manner (2:14–16). Yet, it is not often noted how altogether unlikely this interaction was in the first place.

There is no obvious reason why Boaz asked about Ruth's identity (2:5), especially since the female dress of the day ruled out viewing physical attractiveness. Nor is there a clearcut rationale as to why Boaz granted Ruth permission not just to glean, as stipulated by the law (Deut. 24:19), but, as she requested, to gather "among the sheaves" (2:7, 15 NASB). Finally, there also is no apparent basis for the invitation to eat the noon meal with Boaz and his reapers (2:14).

Given the apparent literary reflection on the Lord's unseen role in this scene in 2:3–4, perhaps it is best to view Boaz's initial question as divinely-stimulated curiosity. Such curios-

18. Huey, "Ruth," 532.

ity might have had a timely ally in the information about Ruth and Naomi that was making the rounds in Bethlehem (2:11–12).

It would also seem that, along the trail between her dwelling place (2:2) and arrival at Boaz's field (2:3), Ruth decided to ask for the extraordinary privilege of gleaning among the sheaves (2:7). The only text-related explanation would seem to be that Ruth concluded that such an unusual request was the best, and quickest, way to determine whether she had found favor in a landowner's eyes (2:2, 10). Still, her choice reflects a holy boldness that was likely founded on her commitment to the Lord (1:16–17) and prompted by him. That fits well with Ruth's apparent confident patience in working, while waiting for a decision on her request,[19] in 2:7.

Gracious Provision and Inclusion (2:14–16)

Visualize an unemployed worker who goes to work for a large company on a day-to-day basis for no guarantee beyond minimum wage. Then imagine, if you can, that the president of the company approaches that "temp," who has not yet completed a morning's work, and extends an invitation to join him and some other longstanding staff for lunch. In such circumstances, how many people would be speechless or prone to faint?

This is what happened to Ruth. While Ruth was still basking in the glow of her conversation with Boaz (2:8–13), Boaz strode across the field to ask her to join him and his workers for lunch (2:14).

Two more wonderful blessings come Ruth's way as a result of this lunch with Boaz, the boss. The leftovers of "bread" and "roasted grain" (2:14) could be taken back to a hungry Naomi (2:18), who could eat without the normal time-consuming preparation. And, furthermore, Ruth had the assurance that Boaz accepted her as one of his trusted reapers,[20] since "she sat beside the reapers, and he served her" (2:14 NASB).

19. Hubbard, *Ruth,* 149–52, provides an excellent detailed discussion of the difficulties in translating, then understanding, Ruth 2:7.

20. Hubbard, *Ruth,* 172–74, expertly treats the cultural aspects of these actions.

As if that were not more than enough favor for one day, after lunch Boaz issued two startling commands to his servants: allow Ruth an additional advantage in her gleaning by throwing harvested grain in her path (2:15a, 16a); and do not harass her in any way (e.g., whether as a woman, a hated Moabitess, or a resented privileged gleaner; 2:15b, 16b). These two factors probably account for the bulk of the ephah that Ruth joyfully carried home that evening (2:17).

A "Why" Question for the Ages (2:8–10)

Many people might reason that the lunch and enhanced afternoon gleaning (2:14–16) were the highlight of Ruth's day. But, that is not the impression left by the crafted structure of Ruth 2. Rather, the focus of this scene is on the midpoint interchange between Boaz and Ruth, as seen clearly in the structural diagram. All the amazing "good luck" that came Ruth's way in the second half of the chapter flows out of this brief chat. Also, in contrast to most "why" questions, one that should be asked more frequently (2:10) is strikingly answered (2:11–12).

Upon hearing of Ruth's request (2:7), Boaz proceeds to personally approve her gleaning (2:8). That was music to her ears. Unexpectedly, though, he also asks her to glean in his field throughout the harvest season, promising Ruth protection and water to quench her thirst[21] (2:9).

Such respect and graciousness astonished and overwhelmed Ruth!

Her prostration before Boaz and the wording of her question (2:10) indicate that she was amazed at Boaz's response to her bold request. Her prayer-like wish at the beginning of the day (2:2) had surely come to fruition, but it never occurred to her that even unrequested blessings would be bestowed on an alien, especially one with no track record in Bethlehem.

This question cuts across the grain of proud humanity, ever ready to take credit for any recognition, accomplishments, or

21. A walk back into Bethlehem, or to another source of water outside the field, would be quite time-consuming, detracting significantly from the amount Ruth could glean. Thus, Boaz's thoughtful and generous provision of water was no small favor.

success that occur in the vicinity. *Why?* usually gets asked in the context of *pain*, but is at least as useful at times of *gain*, if realistic insight is to develop.

Finding Favor Through Faithfulness (2:11–13)

Boaz's answer (2:11–12) was highly affirming to Ruth (2:13) and, most significantly, pointed her back to the Lord God in whom she had believed (2:12; cf. 1:16–17). Ironically, Boaz's figurative reference to God's "wings" of protection over Ruth (2:12) points ahead to how that protection would be practically expressed. In 3:9 Ruth—possibly recalling Boaz's wording in 2:12—would ask for protection through marriage under Boaz's "covering" (NASB).[22]

Boaz knew more about Ruth than she had anticipated, and he greatly respected everything that he had heard (2:11–12). What he had heard about Ruth's *faithfulness* to Naomi is where he begins, but her *faith* in "the Lord, the God of Israel" (2:12 NASB) is even more central in Boaz's thinking.

What began as a simple answer (2:11) soars to a heartfelt prayer for God's blessing on Ruth (2:12). Based on her exemplary behavior and undergirding faith, Boaz requests that the Lord *reimburse* Ruth for what she had traumatically lost through the very process by which she had become a believer.[23]

This incredibly kind answer and blessing "comforted" Ruth, though she apparently still viewed her status as at the bottom of the social ladder in Bethlehem (2:13). But, things would be changing soon, as will be seen in chapters 3 and 4, with her "promotion" from gleaner to reaper in 2:14 as only the beginning. The Lord of "luck" was on her side!

22. Huey, "Ruth," 530; see also Oswalt, *"kanaph"* in *TWOT,* 1:446–47.

23. The arrangement of "Lord" bracketing the similar concepts of "reward" and "wages" in 2:12 probably indicates another mini-chiasm.

4

Scene 4: A Heavenly—and Godly—Match
(3:1–18)

One of my favorite musicals is "Fiddler on the Roof," which our local church drama ministry put on for a community outreach last year. They did an exceptional job and I thoroughly enjoyed every minute of the production (*especially* my wife, who hammed it up as the deceased wife of Lazar Wolf!).

But, what I found myself humming for the next couple of weeks was the song "Matchmaker." In my mind, I could still hear Leitel and her sisters singing, "Matchmaker, Matchmaker, make me a match, find me a find, catch me a catch . . . make me a perfect match." Her dream was shattered, though, when Yente's best shot turned out to be the financial security of marrying a prosperous local businessman old enough to be her father, although she already loved an impoverished young man.

On the surface of things, one might almost be tempted to think that the matchmaker in "Fiddler" was modeled after Naomi, and her search for "security" (Ruth 3:1 NASB) for her widowed daughter-in-law and her intended match being a well-to-do older[1] landowner in Bethlehem. But, two factors indicate

1. Note Boaz's repeated expression *my daughter* (2:8; 3:10, 11) in referring to Ruth. Since the much older Naomi also refers to Ruth in this way (2:2, 22; 3:1, 16, 18), it is most likely that Boaz is much closer to Naomi's age than Ruth's.

how incredibly different these "matches" really are: much more than "marrying for the money" was involved because Naomi undoubtedly knew Boaz's character well and respected and trusted him implicitly (3:2, 4, 18); and Ruth was not at all interested in any younger men, no matter what their social status was (3:10), and that was readily apparent to Boaz.

So, to whatever extent Naomi was playing the role of matchmaker,[2] she was eminently successful. Despite the obvious massive differences in their backgrounds, Boaz and Ruth were well-matched. They were two of a kind in regard to excellent moral character (2:1; 3:11).

That is a crucial principle that can be learned from that "middle of the night"[3] (3:8) encounter between Ruth and Boaz that needs to be trumpeted in the bright light of high noon for all to see: *Personal integrity commands at least as much respect and admiration under cover of darkness as in broad daylight.*

Overview of a Discreet Proposal

Sadly, even some evangelicals are among those who lend much more stock to inconclusive circumstantial evidence and implications about what took place between Ruth and Boaz in chapter 3 than is warranted. One initially charges that "the chapter teems with . . . sexual innuendo. In ancient Israel, a threshing-floor setting suggested sexual compromise."[4] That same scholar concludes his discussion with wording that surely influences the understanding of modern readers virtually the same way as he *claims* the writer of Ruth did the original audience: "He creates a strong impression that Ruth and Boaz might have had sexual relations that night, *yet he never actually says so.*"[5] Even though he backed off, he still leaves the strong

2. F. B. Huey, Jr., "Ruth," in *Expositor's Bible Commentary,* ed. Frank E. Gaebelein (Grand Rapids: Zondervan, 1992), 3:535, cautions, "One must resist an inclination to caricature Naomi as a 'matchmaker,'" but Huey is quick to admit, "Obviously she had been giving the matter some thought."

3. The Hebrew says literally, "in the half of the night" (3:8), apparently meaning *about midnight.*

4. Robert L. Hubbard, Jr., *The Book of Ruth,* New International Commentary on the Old Testament (Grand Rapids: Eerdmans, 1988), 196.

5. Hubbard, *Ruth,* 196. Similarly, Huey, "Ruth," 535, is only willing to say that the interpretation of "sexual intercourse" in Ruth 3 "is not unequivocal here."

impression that Ruth made her feminine charms available to Boaz and that he took advantage of the situation. The tragedy of such an outlook is that, like the sleazy tabloids next to the grocery-store checkout stands, it assumes the most lurid behavior without even taking into account a spotless previous record.

In the case of Ruth and Boaz in the scene before us, any hint of moral impropriety is "unfounded."[6] Exactly the opposite proves to be the case when the clear picture of the overall structure of the chapter emerges. As will be seen, Ruth carries out Naomi's plan in an appropriately discreet manner (3:1–9). And, for his part, Boaz agrees to cooperate, but is concerned that nobody know about (i.e., and possibly misconstrue)[7] Ruth's presence during the night (3:10–14). Both are acutely aware of, and careful to protect, the other's sterling reputation.

Protecting an Excellent Reputation

A Naomi's objective: "Rest" for Ruth, with Boaz as kinsman-redeemer (3:1–2)
  B Naomi's plan: Ruth lies secretly at Boaz's feet (3:3–5)
    C Ruth's part: Carries out Naomi's plan, including "proposing" Levirate marriage to a startled Boaz (3:6–9)
      D Boaz's response: Ruth showed admirable *restraint* toward security in marriage (3:10)
      D′ Boaz's response: Ruth has a deserved *reputation* as a woman of excellence (3:11)
    C′ Boaz's response: Agrees to Naomi's objective, then startles Ruth with other closer kinsman (3:12–13)
  B′ Naomi's inquiry, after Boaz keeps Ruth's presence secret (3:14–16)
A′ Ruth's report, Naomi's response: No "rest" for Boaz until he's done his best to accomplish Naomi's objective (3:17–18)[8]

6. Cyril J. Barber, *Ruth: A Story of God's Grace,* rev. ed. (Neptune, N.J.: Loizeaux, 1989), 88.

7. Besides the practically inevitable gossip, Leon Morris (*Judges and Ruth,* Tyndale Old Testament Commentaries [Grand Rapids: Eerdmans, 1968], 293) cites the *Mishnah* to the effect that a Jewish man suspected of having sexual relations with a Gentile woman was banned from entering a Levirate marriage with her.

8. This outline and other material in the chapter is adapted from A. Boyd Luter and Richard O. Rigsby, "Protecting Ruth's Good Name: The Significance of the Inverted Structure of Ruth 3," Evangelical Theological Society paper, 1993.

The literary structure of 3:1–18 underlines how Naomi's objective of approaching Boaz to serve as kinsman-redeemer (3:1–4) is accomplished without betraying Ruth's moral reputation (3:10–11). If anything, her moral excellence is all the more striking against the backdrop of an immediate setting in which immorality was commonplace. She and Boaz both also stand out in sharp contrast with the overall morally dark society of the era of the judges in which they lived (Judg. 21:25; Ruth 1:1), a period much like permissive contemporary society.

For the "Rest" of Your Life (3:1–2)

As the harvest proceeded (2:23), Naomi and Ruth were undoubtedly much better off in terms of their basic needs because of Boaz's generosity (2:8–9, 15–16). However, the harvest would come to an end all too soon,[9] and the future for the two widows was nothing if not uncertain.

In light of this open-ended uncertainty, Naomi came up with a plan to find Ruth a "permanent home" (Hubbard)[10] so that she would be "well provided for" (3:1 NIV). In other words, she was intent on attempting to broker a marriage for her daughter-in-law, something normally done by parents (note Naomi's custom of calling Ruth "my daughter"; e.g., 3:1, 16, 18) in that era (e.g., Judg. 14:2).

Nothing is said about how Ruth felt as she initially heard about Naomi's stratagem. However, with Boaz's name added to the mix (3:2), Ruth listened intently (3:2–4) and consented to go along with Naomi's plan (3:5).

Initially, all that can be inferred about Naomi's and Ruth's gameplan was that it had to do with Boaz's kinsman-redeemer[11] relationship to Naomi and Ruth ("*our* kinsman," 3:2); and it

9. The mention of "barley" in 3:2, 15, 17 presents a chronological problem. The wording in 2:23 implies that chapter 3 occurs at "the end of the barley harvest and the wheat harvest" (NASB). However, the wording in 2:23 does not exclude Ruth 3 occurring during the middle of the seven-week harvest period (Deut. 16:9), since it only observes Ruth's *intent* to glean through the entire harvest season (Ruth 2:21) and her *presence* with Naomi.

10. Hubbard, *Ruth,* 197–98, correctly infers this rendering from the Hebrew phraseology *a resting place.*

11. For a full discussion of this role in Jewish society, see Donald A. Leggett, *The Levirate and Goel Institutions in the Old Testament with Special Attention to the Book of Ruth* (Cherry Hill, N.J.: Mack, 1974).

would require approaching Boaz while he was at the threshing floor (3:2), likely to guard his harvest from thieves. If this were a military strategy, these elements of quickness and secrecy would likely be effective. But, this was not military warfare; it was *marital welfare*. There was no way to forecast the outcome; it had to be played out near that threshing floor on the outskirts of Bethlehem.

No Rest for the Sleepy (3:17–18)

Back in town early the next morning (3:14, 16), Ruth explained to Naomi the significance of the six "measures"[12] of barley that she had hauled home in her shawl from the threshing floor (3:15, 17). Ruth's words indicate that Boaz was apparently concerned about Naomi's ongoing sense of emptiness (3:17; cf. 1:21). Perhaps he wished to assure her that he also took seriously his role as *her* kinsman (3:2). But, it could well be that Boaz wanted to thank Naomi for formulating the plan that was now set in motion.

These are the final spoken words of Ruth recorded in the narrative. At first glance, that may seem odd. But, since the issues in 4:1–12 focus on Boaz and in 4:13–17 on Naomi, this is a logical point in the Book for Ruth to utter her last—and *lasting*—words. What a way for anyone to deliver their final lines: relaying words of compassion that reflect positively on another!

Naomi's response is that there is nothing else they could do except "sit tight"[13] (3:18) until they learn how Boaz's interaction with the closer kinsman shakes out. Of one thing they could be sure, though. Even if Boaz was tired and bleary-eyed from lying awake the rest of the night after talking to Ruth (3:9–13), he would not be deterred from his appointed mission, whether for a cat nap or any other respite.[14]

If Boaz had been a letter carrier, he would have delivered the mail in spite of the blizzard. If Boaz had been a basketball coach, he would have implemented a full court press until the game was decided, one way or another. "The man" (3:18) had promised

12. Hubbard, *Ruth,* 222, is almost certainly right in concluding that this "measure" is a seah, six of which would weigh fifty-eight to ninety-five pounds.

13. This perceptive paraphrase is by E. F. Campbell, Jr., *Ruth,* The Anchor Bible (Garden City, N.Y.: Doubleday, 1975), 116, 129.

14. Hubbard, *Ruth,* 227.

Ruth that he *would* get the job done (3:13), and you could take that promise to the bank!

Under Cover of Darkness (3:3–5)

Naomi's instructions to Ruth in 3:3 to bathe, perfume herself, and dress as well as possible are very similar to the description of a bride in Ezekiel 16:9–10. Thus, it is reasonably likely that Ruth was presenting herself to Boaz as a bride-in-waiting.

But, it was not as easy as just walking out to the threshing floor to engage Boaz in conversation. In order to avoid embarrassment for either party if he said no, or the misunderstanding that Ruth was willing to compromise herself sexually, she remained secreted in the darkness until Boaz had fallen asleep (3:4) after dinner (3:3). Then she could position herself at his feet to discreetly "propose" to "the man" when he woke up (3:4).

Much has been made of the phrase *uncover his feet* as a possible euphemism for sexual intercourse.[15] However, that is far from certain, especially when the spotless reputation of both Boaz (2:1) and Ruth (3:11) is taken into account sufficiently.

The Woman and *the* Man (3:14–16)

In 3:3–4 Ruth was instructed by Naomi to secret herself in the darkness near the threshing floor until the right time. In 3:14–15 Boaz told her that she needed to continue the secrecy by laying next to him through the night, until the right time at early dawn. In both cases the tendency of human nature for wagging tongues was undoubtedly a primary consideration, as is strongly implied in what appears to be Boaz thinking out loud about the necessity of secrecy (3:14).

In 3:3 Boaz was referred to by Naomi as "the man," probably indicating Naomi's single-minded focus on Boaz as kinsman-redeemer[16] (cf. 2:20). That corresponds beautifully not only to him being called "the man" in the parallel section (3:16), but also to Boaz calling Ruth

15. Huey, "Ruth," 535.

16. The confusing point is that Naomi almost certainly knew of the existence of the closer kinsman from her previous life in Bethlehem (1:1–2). There is no obvious explanation as to why she would not have mentioned him to Ruth before Boaz did (3:12).

"the woman" (3:14). Perhaps Boaz's care for—and attraction to—Ruth had already been deeper than is obvious from the narrative. Or, perhaps it is that his just-promised intent to serve as kinsman-redeemer (3:13) made his focus as single-minded as Naomi's.

A Shocking Proposal (3:6–9)

If one takes the view that sexual fireworks erupted between Boaz and Ruth at the threshing floor, it makes about as much sense to conclude that Boaz was drunk before going to sleep (3:7). However, since "Boaz had eaten and drunk and his heart was merry" (NASB) is vague, and his alertness and integrity are notable just a short time later (3:10–13), such an understanding is highly doubtful. It is considerably more likely that Boaz was simply in a happy mood as he retired for the evening.[17]

The double shock that Boaz received at midnight could, unfortunately, also be subject to misunderstanding. The initial start of waking in the middle of the night to find a person at your feet (3:8) would hardly compare to hearing that person propose marriage, as is alluded to by the protecting garment of the kinsman-redeemer (3:9). That would get your adrenaline pumping!

Ruth "lying at his feet" (3:8) might imply sexual misconduct in certain contexts. However, given the character of both individuals (2:1; 3:11), it surely points to Ruth's humility, as does her calling herself "your maid" (NASB) twice in 3:9.[18]

An Unexpected Complication (3:12–13)

So far, so good! Ruth has proposed Levirate marriage (Deut. 25:5–10) to Boaz and he has profusely praised her godly restraint and reputation (Ruth 3:10–11). But, there is a "catch"—and not just a small hangnail detail, either! There is another kinsman-redeemer who is even closer kin to Naomi's family than Boaz (3:12).

This surely was just as big a shock to Ruth as the proposal of Levirate marriage was to Boaz (3:9). At that moment, questions likely raced through Ruth's mind: "Has this whole episode been for naught?" and "Why didn't Naomi tell me about the other kinsman?"

17. Huey, "Ruth," 537.

18. Hubbard, *Ruth,* 211, helpfully notes that the term for "maid" here refers to a marriageable category in Israel.

There were no immediate answers to the dilemma. But, it was some comfort that Boaz was willing to commit himself to resolving the conflict over who would serve as Ruth's redeemer the next morning (3:13). The wording here ("If he will . . . But if he does not . . ." [NASB]) may indicate that Boaz was already planning the shrewd approach he would employ the next morning (cf. 4:4).

Refusing to Take the Easy Way Out (3:10)

After Ruth's proposal (3:9), Boaz wastes no time in letting her know that he is extremely flattered, and he does so in a very godly manner (3:10). He asks the Lord's blessing on Ruth, particularly for her restraint. Obviously, it is not easy being a young widow. But, it is almost always unwise to take the easy way out by marrying the first man who comes along, of whatever status (3:10).

Boaz also comments that Ruth's "last kindness" (i.e., to *him*, by proposing Levirate marriage) was "better than the first" (apparently Ruth's kindnesses toward Naomi, based on 2:11). If Boaz were alive in our culture, he might call himself (excuse the pun!) "a lucky man."

Admiring a Spotless Reputation (3:11)

When Boaz gets around to beginning to answer Ruth's request about Levirate marriage, he promises to help in any way that he can[19] (3:11). But, he does so for a very good reason: Ruth's reputation in Bethlehem is impeccable! Boaz knows that he would be getting just as good a deal in having Ruth as his wife (3:11) as Ruth would in having him as her husband (2:1). Perhaps the wisdom that later noted how rare "an excellent wife" (Prov. 31:10) truly is was already embodied in Boaz's life!

Everything would be wonderful for this spiritually dynamic duo if the closer kinsman didn't have first right of refusal in regard to Ruth's redemption (3:12–13). In the meantime, Ruth could lie at Boaz's feet and sleepily bask in the glow of knowing that he cared deeply about her welfare (3:13). At the same time, Boaz was largely preoccupied with brainstorming toward that providential court date that awaited him and the other kinsman the next morning (4:1).

19. This broader wording probably previews the issue of the redemption of the family land that is the initial focus of the next scene (Ruth 4:1–9).

Another Perfect Match

Not only are Ruth and Boaz a wonderful match in regard to the possibility of marriage that looms uncertainly before them. So are the beautiful scene just discussed (Ruth 3) and the one that precedes it (Ruth 2).

The following listing of parallels (i.e., comparable, contrasting, and complementary ideas) clearly demonstrates how extensive the interplay of ideas between the two chapters is.[20]

Ruth 2 and 3 "Face-to-Face"[21]

Elements in Ruth 2	*THEMES*	*Elements in Ruth 3*
Naomi, Ruth, and Boaz	CHARACTERS	Naomi, Ruth, and Boaz
Start of harvest	TIMING	End or middle of harvest
Harvesting grain	ACTIVITY	Threshing grain
Ruth present, Boaz arrives	INITIAL INTERPLAY	Boaz present, Ruth arrives
Ruth asks to glean	REQUEST	Ruth asks to marry
Boaz agrees	RESPONSE	Boaz agrees, if possible
Full report	BOAZ'S INSIGHT	Knowledge of all his people
Boaz: A man of excellence	CHARACTER DESCRIBED	Ruth: A woman of excellence

20. Though failing to notice the overall inverted structure of Ruth, or that of the individual scenes of the narrative, Hubbard, *Ruth,* 196, does clearly recognize that Ruth 3 "parallels ch[apter] 2 quite closely."

21. A longer, slightly different listing of parallels between these two scenes is found in Luter and Rigsby, "Ruth 3."

No apparent provider	LOOMING PROBLEM	Closer kinsman-redeemer
Physical needs	BOAZ'S PROTECTION	Excellent reputation
Working all day	DURATION	Waiting all night
Ephah of grain	PAYLOAD	Six measures of grain
Naomi's hope	FINAL OUTLOOK	Naomi's patience

Ruth requests extraordinary "favor" from Boaz (2:7; 3:9), and he replies in a totally cooperative, but unexpected, way (2:8–9; 3:10–12), as well as with great generosity (2:9, 14–17; 3:15). In so doing, Boaz has taken an Olympic long jump toward possibly being the answer to his own prayer that Ruth be fully recompensed by the Lord (2:12). In spite of all that, the presence of the closer kinsman (3:12) looms up before them as a chasm that cannot be leaped over or traveled around.

Will Ruth's and Boaz's budding relationship be nipped in the bud in the early hours of the new day (3:14–4:1),[22] or is the best yet to come? Stay tuned for the "rest" (3:1, 18) of the story!

22. Hubbard, *Ruth*, 232–33, notes that, while the exact sequence of events between the end of chapter 3 and the beginning of chapter 4 is not entirely clear, the "early morning" setting of 4:1–12 is not open to question.

5

Scene 5: The Old Trap Play

(4:1–12)

Perhaps my lowest point of a decent high-school football career took place on what has long been called a "trap" play. I turned out to be the "goat" on the one play of the entire game on which the momentum shifted from our team to our arch rivals.

Leading in a tight game against a much better team, our punter kicked the ball dead on their two-yard line. Then, we held the first two plays for no gain. But, confusion reigned as our opponents set up in a never-before-seen unbalanced line and full-house backfield to the left, even putting the fullback in motion in that direction. Playing right defensive tackle, I anticipated an outside sweep to that side and inched into the gap to the right, then blew past the offensive tackle untouched as the ball was snapped. So far, so good, right?

Wrong! Just as I reached out to try to tackle their all-state halfback behind the line of scrimmage, I got blind-sided by one of their lineman, pulling across from the opposite side. I rolled over just in time to see the ball carrier go right through the hole that was my responsibility, on his way to a ninety-eight-yard touchdown.

What had happened? I had allowed myself to be suckered by an optical illusion: what looked like a unimpeded route to the ball carrier was actually a trap.

Now, this is not just a quaint story from an over-the-hill ex-jock. In real life people are constantly falling prey to variations on the old trap play. The unnamed kinsman in Ruth 4:1–12 certainly did. He learned a crucial lesson the hard way: *Following your instinct, instead of finding out what you're getting yourself into, often gets you "trapped."*

The Shape of Boaz's Strategy

As in the case of every other scene in Ruth, 4:1–12 is inverted in structure. The following diagram[1] reflects the ongoing and centered contrast between the unnamed kinsman (4:1) and Boaz at the point of Levirate responsibility (4:5–8).[2]

A Convening the needed "quorum" of witnesses (4:1–2)
  B Premature public offer to "redeem" by unknown kinsman (4:3–4)
    C Boaz describes responsibility, unknown kinsman backpedals (4:5–6)
    C′ Boaz accepts responsibility, unknown kinsman evacuates (4:7–8)
  B′ Solemn public choice to redeem by Boaz (4:9–10)
A′ The witnesses testify for a fruitful future (4:11–12)

The witnesses gather in 4:1–2, wondering what is going on. When the dust settles, they are heard cheering for Boaz in 4:11–12. The half-baked offer of the other kinsman is set forth in 4:3–4, in striking contrast to the eyes-wide-open commitment of Boaz in 4:9–10. The unnamed figure then slips the noose (4:5–6) and passes the kinsman-redeemer responsibility on to Boaz (4:7–8).

Though he did so with decency and in an orderly manner (cf. 1 Cor. 14:40), and showed full respect, Boaz still blind-sided the

1. This schematic is adapted from A. Boyd Luter and Richard O. Rigsby, "An Adjusted Symmetrical Structuring of Ruth, with Implications for the Dating and Purpose Questions," forthcoming in the *Journal of the Evangelical Theological Society,* 1995.

2. For a thorough discussion, see Donald A. Leggett, *The Levirate and Goel Institutions in the Old Testament with Special Attention to the Book of Ruth* (Cherry Hill, N.J.: Mack, 1974).

kinsman and made the equivalent of a ninety-eight-yard touchdown gallop to the goal line (i.e., being able to marry Ruth), where Ruth and Naomi were waiting to hear (Ruth 3:18) about the outcome of Boaz's day in court.

The Right Way to Get It Done (4:1–2)

I often counsel my students that it is possible to do the right thing in the wrong way and cause almost as much trouble as doing the wrong thing. In fact, you can even do the right thing in the right way at the wrong time and create a lot of difficulty!

Never fear for our heroines, Ruth and Naomi! Boaz went into Bethlehem early that fateful day (3:18; 4:1) and did the right thing in the right way at the right time. The Lord would have praised him for his shrewdness (Luke 16:8), though, unlike the unrighteous steward, he sacrificed nothing in terms of ethics or justice.

The city gate (4:1) was "the open area inside the town entrance where business was generally transacted."[3] It also was the setting for local judicial proceedings (Deut. 22:15), including Levirate marriage (Deut. 25:7).

The references to "the gate" and the "elders" (4:2) here are usually taken as evidence that Boaz was convening a Levirate marriage proceeding.[4]

It is interesting that the writer chooses to refer to the other kinsman as "Mr. So-and-so" (4:1).[5] He almost certainly knew the man's name, but deleted it so as not to further embarrass him and his descendants. If Jack Webb saw fit to "change the names to protect the innocent" in *Dragnet,* there's certainly no good reason to have a *National Enquirer*-style splash in this case!

3. R. K. Harrison, "Ruth" in the *Evangelical Commentary on the Bible,* ed. Walter A. Elwell (Grand Rapids: Baker, 1989), 186.

4. Robert L. Hubbard, Jr., *The Book of Ruth,* New International Commentary on the Old Testament (Grand Rapids: Eerdmans, 1988), 57, is a glaring exception to that rule. He holds that only broader kinsman-redeemer responsibilities are in play in Ruth, not Levirate marriage.

5. This rendering is favored by F. B. Huey, Jr., "Ruth," in *Expositor's Bible Commentary,* ed. Frank E. Gaebelein (Grand Rapids: Zondervan, 1992), 3:541. Translations such as "friend" (NASB, NIV) are inadequate.

The need for ten elders (4:2) marks this scene as a "proper legal ceremony."[6] Apparently Boaz's echoed request for the kinsman (4:1) and the ten elders (4:2) to sit down "convened" the court, so to speak.[7]

Best Wishes for a Great Future! (4:11–12)

For all the legal maneuvering in between (4:3–10), the conclusion of this court (4:11 NASB; lit., gate) scene is straightforwardly joyful! The gathered "witnesses" (4:11), the panel of elders, and other curious onlookers (4:11), all joined in pronouncing extraordinary prayerful blessings on Ruth, Boaz (4:11), and their *anticipated* descendants (4:11–12).

Since Rachel and Leah (4:11) were the esteemed mothers (physically or legally; Gen. 35:22–26) of the founders of the twelve tribes of Israel, any comparison with previously childless Ruth seems amazing. However, the Lord could still finally act in Ruth's life, as in Rachel's (Gen. 30:22), by "opening her womb."

The next two blessings seem to work together. The elevation of Boaz to rightly deserved fame and fortune in Bethlehem (4:11) coupled with comparison to the dominant Perizzite clan[8] of the ascendant tribe of Judah (4:12; cf. Gen. 46:12; 49:8, 10; Num. 26:20–21) through Ruth's *projected* child would place them among the elite of Israel. Now, there's a deal: by becoming a husband and father (4:11–13), you also get proclaimed a local and national hero (4:11–12)!

Going Off Half-Cocked (4:3–4)

If Boaz lived today, he could easily be an expert at fly fishing. He certainly demonstrates in Ruth 4:3–4 the ability to get his fish to take the bait. He skillfully casts upon the waters a mention of Naomi's land to be sold (4:3–4a) and the other kinsman immediately bites (4:b).

It might have been expected that Boaz would lead with mention of Ruth, who was already highly respected throughout Bethlehem (3:11), especially since no previous reference to

6. Harrison, "Ruth," 186. It may be significant, as Huey, "Ruth," 541, notes, that ten later became "the number of men required to constitute a synagogue."

7. This is the considered opinion of Hubbard, *Ruth*, 236.

8. See the in-depth discussion related to the clan of Perez (4:18) in chapter 7.

Naomi's and Elimelech's "land" (4:3) had been made *directly*. Presumably, though, since the family had planned only to "sojourn" (1:1 NASB) in Moab, and since Naomi and Ruth, destitute though they were on their arrival in Bethlehem, apparently had a place to live, the tactic that Boaz chose was not altogether surprising and in no sense inappropriate. That is especially the case since a key responsibility of a kinsman-redeemer had to do with keeping land in the family (Lev. 25:23–28).[9]

As Boaz succinctly laid out the circumstances (Ruth 4:3) and charged the unnamed kinsman with exercising his "first right of Levirate refusal"[10] (4:4a), the kinsman clearly thought he had stumbled into a deal: he could look like a good kinsman and still get a nice piece of land for a bargain price, with no strings attached.[11] Little did he know that he was walking right into Boaz's trap.

The other kinsman's response was emphatic in its acceptance of the Levirate responsibility: "*I* will redeem" (4:4b).[12] It would soon become obvious, though, that he had a serious case of foot-in-mouth disease.

Admittedly, Boaz was subtly pressing[13] him for a decision: "If you will redeem it, do so. But if you will not, tell me, so I will know" (4:4 NIV). Nevertheless, that is not a sufficient excuse not to look before you leap.

A New Lease on Life (4:9–10)

If the closer kinsman had been guilty of talk first, think later, that was not the case with Boaz—not even close! In keeping with the solemn and binding nature of the courtroom setting and the Levirate transaction (4:9–10), Boaz *twice* charged those assembled: "You are witnesses today . . ." (4:9a, 10b).[14]

9. It may also be that Boaz's previously expressed concern that Naomi not be left "empty-handed" (3:17) also comes out here through attempting to liquidate the property of the immediate family, likely the only valuable asset that was left.

10. Harrison, "Ruth," 186.

11. Hubbard, *Ruth,* 242.

12. Huey, "Ruth," 542. Italics added.

13. Hubbard, *Ruth,* 242.

14. It is very likely that these twin charges to the "witnesses" are intended to bracket the two Levirate transactions that Boaz is committing to: the purchase of the family land from Naomi (4:9b), and Levirate marriage to Ruth (4:10a).

It was as public as if Boaz was holding a modern press conference. Everything he said was on the record. There would be no reversing his field, in stark contrast to the other kinsman (4:4–6).

In purchasing "all that belonged to" the family of Elimelech (4:9b), Boaz is, in modern terms, buying the whole family estate. By marrying Ruth (4:10a), he also is "assuming the heirship to Elimelech," and thus to his sons also.[15] All hopes for a future for the family name are now resting squarely on Boaz's shoulders! Through him, the family has the opportunity to get a new lease on life.

Boaz next (4:10) refers to his new wife-to-be as "the Moabitess,"[16] the very background that was hung like an albatross around Ruth's neck when she and Naomi first arrived in Bethlehem (1:22). It also was likely a key element, along with the looming financial burden, that caused the other kinsman to back away from serving as the family redeemer (4:5).[17]

Only now does the reader learn that Mahlon (4:10) was the son of Naomi who was married to Ruth (1:4). Leon Morris is probably right in understanding that, without an heir, Chilion's name would die out and his inheritance would pass to any heir of Mahlon,[18] through Boaz (4:10).[19]

Springing the Trap (4:5–6)

I am not a card player. But, I have watched enough of those Kenny Rogers television movies to figure out that it takes nerves of steel to "know when to hold them and know when to

15. Harrison, "Ruth," 186.

16. It is tantalizing to speculate as to whether the Gentile blood in Boaz's background, through Rahab (Matt. 1:5), had anything to do with Boaz's almost proud reference to "Ruth the Moabitess" here.

17. In terms of the elegant chiastic structuring of Ruth, it is significant to note that the only references to "Ruth *the Moabitess*" are in the parallel scenes (i.e., 1:22 and 4:5, 10).

18. It is probably not possible to be certain whether there is any significance in the reversal of the order of the names of Naomi's sons from their only other mentions in 1:3, 5. One would normally expect the name of the older son to appear first in such a legal context. However, it may be that Mahlon is listed last (4:9b) because his widow, Ruth, becomes the next focus of attention (4:10a).

19. Leon Morris, "Ruth" in *Judges, Ruth,* Tyndale Old Testament Commentaries (Downers Grove: InterVarsity, 1968), 309.

fold them." With the other kinsman's hair-trigger response in Ruth 4:4, it looked like it was time for Boaz to fold it up and walk away. However, the smart money would still have been on Boaz.

The fact that there is not a hint of either surprise or disappointment from Boaz certainly implies that he had anticipated what the other kinsman would do. He knew his kinsman. He knew human nature. He used that wise insight to his own advantage.

With the addition of Ruth (i.e., Levirate marriage)[20] to the deal, the kinsman's perspective changed immediately. What looked like easy street financially before (4:3–4) now looked a lot more like the road to the poorhouse!

Not only would the support of Ruth, a despised Moabite[21] (Deut. 23:3–4), drain the kinsman's resources (4:5). Any children that Ruth might have would be considered legally to be Mahlon's (4:10), according to the broader implications of the Levirate marriage statute (Deut. 25:5–6), which are virtually echoed in Boaz's words in 4:5.

Thus, the kinsman would pay for everything involved in that child's upbringing. Yet the land he was purchasing from Naomi (4:3–4) would eventually revert to that child with no reimbursement after Ruth, Naomi, the child, and the upkeep of the land had drained the estate that he would be able to leave his own children (4:6). This was nowhere near the sweet deal that the unnamed kinsman thought he was getting only seconds before! So, he replies, in effect, "I simply cannot afford it" (4:6).[22]

What a turn-around! In one breath, the other kinsman is jumping at the chance to redeem Naomi's land (4:4). In the next, he cannot jump out of the way quickly enough: he passes the

20. Among recent evangelical commentators, there are those who unequivocally hold that Ruth 4 is an example of Levirate marriage (e.g., R. K. Harrison); take a nuanced Levirate marriage view (e.g., F. B. Huey, Jr.); and do not believe that true "Levirate marriage" in any sense is seen in this passage (e.g., R. L. Hubbard, Jr.).

21. The later Jewish *Midrash Ruth Rab.* 7:7, 10 took the view that the kinsman would not marry Ruth because of her foreign blood. Given that everything else in Boaz's wording is purposeful, that is quite possible. On the other hand, Hubbard, *Ruth,* 243, sees the terminology as "legal precision," not a tactic by Boaz.

22. The discussion in this paragraph (and this interpretive paraphrase of the kinsman's response) is summarized from Hubbard, *Ruth,* 245.

right and responsibility on to Boaz like a hot potato (4:6)! (Congratulations, Boaz! Your ancient forefather of the old trap play worked to perfection!)

Sealing the Deal and Slinking Away (4:7–8)

If this kind of transaction were taking place today, all that would be left to do at this point would be a handshake. Imagine how shocked you would be if you extended your hand, only to have the other party in the deal hand you his shoe.

The writer of Ruth anticipates that his readers might be in the dark as to the meaning of the kinsman's next move (4:7): removing his sandal while urging Boaz to assume his abdicated responsibility as kinsman-redeemer for Naomi and Ruth (4:8). The reason that he offers this parenthetical editorial explanation apparently is the relative distance in time from what Hubbard calls "the Ceremony of the Sandal."[23]

Some commentators have seen in the wording "in earlier times" (4:7 NIV) the passage of many centuries since the event being described. It is true that the term (Hebrew *lephanim*) is occasionally used to speak of a point very long ago (e.g., Ps. 102:25). However, it need not mean anything more than "in previous generations," as is the case in Judges 3:2,[24] a passage that is almost certainly the closest scriptural usage in the timing of both the event and the writing about it.[25]

If this is indeed a Levirate marriage, why didn't Ruth, the spurned widow, go and take the sandal off the foot of the *irresponsible* kinsman-redeemer and spit in his face, as Deuteronomy 25:7–9 lays out? There are at least four reasons: Ruth was not present at the proceeding, in contrast to Deuteronomy 25:7; there was also land involved and there needed to be a *clarification* of wider kinsman-redeemer status *beyond* the immediate family relationships (Deut. 25:5–7) in this case (Ruth 3:18–4:4); what Ruth hoped would happen was "rejec-

23. Hubbard, *Ruth,* 247.

24. Herbert Wolf, "Judges," in *Expositor's Bible Commentary,* 3:396.

25. Both Wolf, "Judges," 378, and Andrew Bowling, "Judges," in *Evangelical Commentary on the Bible,* 158, date Judges around 1000 B.C. See the discussion on the early dating of Ruth related to the concluding genealogy (4:18–22) in the next chapter.

tion" by the other kinsman so that she could marry Boaz (Ruth 3:11–13; 4:7–10), the opposite outcome of that envisioned in Deuteronomy 25; and the kinsman's sandal gets removed anyway (Deut. 25:9–10), even though it is as much in regard to the settlement of the land transaction as in relation to the Levirate marriage (Ruth 4:7), though in this case they are interrelated issues (4:5, 9–10).

It may also be that Boaz and Ruth were such gracious people that they saw no need to embarrass the other kinsman (e.g., Ruth coming forward and spitting in his face) any more than he had already embarrassed himself. That certainly was the case with the writer of Ruth, who did not specifically name the kinsman (4:1), but allowed him to fade quietly from view once his decision was made. Thus, the kinsman quickly exits stage left from the ensuing action (4:9–12), much as Orpah had done in 1:14.[26]

First Steps, Final Steps

When Naomi and Ruth took their first exhausted steps through the gate of Bethlehem only a few weeks earlier (1:6–22), they had no idea that a courtroom scene at that same location would soon permanently alter their lives for the good. The following chart depicts how the final legal steps that Boaz undertook (4:1–12) were undoubtedly expertly shaped by the writer to echo the earlier "commitment" scene.

"Till Death Us Do Part":
Mirroring Commitment Scenes

Ruth 1:6–22	*THEMES*	*Ruth 4:1–12*
Naomi, Orpah, and Ruth (3)	MAIN CHARACTERS	Boaz, unnamed kinsman, and Ruth (3)

26. The symmetrical literary parallel between the logical decisions made by Orpah and the unnamed kinsman is often missed by students of Ruth. It serves to further emphasize the costly commitments made by Ruth (1:16–17) and Boaz (4:9–10) in the respective scenes. See the following chart for further development of this beautiful parallelism.

To Bethlehem	TRAVEL	To gate of Bethlehem
No possible heirs	COMPLICATION IN PLOT	possible heirs (inheritance)
Withdrawal by uncommitted one	HINGE EVENT	Withdrawal by uncommitted one
Ruth toward Naomi	COMMITMENT	Boaz toward Ruth
Women of Bethlehem	"CHORUS"	People at the gate of Bethlehem
Bitterness	CLOSING ATTITUDE	Joy
*The Moabitess	DESCRIPTION OF RUTH	*The Moabitess (* only uses in book)
Deuteronomy 23:3 (24:19)	RELEVANT SCRIPTURE	Deuteronomy 25:5–10

When Ruth committed herself to Naomi and Naomi's God in 1:16–17, there was considerable uncertainty as to what would happen in the future. When Boaz committed himself to Ruth (4:10a), her personal "security" (3:1 NASB)—and that of Naomi (4:9)—was no longer in question. Yet, the problem of the future of the family still loomed large (4:10b).

Would the Lord see fit to revive the family name by blessing the new marriage of Ruth and Boaz (4:10)? That is the aspect of this otherwise happy drama that is still to be resolved!

6

Scene 6: Getting the Pressbox Perspective *(4:13–17)*

The football season previous to the one in which I got trapped, I also suffered a fractured hand and missed three games. During that time I was assigned to be the spotter for the public address announcer in the pressbox.

I soon found out that the pressbox offers an amazing perspective on a football game. I particularly enjoyed being able to tell what was coming together in two situations during the final quarter of games: the do-or-die third- and fourth-down plays on ball-possession "marches" that resulted in a decisive score, and the unexpected so-called gadget plays, where the element of surprise made for a spectacular touchdown that turned a game around.

If the Book of Ruth were a football game, Ruth 4:13–17 is the final, and determinative, stanza. This is where the family of Elimelech (1:2–3; 4:3) converts the crucial fourth down in regard to the future of its name (4:13), due to the action of the divine "Coach." This is also where the Lord's surprise play, held to the last verse of the narrative (4:17), is, so to speak, a long pass caught by an unexpected figure to gain the crown.

The Pressbox View of Ruth's "Last Hurrah"

The following diagram looks down from the scriptural pressbox and shows what is at the center of the inverted structuring of the final scene in this wonderful drama (4:13–17). In looking ahead to the resurrected future of her family, Naomi finds out that her loving and loyal daughter-in-law, Ruth, is more important than having her sons back, or even having the culturally perfect number of sons (4:15b).

A The family's *immediate* future: Marriage, conception, birth (4:13)
  B Women bless name of Naomi's redeemer: *Greatness* (4:14)
    C Newborn child will sustain Naomi's old age (4:15a)
      D Ruth better than seven sons (4:15b)
    C′ Newborn child nursed by Naomi (4:16)
  B′ Women give name to Naomi's redeemer: *Servant* (4:17a)
A′ The family's *longer-term* future: Obed, Jesse, David (4:17b)[1]

This passage teaches even modern readers an important principle: *God can use unexpected people and unlikely means to accomplish amazing things in and through your life.* Let's see how that worked out over time in Naomi's life.

The Future: Up Close and Personal (4:13)

Immediately after declaring publicly that he would marry Ruth (4:10), Boaz made good on his promise (4:13a)[2] and "took Ruth home as his wife."[3] The narrative of this verse includes no

1. This structural chart is adapted from A. Boyd Luter and Richard O. Rigsby, "An Adjusted Symmetrical Structuring of Ruth, with Implications for the Dating and Purpose Questions," forthcoming in the *Journal of the Evangelical Theological Society,* 1995.

2. Interestingly, there is no mention of the normally festive Jewish wedding, which may have continued for days (R. K. Harrison, "Ruth," in *Evangelical Commentary on the Bible,* ed. Walter A. Elwell [Grand Rapids: Baker, 1989], 186).

3. This helpful paraphrase is from Robert L. Hubbard, Jr., *The Book of Ruth,* New International Commentary on the Old Testament (Grand Rapids: Eerdmans, 1988), 266. F. B. Huey, Jr., "Ruth" in *Expositor's Bible Commentary,* ed. Frank E. Gaebelein (Grand Rapids: Zondervan, 1992), 3:547, correctly notes that the word used here for marriage (Hebrew *laqah*) is "unusual." However, all the circumstances involved in this story are unusual. Also, 4:13, which spans at least nine months, seems intent on moving forward to the point when Ruth's and Boaz's child is born as quickly as possible.

dialogue,[4] just tastefully observing that the marriage was consummated ("he went to her," NIV).

If this marriage were taking place in the 1990s, both parties would have set up sessions with a fertility specialist as soon as possible. However, in spite of Ruth's previous years of childless marriage (1:4), there is no mention of difficulty in becoming pregnant.

The wording of the verse moves briskly and succinctly from marriage to intimate relations to conception to birth (4:13), slowing down only to triumphantly state "the Lord enabled her to conceive."[5] Amazingly, after Ruth 1:6–4:12 covers at most a few months, 4:13 leaps over the better part of a year. Thus, the impression is strong that, although the new marriage was indeed a wonderful one, the writer is much more concerned with the child it produced.

The Future: A Crown on the Horizon (4:17b)

So, you thought 4:13 was a fast run around the block! You ain't seen nothing yet! That verse at the beginning of the final narrative scene overviews something over nine *months* of time. By contrast, 4:17b spans three *generations,* from Obed, the child born to Boaz and Ruth (4:13–17a), through his son, Jesse, to (surprise!) David, his grandson (4:17b).[6]

Only now does it become clear that this touching story of an endangered family name in the little town of Bethlehem in Judah (1:2, 22) is about a previous generation in the life of that nationally famous leader, David. The prayerful wishes of the onlookers in 4:11 (for Boaz) and 4:14 (for Obed) for a famous name turns out to be eerily prophetic![7]

4. This is another parallel between 4:13–17 and the first scene in the book (1:1–5), which has no dialogue at all. See the chart near the end of this chapter which notes a number of striking additional parallels between 1:1–5 and 4:13–17.

5. The miracle here, while not on the order of the virgin birth (Matt. 1; Luke 1–2), is nevertheless still every bit as much a miracle, as were the "eleventh-hour" conceptions of Rachel (4:11) and Tamar (4:12).

6. Huey, "Ruth," 547, holds that the "Moabite connection" in David's family background explains why David asked the king of Moab for refuge for his parents in 1 Sam. 22:3–4, while David was fleeing from Saul.

7. Hubbard, *Ruth,* 278.

What's in a Name (i): Greatness (4:14)

For many of my younger years, I chafed at having been named Asa Boyd Luter, Jr. The only thing that kept me from being made fun of *to my face* when I was young was that I was considerably bigger than anyone else in my class until high school.

Oh, well. With a name like this, I have never gotten mixed up with the nondescript "John Smiths" of this life. And, I get to carry on the proud name of my now-deceased father, a career Army officer and astute businessman in his retirement years. My name has finally changed from a burden to the blessing it was intended to be.

This verse does not yet tell us the exact name given to the newborn baby of Ruth and Boaz (4:13b). However, it does tell us two other important angles: the child will, in time, take over the role of kinsman-redeemer for Naomi from his father, Boaz (4:14a), and in the minds of the women of Bethlehem, who chime in at this point, this child is (prayerfully) destined for national greatness (4:14b)![8]

What's in a Name (ii): Servanthood (4:17a)

It's almost as if the writer of Ruth had been reading Matthew 20:26: "Whoever wishes to become great among you shall become your servant."

Or, perhaps Jesus partly saw that principle embodied in the lives of his forebears, Boaz and Ruth (Matt. 1:5), and the name given to their newborn son: Obed (Ruth 4:17a), meaning "one who serves."[9]

Obed was almost certainly given his name because he would be serving Naomi, both as her kinsman-redeemer (4:14–15a) and her (grand-) "son."[10] The interesting angle here is that it is the chorus of "neighbor women" that again pipes up and "named him Obed" (4:17a NASB).

8. Attempts to either understand the *goel* as Boaz or the famous one as the Lord in 4:14 fall flat in light of the "him" in 4:15 clearly referring to the newborn child.

9. Hubbard, *Ruth,* 276–77; Huey, "Ruth," 547; Harrison, "Ruth," 187.

10. There is an extraordinarily close relationship between Naomi and Obed envisioned in 4:15–17, but there is no compelling evidence that she officially adopted him.

Interestingly, this is the only place in the Old Testament in which "a child is named by someone other than the immediate family,"[11] though it happened with John the Baptist (Luke 1:13) and Jesus (Matt. 1:21) in the New Testament. But, if those women are as good at naming babies as they are at predicting future greatness (Ruth 4:14), let 'em take a shot at it![12]

A Newborn Retirement Plan (4:15a)

Here we see one of the rare "two for the price of one" deals that is totally on the up-and-up. In the years ahead, Naomi will receive both emotional solace ("renew your life," NIV) and physical sustenance (4:15a)[13] from the grown son of Ruth and Boaz (4:13–14). However long Naomi lived in her "old age," Obed (4:17) would be there for her, providing great encouragement to her beyond the necessities of life.

Where did the capacity for this kind of ongoing "service" (4:17) come from? *Good genes and good examples!* This is precisely the same kind of tenacious loyalty seen in the lives of Obed's mother, Ruth (1:16–17), and father, Boaz (3:13; 4:9–10).

Nursing the Redeemer Along (4:16)

It would be some time, though, before baby Obed (4:17) would be able to assume his duties in "serving" Naomi. In the meantime, though, Naomi joyfully held in her arms the child who legally took the place of her own deceased sons (1:5). What a delight, watching the future of the family that not long ago had no future grow up!

It is impossible to know from the scant evidence in this scene whether Obed went to live with Naomi, or whether "cared for him" (4:16 NIV) means acting as "his nurse" (NASB), as a guardian, or simply as a proud grandmother (4:17a).[14] It is intriguing to note, however, that Ruth and Boaz fade from view, in terms of actions, after 4:13. Whatever the exact nuance of Naomi's role, it means that she

11. Huey, "Ruth," 547.

12. Luke 1:59 may indicate that a custom had developed among the Jews that included "neighbors" in the naming of children.

13. Hubbard, *Ruth,* 272.

14. See the helpful discussion in Hubbard, *Ruth,* 274–75.

would lovingly take care of Obed up to a certain age, then he would lovingly care for her the rest of her life (4:14–15a, 16).

Better Than Perfection (4:15b)

This is the crowning glory of the Book of Ruth until you get to the part that looks ahead to David being crowned as the rightful king of Israel (4:17, 22; 1 Sam. 16:12–13)! Earlier in the narrative, Boaz has paid Ruth some wonderful compliments, in terms of her family loyalty and faith (Ruth 2:12–13) and her sterling reputation (3:11; see Prov. 31).

But, now, it is the women of Bethlehem who give her the ultimate accolade in a patriarchal society: not only did she dearly love their friend, Naomi; she had turned out to be more valuable to Naomi "than seven sons" (4:15b).

Having seven (the biblical number of completeness, or perfection) sons was "the ideal of all Hebrew families."[15] So, in the happiest of happy endings, Naomi's family is realized to be maximally blessed, but not by the presence of a "quiver full" (Ps. 127:5) of sons. Rather, it is a Moabite woman (4:10) who is the source of that blessing! When you've got a daughter-in-law—or a wife—like that, you've got a priceless gem sparkling in your life (Prov. 31:10)!

Coming Full Circle

The garments of mourning of Ruth 1:5 have finally given way to the glad rags of 4:14–17. The gnawing emptiness has been replaced by grateful (4:14) fulfillment! The following chart reveals the extensive thematic interplay between these scenes of complete devastation (1:1–5) and miraculous restoration (4:13–17).

Naomi Emptied and Filled:
Ruth's Literary Low Point and High Point

Ruth 1:1–5		*Ruth 4:13–17*
Famine in Bethlehem	Initial circumstances	Wedding in Bethlehem

15. Harrison, "Ruth," 187.

Leaving land; land endangered	Family status	Back in land; land reestablished
Marriages and then deaths	Family events	Marriage, then birth
Withheld: Barrenness	Blessing	Bestowed: Birth
No hope in sight	Possibility of help	Redeemers: Boaz, Obed
Widow of deceased son	Status of Ruth/ significance to Ruth	Better than seven sons
Emptiness/grief from husband's death	Naomi's emotions	Joyfulness: Obed's birth
Introductory "bookend"	Literary function	Concluding "bookend"

This is the end of the "short story" part of the Book of Ruth. But, there is a very good reason that you do not yet see "The End" and the rolling of the credits. The epilogue (4:18–22) is still to come. That's where the press-box view gives way to a breathtaking helicopter view. After a brief break (to turn the page!), I'll join you in climbing to the top of Ruth's concluding family tree, where we'll get the lowdown on the higher-ups in the most scripturally prominent family in Bethlehem.

7

Epilogue: Limbs on the Original Christmas Tree *(4:18–22)*

As a child growing up near Jackson, Mississippi, for me one of the highlights of the Christmas season was Belhaven College's presentation of "The Living Christmas Tree." It was thrilling to watch the choir members move up onto the large tree-shaped stand in their green robes. From a distance, it looked as if the "tree" was actually growing before your eyes!

Viewing the family tree at the end of the Book of Ruth is much like that. You get to see the family tree of David, the greatest king of Israel, grow from its roots, the generation that heard the promise of the royal "scepter" and the "ruler's staff" (Gen. 49:10 NASB) given to the tribe of Judah. In fact, within the wider biblical context, it is not too much to say that this ten-person genealogy in Ruth are *limbs on the original Christmas tree that are moving up toward the "star," Jesus Christ.*

There is another sense in which Ruth 4:18–22 is like a beautiful live Christmas tree. As will be clearly seen, it is shaped with remarkable balance,[1] though it carries the marks of surviving through the difficult seasons.

1. Much of the material in this chapter is adapted from A. Boyd Luter and Richard O. Rigsby, "An Adjusted Symmetrical Structuring of Ruth, with Implications for the Dating and Purpose Questions," forthcoming in the *Journal of the Evangelical Theological Society,* 1995.

Lingering Doubts

But, there is a foundational problem in dealing with the concluding family tree (4:18–22): some scholars do not believe that it was originally part of the book. For example, as recently as 1975 the influential voice of E. F. Campbell, Jr., confidently stated: "There is all but universal agreement that verses 18–22 form a genealogical appendix to the Ruth story and are not an original part of it."[2] To his credit, Campbell was also wise enough to quickly admit, "The addition of a genealogical appendix to Ruth is unique; we are therefore hard put to assess its precise significance."[3]

Since Campbell's assessment, however, a chorus of voices from different parts of the scholarly community have argued that the genealogy is, in fact, an integral part of Ruth.[4] Things have now changed to the extent that Phylis Trible could recently cautiously affirm: "Most exegetes affirm the unity of the book, though the genealogy at the end (4:18–22) remains a problem."[5]

Links That Are *Not* Missing

The present study will not argue directly for the unity of the Ruth narrative and genealogy. Rather, it will put on display some of the

2. E. F. Campbell, Jr., *Ruth,* The Anchor Bible (Garden City, N.Y.: Doubleday, 1975), 172.

3. Ibid.

4. A chronological short list of such significant works includes J. M. Sasson, *Ruth: A New Translation with a Philological Commentary and a Formalist-Folklorist Interpretation* (Baltimore: Johns Hopkins, 1979), 178–87; Robert L. Hubbard, Jr., *The Book of Ruth,* New International Commentary on the Old Testament (Grand Rapids: Eerdmans, 1988), 33–38; Phylis Trible, "Ruth," in *Anchor Bible Dictionary,* ed. D. N. Freedman (New York: Doubleday, 1992), 5:843, 845; and F. B. Huey, Jr., "Ruth," in *Expositor's Bible Commentary,* ed. Frank E. Gaebelein (Grand Rapids: Zondervan, 1992), 3:548–49. Adele Berlin, "Ruth," in *Harper's Bible Commentary,* ed. Wayne A. Meeks (San Francisco: Harper and Row, 1988), 262, is of the opinion that there is currently "no consensus" on the unity of the Book of Ruth. See also C. McCarthy, "The Davidic Genealogy in the Book of Ruth," *Proceedings of the Irish Biblical Association* 9 (1985): 53–62.

5. Trible, "Ruth," 843. It has even been thought by some that the family tree in Ruth was adapted from the genealogy in 1 Chron. 2:1–15 at a late date, though there is no hard evidence for such a view.

additional literary touches[6] beyond the grand chiastic structure laid out throughout the exposition that the writer of Ruth skillfully utilized in previewing the climactic genealogy throughout the narrative. The following chart highlights a number of these:

Literary Links Between Ruth's
Story (1:1–4:17) and Family Tree (4:18–22)

Preview in the Narrative	*Parallel in the Genealogy*
1. Days of the judges (1:1)	Salmon to Jesse (4:20–22)
2. Famine (1:1)	Reason to go to Egypt: Perez, Hezron (4:18)
3. Bethlehem in Judah (1:1)	Boaz to David (home of family; 4:21–22)
4. Leaving the land (1:1)	Perez, Hezron (4:18)
5. Returning to the land (1:6–22)	Exodus and conquest: Nahshon, Salmon (4:20–21)
6. Emphasis on Boaz in central chiastic layer (chaps. 2, 3)	Boaz in honored seventh position in family tree (4:21)
7. Child by "Levirate" relationship after kinsman's reneging (4:6,13)	Birth of Perez (4:18) after Judah's reneging (see Gen. 38)
8. Become "famous" in *Bethlehem* (4:11)	Boaz and David (4:21–22)
9. Fame in Israel (4:14)	Obed and David (4:21–22)
10. Obed, Jesse, David (4:17)	Obed, Jesse, David (4:21–22)

The key observation here is that every part of the narrative of Ruth points ahead to the genealogy, whether obviously or with exquisite subtlety. And, because the literary interplay between the family tree (Ruth 4:18–22) and the narrative of the book (1:1–4:17) is apparently even more

6. Note here the perspective of Campbell, *Ruth,* 13, that inclusios are the "chief building blocks" of Ruth.

extensive than has been previously recognized, the case for the original unity of Ruth 1:1–4:22 is strengthened.

A Beautifully Shaped (Family) Tree

As far as the purpose of the concluding family tree in Ruth (4:18–22) is concerned, commentators from as least as early as Keil and Delitzsch have spoken of: ". . . The limitation of the whole genealogy to ten members, for the purpose of stamping upon it through the number ten as the seal of completeness the character of a perfect, concluded, and symmetrical whole."[7]

It is also common for 4:18–22 to be viewed as a royal genealogy[8] designed to "legitimate David and his monarchy."[9] This effectively explains the climactic positioning of the name *David* in 4:17 and 4:22.

But, there may well be more. After all, Campbell is correct in calling the location of this genealogy "unique,"[10] and that combined with its internal chiastic structure, as will be seen, implies a role more significant than has been previously understood.

Two other angles on the purpose of the family tree that merit fair consideration are suggested by M. D. Johnson: "to bridge the time gap between the conquest and the onset of the Davidic monarchy" and to "provide an individual of rank with connections to a worthy family or individual of the past."[11] It is better, however, to view the "bridging" *from* the time when Perez—to whose clan Elimelech, Naomi's deceased husband, and Boaz belonged (2:1; 4:18)—became recognized as the heir (Gen. 46:12) to the promise of the "scepter" and "ruler's staff" to Judah's descendants (Gen. 49:10), in spite of the odd, embarrassing Levirate-like circumstances of his birth (Gen. 38).[12]

7. C. F. Keil and F. Delitzch, "Ruth," in *Commentary on the Old Testament,* trans. J. Martin (reprint; Grand Rapids: Eerdmans, 1973), 2:493.

8. Hubbard, *Ruth,* 39.

9. Trible, "Ruth," 846.

10. Campbell, *Ruth,* 172.

11. M. D. Johnson, *The Purpose of the Biblical Genealogies with Special Reference to the Setting of the Genealogies of Jesus,* SNTSMS 8 (Cambridge: Cambridge University Press, 1969), 78–79. See also R. Wilson, "Old Testament Genealogies in Recent Research," *Journal of Biblical Literature* 94 (1975): 169–89.

12. C. F. Mariottini, "Perez," *Anchor Bible Dictionary,* 5:226, concludes that Gen. 38 is designed to explain "the preeminence of the younger clan Perez over the older clans of Judah."

The following chart visualizes this bridging and serves to clarify the crucial, and striking, comparison between David and Nahshon (4:20) that is highlighted. Both emerged from this clan of expectant royalty (Gen. 49:10) to highly responsible positions of military command in Israel at the conclusion of extremely difficult periods in Israelite history: for Nahshon, the Egyptian captivity; for David, the era of the judges and the uneven beginning of a united monarchy in Israel under Saul. Both not only represented hope for the future through their strong leadership, but also a reminder of the ongoing "royal promise" (Gen. 49:10) to the emerging family line.

The Lives and Times[13] of the Perezite Clan (Ruth 4:18a):
The "Leading" Family of Judah (Ruth 4:20, 22)

From the "Promise of Royalty" to Judah's Descendants (Gen. 49:10) until Leadership in the Exodus	*From Entry into the Promised Land until the Anointed (1 Sam. 16:1–13) Founder of the Judahite Royal Line*
1. Perez	6. Salmon (or Salma)
2. Hezron	7. (Honored Position) Boaz
3. Ram	8. Obed
4. Amminadab	9. Jesse
5. Nahshon: "Leader of the sons of Judah" (Num. 2:3) militarily in the exodus period under Moses	10. David: Leader of Israel's armies under Saul (1 Sam. 18:5) after being anointed next king by Samuel
Approximate Span of First Half of Genealogy: 430 years (Exod. 12:40), *plus* perhaps much of the wilderness generation (40 years; Num. 14:27)	*Approximate Span of Second Half of Genealogy*: 476 years to end of David's reign (1 Kings 6:1), *minus* 40 years to its start (2 Sam. 5:4)

13. P. R. Gilchrist, *"toledot," Theological Wordbook of the Old Testament* 1:868, affirms that the important term *generations* (e.g., Ruth 4:18) refers to "the events" as well as "what is produced or brought into being by someone" (here, the Perezites).

From the Promise to the Exit (4:18–20a)

As can be seen, apparently as an extension of the elegant symmetrical crafting of the narrative (1:1–4:17), the final genealogy of ten names is also symmetrical: five names (Perez to Nahshon) bridging from Israel's entry into Egypt until the exodus period; and five (Salmon to David) from the conquest of the land to the first king of the Judahite (through the Perezites) "royal line" (Gen. 49:10).

The first five follow the emerging clan of the Perezites. Having been recognized as the most prominent line of Judah's descent as early as Genesis 46:12, their role is again underscored at the end of the forty years in the wilderness (Num. 26:20–21), which coincides with the transition in the genealogy from Nahshon to Salmon (Ruth 4:20).

Hezron (4:18–19) accompanied his father, Perez, his grandfather, Judah, and his great-grandfather, Jacob, to Egypt for protection from the famine (Gen. 46:8, 12). Ram,[14] Amminadab, and Nahshon (Ruth 4:19–20) were all born in Egypt, where they soon became slaves (Exod. 1:8–11), with Amminadab becoming the father-in-law of Aaron (6:23).

As "leader of the sons of Judah" (Num. 2:3) in the exodus-Sinai period, Nahshon presented their tribal offering *first* (7:12). He then led the armies of Judah, as well as the entire column of Israel, when the nation struck camp to leave Sinai (10:11–14). Nahshon was the acknowledged leader of the leading clan of the leading tribe of Israel! (How incredibly *David-like*!)

From the Entrance to the Throne (4:20b–22)

Salmon (4:20–21) participated in the conquest of the Promised Land under Joshua, and may be the figure who originally got the family settled in Bethlehem.[15] Then the family baton is handed to our heroes, Boaz (where we might have expected Elimelech's or Mahlon's name, from a Levirate perspective) and

14. There is a generation skipped at this point in the family (1 Chron. 2:25, 27), and perhaps elsewhere, in order to shape the family tree to the perfect number of ten.

15. Since only four generations of this family span some 360 years (i.e., from the conquest [ca. 1406 B.C.] to David's birth [1040 B.C.]), there may be another gap at this point in the genealogy.

Obed, (4:21–22) who run strong legs of the race before Jesse, who passes it on to the anchor figure, David (4:22).

The parallelism of the family tree seems to work at two levels.[16] First, and most direct (because of the preceding short story), the general flow of the story of Elimelech's family is quite similar to broader events in Israel's history during the "generations" (Ruth 4:18–22) in the genealogy, with the two virtually merging at the honored seventh position: Boaz, whose name and descent would become "famous" in Israel (4:11, 14).

Second, the strong leadership of Nahshon—in the emphasized fifth position in the symmetrical genealogy (4:20)—during the emergence of Israel from slavery in Egypt, is mirrored by the role of David's leadership in decisively putting the era of the judges (1:1) behind Israel. In reality and in the parallelism of this genealogy, Nahshon is *the unique* prototype model for leadership in Judah until David's exploits.

So, *When* Are We Talking about?

An important implication for the date when Ruth was written emerges here. The combination of the recognition of the form of Ruth 4:18–22 as a royal genealogy, its duration (i.e., bridging from Perez to David), and its paralleling of Nahshon and David—which must be limited to leadership and military exploits (Num. 10:11–14), since Nahshon is never anointed or viewed as royalty—fits best in the time between David's anointing as king by Samuel (1 Sam. 16:12, 13) and his actual recognition as king, first by Judah (2 Sam. 2:1–4), then seven years later by "all the tribes of Israel" (5:1 NASB). Thus, it would seem that at least an initial draft[17] of Ruth dates from about 1010 B.C., when David became king, or possibly earlier.[18] If it was written before Samuel's death (1 Sam. 25:1), it

16. Berlin, "Ruth," 262, believes that, in general, the Book of Ruth communicates at several levels, and Trible, 846, declares, "Many levels of meaning intertwine . . . ."

17. Huey, "Ruth," 511, conjectures that Ruth might have existed as a poetic story during the period of the Judges before being published in its present form at a later date.

18. This implication assumes that *at least* three (given the selective nature of the family tree) generations (i.e., Boaz to David) is a sufficiently long time span for an old custom to require explanation (Ruth 4:7).

would make sense that Samuel would follow up the anointing by carefully investigating the family background of the new king whom the Lord showed him would succeed the rejected Saul (1 Sam. 16:1).

A Purpose in His Sanity

The closing family tree of Ruth has been confusing to many. After the preceding discussion, we could conclude that the writer had a method in his madness. But, that wording does not even come close to reflecting how logically purposeful the genealogy is within the whole book. It is much closer to the mark to say that he had a purpose in his sanity.

If the reasoning regarding dating is valid, the "royal" purpose of Ruth can be further clarified. Hubbard represents a growing number of scholars who have painstakingly discerned a "political" purpose[19] for Ruth: "to win popular acceptance of David's rule by appeal to the continuity of Yahweh's guidance in the lives of Israel's ancestors and David."[20]

Dating Ruth before David's ascension to the throne of united Israel (2 Sam. 5:1–3) strengthens the force of that purpose. It is not at all unrealistic to view the Book of Ruth as a crucial credential for David, first to Judah (2 Sam. 2:1–4), then in Israel's bewildering choice between the existing royal family of Saul (2:8–4:12) and the long-promised Judahite line (Gen. 49:10).

Thus, it is clear that the family tree that crowns the Book of Ruth plays an indispensable role. It is only here that what is riding on the events in the Book of Ruth becomes clear. Though those events, of course, have significance in their own right, the wider purpose of the Book of Ruth is to chronicle *the providential prevention of a "missing link" in the royal line (Gen. 49:10) from Perez to the anointed family member, David (1 Sam. 16:12–13).*

The Star on the First Christmas Tree

This is where the Book of Ruth stops, but it not where the family tree ends. The genealogy (Ruth 4:18–22) is lifted like

19. Hubbard, *Ruth,* 39–42, provides an extended thematic interweaving that converges on this overarching purpose.
20. Ibid., 42.

a slice of pie and placed—with a few beautiful decorations—in the messianic family tree of the Lord Jesus Christ in Matthew 1:3–6.

This means that Ruth's marriage to Boaz accomplished even more than providing the link in the chain to King David. It also maintained the family movement ahead to ultimately "the son of David" (Matt. 1:1), the rightful eternal king. He is truly the Star who crowns the family tree that proves to be the real tree at the heart of Christmas and the Christian faith.

Remembering God's Providential Grace

Before closing, let's take one parting look at those decorations that Matthew added to Ruth's family tree. They are the names of four women: Tamar (1:3), Rahab and Ruth (1:5),[21] and Bathsheba (1:6). Two (Tamar and Rahab) had played the roles of prostitutes and a third had a tragic illicit affair (Bathsheba). Only our heroine, Ruth, is untainted by scandal.

All four women were likely Gentiles, probably pointing ahead to the time when the gospel of Jesus Christ would be offered to "all the nations" (Matt. 28:19 NASB), not just Israel. But, there is one other huge reason why these names were included: In the lives and families of each of these four women the incredible providence and grace of God is seen in remarkable ways, as he fits them beautifully into his messianic plan.

All along, the Lord knew that Joseph and his bride, Mary, would enter the gate of Bethlehem (Luke 2:4), just as Naomi and Ruth did, and that there Boaz would receive the right to marry Ruth; that Jesus would be born and laid in a feed trough (Luke 2:7) not far from the field where his great-great-great-great-great (you get the idea!) grandmother, Ruth, had gleaned and the threshing floor where she proposed marriage to Boaz; and that the shepherds who came to see the newborn Jesus (Luke 2:8–16) tended their flocks in the same fields

21. A slightly different discussion of the inclusion of Ruth's name in Matthew 1:5 can be found in A. Boyd Luter, "Ruth," in *The Complete Who's Who of the Bible,* ed. Paul Gardner (Grand Rapids: Zondervan, 1995).

where Ruth's great-grandson, David, had protected his family's sheep (1 Sam. 16:11; 17:34–35).

You can count on it: God's unseen providence always triumphs! No wonder Ruth had such an easy time finding the right job (Ruth 2:3), then getting an interview (2:7–8) and making a *favor*-able impression on the boss (2:11–12)!

Select Bibliography on Ruth

Atkinson, David. *The Wings of Refuge: The Message of Ruth.* The Bible Speaks Today. Downers Grove: InterVarsity, 1983.

Baldwin, Joyce G. "Ruth." In *New Bible Commentary: Revised,* edited by Donald Guthrie and J. A. Motyer. Grand Rapids: Eerdmans, 1970.

Barber, Cyril J. *Ruth: A Story of God's Grace.* Rev. ed. Old Tappan, N.J.: Loizeaux, 1989.

Beattie, D. R. G. *Jewish Exegesis of the Book of Ruth.* Sheffield: JSOT, 1977.

Berlin, Adele. "Ruth." In *Harper's Bible Commentary*, edited by W. A. Meeks. San Francisco: Harper and Row, 1988.

Bertman, Stephen. "Symmetrical Design in the Book of Ruth." *Journal of Biblical Literature* 84 (1965): 165–68.

Bush, Frederick W. *Ruth and Esther.* Word Biblical Commentary 8. Dallas: Word, forthcoming.

Campbell, E. F., Jr. "The Hebrew Short Story: Its Form, Style and Provenance." In *A Light Unto My Path: Old Testament Studies in Honor of Jacob Myers,* edited by H. N. Bream, R. D. Heim, and Carey A. Moore. Philadelphia: Temple University Press, 1974.

———. *Ruth.* The Anchor Bible. Garden City, N.Y.: Doubleday, 1975.

Chapin, Shelley. "Naomi" and "Women in the Bible." In *The Complete Who's Who of the Bible,* edited by Paul Gardner. Grand Rapids: Zondervan, 1995.

de Waard, Jan, and Eugene Nida. *A Translator's Handbook on the Book of Ruth.* London: United Bible Societies, 1973.

Enns, Paul. *Ruth*. Bible Study Commentary. Grand Rapids: Zondervan, 1982.

Gow, M. "The Significance of Literary Structure for the Translation of the Book of Ruth." *Bible Translator* 35 (1984): 309–20.

———. "Structure, Theme and Purpose in the Book of Ruth." Ph.D. dissertation, Cambridge University, 1983.

Gray, John. *Joshua, Judges, Ruth*. Rev. ed. New Century Bible. Grand Rapids: Eerdmans, 1986.

Hals, Ronald M. *The Theology of the Book of Ruth*. Philadelphia: Fortress, 1969.

Harrison, R. K. "Ruth." In *Evangelical Commentary on the Bible*, edited by Walter A. Elwell. Grand Rapids: Baker, 1989.

Hubbard, Robert L., Jr. *The Book of Ruth*. New International Commentary on the Old Testament. Grand Rapids: Eerdmans, 1988.

Huey, F. B., Jr. "Ruth." In *Expositor's Bible Commentary*, edited by Frank E. Gaebelein. 12 vols. Grand Rapids: Zondervan, 1992.

Johnson, M. D. *The Purpose of the Biblical Genealogies with Special Reference to the Setting of the Genealogies of Jesus*. Society of New Testament Studies Monograph Series. Cambridge: Cambridge University Press, 1969.

Keil, C. F., and F. Delitzsch. *Commentary on the Old Testament*. Translated by James Martin. Grand Rapids: Eerdmans, n.d.

Kennedy, Hardee. "Ruth." In *Broadman Bible Commentary*, edited by Clifton Allen. Nashville: Broadman, 1970.

Leggett, Donald A. *The Levirate and Goel Institutions in the Old Testament with Special Attention to the Book of Ruth*. Cherry Hill, N.J.: Mack, 1974.

Luter, A. Boyd. "Boaz" and "Ruth." In *The Complete Who's Who of the Bible*, edited by Paul Gardner. Grand Rapids: Zondervan, 1995.

Luter, A. Boyd, and Richard O. Rigsby. "An Adjusted Symmetrical Structuring of Ruth, with Implications for the Dating and Purpose Questions." Forthcoming in the *Journal of the Evangelical Theological Society*, 1995.

———. "The Chiastic Structure of Ruth 2." *Bulletin for Biblical Research* 3 (1993): 49–58.

———. "Protecting Ruth's Good Name: The Significance of the Structure of Ruth 3." Evanglical Theological Society paper, 1993.

Morris, Leon. "Ruth." In A. Cundall and L. Morris, *Judges, Ruth*. Tyndale Old Testament Commentaries. Downers Grove: InterVarsity, 1968.

Murphy, Roland E. "Ruth." In *Wisdom Literature*, Forms of Old

Testament Literature 13, edited by Rolf Knierim and Gene Tucker. Grand Rapids: Eerdmans, 1981.

Radday, Y. T. "Chiasmus in Hebrew Biblical Narrative." In *Chiasmus in Antiquity,* edited by John W. Welch. Hildesheim: Gerstenberg, 1981.

Reed, John. "Ruth." In *Bible Knowledge Commentary: Old Testament,* edited by John F. Walvoord and Roy B. Zuck. Wheaton: Victor, 1985.

Sasson, Jack M. "Divine Providence or Human Plan?" *Interpretation* 30 (1976): 415–19.

———. *Ruth*. Johns Hopkins Near Eastern Studies. Baltimore: Johns Hopkins University Press, 1979.

Slotki, Judah J. *The Five Megilloth*, edited by A. Cohen. London: Soncino, 1946.

Smith, Louise Pettibone. "The Book of Ruth: Exegesis." In *The Interpreter's Bible*, edited by George A. Buttrick. 12 vols. New York: Abingdon, 1953.

Thompson, Thomas, and Dorothy Thompson. "Some Legal Problems in the Book of Ruth." *Vetus Testamentum* 18 (1968): 79–99.

Trible, Phylis. "A Human Comedy: The Book of Ruth." In *Literary Interpretations of Biblical Narratives,* edited by K. G. Louis and J. Ackerman. Nashville: Abingdon, 1982.

———. "Ruth." In *Anchor Bible Dictionary*, vol. 5, edited by David Noel Freedman. New York: Doubleday, 1992.

Wilson, R. "Old Testament Genealogies in Recent Research." *Journal of Biblical Literature* 94 (1975): 169–89.

Part 2

Expositions of the Book of Esther

Barry C. Davis

Introduction to Esther

Something is missing."

One of the most frustrating things in life is looking for something you know you have but can't find.

Recently, while preparing to teach a theology class, I was unable to locate some papers that I needed. I scoured my study but couldn't find them, so I invaded the living room, the dining room, and then my study once again on the odd chance that somehow the papers crept back in there on their own—no such luck. After asking my wife if she knew where they were, I set out to recheck the living room and dining room, as well as my previously-searched briefcase. Still no papers. In frustration I returned to my study and sat down in front of my computer to continue working without them. Would you believe . . . there were my papers, right in front of me at the bottom of a pile of papers and books that I had already checked.

Somehow those papers must have sneaked in and hidden themselves . . . or were they there all of the time? Couldn't have been. Must have been Dickens, our cat, who stashed them there. Her ways have always been mysterious.

Not to Be Found

My frustration in searching in vain for something right under my nose is the same as that experienced by the reader of the Book of Esther. Where is God hiding? Nowhere is he mentioned, or even hinted at, in any of the ten chapters of the book.[1] Where, too, are the righteous people of God?[2] There is no mention of prayer[3] or of sacrifice, no indication of praise or the quotation of Scripture.

Despite what some well-intentioned commentators have said, neither Esther nor Mordecai (the main characters of the book) gives any evidence of being particularly righteous or spiritual.[4] Mordecai, a Jew, does the unthinkable (2:8–11)—he encourages his cousin (and "adopted" daughter) Esther to marry a heathen king, even though he knows that God strictly forbade his people the practice of mixed religious marriage.[5] Mordecai also knows full well that should Esther fail in her highly unlikely bid to become queen,[6] she would become the concubine of the king (2:12–14). Not

1. Esther is the only book in the Scripture that makes no direct reference to God. See, however, Esther 1:20; 5:4, 13; 7:7 for possible hidden acronyms of the divine name, YHWH.

Note: Many English versions of the Song of Songs contain no reference to God. The Hebrew of 8:6, however, includes the word *šalhebetyāh* which may be translated as "a flame of the Lord." Such a translation assumes that the final syllable, *yāh,* is the short form of the divine name, a form which occurs frequently throughout the Scripture. The intent of that final syllable, however, may be to convey the idea of might or vehemence, rather than to be a specific reference to God. If such is the case, then the entire word could be translated as either "a mighty flame" or "a vehement flame." Franz Delitzsch, *Commentary on the Song of Songs and Ecclesiastes*, trans. M. G. Easton (reprint; Grand Rapids: Eerdmans, 1968), 147; Dennis F. Kinlaw, "Song of Songs," *Expositor's Bible Commentary,* ed. Frank E. Gaebelein, 12 vols. (Grand Rapids: Zondervan, 1991), 5:1241.

2. The Book of Esther devotes more space than any other book in the Bible to a discussion of a heathen nation prior to ever mentioning either God (which it does not) or the people of God (first mentioned in 2:5, twenty-seven verses after the book begins).

3. Fasting is mentioned in Esther 4:3, 16, but prayer is conspicuous by its absence.

4. At the same time, the Book of Esther does not depict either Esther or Mordecai as being immoral or antagonistic toward God. It "simply relates what took place without blame or approval." C. F. Keil, *The Books of Ezra, Nehemiah, and Esther*, Biblical Commentary on the Old Testament, trans. Sophia Taylor (reprint; Grand Rapids: Eerdmans, n.d.), 316.

5. Technically, according to Exod. 34:11–16 and Deut. 7:1–4, the people of Israel were only forbidden to marry the people whom they conquered in the Promised Land. Yet Nehemiah (13:23–27), writing about a period of time perhaps less than forty years after the events of this story, and writing perhaps about the children of the Jews of Esther's time, issues a scathing indictment of any such practice.

6. Keep in mind that Esther was competing against all the other beautiful women of the realm (2:3–4) and that, being a Jewess, her physical features

only that, Mordecai commands Esther to hide, rather than to reveal, her Jewishness (i.e., her relationship to the Hebrew God) for fear that the king might disapprove of her religion (2:10, 20).

But what about Esther, the namesake of this book of the Bible? It is true that she respectfully submitted in total obedience to the commands of her adopted father, first to hide her heritage (2:10, 20) and then to reveal it (4:8). Yet in her *own* mind, she could not have misunderstood the ultimate purpose of the deceit—to please and flatter her heathen king to the extent that he might marry her[7] (2:10) or, after they are married, to remain in his good graces (2:20). Had she immediately revealed her Jewishness, she might have been summarily excluded from the king's contest and then would have been able to honor God by marrying according to his standards alone.[8] Furthermore, had she been able to speak about her faith immediately after her marriage, while the king was still enthralled with her (2:17), she might have averted the potential destruction of her people before Prime Minister Haman's edict against them could have been issued (3:8–15). The king undoubtedly would not have permitted Haman to draft such an order that would have condemned his (the king's) own beloved wife to death.[9] Interestingly, though, it was only under threat of death by Mordecai (4:14) that Esther finally revealed her Jewish bloodlines in hopes of saving her people from extermination.

---

might appear somewhat foreign and possibly less desirable to the Persian king, Ahasuerus. Perhaps to a non-Middle Easterner "all Middle Easterners look alike," but it is unlikely that a Persian would have assumed that Esther was Persian unless she had become thoroughly acculturated in her dress, speech, and body language to that of the local Gentile population.

7. How was Esther able to hide her Jewishness from the king's attendants when they offered her nonkosher food during the year of preparation? See the discussion regarding 2:8–10, 12.

8. Lest we worry that God's people would have been destroyed had Esther not become queen, we need only to parrot Mordecai's words in 4:14: "deliverance will arise for the Jews from another place."

9. Haman surely was a shrewd man since, despite being a foreigner, he was able to rise to the position of second in command of the kingdom (3:1). Being wily, Haman most likely would not have suggested to the king to have the queen's people destroyed but most probably would have worked behind the scenes to eliminate Mordecai, whom he hated (3:5), and as many other Jews as possible.

A further point of interest is that the author refers to Esther by her Persian name, Esther, rather than by her Hebrew name, Hadassah (2:7). Is the author attempting to convey by this subtle means a half-hearted commitment on the part of the Jews of the exile to Jewish values and to the God of Israel? This could explain Mordecai's and Esther's willingness to compromise their relationships to the one true God. Employing this nomenclature as a stylistic device to convey a turning back to God, the author could legitimately have recorded the name *Esther* in the first half of the book prior to the disclosure of her Jewishness and then have reverted to her Jewish name, Hadassah, after her admission was made. Yet, such is not the case.[10]

One also wonders why so many Jews, despite the proclamation made fifty years earlier by King Cyrus that allowed them to return to their homeland, still remain in exile in the various regions of Medo-Persia. Traditionally, the Jews throughout their history of exile have always desired to return to the Promised Land, yet *these* Jews choose to remain in exile. Regarding this situation, Ronald W. Pierce writes that many "had forgotten their calling to separateness and had chosen to compromise their heritage for the sake of personal advancement."[11]

Of all people, Mordecai should have returned to Israel, for he was a "Jew of Jerusalem"—his great-grandfather had been taken into exile from there at the time of Jeconiah, King of Judah (2:5–6). Mordecai, however, continued to live in exile away from the land of God's blessing. Had he returned to Jerusalem and taken Esther with him, the events of the Book of Esther most likely would never have taken place.

10. The Book of Daniel reveals a similar situation of Jews in exile who had both Hebrew and foreign names. Hananiah, Mishael, and Azariah (Babylonian, respectively, Shadrach, Meshach, and Abed-nego) are referred to by both names, more often by their Hebrew names when they are depicted in connection with Daniel but more often by their Babylonian names when the Babylonian king is present (particularly when they are about to be thrown into the fiery furnace). Throughout the Book of Daniel, however, Daniel, a man of God, is referred to primarily by his Hebrew name rather than by his Babylonian name, Belteshazzar.

11. Ronald W. Pierce, "Purim: A Time to Mourn or a Time to Dance?" Ms. presented to the Evangelical Theological Society in San Diego, Calif., 18 November 1989, 6–7.

These important and potentially disturbing issues are dealt with in greater depth throughout this commentary. The final chapter, moreover, which should be skimmed at this time and then read in depth after the intervening chapters have been studied, seeks to answer crucial questions that have plagued serious students of the Book of Esther for many years.

Parental Guidance is Necessary

If Hollywood were to make a new movie about the Book of Esther, would the movie receive an X rating? Or would it earn some other rating? Undoubtedly Hollywood is capable of making an X-rated movie of the book,[12] but such a depiction would conflict with Gods intent for the true-life story of Esther. Perhaps the rating that God, as Producer and Director, has determined for the book is PG – parental guidance necessary – since the reader needs to be guided by his or her heavenly parent, God the Father, to understand the book clearly.

What spiritual lessons can we learn from such a book in which the hero and heroine are afraid to give honor to God? What great truths can we discover from a book that avoids even the mention of the name of God? Actually, there are many valuable and practical lessons for those of us who are guided by our heavenly Father!

1. God is *behind the seen*, working for our good even when we cannot see, or do not want to see, him.
2. We get into trouble when we deliberately hide our faith.
3. Our good motives and family ties will not keep us from danger, especially when we rely on human guidance rather than on God's leading.
4. The actions we choose to take or not take at any given time may have far-reaching consequences that may affect not only us but also many others throughout the world.

With these thoughts in mind, we can now turn our attention to the story of Esther and Mordecai.

12. The basic ingredients are all there – a drunken orgy (chap. 1); the sexually explicit scenes (chap. 2); and the violence (chap. 9).

8

The Emperor's New Clothes
(1:1–9)

Remember that classic Hans Christian Andersen tale of "The Emperor's New Clothes"? Remember feeling embarrassed as the emperor paraded through the streets because he was so flattered and fooled by his tailor and by his own vanity that he believed he was wearing elegantly regal clothes when he was wearing nothing at all? The more we think of it, the sillier it becomes. How could an emperor be so deceived? Moreover, how could all who saw him also deny what they were seeing? As you remember, the myth of the royal attire was shattered when an innocent boy—a lad who was not beguiled by the need to impress those in positions of power—openly declared the nakedness of the emperor.

The author of the Book of Esther is much like that little boy. He allows the king to display his finery, his wealth, and his power to impress the people of his world with his assumed greatness. Then that seemingly powerful king is systematically stripped before the sovereign providence of God. What appears to be *the* preeminent mover and shaker in the eyes of the Middle Eastern world is in reality no more than a mere pawn in the hands of the omnipotent God.

He Had It All

Wealth, power, fame, a beautiful spouse—what more could a person want? King Ahasuerus, ruler of the Medo-Persian empire, had all of these things and much more.

Ahasuerus was the most powerful ruler of his day. Not even the prince of Wu, who headed the great Zhou (Chou) Dynasty of China at the same time, could claim to rule over more territory or to possess more wealth than did King Ahasuerus.[1] Furthermore, no other contemporary potentate came close to controlling what Ahasuerus did.

In Esther 1:1–9, the author of the Book of Esther briefly sketches a picture of the extent of Ahasuerus's greatness. In verses 1–3, the author describes the vastness of Ahasuerus's domain and announces the convening of a royal banquet. In verses 4–8, the author makes note of that banquet, a second banquet, and the display of the king's riches. Finally, in verse 9, the author mentions still a third banquet, this one held by Queen Vashti, King Ahasuerus's wife. Yet, despite all of Ahasuerus's wealth and greatness, all is not well in his kingdom, as the author will soon point out.

A House of Cards

As we begin to peer into this section (vv. 1–9), no particular theme seems obvious until we focus our binoculars and look at the passage in the context of the entire story. We then discover that the author has skillfully designed these verses to intimate that, in the midst of what appears to be a well-constructed, smoothly operating kingdom, cracks are developing in the walls of the king's house.

This section fits nicely into a classic chiastic structure (ABCB′A′) in which the first and the last subsections parallel each other, as do the second and the fourth. The middle subsection, however, stands alone as that component which is being emphasized as the central point of the passage:

A A power player (1:1–3)
  B A power play (1:4–5)
    C A power display (1:6)
  B′ A power play (1:7–8)
A′ A power player (1:9)

1. Kenneth Scott Latourette, *The Chinese: Their History and Culture*, 4th ed. (New York: Macmillan, 1972), 39.

The author of Esther uses such a scheme to juxtapose the king (vv. 1–3) with the queen (v. 9), who as the initial key participants in the story set the stage for what is to come. The author also presents the king in two distinct acts of attempting to curry the favor of his subjects: the hosting of a party (vv. 4–5) and the offering of free drinks with no strings attached (vv. 7–8). Finally, the author highlights the opulence of the king's possessions (v. 6). This display functions as a fulcrum—what precedes it is the generous layering of card upon card to create an elaborate but fragile house of cards, what follows are the warning signals of an impending earthquake.

The Man at the Top (1:1–3)

As we begin the Book of Esther, we need to place ourselves in the sandals of the author and the first readers. What did they expect to see conveyed in the book? Would it be a book of hope or of tragedy, a book of wisdom or of warning? Although early postexilic[2] readers undoubtedly hoped for a note of encouragement, the first two Hebrew words that they read must have caused their hearts to sink in despair. The Hebrew[3] begins with *wayhî bîmê* (and it came to pass in the days of)—words which, without exception, in all five occurrences in Scripture, introduce impending catastrophe or doom.[4] Yet, on all five occasions the ending to each story is happy, but before that happy ending is realized, much grief occurs. The grief of

2. The events of the Book of Esther take place ca. 484–473 B.C. and thus the writing of the book occurs sometime thereafter. No definite information regarding the author of the book, however, is currently available. The Talmud indicates that the Book of Esther was written by the men of the Great Synagogue, but this has no historical foundation. Other sources have suggested Ezra, Nehemiah, or perhaps even Mordecai (highly unlikely, for reasons to be discussed later). Yet the truth of the book's authorship remains shrouded in the mystery of antiquity. C. F. Keil, *The Books of Ezra, Nehemiah, and Esther,* Biblical Commentary on the Old Testament, trans. Sophia Taylor (reprint; Grand Rapids: Eerdmans, n.d.), 312–13.

3. All references to the Hebrew text or to the Masoretic Text are taken from *Biblia Hebraica Stuttgartensia*, ed. K. Elliger and W. Rudolph (Stuttgart: Deutsche Bibelgesellschaft, 1984).

4. The other four occurrences are in Gen. 14:1; Ruth 1:1; Isa. 7:1; and Jer. 1:3.

the Book of Esther is not only that the people of Israel are in captivity but also that they are at the brink of extinction at the hands of their captors (3:1–15).

The author states that the events of the book take place "in the days of Ahasuerus" (1:1). Ahasuerus is more commonly known by his Greek name, Xerxes. Statements in the book confirm that Xerxes, rather than some other Persian king, is the man in control: he reigned over both Persia and Media (1:3, 14, 18); his empire extended from the subcontinent of India to the northern regions of the continent of Africa (1:1; 8:9), consisted of 127 provinces (1:1; 8:9; 9:30), and included islands in the Mediterranean (10:1), and his palace was established in Susa (Shushan) in the land of Elam (1:2).

History depicts Ahasuerus as physically towering over his contemporaries but emotionally lacking in tolerance and sensitivity. His mental and leadership capabilities, moreover, were considered no match for those of either his father, Darius the Great, or his grandfather, Cyrus the Great.

Soon after his ascension to the throne in 486 B.C. and prior to the events in the Book of Esther, Ahasuerus brutally crushed revolts in Egypt and Babylon. His military success, however, was short lived, for soon thereafter he was greatly humiliated twice (in 480 and 479 B.C.) by the Greeks whom he had attacked. After those devastating defeats, he ceased his military exploits and concentrated on the construction of buildings at Persepolis and Susa. The vital and dynamic empire that he had inherited was left at his death (by assassination) in 465 B.C. with its growth stunted and its original luster tarnished.[5]

Continuing in verse 1, the author again strikes fear in the hearts of his original readers. Through the repetition of the name *Ahasuerus* and the inclusion of the personal pronoun *he,* the author emphasizes that the first source of terror to be encoun-

5. For general descriptions of the life of Ahasuerus see Lewis Bayles Paton, *The Book of Esther,* International Critical Commentary, ed. Samuel Rolles Driver, Alfred Plummer, and Charles Augustus Briggs (Edinburgh: T. and T. Clark, 1908), 53–54, 121–22; R. E. Hayden, "Xerxes," *International Standard Bible Encyclopedia*, ed. Geoffrey W. Bromiley (Grand Rapids: Eerdmans, 1982), 4:1161; and "Ahasuerus," *Baker Encyclopedia of the Bible,* ed. Walter A. Elwell (Grand Rapids: Baker, 1988), 1:40.

tered in the story is none other than Ahasuerus—the king who wrote of himself, "I, the mighty king, king of kings, king of populous countries, king of this great and mighty earth, far and near."[6] This was the king who, because a storm destroyed a bridge that he had commanded be built across the Hellespont (Dardanelles), ordered that three hundred lashes be given to the Hellespont and that the heads of the bridge-building engineers be cut off.[7] More importantly, this was the king in whose reign the people of God were almost destroyed. The name *Ahasuerus* would understandably send a shiver down the collective Hebrew spine because he was, by reputation and by deed, a king to be feared.

Prior to World War II, a statement that was frequently uttered was that "the sun never set upon the British empire." The author of the Book of Esther makes a similar statement here regarding the lands ruled by Ahasuerus when he writes that they extended from Hodu to Cush, that is, from the Indus River in the east to northern Sudan in the west.[8] Saying "from Hodu to Cush" is like saying from the sunrise to the sunset, the "boundaries" of the then civilized Persian world.

The author further impresses upon his readers the geographical vastness of Ahasuerus's empire by citing the larger number of provinces (127) that it encompassed rather than the smaller number of satrapies (31) involved.[9] Thus not only is Ahasuerus himself of great importance in the eyes of the world, but so also is his kingdom.

In 1:2, the author shifts his readers' attention from the broad expanse of the empire to the narrower perspective of the sea-

6. Paulus Cassel, *An Explanatory Commentary on Esther*, trans. Aaron Bernstein (Edinburgh: T. and T. Clark, 1888), 6, here cites a cuneiform inscription.

7. Hayden, "Xerxes," 1161.

8. Some translations read "from India to Ethiopia," but most authorities consider the actual meanings of "Hodu" and "Cush" to be references to modern-day Pakistan and northern Sudan, respectively.

9. The term *satrapies* refers to the division of the empire into the various nations of which it is comprised. By contrast, "provinces" are the geographical regions of the empire that are identified according to the races that inhabit them. Keil, *The Books of Ezra, Nehemiah, and Esther*, 321. The reference in Dan. 6:1 to 120 divisions of the kingdom apparently denotes only those areas not part of Persia proper. Persia itself had 7 divisions. Thus when that figure is added to Daniel's 120 divisions, it accounts for the figure in Esther.

sonal palace at Susa.[10] There at the winter/spring palace, King Ahasuerus firmly established himself as ruler of the Medo-Persian empire after having suppressed the Egyptian and Babylonian rebellions.

The infinitive form of the Hebrew verb *yšb* (to sit) as used in verse 2 does not focus on the continuing reign of the king as does the participial form of the verb *mlk* (to rule) in verse 1. Rather, it suggests that it was at Susa that the king was *ceremonially* crowned ruler of the empire.[11] Ahasuerus has already been king in title and authority for three years. Now, however, he is able to celebrate that reality in full royal splendor.

Susa itself was considered to be a garden paradise, a capital truly fit for a king. It abounded in fruits and flowers and was particularly famous for a specific kind of lily from which the city received its name. This fortified city was surrounded by streams and mountains that added to its beauty and attraction as a royal citadel during the cooler months of the year (Susa was intolerably hot during the summer). Furthermore, the term *bîyrā(h)* (often translated "capital") is best understood to mean "acropolis," which in the Persian culture indicated an elevated palace complex within a city that was designed both to suggest the majestic grandeur of the king and to provide for his protection.[12]

In the midst of such a luxurious environment, King Ahasuerus holds a banquet (lit., "drinking feast"). He invites the leaders of his kingdom—princes, nobles, and military leaders—to celebrate with him. He also wisely includes the courtiers of his royal household, since they are the people whose loyalty he has to depend upon for the day-to-day operations of his palace and, more importantly, for his personal protection.

10. The rulers of the Medo-Persian empire had their choice of four different palaces to suit their whims and the weather. Those palaces were located in Babylon, Ecbatana, Persepolis, and Susa.

11. The fact that the Septuagint uses the aorist passive form of *ethronizō* (to enthrone) supports this idea of coronation. All references to the Septuagint are taken from *Septuaginta*, ed. Alfred Rahlfs (Stuttgart: Deutsche Bibelgesellschaft Stuttgart, 1979).

12. Joyce G. Baldwin, *Esther: An Introduction and Commentary*, Tyndale Old Testament Commentaries, ed. D. J. Wiseman (Downers Grove: InterVarsity, 1984), 56.

All in all, the beginning of Ahasuerus's reign exhibits much promise for him. But such an auspicious beginning for Ahasuerus does not bode well for the captive people of God. They could expect no favors from a notoriously intolerant ruler who had brutally suppressed the desire for freedom yearned for by other captive groups. What is cause for a joyous celebration by the Medes and the Persians undoubtedly is cause for serious concern by the exiled nation of Israel. The simple words that begin the book, when combined with the remaining words of this section, signal an ominous beginning—a beginning that offers little hope with no redemption or redeemer in sight.

Lifestyles of the Rich and Famous (1:4–5)

Although some people are great money managers, there are others who, whether they earned it themselves or were given it, are not able to handle large sums of money. King Ahasuerus appears to be one of the latter. He has wealth, and he flaunts it. That Ahasuerus has a great storehouse of wealth cannot be denied. Lewis Bayles Paton states that when the Spartans defeated Ahasuerus, they found in the spoil of the camp "tents covered with gold and silver, golden couches, bowls and cups, and even gold and silver kettles."[13] If Ahasuerus took that much gold and silver with him when he went into battle, what he left behind in his palaces and storehouses must have been incredible.

To describe Ahasuerus's wealth, the author uses a phrase that graphically depicts the immensity of that wealth. He states that the king openly showed "the riches of his royal glory" (1:4). The key word is "glory" *(kābôd)*. The basic sense of the term is "to make heavy," thus indicating anything that makes a person heavy, that is, important or prestigious (even today we speak of those who show off their wealth as those who "throw their weight around"). What made a person "heavy" in biblical times was the possession of much gold and silver. Although the Scripture teaches that graciousness (Prov. 11:16), humility (Prov. 15:33), cessation of strife (Prov. 20:3), righteousness and loyalty (Prov. 21:21), and fearing the Lord (Prov. 22:4) will bring a per-

13. Paton, *The Book of Esther*, 129.

son *kābôd* (honor or glory), the world is far more impressed by the *kābôd* that accompanies riches and fame.

By this display of riches, Ahasuerus undoubtedly increased his *kābôd* not only in the eyes of the commoners but also in the minds of the social, political, and military leadership. They would now attribute to him a greater sense of power and importance than ever before.

Such a statement ("the riches of his royal glory") in and of itself would seem sufficient to declare Ahasuerus's greatness in the world, but the author includes the phrase "the splendor of his great majesty." In some ways these words seem redundant, yet in fact they add a different dimension to our understanding of Ahasuerus's wealth. The term *splendor (yeqār)* implies a rarity or a uniqueness, hence a thing that is highly prized. The term *majesty [tip'ārā(h)]* is elsewhere translated "beauty" or "pride" and thus emphasizes the pleasure to the eyes brought about by what one sees. Ahasuerus's wealth, therefore, is impressive not merely for its seeming limitlessness but also for the physical beauty that it produced.

The immensity of Ahasuerus's fortune is such that even after being on exhibition for 180 days its *kābôd* (glory) or its *tip'ārā(h)* (majesty) is undiminished. His riches made such a lasting impression that their display was recorded in the Book of Esther many years after the event. Some items (1:6) were so impressive that time could not blur the detail with which they were remembered.

Regarding the 180-day period, some commentators believe that it refers only to the exhibition of Ahasuerus's wealth and not to the length of the banquet. The Hebrew text, however, clearly indicates that both the feast and the display of riches lasted the full 180 days.[14] Esther 1:4, therefore, should not be considered as parenthetical[15] but as a temporal clause that is connected to and continues the thought of 1:3. Although it is

14. From the standpoint of the efficient functioning of the empire, it is highly unlikely (although possible) that all of the people invited to the banquet remained there for the entire 180 days. More likely, they attended in shifts, with only one group being at the banquet at any given time.

15. Baldwin, *Esther: An Introduction and Commentary*, 57.

difficult to fathom a six-month party, it apparently was not unheard of in ancient times.[16]

Amazingly, upon the completion of the 180-day banquet, the king holds a "private" outdoor party for all the residents of Susa and for everyone else present in the city at that time (1:5). This feast lasts a "mere" seven days. The same Hebrew word for "banquet" is used in 1:3 and 1:5, yet the context (cf. 1:7–8) seems to place greater emphasis on drinking in 1:5 than in 1:3.[17]

This second banquet includes all "from the greatest to the least," a reference not to age but to rank. It may have been limited to those in the employ of the king,[18] but the Hebrew places no such limitation and seems to imply *all* who were in the city at that time. Lest we worry that a banquet (i.e., drinking bout) that included everyone in the city would be beyond reason and beyond the managerial capacity of even a Persian king, we need only be reminded that "according to Ctesias, the court physician to Artaxerxes Mnemon (405–359 B.C.), no less than 15,000 feasted at the table of the Persian kings . . . and . . . Assurnasirpal had a ten-day celebration for 69,574 guests."[19]

Needless to say, Ahasuerus put on a performance that was one for the history books, a performance that would impress even the most skeptical. His power as supreme ruler would remain unchallenged for many years. Ahasuerus had accomplished his purpose . . . and so has the author of the Book of Esther.

Baubles, Bangles, and Beads (1:6)

Verse 6 is grammatically unconnected to those surrounding it. The author may have intentionally designed this verse to be detached from the section of which it is a part in order to reveal that the king's wealth also is detached from reality—far beyond imagining and yet at the same time unable to bring a halt to the

16. Carey A. Moore, *Esther*, The Anchor Bible, ed. William Foxwell Albright and David Noel Freedman (Garden City, N.Y.: Doubleday, 1971), 6.

17. The Septuagint suggests that such is the case since it translates the Hebrew word for banquet in 1:3 as *dochē* (a feast) and in 1:5 as *potos* (a drinking party or a carousing).

18. Paton, *The Book of Esther*, 136.

19. Moore, *Esther*, 6.

events that follow.[20] What the king was trusting in (i.e., his riches) could not prevent the raggedness of the rule of his kingdom.

Along with composing a sentence unconnected from the remainder of the passage, the author chooses numerous Hebrew words that occur only here in the Bible to suggest a uniqueness and an exquisiteness to the decor. The purple used to dye the linen was "obtained from the mollusk *Murex Trunculus,* found on the Phoenician coast, and from the *Murex Brandaris,* found in the western Mediterranean."[21] This dye was quite expensive, since its closest source was a minimum of 650 miles from Susa and since the work required to extract and purify sufficient quantities of the dye for commercial use by the king was extensive.[22]

The marble columns were immovable pillars that the ancient Hebrew commentary known as the *Midrash Esther Rabba* implies were part of the spoil of the Solomonic temple carried off by Nebuchadnezzar to Babylon (ca. 604 B.C.).[23]

The couches or beds most likely were covered with pillows or cushions on which people would sit or recline. The mention of couches or beds should not be construed as referencing sexual activities that may have taken place in association with the banquet. These couches are found in the courtyard of the palace (1:5) and would have been used more naturally for conversation or feasting purposes.

The geometric patterns of the mosaic floor of the garden consisted of four different kinds of stones of four different colors: porphyry typically was a purple- or maroon-colored rock; the marble was white; the mother-of-pearl was the lustrous, iridescent internal layer of the mollusk shell; and the precious stones were black or black marble with shield-like

20. Interestingly, the author places this verse at the center of the chiastic structure of 1:1–9 (see p. 106). By doing so, he gives additional weight to the significance of the contents of the verse.

21. Paton, *The Book of Esther*, 145.

22. "This red-purple and violet dye was, in fact, the most highly valued of ancient times, and . . . was prepared by boiling certain tissues of the mollusc in a salt solution for a period of three days." G. I. Emmerson, "Dye," *International Standard Bible Encyclopedia*, ed. Geoffrey W. Bromiley (Grand Rapids: Eerdmans, 1982), 1:1000.

23. Paton, *The Book of Esther*, 139.

flecks. A pavement of this design and composition was highly prized in the ancient Middle East.[24]

There is no mistaking the fact that the author desires his readers to be impressed by the possessions of the king. Yet the author establishes Ahasuerus's greatness only to show how it pales in comparison to the providence of God.

The Drinks Are on the House! (1:7–8)

Ahasuerus's second power play (the first was the hosting of lavish banquets) is his declaration that guests at the seven-day banquet do not need to adhere to the custom that required them to drink without exception whenever the king drank or served drinks. Although the king's declaration might appear to be an act of grace, it is in fact a subtle sign of weakness. Whereas other Persian rulers demanded unyielding adherence to this custom, Ahasuerus, perhaps being unsure of his power base, finds it necessary to relax this custom as part of his efforts to win the favor of his people. The subtlety is highlighted by the fact that in 1:7 the author provides additional information substantiating the extent of the king's wealth, thereby seemingly making the king appear invincible and in need of no one else's help. Yet immediately thereafter, in 1:8, the author begins to unravel the first stitch of thread in the king's "power suit."

In 1:7, the author presents four evidences of that stupefying wealth:

1. The drinking goblets are made of gold. Persian drinking vessels typically were exquisitely crafted into the shape of drinking horns with handles often fashioned into the figures of animals.[25] These royal goblets are without doubt the finest and most expensive in the empire.
2. No two of the drinking cups are alike (lit., "vessels from vessels," an idiomatic expression that indicates that the vessels were different from one another). When one con-

24. Keil, *The Books of Ezra, Nehemiah, and Esther*, 326; Paton, *The Book of Esther*, 140.

25. Baldwin, *Esther: An Introduction and Commentary*, 58.

siders the immense proportions of this gathering, the fact that it is dedicated primarily to drinking and continues for a stretch of seven days, and the Persian tradition of frequently changing the drinking cups at a royal party,[26] one gains an even greater appreciation for the seeming inexhaustibility of Ahasuerus's treasury.
3. The wine is royal wine, that is, the best and most expensive in the empire.
4. The royal wine flows according to the king's ability to provide it (lit., "according to the hand of the king"). In other words, the wine never runs out.

At first glance, 1:8 appears to present an interpretative difficulty. How is it possible that the drinking is done "according to the law," while at the same time each person is free to drink as he or she likes?[27] Perhaps the easiest solution to this dilemma is to understand the Hebrew word *dat* (law) not as a reference to the formal law code of the Medes and Persians, which was inviolable even by the king (cf. 8:8), but to a law, decree, or regulation made by the king specifically for the party.[28] Then the two discrepant elements fit together as follows: "drinking was *done* according to the decree (law) that stated that there was no compulsion." Such an interpretation parallels most closely the second half of the verse that indicates that the king gives his guests freedom to drink as they desire.

The king's reason for not demanding adherence to the traditional drinking custom is not stated. The author, however, has recorded this event to reveal something of the character of the king, a character that is not as strong as it appears to be on the surface.

The Beauty and the Feast (1:9)

The first section of the Book of Esther draws to a close with the introduction of a second power player: Queen Vashti. Precisely who she was in the history of the Persian empire is

26. Cassel, *An Explanatory Commentary on Esther*, 23.

27. Persian custom required the guests of the king to drink whenever the king's servants served the wine.

28. See Baldwin, *Esther: An Introduction and Commentary*, 58–59; Moore, *Esther*, 7–8; and Paton, *The Book of Esther*, 141.

unclear because the name *Vashti* (variously translated "best," "beloved," or "beautiful") was not recorded in the annals regarding the reign of Ahasuerus (perhaps due to the shortness of her reign).[29]

Speculation also abounds as to why Vashti hosts a feast separate from Ahasuerus's banquet. Some scholars suggest that she does so because the king is magnanimous and desires to grant the women freedom to hold their own party. Others surmise that the queen is acting in defiance against the king, who apparently has snubbed her by not inviting her to his banquet. Still others maintain that she is following a Persian tradition of parallel banquets, that is, a separate party for females when they are excluded from the one held by the king. The true reason for this separate banquet, however, is once again lost in antiquity.[30]

However, the information provided by the author of the Book of Esther regarding the definite fact of Vashti's banquet at this point in the story serves several functions. First, it records an interesting event in history that might otherwise be missed. Second, it completes the chiasm of the initial section of the book, introducing a second power player to balance the first (Ahasuerus, 1:1–3). Note that both power players have their own banquets. Third, it portends a future event that will pit the two power players against each other (1:10–22).

A Launching Pad

As is necessary for deep-space network probes, so too a foundational launching pad is essential for the Book of Esther so that we may probe deeply into the truths it contains. This section (vv. 1–9) is such a launching pad. It is not the most important element in our journey, but it is a significant one. The

29. Some argue that Vashti was Queen Amestris, the daughter of Otanes, and that the word *Vashti* was her title or nickname. See F. B. Huey, Jr., "Esther," *Expositor's Bible Commentary*, ed. Frank E. Gaebelein, 12 vols. (Grand Rapids: Zondervan, 1988), 4:790; and Baldwin, *Esther: An Introduction and Commentary*, 59–60.

30. Sandra Beth Berg, *The Book of Esther: Motifs, Themes and Structure* (Missoula, Mont.: Scholars, 1979), 32, 34, 49–50; Cassel, *An Explanatory Commentary on Esther*, 25, 26; and Paton, *The Book of Esther*, 142–43.

truths to which it propels us are valuable ones to learn, but greater truths are yet to be discovered.

Focusing solely on this passage, we discover two important concepts. The first is that some people live off the coattails of others. Not only did the people live off the generosity of the king, but the king himself also lived off the riches of his father. Specifically, King Ahasuerus did not earn from his own efforts the wealth that he displayed but rather inherited it from his father, Darius the Great, who was a great empire builder.

The second point is that excluding one's spouse from one's activities may be symptomatic of marital disharmony. Unlike some other ancient societies, the Medes and the Persians had no laws that required wives to be excluded from the parties hosted by their husbands.[31] So the seeds of family discord may have been sown.

Fully developing this idea of marital disharmony, however, would require analyzing the information contained in the next section of Esther, and this leads me to interject a warning here. Going beyond this immediate passage to discover and develop principles for life in relation to the truth may appear to be more profitable than sticking to the passage at hand. Yet we must be careful not to engage in what is called eisegesis, that is, reading truths gained from other sources into this passage where those truths do not exist.

However, if we use 1:1–9 as our launching pad for the discovery of truth and add to it truth gleaned from the rest of the Book of Esther, we find the following:

1. God is in ultimate control, despite any power or wealth that humans may have at their disposal to manipulate people and events. Even though King Ahasuerus is a pagan ruler who controls much of the riches and land of his world, the entire Book of Esther demonstrates that God still is able to work out everything for his glory.
2. What looks like power or greatness may actually be a veneer that, once penetrated, reveals the vulnerability of the person hiding behind it. King Ahasuerus seems to be in complete control at the outset but is easily influenced by

31. Berg, *The Book of Esther,* 49–50.

the advice of whoever is around him. In 1:13–2:3, it is his counselors who sway his thinking. In 3:1–15, it is Haman, the prime minister; in 7:1–7, Queen Esther; in 7:9–10, a servant; and in 8:1–9:15, both Esther and Mordecai, the newly appointed prime minister.

3. Husband-wife relations must be nurtured carefully and not taken for granted.[32] King Ahasuerus again is the focal point of this principle, which is borne out in his relations with his first wife, Vashti (1:9–22), and with his second wife, Esther (4:11).

We've Only Just Begun

The author of Esther has woven his story masterfully to frighten, enthrall, and tantalize his readers. By this point in the story, first-time readers would be whistling in astonishment at the riches of the king. They also would be curious to know more about Queen Vashti and the relationship between her and the king. All the while they would be remembering the foreboding beginning in 1:1 and wondering when the other shoe will drop, what disaster will befall Israel.

The first section of the Book of Esther has shown the way of the world—the glitz, the glamour, and the fluff. The remainder of the book will silently interweave the overriding providence of God into the activities of the subjugators and the subjugated, and into those events affecting both the Jews and the Gentiles of Medo-Persia.

The pace will pick up! The plot will thicken! The adventure has begun.

32. Marital or family relationships are neither the primary focus nor a major theme of the Book of Esther, but they provide an interesting backdrop to the more significant issues of the book.

9

Pose or Be Deposed
(1:10–22)

Choices, choices, we are constantly faced with choices—what to wear, where to go, when to eat, what to be. Sometimes, even those decisions that we consider to be of little consequence are those that later prove to have the most significant impact on us and on our world. For example, the decision I made to wear a suit on a date on a warm June evening in Hawaii several years ago has transformed my life. The girl whom I was dating "fell in love with my suit" that evening and decided that I might be the right one to marry. Approximately six months later we were married and she has had a transforming effect for the good on my life ever since. That one small decision made a difference for me.

This section of the Book of Esther (1:10–22) in particular and numerous other sections in general reveal that even minor decisions have the potential for initiating events that have not only personal but also worldwide consequences. Fortunately, those consequences are under the watchful care of the unseen God. He moves those outcomes (as well as the choices themselves) to achieve his goals for his purposes and for the good of his people. What makes this particular section all the more amazing is that the decisions are being made by unbelievers, that is, by those who have no comprehension of or interest in who God is and how he is controlling the destiny of a still-as-of-yet-unmentioned people in the Book of Esther, that is, the Jews.

Fighting Mosquitos with Patriot Missiles

One of the most frustrating sounds on a sultry summer evening is the buzz, buzz, buzzing of a single mosquito divebombing our ears. Swatting and sprays never seem to work and only add to our misery. What about a flame-thrower or a howitzer? Maybe a heat-seeking missile? The only problem with taking such drastic measures is the residual damage to the surrounding terrain and to the civilians who get caught in the crossfire.

Such drastic measures, however, are used by the king of the Medo-Persian empire. What appears to us as a minor irritant becomes the grounds for bringing out the big guns. "Overkill" becomes the operative word to the king and his counselors. A domestic problem between the king and his wife is blown all out of proportion and affects all husbands and wives in the empire.

We're Moving, But Where Are We Going?

The pace of the story is beginning to pick up. We are moving now but we are not sure yet where the author is taking us. We are still interacting with pagans and there is no indication of the presence of God or of the existence of God's people. Yet, this story, as does each episode in the entire Book of Esther, has a purpose, a divine purpose, for being included.

King Ahasuerus invites his wife, the beautiful Queen Vashti, to his banquet (vv. 10–11). She refuses, enraging the king. He then convenes a meeting with his closest advisers to determine what measures should be taken against her (vv. 12–15). The royal counselors propose, and the king agrees, that an irrevocable law be enacted that removes Vashti from her position as queen and dictates that all wives in the empire are to recognize their own husbands as being the sole masters of their respective homes (vv. 16–22).

From one perspective, the story of Vashti's dethronement is a sociological study in the escalation of problems. A small domestic matter between two people (vv. 10–12) expands to draw a larger group into the fray (13–20) and finally involves an entire nation (vv. 21–22). Several factors—factors that are typically found in the escalation of many problems—reveal why this situation got out of hand: the unnecessary involvement of additional people beyond the primary disputants in the case; the bringing into public matters that could better be handled in private;[1] the failure to investigate the root cause(s) of the problem; the use of hyperbole in presenting the arguments; the emphasis of fear over reason to make one's point; and the proposal of a solution that far exceeds the demands of the original situation. Interestingly, most of these components by which a situation is escalated to worldwide proportions arise again in a prime minister's (Haman's) proposed solution to the king for dealing with a problem of a single, recalcitrant individual, Mordecai (3:8–15).

From the perspective of the storyline of the book, this incident opens the door for Esther's rise to power (2:8–18) and for Mordecai's promotion to a position in which he becomes involved in an interpersonal crisis that ultimately has empire-wide consequences (2:19–3:15). These verses, moreover, depict the king as an individual who desires harmony at any cost but who apparently has neither the wisdom nor the ability to use his power effectively. In revealing those character flaws and in advancing the author's story, this section may be understood structurally as follows:

A The king is happy and all is well (1:10–11)
  B The queen chooses not to come into the king's presence (1:12)
    C The king seeks advice to ensure that all will be well again (1:13–15)
  B′ The queen is not allowed to come into the king's presence (1:16–20)
A′ The king is happy and all is well (1:21–22)

Interestingly, the structural outline of this section reflects a pattern that is repeated in various instances throughout the Book of Esther[2] and that forms the overall outline for the book itself (see chap. 22). That pattern follows the general format of (A) all being at peace, (B) a conflict arising that disturbs that peace, (C) a proposal being offered to resolve the problem, (B′) the proposal being enacted, and (A′) all returning to a state of peace.

1. Although the original domestic difficulty occurred in public, it should have been dealt with in private, or at most in that relatively small public gathering, rather than being played out before an international audience.

2. Examples can be found in 3:1–15; 4:1–17; and 9:1–17.

The Jewel and Her Crown (1:10–11)

The author of the Book of Esther is a master of detail and a master at constructing a tightly-knit story through the use of appropriate literary techniques. In these two short verses he establishes not only the prominence of the people involved but also the time, the emotional climate, and the purpose of the events taking place. What is more, in doing so he answers the six journalistic questions of who, what, when, where, why, and how.

The event that sets off an international crisis takes place on the final day of a seven-day royal drinking party,[3] at a time when the king is far from sober (lit., "when the heart of the king was good[4] with wine") and his reasoning power could be described as being "not fully rational."[5] As Lewis Bayles Paton states, this remark "indicates the opinion of the author that he [the king] would not have acted so if he had been in his right mind."[6] In other words, what the author records between 1:10 and 1:22 reveals events that take place when the king and undoubtedly his counselors are not functioning properly—the drunk leading the drunk. The outcome of the decisions noted in these verses confirms the author's perspective.

The king sends seven eunuchs to convey his command to his wife, Queen Vashti, that she is to appear before him at the men's banquet. These eunuchs are no mere errand boys who convey a message; they are powerful men within the government of the king. That power is noted in four ways: they are specifically

3. Huey (along with others) correctly states that the seventh day is a reference to the last day of the feast and not to the Sabbath day. F. B. Huey, Jr., "Esther," *Expositor's Bible Commentary,* ed. Frank E. Gaebelein, 12 vols. (Grand Rapids: Zondervan, 1988), 4:800.

4. The idiomatic use of the Hebrew word *tôb* (good) occurs throughout the Book of Esther (cf. 1:10, 11 [2x], 19; 2:2, 3, 7, 9; 3:9, 11; 5:4, 8, 9; 7:3, 9; 8:5 [2x], 8, 17; 9:13, 19, 22; 10:3). Here it introduces the pericope that concludes with another idiomatic use of *tôb* (a verbal use) in 1:21, where the decision to banish Vashti is *tôb* (good) to the king (i.e., "and *this* word pleased the king").

5. Michael V. Fox, *Character and Ideology in the Book of Esther* (Columbia, S.C.: University of South Carolina Press, 1991), 19.

6. Lewis Bayles Paton, *The Book of Esther*, International Critical Commentary, ed. Samuel Rolles Driver, Alfred Plummer, and Charles Augustus Briggs (Edinburgh: T. and T. Clark, 1908), 148–49.

identified by name,[7] they are denoted in the Hebrew as "the seven eunuchs" and not merely as "seven eunuchs," they serve before the face of the king (cf. 4:11), and they are mentioned twice later in the story in connection with this incidence—once in the narration of the story (1:12) and once in a quotation of the king, who cites the method by which his command was transmitted to the queen (1:15).

The eunuchs are commanded to escort to the king's banquet the queen, who is to be dressed in full royal regalia. They are to do so because the king, who previously had shown off his riches and his generosity (vv. 4, 8), now desires to display his most prized possession, Queen Vashti (v. 11).[8] As Yehuda T. Radday states: "Instead of fireworks, the *pièce de résistance* on the seventh day of the feast is to be . . . the spectacle of Queen Vashti accompanied by a bodyguard of seven eunuchs."[9]

Some scholars have debated whether Queen Vashti is being summoned to appear in her full royal dress or simply to wear her royal crown (i.e., royal turban) and nothing else. The Jewish *Midrash* holds that the queen is expected to arrive "unclothed, so her true beauty could be appreciated."[10] The argument favoring Vashti being unclothed is based on the fact that Persian women did not cover their faces with veils and that Vashti, as queen, must have appeared in public, at the side of the king, on numerous state occasions. Thus, the adherents of this view reason that the drunken men of the banquet would not have been overly excited by merely catching another glimpse of that face, no matter how beautiful.

Most commentators, however, believe that the king commands Vashti to come to the banquet fully clothed in her finest

7. Cassel maintains that the names indicated here are actually titles: chief officer or cabinet minister, treasurer, chief of the bodyguard, guard of the harem, chief baker, chief butler, and chief commander of the castle or tower, respectively. Paulus Cassel, *An Explanatory Commentary on Esther,* trans. Aaron Bernstein (Edinburgh: T. and T. Clark, 1888), 27.

8. Paton, *The Book of Esther*, 148.

9. Yehuda T. Radday, "Esther with Humor," in *On Humor and the Comic in the Hebrew Bible*, ed. Yehuda T. Radday and Athalya Brenner (Sheffield: Almond, 1990), 296.

10. Meir Zlotowitz, trans. and comp., *The Megillah: The Book of Esther: A New Translation with a Commentary Anthologized from Talmudic, Midrashic and Rabbinic Sources* (Brooklyn: Mesorah, 1981), 46.

royal garments, along with her royal turban.[11] Such a position accords with the silence of the author of the Book of Esther on the matter.

Although many have debated Vashti's attire, few have ever questioned Vashti's beauty. The author of the story draws attention to that beauty, mentioning it twice in this verse, the second time being for emphasis. By contrast, the author mentions the beauty of Esther, the heroine of the story, only once (cf. 2:7).[12] Vashti undoubtedly was one of the most beautiful women of the ancient world.

An Unexplained Refusal (1:12)

Unexpectedly and without stating a reason, Queen Vashti refuses to heed the king's summons to attend the men's feast. Immediately the true character of the king bursts through; he becomes outraged at such an act of rebellious disobedience.

Many scholars have speculated throughout the centuries as to why Queen Vashti refused to obey the king's command. Any of seven different reasons have generally been espoused, some of which have considerably less merit than the others:[13]

1. Vashti, being the granddaughter of King Nebuchadnezzar, considered herself to be the legitimate heir to the throne rather than Ahasuerus, whom she deemed to be a usurper.
2. Vashti resented being called "Vashti the Queen," rather than "Queen Vashti," because the former declaration im-

11. Carey A. Moore, *Esther*, The Anchor Bible, ed. William Foxwell Albright and David Noel Freedman (Garden City, N.Y.: Doubleday, 1971), 9; Howard, F. Vos, *Ezra, Nehemiah, and Esther,* Bible Study Commentary (Grand Rapids: Lamplighter, 1987), 150; and Paton, *The Book of Esther,* 148.

12. Apparently what attracts the king to Esther is more than simply her physical beauty (cf. 2:17), which is not even mentioned specifically when she is chosen to be queen (2:2, however, suggests that she was beautiful, since that was a prime qualification for those who were to enter the king's harem and to be part of the contest).

13. For a presentation of these various positions see Cassel, *An Explanatory Commentary on Esther*, 29; Fox, *Character and Ideology in the Book of Esther*, 20; Moore, *Esther*, 13; Paton, *The Book of Esther*, 149–50; Friedrich Weinreb, *Chance: The Hidden Lord: The Amazing Scroll of Esther* (Braunton, U.K.: Merlin, 1986), 99; and Zlotowitz, *The Megillah*, 46.

plied that her title was of secondary importance and that Ahasuerus saw her merely as a commoner whom he had elevated to the throne.

3. Vashti had leprosy or a much worse, contagious skin disease, and thus did not want to be ridiculed in front of the men.
4. Vashti did not want to display herself before a gathering of drunken men for fear of being insulted by them.
5. The angel Gabriel had caused a tail to grow on Vashti—thus she was utterly humiliated.
6. Vashti chose not to obey the command: that is, it was a whim on her part.
7. The king expected Vashti to appear naked before the gathering of males (see pp. 125–26), but Vashti's modesty prevented her from doing so.

None of these possibilities is very satisfying and most can be dismissed quite easily. The safest answer is to say that as of yet we do not know what motivated Vashti's refusal. The author apparently believed that the reason for Vashti's refusal had nothing to contribute to the story he was developing—or perhaps (although unlikely because of the detail with which the story is written) he did not know the reason.

One thing is for certain, however; Vashti's refusal brought on the immediate onset of the king's anger. Quite understandably, after 180 days of one party and 6 days of another very successful party, the king did not want this final day of revelry to be ruined by an act that he considered an affront to, and perhaps even a direct attack against, his authority.

The author notes the king's fury by means of a literary device known as parallelism—the king's anger being conceptually parallel to his wrath. Here we note two additional means the author uses to reveal the extent of the king's wrath: the addition of the term *m*^{eʾ}*od* (exceedingly) to the first clause ("then the king became exceedingly angry") and the positioning of the term *waḥămātô* (and his wrath) at the beginning of the second clause.[14]

14. Hebrew narrative grammar typically places the verb at the beginning of a clause, followed by the subject of the clause. Here the order is reversed for emphasis.

A drunk king is not the kind of person you want to anger, and a drunk and angry king is not the type of person you would want to face as your judge, as Vashti (and the empire) would soon discover.

Oh No, What Do We Do Now? (1:13–15)

Like a child who has been hurt by another child, King Ahasuerus acts emotionally rather than rationally, seeking revenge rather than reconciliation. He wants justice and he wants it now, irrespective of the facts and irrespective of the impact on the empire.

Drunk, the king considers even this "trifling"[15] matter to be monumental, as serious as any state affair that cries out for his attention in the imperial throne room. Yet, this injustice took place in the royal banquet hall, and that is where it is to be resolved.

The king (v. 13) convenes a meeting with his wise men *(ḥăkāmîn)* to determine what action should be taken against Vashti. Who exactly these wise men are is debated. Some scholars argue that the wise men are astrologers, since they "understood the times," whereas others believe that the title of legal advisers better suits these individuals "who knew law and justice."[16] Such individuals could be astrologers, yet the context implies that they are more than mere students of the times; they are also experts in legal matters. Perhaps in an age of pre-science, astrologers and legalists are one and the same.

Even though the king is under the influence of much wine, he adheres to his usual practice of conferring with these wise

15. Whether this affront could truly be called insignificant is a matter of debate. We need to keep in mind that Vashti's refusal, rightly or wrongly, was a direct offense against the king that took place in public, in the presence of important government officials whom the king wanted to impress.

16. Cassel, *An Explanatory Commentary on Esther,* 30; Fox, *Character and Ideology in the Book of Esther*, 21; Moore, *Esther*, 9; Paton, *The Book of Esther*, 151–52; and Vos, *Ezra, Nehemiah, and Esther,* 150–51. The same term is used of members of one of the twelve tribes of Israel, the tribe of Issachar (1 Chron. 12:33), and is used in such a way as to imply the legitimacy of that profession for those individuals. Since, in Lev. 20:6 and Isa. 47:13, Israel was strictly forbidden from associating with mediums, spiritists, astrologers, and the like, the term as used in 1 Chron. 12:33 cannot mean "astrologers." Here, however, the term is found in connection with the Persians—non-Jews who do not understand the law of God.

men to gain their insight into the matter at hand. These seven men listed by name (1:14) are important leaders in the Persian government, having both high status and special access to the king, who was physically inaccessible to all but a few chosen people in the empire. They literally "saw the face of the king," that is, they conversed with him directly without going through standard bureaucratic procedures.[17] Furthermore, that they sit in the first place in the kingdom is interpreted by Paton to mean that "[t]heir thrones were probably set in the same relation to that of Xerxes [Ahasuerus] as those of the Amesha-Spentas to that of Ahura-Mazda [Persian deities], namely, three on each side and one in front of the King"[18]—another indication of their importance.

Ahasuerus's concern (v. 15) is to discover what law applies to the given situation that might be invoked against (i.e., inflicted upon)[19] Vashti. The emphatic position in the sentence of the phrase *according to law (k^edāt)* is instructive, for it suggests that legality or technicality is on the mind of the king. The king's excessive emphasis on the law here in this minor domestic matter, in contrast to his failure to consult the law in far more important matters later (3:8–15), is a serious flaw in his ability to rule.[20] Thus, although he is powerful, King Ahasuerus does not know how to rule effectively.

The Sky Is Falling (1:16–20)

Although Ahasuerus may be weak, his advisors are not, for they do not fail to take advantage of the situation to upset the balance of power within the palace.

Memucan, one of the seven princes of Persia and Media (cf. v. 14), addresses the king on behalf of the group of counselors of which he is a part. He has one chance and one chance only to deliver a persuasive speech that will carry the day. He cannot afford to have his speech backfire. Should he fail to realize his

17. Moore, *Esther,* 10.
18. Paton, *The Book of Esther*, 153.
19. C. F. Keil, *The Books of Ezra, Nehemiah, and Esther*, Biblical Commentary on the Old Testament, trans. Sophia Taylor (Grand Rapids: Eerdmans, n.d.), 329.
20. Zlotowitz, *The Megillah*, 48.

goals, he (and perhaps the other six advisers as well) would be faced with a career-limiting and potentially life-shortening situation. Memucan obviously understands that fact, and therefore designs his speech to achieve the maximum effect.

Memucan's speech is a study in effective communication in the midst of a crisis; it is brilliant in its simplicity. In his speech, Memucan wastes no words as he presents in part 1 (vv. 16–18) "a statement of the problem" and in part 2 (vv. 19–20) "a solution to the problem." Using the most effective psychological weapons at his disposal for a speech as brief as this, Memucan subtly (and at times not so subtly) interweaves concerns about moral (vv. 16, 19), sociological (vv. 17, 20), and political (vv. 18–19) matters. Furthermore, having correctly evaluated the personality of the king, Memucan designs this speech to meet the needs of such an individual who constantly seeks to please and who desires harmony above all.

In setting forth the problem (vv. 16–18), Memucan focuses on that which would drive an already emotional king to accept a solution that he might not accept under different circumstances.

Memucan neither oversells his position nor undersells the king on the seriousness of the crisis. According to Memucan, what the king and the entire Medo-Persian empire face is a radical overthrow of traditional Medo-Persian values. If the matter of Vashti's disobedience is left to stand, then family structures will be fractured and there will be dissension among those whom the king sought to impress over the last 187 days of partying. Thus Memucan depicts Vashti's act not as an isolated event but as the forerunner of a rebellion throughout the empire. Other women too will rise up against their husbands, and discord and contention will be the order of the day. Hence, the outcome of the decision made this day will affect not merely one nuclear family, nor even just the most powerful households of the empire, but all families throughout the empire. Drastic measures therefore must be taken to eradicate this most divisive of problems.

Memucan begins his speech (v. 16) by avoiding any reference to the existing laws of the land, because apparently he can find none that apply to the current situation. He stresses, therefore, the worldwide ramifications that Vashti's "moral" perversity[21] will have if left unchecked. In the emphatic position in the sentence, Memucan declares: "not against the king alone" has Vashti rebelled. Such a statement would arrest the king's attention immediately, causing him to wonder what other illegal acts has Vashti done and against whom else has she perpetrated them. Memucan quickly resolves that dilemma—against "*all* the princes, and *all* the peoples who are in *all* the provinces of King Ahasuerus." Vashti's offense is colossal. As Michael V. Fox states, "In Memuchan's frantic misinterpretation, Vashti's act signals a universal crisis, a rebellion against the sexual and social order, a violation of the harmony of every home and marriage."[22]

Memucan next (v. 17) draws the king's attention to the consequences of Vashti's disobedience—all wives everywhere will look upon their husbands with contempt.[23] The verb (*l^{e}habzôt,* to have contempt) carries within it the idea of "trampling with the feet," and is the opposite of *l^{e}kabēd,* which means to honor.[24] Thus, Memucan argues, men throughout the empire would no longer have places of leadership or respect within their homes because the king himself is not honored in his own home. Furthermore, the battle cry of all the rebellious women of the empire would be, "*King Ahasuerus* commanded Queen Vashti to be brought into his presence, but she did not come" (emphasis part of the original text). King Ahasuerus himself would be a contributor to the rebellion—guilty by complicity—if he does not take the appropriate steps to halt this incipient insurrection now.

Memucan concludes his statement of the problem (v. 18) by invoking the domino theory of politics and by making use of

21. The Hebrew term *ʿāw^{e}tā(h)* (she has wronged) conveys the sense of twisting or distorting something, acting perversely, or sinning. William Gesenius, *Hebrew and Chaldee Lexicon to the Old Testament Scriptures*, trans. Samuel Prideaux Tregelles (reprint; Grand Rapids: Eerdmans, 1967), 611; Ludwig Koehler and Walter Baumgartner, eds., *Lexicon in Veteris Testamenti Libros* (Leiden: Brill, 1985), 691–92.

22. Fox, *Character and Ideology in the Book of Esther*, 21.

23. Gordis correctly notes that the phrase *all the women* in v. 17 refers specifically to the women not present at the court, that latter group being identified in v. 18. Robert Gordis, "Studies in the Esther Narrative," *Journal of Biblical Literature* 95 (March 1976): 45–46.

24. Gesenius, *Hebrew and Chaldee Lexicon,* 110.

ambiguity. The rebellion mentioned in verse 17 would not remain in the provinces of the empire but would reach in a widening ripple effect even to the highest ruling body of the land. Rebellion would occur within the homes of the king's closest supporters (who potentially have the power to overthrow him as well). Memucan subtly makes this point clear by saying "the king's princes" and not merely "the princes." Thus Memucan carefully reminds the king that as king he has a direct responsibility for the well-being of these princes—a responsibility that in this case demands immediate royal attention.

Furthermore, Memucan strategically leaves ambiguous the subject of the final clause of this segment of his speech. There would be much contempt and anger, but from what corners of the empire would those potentially damaging emotions arise? Memucan craftily implies that danger would lurk everywhere for the king, if he does not respond in the way that Memucan proposes.

In verses 19–20, Memucan offers a solution to the problem of what to do with Vashti and how to halt an empire-wide insurrection before it begins. He stresses two points: the edict should be irrevocable (v. 19), and the results would be unstoppable (v. 20).[25]

Beginning by paying formulaic deference to the king—"if it pleases the king" (lit., "if it is good unto the king")—Memucan proposes that an edict go forth directly from the presence of the king. Such an edict would carry far more weight than a similar one sent out by the wise men or the princes. Such an edict, moreover, would be irreversible. Hence the edict must be placed among the written, irrevocable laws of Persia and Media.

Memucan has structured this portion of his speech to balance the danger he portrays in verse 17.[26] The concern that "the queen's deed will go forth" [*yēṣēʾ dᵉbar hammalk(a)h*] is counteracted here in verse 19 by the clause *a royal deed (order) will go forth (yēṣēʾ dᵉbar malkût)*.

25. The initial consonants of four consecutive Hebrew words in this verse when read backward form an acrostic that spells out the proper name of God, YHWH. See 5:4 for the significance, or lack thereof, of such a finding.

26. Roland E. Murphy, *Wisdom Literature: Job, Proverbs, Ruth, Canticles, Ecclesiastes, and Esther. The Forms of the Old Testament Literature*, 13, ed. Rolf Knierim and Gene M. Tucker (Grand Rapids: Eerdmans, 1981).

That Memucan suggests this edict should be made into an imperial law appears, at first glance, to be overkill for dealing with a seemingly minor domestic offense. The text of his speech and of the rest of the Book of Esther unfortunately do not provide us with his reasoning. There is, however, a logical scenario to explain his suggestion.[27] Simply stated, Memucan and his cohorts could not be certain to remain in power (or alive) if, after they proposed the deposal of Vashti, she at some later date regained her power and position within the palace.[28] The irrevocable edict protects them.

Note that Memucan here for the first time refers to Queen Vashti simply as Vashti.[29] Memucan is taking a calculated risk by referring to the queen of the Persian empire without using the formality of her title. His strategy, apparently, is to plant subconsciously the thought in the king's mind that Vashti no longer should be called "queen" because Vashti, who is rebelling against the king, is no longer acting like a queen.

Memucan's proposal ironically is "to forbid Vashti to do precisely what she had refused to do—to come to the king."[30] Interestingly, Memucan does not propose either her execution or her exile, nor does he even intimate that she be made a public spectacle. He does, however, suggest prudently that she be removed from her position in the palace.[31] Memucan further desires that Vashti's position be given to another individual (lit., "to her neighbor" or "companion"), but does not identify whom that individual should be.[32] He encourages the king by saying that

27. Moore, *Esther,* 10–11; Paton, *The Book of Esther,* 157.

28. Now the exaggerations of vv. 16–18 make sense. Without establishing the empire-wide nature of Vashti's offense, Memucan would not be able to propose this irrevocable solution with any serious hope for success in seeing it implemented.

29. Prior to this point in the story all references (1:9, 11, 12, 15, 16, 17, 18) to Vashti included her title; subsequently in all other citations in the story (2:1, 4), that title is conspicuously missing.

30. Fox, *Character and Ideology in the Book of Esther*, 22. As Baldwin concludes: "There is an appropriateness about her punishment. If she will not come when summoned, let her not come ever again." Joyce G. Baldwin, *Esther: An Introduction and Commentary*, Tyndale Old Testament Commentaries, ed. D. J. Wiseman (Downers Grove: InterVarsity, 1984), 62.

31. The phrase *her royal position* is emphasized by its location in the text.

32. Whether Memucan has someone specifically in mind to replace Vashti as queen is not clear. His choice of words does not limit the king's options in any way, much less direct the king to any specific woman or group of women.

the one chosen should be a woman who is "better" or "more worthy" than Vashti, but here again Memucan leaves room for the king's mind to roam in any direction that it pleases. The phrase may mean "better" or "more worthy" in beauty, intelligence, submissiveness, moral goodness, or potentially any other qualification that the king desires in a wife.

Having provided an overview of the proposal that he wants the king to adopt (v. 19), Memucan points out the benefits of implementing such a proposal—order will be restored to all families in the land (v. 20).

Memucan wisely "turns back" the reins of the proposal to the king. Never throughout his speech does Memucan identify the proposal as his own, and here, at a crucial juncture, he assures the king that the proposed edict[33] is to be the king's, that is, to be written and delivered with the king's seal of approval. Such an edict, royal in its origin, is needed for the great empire that King Ahasuerus rules.[34]

As a result of the king's edict, all women of the empire would show respect *(y^e^qār)* to their husbands, that is, treat them as priceless or magnificent treasures.[35] The results of the royal edict, moreover, would benefit all husbands in the empire; none would be left out from receiving the blessings that flow from the enactment of the king's order.[36]

Memucan's speech ends as it begins, focused on all of the people throughout all of the empire. Whereas in verse 16 it identifies strife and contention within that empire, here it sees only peace and harmony. Whereas in verse 16, the queen is the one

33. Keil notes that the term Memucan chooses, *pitgām*, permits a latitude of ambiguity to exist, since the term "signifies not only edict, decree, but also thing (see on Dan. iii. 16): to do a thing. In the present verse also it might be so understood: when the thing is heard which the king will do in his whole kingdom." Keil, *The Books of Ezra, Nehemiah, and Esther,* 331.

34. Although Memucan indulges in a little flattery, he does not stray from the truth or from his purpose. The flattery of calling the kingdom great is used judiciously as a reminder to the king of the importance and necessity of the action that he is being called on to implement.

35. Gesenius, *Hebrew and Chaldee Lexicon*, 363. This term is also found in 1:4, where, used in reference to the king's great majesty, it is translated variously as "magnificence," "splendor," "honor," or "pomp." See also 6:3, 6 (2x), 7, 9 (2x), 11; 8:16.

36. "From great to small" is a merism meaning everyone.

who sends a message and the king and the rest of the empire are merely recipients of that destructive communication, here and in verse 19 the tables are turned, for the king himself sends a message and the queen and the rest of the empire are the recipients of a message that eradicates the fast-spreading cancer of verse 16. Whereas once (v. 16) all was wrong, now once again, according to Memucan, all will be right.

DUI: Decision-Making Under the Influence (1:21–22)

Much like the headline of an article in the sports section of a newspaper that highlights the achievements of a baseball or football star, verse 21 provides an overview of the events that take place in the life of the king as an immediate result of Memucan's speech. Likewise, verse 22 functions in a similar fashion to the lead paragraph of that sports article, spelling out some of the key details of those events.

The king, whose heart is still "good with wine" (v. 10), finds (as do the princes) the words of Memucan also to be "good in his own eyes" (v. 21). What Memucan propounds in verses 16–20 the king accepts here, that is, the belief "that disobedience of wives to their husbands was dangerous to the peace of the State."[37] Thus, that which might not make much sense under different conditions is "pleasing" to the king (and the princes) now. Thus he acts in full accordance with the words of Memucan.

The king (v. 22) has letters drafted in each of the four official languages used at the provincial level—Persian, Elamite, Babylonian, and Aramaic[38]—and in each of the major ethnic languages used at the local level. He then utilizes the highly efficient pony and camel express system of the Persian empire to transmit those letters throughout the 127 provinces of the realm.[39]

The specific message that the king sends is divided into two parts. The meaning of the first is clear—that a husband is to rule in his house; the meaning of the second, however, is somewhat unclear. The Hebrew of the second clause is

37. Cassel, *An Explanatory Commentary on Esther*, 39.
38. Vos, *Ezra, Nehemiah, and Esther*, 152.
39. See also 3:13 and 8:10.

generally interpreted in one of two ways:[40] the language of the home should be the language of the husband in cases of mixed ethnic marriages, and the husband should have the final authority in the home. Both interpretations fit the general context of verses 10–22, and perhaps both are intended. Quite probably, however, since the first part of the message addresses the issue of mastery within the home, the second part focuses on the use of the ethnic language of the husband—a view that accords well with the king's effort to have the edict disseminated in the various languages of the people and not merely in the official language of a given region.[41]

Putting It All Together

Chocolate chip cookies are a specialty of mine—both baking and eating. One thing I have learned about baking chocolate chip cookies is that the individual ingredients placed on the kitchen counter do not miraculously come together on their own to form a cookie. There must be a mixing of the proper ingredients in the proper way to ensure a great-tasting outcome, that is, the purpose for the existence of the individual ingredients. Such is the case with any text of Scripture. Once the individual ingredients have been determined, they must be brought together with the mixer known as "so what?" Why then is 1:10–22 included in the story of Esther? What lessons can we learn from it?

Perhaps Vilna Gaon, an eighteenth-century Jewish rabbi, captures best the overall purpose for this section: "All this was written in such detail to teach us how the Almighty weaves a web of intrigue and paradox to accomplish miracles for Israel!"[42] Vilna Gaon is right, God is at work—the unmentioned God, the almost forgotten God, is accomplishing his goals despite humanity running headlong into foolish distraction.

In relation to the storyline, however, this section provides background information on the character of the king—to

40. Baldwin, *Esther: An Introduction and Commentary*, 62; Huey, "Esther," 803; and Vos, *Ezra, Nehemiah, and Esther*, 152.

41. Keil, *The Books of Ezra, Nehemiah, and Esther*, 332.

42. Zlotowitz, *The Megillah*, 51.

show his susceptibility to outside forces and his desire to please people—and on the events that paved the way for Esther to become queen.

The storyline of this section, when viewed from its overall perspective, yields a minimum of four general principles that may be of value to us today:

1. We face the consequences of our decisions, whether or not they are correct, and whether or not we are in our right senses when we make them.
2. The magnitude of the consequences or results of our actions may be far greater than we imagined. The story of Esther takes place, to a great extent, because of the decision made by the king to depose Vashti. That decision sets off a chain of events that topples the governmental leadership of the entire empire, and causes more than seventy-five thousand people to face an early death.
3. Leaders set examples for their followers; leaders have an impact on the well-being of those under them (cf. 3:15).
4. A well-executed speech given at the right time can have worldwide consequences.

A Mountain Out of a Molehill

Viewed from one perspective, the author of the Book of Esther appears to be writing 1:10–22 as a straightforward description of events that set the stage for even more important stories to come. He provides much detailed information regarding the social, political, and emotional climate of ancient Medo-Persia. His story is believable and interesting, captivating the readers of his day as well as readers today.

Viewed from another perspective, however, 1:10–22 (and in fact the whole chapter and, perhaps, as some think, the whole book) reads like a political and sociological satire.[43] The satire

43. David J. A. Clines, "The Esther Scroll: The Story of the Story," *Journal for the Study of the Old Testament: Supplement* 30 (Sheffield: University of Sheffield, 1984), 31–32; S[hemaryahu] Talmon, "Wisdom in the Book of Esther," *Vetus Testamentum* 13 (1963): 451; and Zlotowitz, *The Megillah*, 52.

is directed toward an empire whose main leaders function in a world of exaggeration and tragic farce. It is an empire that for the most part is governed foolishly, without the wisdom of the Scripture to guide it.[44]

The comedy of 1:10–22 occurs primarily in the exaggerated seriousness with which the king and his underlings take the simple offense of Queen Vashti. What is a private domestic affair becomes an international crisis that swallows up the time, effort, and resources of the leaders of the largest empire of the world. Even the manner of resolution of the story is farcical, that is, the dictation of what can and cannot be done within each and every household of this empire, with the ultimate goal being the preservation of peace and harmony throughout the empire.[45]

The comic farce of 1:10–22 plays out in grandiose fashion in 2:1–16. In chapter 2, the king finds a wife to replace the deposed Queen Vashti. Yet, he does not select a bride from among the leading families of the empire or even from the royal families of other nations in order to make a political alliance. Instead, he initiates an empire-wide search[46] for a bride—for the most beautiful virgin among all of the people of the land.

44. Prov. 20:1–2 functions almost as a commentary on the events of Esther 1:10–22. Prov. 20:1 warns of the dangers of making decisions while under the influence of strong drink; 20:2 warns of the dangers of provoking the anger of a king. Both warnings are forsaken here in Esther 1:10-22 with tragic results.

45. Fox astutely points out that 1:10–22 functions together with 1:1–9 as a "dramatic unit . . . framed by an ironic inclusio playing on the theme of the royal and masculine will: The great emperor, who rules 'from India to Nubia, 127 provinces' (v. 1), declares by imperial edict that every man shall be 'ruler in his own household,' in other words, have his wife obey him (v. 22), something the king has proved unable to enforce himself." Fox, *Character and Ideology in the Book of Esther*, 24. An inclusio is a literary device whereby the same words or themes are found at the beginning and end of a literary unit. An inclusio functions to identify all that is contained within its borders as a separate unit of thought or action from that which is outside of it.

46. Nothing in the empire of King Ahasuerus seems to be done in a simple, straightforward manner. In chapter 1 the king hosts a 180-day banquet (1:3–4) and issues an edict that impacts the social fabric of the entire empire (1:19–22). In chapter 2 there is an empire-wide program to secure a wife for the king (2:1–4, 8–17); in chapter 3, an empire-wide edict to eradicate a race of people (3:8–15). In chapter 5 the king offers to give his wife up to half of his kingdom (5:3, 6) and a seventy-five-foot gallows is built (5:14). In chapter 6 there is an ostentatious honoring of a citizen of the realm (6:7–11); in chapter 8 an empire-wide

Chapter 1 concludes with a once happy king (vv. 10–11) becoming happy again (vv. 21–22), but will he always remain that way? A once stable empire (vv. 1–9) becomes stable again (vv. 21–22), but will it always remain that way? A once forgotten God is still forgotten, but will he always remain that way? Will God's people ever appear in the book and will they fare better than the Gentiles just described? These and other questions are addressed by the author of the Book of Esther as he proceeds from the telling of the story of Vashti to the telling of the story of Esther that begins in the next chapter.

edict (8:9, 13, 17); in chapter 9 the slaughter of more than seventy-five thousand people (9:6–10, 15–16) and the creation of a holiday that is to last for all time (9:20–32); and in chapter 10 the enactment of an empire-wide tax (10:1).

10

And the Winner Is . . .
(2:1–16)

In the old days, the Miss America Pageant was primarily a beauty contest—an annual search for the most beautiful, unmarried young woman in the United States. The emphasis was on the physical attributes of the contestants as they appeared in swimsuits and in evening gowns. Although the wrapping on the package—the beauty of the women—is still considered important, the inner character of the women takes on equal or even greater weight in the judges' consideration. Intelligence, social concerns, worthy career choices, and communication skills are among some of the more highly prized traits in contemporary pageants.

These modern pageants are a far cry from the one that King Ahasuerus, ruler of the Medo-Persian empire, initiates to find his future wife. When his aides (2:1–4) suggest that he hold a contest to determine who the next queen should be—the queen to replace the deposed Vashti (1:15–21)—the king readily embraces the idea (and the women). He jumps at the chance to be not simply a spectator at the pageant, but the sole judge and jury, and thus the contest begins.

King Ahasuerus's pageant requires all contestants to do all that they can to satisfy the sexual desires of the judge (2:4, 12–14). The more they please him in that category, the higher are their scores and the greater is their chance of being called back for another round of judging (v. 14). The ultimate prize in this pageant—there are no runners-up—is the right to marry the king and to be crowned queen.

This pageant forms the backdrop for this section (2:1–16) and for the introduction of the two lead characters of the book. It shows the means by which an orphaned Jewish girl could rise to the position of queen of one of ancient history's largest and most powerful empires—an empire governed by non-Jews. This section, moreover, provides information regarding a close relative of that orphaned Jewish girl who would one day become prime minister of that same Medo-Persian empire.

Bon Appétit

Eating an artichoke involves extracting the tender edible meat off the outer leaves, discarding the cone of young leaves and the fuzzy center, and delving into the heart of the vegetable for additional tasty morsels. In a similar way, this section of the Book of Esther produces increasing taste treasures of truth as one digs further down to the heart of the passage.

The overall structure of 2:1–16 is easily discernible. There are three major divisions: the establishment of the contest (vv. 1–4), an introduction of one of the players in the contest (vv. 5–7), and the rules and procedures of the contest (vv. 8–16). In essence, then, we encounter a plan, a person, and a process—a plan to secure a new queen, the person who will be the new queen, and the process by which she becomes that new queen.[1]

A detailed breakdown of the structure of this section, however, poses more of a challenge. When verses 1–16 are studied from the perspective of the interpersonal relationships presented, the structure of the passage appears to follow an AB—A′B′—CC′ format:

A Concern for the welfare of another (vv. 1–4)
  B Concern for the preservation of another (vv. 5–7)
A′ Concern for the welfare of another (vv. 8–9)
  B′ Concern for the preservation of another (vv. 10–11)
    C Concern for the welfare of self (vv. 12–14)
    C′ Concern for the welfare of self (vv. 15–16)[2]

1. The third section (vv. 8–16) may be divided into the process (vv. 8–11) and the presentation (vv. 12–16). Thus the outline could read: a plan (or a proposal), a person, a process, and a presentation.

2. Note that Esther, like each of the other women in the harem, does everything she can to enhance her position before the king.

This format highlights the intimacy that is to follow for each of the women as she goes before the king to win his favor by her sexual prowess.

The structure of this section, however, is changed somewhat if the verses are viewed from the vantage point of the situations that occur. When that perspective is take, the structure follows an AB—A′B′—B″A″ pattern:

- A Successful state of affairs (vv. 1–4)
  - B Sad state of affairs (vv. 5–7)
- A′ Successful state of affairs (vv. 8–9)
  - B′ Sad state of affairs (vv. 10–11)
  - B″ Sad state of affairs (vv. 12–14)
- A″ Successful state of affairs (laid overtop of a sad state of affairs) (vv. 15–16)

The reversal of the order of the elements in the last couplet suggests the upside-down nature of the events that the author is portraying. Life for the people of God is out of synchronization with what God intends it to be.

In addition, in this section the author shifts his attention back and forth from those who are non-Jews to those who are Jews. Verses 1–4 deal with the non-Jews, verses 5–7 with the Jews, verse 8a with the non-Jews, verses 8b–11 with the Jews, verses 12–14 with the non-Jews, and verses 15–16 with the Jews. Such a pattern could be expected to be used to reveal contrasts between the unspiritual heathen and the spiritual Jew, between those who do not know God and those who serve him faithfully. Such, however, is not the case. Instead of showing contrasts, the author shows similarities. By making these shifts, the author seems to suggest an intermingled state of affairs of the two groups, almost as if to say that there is no difference in the way the two groups live, or that their "fates"[3] are intertwined.

Interestingly, in each of the sections dealing with the Jews, the state of affairs of those Jews is greatly affected by the

3. The term *fate* is used here and elsewhere in this commentary in a popular sense rather than in a theological sense. "Fatalism" is not a theological tenet of a biblical Jewish faith.

actions of non-Jews. In verses 5–7, Mordecai's (and Esther's) family is in exile, away from the Promised Land, away from the physical center of their faith (i.e., Jerusalem) because of the actions of non-Jews. In verses 8b–11, Esther's living conditions and welfare depend to a large extent on how she pleases a Gentile harem-master, and in verses 15–16 Esther's success is bound up in how well she takes guidance from a Gentile harem-master in how to please (read: seduce) a heathen king.

Another intriguing aspect of this Jew-Gentile division of the chapter is that sensuality seems to be the core theme of each Gentile passage, whereas sensitivity mixed with sensuality is at the center of each of the Jewish passages.

The sensuality of the Gentile passages is clear. The sensitivity-sensuality of the Jewish passage, however, needs some discussion. In verses 5–7, for example, the author depicts the Jewish hero Mordecai as displaying a caring attitude toward his cousin Esther, and at the same time describes Esther as being both beautiful and shapely. In verses 8b–11, the writer presents Esther as being responsive not only to Mordecai but also to Hegai, the non-Jewish harem-master. All the while, Esther is involved in a year-long course of preparation for a one-night meeting with the king in his bedchamber. In the final passage in which a Jew is prominent (vv. 15–16), the author pictures Esther as being sensitive to the guidance of Hegai and as acting in such a way that all who see her are impressed by her demeanor. Yet the author also discreetly mentions that Esther is escorted to the palace (for her turn to please the king).[4]

4. What makes these verses seem so strange is the manner in which the author treats the events that lead up to Esther's night with the king. First he mentions her Jewish heritage, second her faithful trust in Hegai the harem-master, third the accolades of those who see her, and finally her journey to the king. The author makes everything seem so beautiful, yet in a surrealistic way. Not once does he mention the immorality being committed. Not once does he remind the reader that Esther in no way should be seeking to join herself with a heathen. Not once does he specifically point out that all of Esther's praise and guidance come from unbelievers and that the only advice she receives from a believer (Mordecai) is, in essence, "keep quiet about your faith." All of those unspoken implications are left to fall on the reader at later reflection.

Are You Lonely? Call "Dial-a-Wife" (2:1–4)

In recent years, telephone hotlines have been springing up, offering callers everything from wake-up calls to tips on what their future supposedly will be like, from a "listening ear" to "a dream date." If telephones existed in the Medo-Persian empire, the marketing agents of King Ahasuerus's time would have had a field day. King Ahasuerus was desperate to find some comfort for his loneliness; he needed a(nother) wife. They, the marketing agents, probably could have sold him on the idea of dialing any of a number of telephone numbers such as 1- ### -FIND-LUV or 1- ### -HOT-TIME. Unfortunately for those marketers, no such technology was available, but that did not stop them from marketing a new concept to the king—a "find-a-bride" service. The idea excited the king, and the author of the Book of Esther tells his readers how such a wife-finding service began.

Some time has passed (2:1) from the events of the previous chapter—the pleasures of the banquets are a distant memory to the king, but he senses a yearning for Vashti, the queen whom he deposed (1:15–21). The author provides only an imprecise way of dating the time—"after these things"[5]—when the king's anger subsided and his thoughts turned again to Vashti. The timing apparently is not crucial to the author; the events, however, are.

The verb *subsided* or *abated (šākak)* occurs only five times throughout the Old Testament.[6] According to Joyce G. Baldwin, the fact that this verb is used twice in the same book—here and in 7:10—tends to link the two incidents.[7] The word order, however, is different in the two verses. Here the standard Hebrew order (temporal marker followed by verb, then subject) suggests a natural flow in the process of the anger subsiding, whereas, by

5. The timing of these events is a bit convoluted. King Ahasuerus holds the banquet in the third year of his reign (1:3) and Esther is crowned queen in the seventh year of his reign (2:16). History records that in the fifth year of his reign, he attacks the Greeks unsuccessfully. Thus several possibilities exist, the most likely scenario being that "after these things" means approximately three years later or that time after the king had returned from his unsuccessful battle.

6. This verb is also found in Gen. 8:1; Num. 17:5 (Heb. 17:20); and Jer. 5:26.

7. Joyce G. Baldwin, *Esther: An Introduction and Commentary*, Tyndale Old Testament Commentaries, ed. D. J. Wiseman (Downers Grove: InterVarsity, 1984), 64.

contrast, the word order in 7:10 (temporal marker followed first by subject and then by verb) emphasizes the "anger." The word order, therefore, appears to imply a quicker reduction in the expression of the king's anger after the hanging of Haman than after the loss of Vashti as his wife.

The fact of the word order of 2:1 (contrasted to that of 7:10), when coupled with the lack of any mention of Vashti's execution, supports the notion that Vashti is merely deposed, rather than executed as some think.[8] If she is alive at this time, then the potential for her to return to power (despite the irrevocable law of the Medes and Persians, which in various ways could be undermined [cf. 8:8–12]) remains a grave danger to those servants of the king who favored her disposal. That potentiality may have provided the impetus for the quick thinking of the servants causing them to suggest to the king the option of a wife-finding contest.[9]

The servants suggest three criteria for those who are to be part of the wife-search contest: beauty, youth, and virginity. Only those who meet these three criteria would be considered worthy to be possible candidates for the position of the king's wife.[10] Furthermore, all women throughout the empire who meet these three qualifications are to be sought out[11] and are to

8. Paulus Cassel, *An Explanatory Commentary on Esther*, trans. Aaron Bernstein (Edinburgh: T. and T. Clark, 1888), 45; Meir Zlotowitz, trans. and comp., *The Megillah: The Book of Esther: A New Translation with a Commentary Anthologized from Talmudic, Midrashic and Rabbinic Sources* (Brooklyn: Mesorah, 1981), 52.

9. If Vashti, however, is dead, then, as Fox points out, the passive verb (had been decreed) reminds the reader of the fact that the decision to remove Vashti was not an independent action of the king. The advisers too are responsible for her departure. They then are in a precarious and potentially life-threatening position since, as Fox continues, "this sentence paraphrases his [the king's] thoughts, . . . [and thus] suggests he is transferring blame to his advisers—a habit he will manifest again." Michael V. Fox, *Character and Ideology in the Book of Esther* (Columbia, S.C.: University of South Carolina Press, 1991), 26.

10. Chandler states that these maidens would not have been consulted as to whether they agreed to the king choosing them or not. Lucinda B. Chandler, *Comments on Esther,* The Woman's Bible, ed. Elizabeth Cady Stanton and Lucinda B. Chandler (reprint; New York: Arno, 1974), 2:91.

11. Despite Huey's contention that the "[f]athers . . . [of such women would] not voluntarily present their daughters" and thus the women had to be sought out, the text does not suggest that there would be any difficulty implementing the process. The basic meaning of the Hebrew verb *bāqaš* is to seek, to find. The

be gathered into the king's harem to proceed with their beauty treatment to make them presentable to the king (2:3).

Tantalizing the king by the repetition of the words *beautiful young virgins* (v. 3), the servants assure the king that every[12] single one of those beautiful young virgins in all of the 127 provinces of the kingdom would be gathered; none would be missed. The king, therefore, would be able to choose the best of the best.

The plan that the servants offer includes both the appointing[13] of those who are to gather qualified virgins and the establishment of the process by which those virgins who are gathered are made ready to meet the king. An important part of that process, moreover, is the placing of the virgins who are brought to the capital city into the hands of the eunuch Hegai, who knew how best to prepare them for their special evening.[14] Ultimately, as verse 4 reveals, the choice of the winner—the one who would become queen in Vashti's place—is determined by whoever sexually pleases the king most during the night that she has with him (cf. vv. 13–14).[15]

The king approves of the idea of his attendants and implements their plan. Note that the king in no way challenges the suggestion of his servants. The whole affair sounds exceptional to him. The Hebrew grammar of this passage, moreover, does

---

search thus is for those who are beautiful, young, and virgin. F. B. Huey, Jr., "Esther," *Expositor's Bible Commentary,* ed. Frank E. Gaebelein, 12 vols. (Grand Rapids: Zondervan, 1988), 4:804.

12. Note the addition of the word *every (kol),* which is not found in the servants' initial declaration in 2:2.

13. Keil notes that "the infin. abs. [infinitive absolute], [is] used instead of the verb. fin. [finite verb] to give prominence to the matter: let them appoint." C. F. Keil, *The Books of Ezra, Nehemiah, and Esther*, Biblical Commentary on the Old Testament, trans. Sophia Taylor (Grand Rapids: Eerdmans, n.d.), 334.

14. Eunuchs, for obvious reasons, typically were placed in charge of harems in ancient times.

15. Herodotus writes that Persian custom required that the queen be selected from one of the seven noble families. Herodotus 3:84. This requirement apparently is not in effect here, since the Book of Esther does not indicate that the contest winner would be either the first-in-rank queen (Vashti herself may not have been first in rank) or the queen through whom the royal heir was to come. In fact, an heir had already been born, as Fox notes: "[Queen] Amestris had Xerxes' [Ahasuerus'] third son in about 483, before Esther came on the scene in 480 (according to 2:16)." Fox, *Character and Ideology in the Book of Esther*, 136. Hence, the proper family background of the virgins in the Book of Esther would not be an issue.

not imply the existence of any hesitation on the part of the king; if anything, the word order suggests that immediately upon hearing the plan, the king is pleased and sets out to take action.

The Private Lives of Public People (2:5–7)

Esther 2:5–7 comes as a surprise. We would naturally expect the contents of 2:8 to follow immediately after 2:4, yet the author interposes a seemingly innocuous parenthetical discussion about a man and his adopted daughter. From the beginning of the book all the way through 2:4, the author has focused solely on Gentiles in the Persian empire. What is more, from 1:9 through 2:4, he has directed his readers' attention to a particular woman or to women (beautiful young virgins) in that empire. Thus the first word of 2:5, *ʾîš* (a man) is totally unexpected. The next word is no less surprising: *y^ehûdî* (a Jew). If anything, the readers would have been anticipating the words to be "a Persian woman," not the idiomatic phrase meaning "a Jew."

The author further arrests our attention by placing these two nouns at the beginning of the verse, before the verb, and thus disrupting the normal word order for a Hebrew sentence. In addition, the author does not use a conjunction to connect this verse with those that precede it as would normally be expected. The author therefore makes certain that his readers recognize that a significantly different subject is now under consideration.[16]

One additional surprise exists in this verse: this Jew is living in Susa during the time of Ahasuerus. What makes this fact so startling is that Cyrus the Great, a previous king of the Medo-Persian empire, had declared fifty years earlier that the Jews could return to their homeland. Yet this Jew (whose

16. This transition is all the more striking because the use of the term *Jew* (including the terms *Jews, the Jew, the Jews,* and *Jewish*), is quite rare within the Hebrew Scriptures, and extremely rare outside of the Book of Esther. Of the seventy-six uses of the term *Jew* (and its related terms) in the Hebrew Scriptures, fifty-two are found in the Book of Esther. Such a high preponderance of usage within the book suggests that the Jews and the Gentiles had intermixed within Persian society so much that telling the Jews apart from the Gentiles is almost impossible without the author making a special effort to distinguish between the two groups.

ancestors came from Jerusalem, 2:6) is living not only in exile but at the very heart of the heathen kingdom, in its capital.

Note that the name of the Jew is Mordecai,[17] a Persian name, not a name of Hebrew origin. In fact, no Jewish name is given for Mordecai,[18] nor is any mention made of his immediate family relations (i.e., a wife or children), although his Jewish ancestry is briefly spelled out.

The list of ancestors poses a bit of a conundrum. Exactly who Jair, Shemei, and Kish are is unknown. They may be the immediate ancestors of Mordecai or they may be a representative group of men who are part of Mordecai's lineage going back to Kish, the father of Saul, the first king of Israel.[19] Apart from this verse, nothing is known of Jair;[20] Shemei, however, may be the son of Gera (of the lineage of Saul) who cursed David when David was fleeing from his own son Absalom (2 Sam. 16:5–13; 19:16–23; 1 Kings 2:8, 36–46).[21]

Esther 2:6 poses another problem: who specifically is the one "who had been taken into exile from Jerusalem" when Jeconiah was king of Judah? If Kish is the father of King Saul, then he cannot be the one; if Kish, however, is the great-grandfather of Mordecai then he conceivably could be the one who was "exiled with Jeconiah king of Judah." The natural referent to the term *who,* in the phrase *who had been taken into exile,* is Mordecai. Yet, as

17. Outside of the Book of Esther, there is no mention of Mordecai. Another man bearing the same name, who is to be differentiated from the Mordecai spoken of here, is listed in Ezra 2:2 and Neh. 7:7.

18. Cassel wisely cautions against assuming that because this Jew bears the name *Mordecai* he is a follower of the pagan Persian religion: that he is a worshipper of the idol Merodach. Cassel, *An Explanatory Commentary on Esther,* 51.

19. The term *son of* (as in "son of Jair") in Hebrew is often used idiomatically throughout Scripture to indicate (among other concepts) the sense of "descendent of." Thus the term may refer to an individual who is the son, grandson, great-grandson, or so on of the individual cited. For example, in Gen. 29:5 (compare Gen. 24:15, 24, 29), Laban, the grandson of Nahor, is called the "son of" Nahor.

20. The name *Jair* occurs in the Scripture in reference to two other individuals, neither of whom would fit appropriately in this context as an ancestor of Mordecai. See Num. 32:41; Deut. 3:14; 1 Kings 5:13; and 1 Chron. 2:22; as well as Judg. 10:3, 5.

21. The name *Shemei* is used to designate several different individuals in the Scripture, none of whom (apart from the Shemei noted here) would make sense here.

Michael V. Fox states, "if it is Mordecai who was exiled with Jehoiachin in 597 B.C.E., he would be over 110 years old in Xerxes' time (487–67 B.C.E.), and his cousin Esther too would be very old."[22]

Although Mordecai may have been "over 110 years old" when the story of Esther began (and thus over 120 years old when he is appointed to the position of prime minister, cf. 8:2 and 10:3), the likelihood of his being appointed prime minister at such an advanced age is minimal, yet it is not beyond the realm of possibility.[23] C. F. Keil, however, presents an appropriate resolution to this dilemma: "For the relative clause: who had been carried away, need not be so strictly understood as to assert that Mordochai himself was carried away; but the object being to give merely his origin and lineage; and not his history, it involves only the notion that he belonged to those Jews who were carried to Babylon by Nebuchadnezzar with Jeconiah, so that he, though born in captivity, was carried to Babylon in the persons of his forefathers."[24] In other words, Mordecai was carried into captivity in the "seed" of his parents, grandparents, or great-grandparents (whoever had been taken into captivity), and then at some time later was born in captivity. Such an understanding of this passage, although strange perhaps to many of us, is a legitimate understanding of Hebrew genealogical records. The ages of Mordecai and of Esther, therefore, cannot be accurately determined from the data currently available.

The primary function of this brief presentation of Mordecai's lineage is to lay a foundation for the major sequence of events that form the crux of the story of the Book of Esther. The author here intimates that Mordecai has some connection, direct or indirect, to King Saul, either through the mention of Shemei and Kish (two names closely associated to Saul) or through the denotation of Mordecai as being a Benjaminite (Saul, too, was of the tribe of Benjamin). In 3:1, the author also sets forth the lin-

22. Fox, *Character and Ideology in the Book of Esther*, 29. See also Lewis Bayles Paton, *The Book of Esther*, International Critical Commentary, ed. Samuel Rolles Driver, Alfred Plummer, and Charles Augustus Briggs (Edinburgh: T. and T. Clark, 1908), 168–69.

23. Esther's age, however, becomes a problem if Fox is correct since, according to 2:2–4, those selected for the contest are to be "young," not middle-aged or old.

24. Keil, *The Books of Ezra, Nehemiah, and Esther*, 336.

eage of another character of the book, Haman, the prime minister who becomes the archenemy of the Jews (3:10).[25] The author in 3:10 identifies Haman as an Agagite, that is, a member of a group of people whom King Saul was to have eradicated at the command of the Lord, but whom King Saul failed to eliminate, and as a consequence lost the right for his family to rule as kings over Israel (1 Sam. 15). Thus the families of the survivors of the Saul-Agag battle understandably had cause for despising each other—Mordecai for having his family line being eliminated from the rulership of Israel, and Haman for having most of his family line destroyed.

The author also indicates (2:6) that Mordecai's ancestors were a part of the upper class of Jewish exiles since they were taken into exile at the time when Jeconiah, king of Judah, was deported. According to 2 Kings 24:10–16, in 597 B.C., Nebuchadnezzar king of Babylon took into exile King Jeconiah, his officials, the leaders of Judah, the mighty warriors, and the craftsmen (and all of their families).[26] Nebuchadnezzar left behind the remainder of the population of Jerusalem, who themselves were removed from the land ten years later (2 Kings 25:1–21).

Quite unexpectedly, Esther 2:7 announces that Mordecai is acting as a foster or adoptive father to his cousin Hadassah. Mordecai, the author notes, adopts Hadassah after both her parents died,[27] caring for her as he would for his own daughter.

Hadassah, we learn, is also (and more commonly) known as Esther—the name she carries with her throughout the rest of

25. The author provides only two genealogies of any consequence, those for Mordecai and Haman. This fact supports the view that a "family feud" fuels the flames of the deadly intrigues pictured in this book. Note that not even King Ahasuerus's ancestry is given. The author does cite a one-person ancestry for Esther, that is, Abihail her father, but that reference appears to be presented more for the purpose of providing the family linkage between Esther and Mordecai than for revealing anything about Esther's family tree.

26. This does not necessarily mean that Mordecai at the time we meet him is rich or famous, but does seem to suggest that he or his family may be better off financially or socially than the masses of people who came into exile at a later date.

27. How old Esther is at the time of her parents death is unknown. The text of 2:7 suggests that she is perhaps at least a teenager when it indicates that she is well developed physically and good-looking, and implies that she displayed both of those attributes at the time of her "adoption."

the book.[28] Hadassah is a Hebrew name; Esther is a Persian name. Hadassah means "myrtle" (a fragrant shrub or tree); Esther, however, is derived from the Persian word meaning "star" or "Ishtar," the Babylonian goddess of love.[29] According to Friedrich Weinreib, the name *Esther,* when brought over into the Hebrew language, means: "'I hide Myself', or 'I am hidden', or 'I have hidden Myself'."[30] If the author of the Book of Esther intends the meaning of the name *Esther* to have significance throughout the book, then there are two different ways in which its meaning could fit his purposes. The *m* on "Myself" could be understood as a capital letter (as Weinreib indicates), thereby reflecting what God is doing in the Book of Esther, that is, working in an unseen fashion behind the scenes. The *m,* however, could be understood as a small letter,[31] thereby implying that Esther has hidden herself, and thus would be suggestive of what she does for much of the book, that is, keep her Jewish origins hidden.

In addition, the author describes Esther as having both a good figure and good looks (v. 7). By doing so he hints at what is about to happen, in light of the qualifications for the competition just mentioned in verses 2–4.

Standing Apart from the Crowd (2:8–9)

In school, there were always one or two students who stood out from the rest of the crowd. Some stood out because they were beautiful or handsome, others because they were athletically inclined or were highly intelligent. A few, however, excelled in more than one arena. In the Book of Esther (2:8–9, 15), the author depicts Esther as one who excelled in more than one category.

28. When specifically Hadassah receives the name *Esther* is unknown—a fact that apparently is not of as much concern to the author as is the fact that Hadassah has a Persian name and is consistently called by it.

29. As is noted in v. 5 in regard to Mordecai's name, the fact that Hadassah is called Esther does not necessarily imply that she worshiped the gods or goddesses of the Persian empire.

30. Friedrich Weinreib, *Chance: The Hidden Lord: The Amazing Scroll of Esther* (Braunton, U.K.: Merlin, 1986), 34.

31. The Hebrew language does not make use of upper-case and lower-case letters in the same way that the English language does. Thus either the capital *M* or the small *m* is a possible rendering.

In verses 8–9, the king's appointed officers gather to Susa, the capital, perhaps hundreds[32] of young beautiful virgins eligible to enter the king's harem, Esther being one of those taken. All of these women are placed under the authority (lit., "into the hand") of Hegai, the harem-master, who is responsible for providing each woman with a year-long beauty treatment and with the other necessities that would prepare her best to meet the king (vv. 9, 12–14).

A question that arises at this point is whether the women are forced to participate in the competition. Interestingly, the Scripture does not address that issue. As Michael V. Fox states: "What is significant—and most oppressive—is that their will, whatever it may have been, is of no interest to anyone in the story. They are handed around, from home to home, to harem, to the king's bed. Their bodies belong to others, so much so that they are not even pictured as being forced."[33]

The Hebrew of the text likewise volunteers no insights. Nothing significant should be made of the fact that the verse reads that the virgins "were gathered" *(hiqqābēṣ),* whereas Esther "was taken" *(tillāqaḥ).* "To gather" does not suggest in any way that these women are viewed as something less than human (e.g., cattle) or that the event is to be deemed as that which is evil. Furthermore, "to take" does not necessarily convey the sense of coercion, that is, that Esther is forced against her will (whereas the others, merely being gathered, go willingly). Note that Mordecai "takes" *(lāqaḥ)* Esther to be his daughter in verse 7, an action that quite probably was not forced upon her. The words *qābaṣ* (to gather) and *lāqaḥ* (to take), as used here, however, should be understood to convey essentially the same general semantic sense, that is, that each and every virgin under consideration is transported in some fashion to Susa to be placed into Hegai's (the harem-master's) care. These women are assembled at "the house of the king," where they are to receive their beauty treatment

32. The text does not indicate how many virgins are gathered. Josephus, a first-century a.d. Jewish historian, however, places the figure at four hundred. Flavius Josephus, *The Complete Works of Flavius Josephus,* trans. William Whiston, 475.

33. Fox, *Character and Ideology in the Book of Esther*, 34.

(v. 12).[34] Carey A. Moore correctly points out that the term *house* refers to the entire palace complex, rather than to the king's personal residence (cf. v. 13).[35]

At this point in the book (2:8) the author is strangely silent about several important issues. He leaves us with many unanswered questions. Why does neither Esther nor Mordecai offer any protest to the process by which Esther at "best" would be married to a heathen, and at worst be confined to a life of concubinage in the king's harem? Why is there no mention of a general outcry from the Jewish population of the empire, from which undoubtedly other unnamed but beautiful young virgins were taken (and ended up as the king's concubines)? Why is there no record of even a single prayer by the Jewish people being lifted up to God for deliverance from this sinful situation? Do the people of God perhaps welcome the possibility of one of their own becoming queen over the heathen empire of Medo-Persia? This silence of the Scripture may be instructive of the spiritual condition of the Jews during this period of exile.

In verse 9, however, the author provides insight into the character of Esther, who makes the most of a difficult situation. She makes Hegai, the harem-master, happy,[36] and she works actively to secure his goodwill, that is, his loyalty.[37]

34. At this royal health spa the goal is not merely to make the women (Esther included) physically attractive but also to make them sexually attractive to the king.

35. Carey A. Moore, *Esther,* The Anchor Bible, ed. William Foxwell Albright and David Noel Freedman (Garden City, N.Y.: Doubleday, 1971), 21.

36. The idiom used here, "to be good in the eyes of someone," is the same as that used in 2:4 in reference to the servants' suggestion to the king. In verse 4, the king likes their idea; here in verse 9, Hegai likes Esther, that is, she brightens his eyes. Nothing of a sensual connotation should be read into these words. See also 3:11; 8:5, 8 for similar examples of this idiomatic expression in the Book of Esther.

37. Both Fox and Moore point out that the author distinguishes between the Hebrew terms *nāśāʾ* (to gain, sometimes translated "to find") and *māṣā* (to find). The former (used *of* Esther here in 2:9 as well as in 2:15, 17; 5:2) implies an active securing of something (in this case "favor"); the latter (used *by* Esther in 7:3; 8:5) conveys a passive notion that suggests a dependency on someone else. Fox, *Character and Ideology in the Book of Esther*, 31; Moore, *Esther,* 21.

Because Hegai likes Esther, he begins her beauty regime of cosmetics and beauty-enhancing delicacies[38] sooner than would normally be expected.[39] In addition, he gives her seven choice maids and the best accommodations in the harem. The author places the definite article *the* in conjunction with the seven select maids to indicate that these women are not merely good maids, but that they are the seven best maids in the king's palace.[40] Thus only Esther of the possibly hundreds of women in the competition received the very best maids and the very best accommodations.

All of this special treatment would spoil many if not most people placed in such an environment. The text (2:10), however, does not portray Esther as having rejected her parental teaching. In fact, when verse 10 is taken in conjunction with verse 15, Esther is seen to display a remarkable loyalty to her foster father Mordecai while at the same time she exhibits those characteristics that endear her to all who encounter her in the harem, that is, the eunuchs, the maids, and even her competition. Such a record of interpersonal relations reveals a truly remarkable young woman.

38. The Hebrew term *mānôt* is translated literally as "portions." Most scholars take the term to mean allotments of special food delicacies, although some have suggested that possibilities such as dresses, ornaments, or jewels. Its use in 9:19, 22 favors the allotment of foodstuffs view.

Whether or not the term is to be understood as an allotment of food raises the issue of Esther's ability to remain kosher in her diet. Unlike for Daniel and his three friends in the canonical Book of Daniel (1:8–16) or even unlike for Judith in the apocryphal Book of Judith (12:1–4), there is no record of Esther ever protesting the eating of nonkosher foods (i.e., foods not sanctioned by Jewish law). Quite the opposite, if she is to keep her Jewish origins hidden (Esther 2:10, 20), she would have to eat nonkosher foods throughout her twelve-month beautification process. Cassel, *An Explanatory Commentary on Esther,* 60; Keil, *The Books of Ezra, Nehemiah, and Esther,* 337; Moore, *Esther,* 22; Paton, *The Book of Esther,* 174.

39. The term *waybahēl* (and he quickly provided, 2:9) suggests that Hegai began Esther's year-long process sooner than he otherwise would have done. This does not mean, however, that she finished in less than one year, since, according to verse 12, the beauty treatment was a fixed twelve-month process for all of the women. Verse 15 confirms that the twelve-month period was not shortened even for the favored Esther. Cassel, *An Explanatory Commentary on Esther*, 60; Fox, *Character and Ideology in the Book of Esther*, 31–32; Moore, *Esther*, 22.

40. Verse 9 implies that all of the women receive seven maids; Esther, however, receives the best ones. Fox, *Character and Ideology in the Book of Esther,* 32.

A Deep, Dark Secret (2:10–11)

Esther 2:10 declares that Mordecai intentionally commands his charge Esther not to reveal the secret of her ethnic background (and hence the secret of her faith). This verse, moreover, does not offer even the slightest hint that Esther protests the command. In his assessment of this verse, Ronald W. Pierce strongly declares that what "one finds here [is] a diaspora Jewess who desires a chance at the throne so greatly that she is willing to betray her heritage at the advice of her cousin without resistance."[41] Pierce may be overstating the case somewhat, yet he has captured the essence of the problem—a yielding to the pressures of the world on the part of both Esther and Mordecai. Neither Esther nor Mordecai seeks God's solution to the dilemma they face.

The author stresses the importance of 2:10, introducing it without the use of the standard Hebrew conjunction. The impact of Esther's decision not to reveal her heritage hits with full force. Whereas everything seemed to be flowing so smoothly in verse 9, something amiss is happening here. In verse 9, Esther pleases the heathen harem-master Hegai and thereby advances along her chosen path. In verse 10, she pleases her foster father Mordecai, but at the expense of her faith.

The next verse (v. 11), on first glance, reveals the concern of a father for his daughter who is in a difficult circumstance. Mordecai daily walks back and forth[42] in an area as close to the harem as he is allowed to walk to learn of Esther's situation. A fuller analysis of this verse in its context, however, unpacks a considerably different story. Mordecai is the one who instructed Esther to keep silent about her faith. Mordecai[43] is the one who,

41. Ronald W. Pierce, "Purim: A Time to Mourn or a Time to Dance?" Ms. presented to the Evangelical Theological Society in San Diego, Calif. 18 November 1989, 9. Interestingly, the only time in the entire book when Esther raises any protest at all to Mordecai is found in 4:11. In that verse, ironically, Esther protests not Mordecai's instruction to keep her heritage hidden, but rather his command (4:8) that she reveal it before the king.

42. The Hithpael verb form used here suggests a habit of doing something, in this case, walking.

43. The fact that Mordecai is in control of the interaction between himself and Esther is emphasized by the position of the name *Mordecai* within the sentence structure of the last half of verse 10.

if he did not get her into the harem in the first place, encourages her to remain in the harem by having her hide her Jewishness (v. 10). Had she left the harem at this point—assuming that the revelation of her Jewish heritage would have disqualified her (which it probably would not)—Esther would not have committed the sin of willful adultery (vv. 15–16) or the sin of marrying a heathen (v. 17). Furthermore, lest the reader be concerned, if Esther does not become queen and yet the edict calling for the elimination of the Jews is still invoked (3:1–15), then (to parallel though not quote Mordecai's words of 4:14) God would provide another means for the deliverance of his people. God then would be able to work through the faithfulness of his people rather than despite their unfaithfulness.

Mordecai's concern for Esther (2:11) is twofold: He is interested in her well-being, literally in her "shalom," and he desires to find out about her success, that is, how well she is doing in her beauty treatment and other preparations. These concerns are natural for a father to have for his daughter, especially since he quite probably is not able to see her at least for a period of a year. That Mordecai expresses these concerns daily reveals a faithfulness that is to be commended—many less concerned parents would have ceased going to the court of the harem on a regular basis, much less on a daily basis.

A Chance to Strut One's Stuff (2:12–14)

Many people enjoy reading about the comings and goings of royalty. They desire to gain insight into the lives of famous people. These verses (vv. 12–14) portray the glamor and the glitz of one palace happening twenty-five hundred years ago; they also reveal the harsh reality of the life for some behind palace walls—a reality that is based on a callous view of the value and sanctity of every human life.

The happening described here indicates that all of the women in the competition underwent a four-step procedure: a year-long beautification treatment; a night of attempting to please the king sexually; a transference to a second harem chamber and, at the same time, receiving the designation of "concubine"; and a period of waiting until being summoned again (if ever) to spend another night attempting to arouse the king sexually.

Eventually, through this process, one of the women presumably would please the king sufficiently to cause him to choose her to be his queen (cf. vv. 2–4).

In verse 12, the author notes that each virgin is given her opportunity to win the king to herself. The specific time of that opportunity is different for each woman, depending largely on when she completes the two-phase beauty treatment. Phase 1 of the beautification program consists of being immersed in myrrh[44] (either in a bath or in a misting spray)[45] regularly over a six-month period. Phase 2, the next six months, involves additional full-body treatments, these treatments involving special spices and cosmetics (cf. v. 9).

When each virgin goes to meet the king (v. 13) she may take with her anything from the harem that she desires (lit., "says" in this case, her wish is the harem-master's command). The author, moreover, emphasizes the "anything," all she asks for, no matter what, whether thing or person (e.g., any of her maids), is given to her.[46] Thus each virgin has at this time in her stay in the harem complete freedom to choose anything that she believes will enhance her chances with the king. Some understand verses 13 and 15 to imply that each woman may have been permitted to keep for herself whatever she took with her and, hence, that many of the women would have been tempted to load themselves down with the finest of clothes and jewels.[47]

Each virgin's encounter with the king (v. 14) begins in the evening[48] and ends in the morning. Although the author discreetly avoids describing what occurs during that night, he indicates that the status of each virgin changes from the time she

44. Cassel believes that this myrrh is the "fragrant resin of balsamodendron myrrha, which was esteemed very precious in olden times" and from which "famous ointments" were made. Cassel, *An Explanatory Commentary on Esther,* 68.

45. Fox, *Character and Ideology in the Book of Esther*, 35.

46. Cassel, *An Explanatory Commentary on Esther*, 69.

47. Paton, *The Book of Esther*, 179.

48. Radday notes that "[t]he Rabbis can find only one good thing to say about the king's promiscuity—that at least nothing took place in the broad daylight . . ." Yehuda T. Radday, "Esther with Humor," in *On Humor and the Comic in the Hebrew Bible,* ed. Yehuda T. Radday and Athalya Brenner (Sheffield: Almond, 1990), 300.

goes into the king's bedchamber until the time when she leaves him the next day. He reports that she does not return to the harem of virgins but to a different harem—the harem of the concubines, for she is no longer a virgin.[49] At that time the responsibility for her care is transferred from the eunuch Hegai to the eunuch Shaashgaz.[50]

The role of the concubine in the second harem is to keep herself ready for the possibility of a return visit to the king's bedchamber. The likelihood of such an event happening, however, was slim because of the size of the harem. Most of the women would never have a second chance (at least not during the competition) to attempt to gratify the king's sexual needs or wants.

Fox rightly sizes up the author's purpose in describing (in greater detail than the plot demands) the preparation of the virgins, their night with the king, and their transfer to the second harem as sensuality for the sake of sensuality. Yet this sensuality has a purpose: "like the burlesque of chapter 1, [this sensuality] softens the mood and puts the reader off-guard, making the coming danger all the more harsh."[51] The author's focus on the earthy sensuality of these events, moreover, is one additional reason for arguing that the leading characters of the story, Mordecai and Esther, have their sights set on earthly affairs and not on spiritual matters.

Curtain Call . . . You're Next (2:15–16)

Unlike a play in which the actors exist in a fantasy world and in which they have the opportunity to correct tomorrow night the mistakes they make tonight, Esther's meeting with the king

49. The author carefully distinguishes between this statement ("who was in charge of the concubines"—v. 14) and the statement of verse 8, which reads "who was in charge of the women." Something transpired in the night to cause the writer to change from the term *women* to the term *concubines,* and that something was sexual intercourse with the king. The reality of this transformation makes one wonder how Mordecai could ever encourage Esther to participate in such an immoral situation.

50. Cassel points out that Shaashgaz's name is, in part, a derivative of the Persian word for "beautiful" and thus that the meaning of his name is appropriately the "minister of the beauties." Cassel, *An Explanatory Commentary on Esther,* 69.

51. Fox, *Character and Ideology in the Book of Esther*, 36.

allows no room for retakes. If she fails to please him on that one night, the efforts of a year's preparation become meaningless—she is unlikely ever to have a second chance to prove herself. She then would be doomed to what Howard F. Vos calls a "living death,"[52] that is, to life in the harem.

Esther now goes to meet the king—not simply as Esther alone, but Esther who is under the authority and direction of Mordecai, her cousin[53] and foster father. Even at this crucial juncture in the story, Mordecai plays a dominant role in Esther's life. It is a role that he, for the most part, maintains throughout the book.

Acting wisely, and not relying simply on what little she knew about how to please the king, Esther seeks and follows the advice of Hegai the harem-master. In trusting Hegai's knowledge of the king's preferences, as Moore states, "Esther not only made herself more appealing to the king, but she also showed herself to be humble and cooperative. . . ."[54] Esther is not too proud to listen to the wisdom of others. The special treatment of being given seven choice maids and the best place in the harem apparently has not gone to her head, for she has remained both humble and teachable.

Much to the chagrin of fashion consultants, the passage gives us no sense of what Esther took with her. She may have been the most modestly dressed of all who saw the king or the most spectacularly (or gaudily to our sensibilities) adorned. We know nothing of either Hegai's or the king's tastes in these matters. What we do see here is Esther submitting herself to the will of Hegai, much in the same way she submitted herself to Mordecai's command in verse 10.[55]

52. Howard F. Vos, *Ezra, Nehemiah, and Esther*, Bible Study Commentary (Grand Rapids: Lamplighter, 1987), 153.

53. The mention (here and in 9:29) of Esther's birth father, Abihail, appears to convey no special meaning other than to remind the reader of the relationship that exists between Esther and Mordecai. Nothing else is known of Abihail, for he is mentioned nowhere else in Scripture. Although four other individuals in Scripture bear the same name (two males and two females—Num. 3:35; 1 Chron. 5:14; and 1 Chron. 2:29; 2 Chron. 11:18, respectively), none can be equated to the Abihail found here.

54. Moore, *Esther*, 24.

55. Whatever Esther wore, she was impressive to all who saw her (v. 15).

As was noted in regard to verse 8, so it is true in verse 16, the fact that Esther "was taken" does not suggest in any way that she was forced against her will. Here, in fact, the verb conveys the idea of being escorted, perhaps by Hegai, and quite probably with her entourage of choice maids who would appropriate assistance throughout Esther's night with the king.

Interestingly, the author draws attention to this memorable occasion by identifying the month and the year in which Esther goes to meet the king: the tenth month (Teveth)[56] of the seventh year of King Ahasuerus's reign. Thus, approximately four years after Queen Vashti is deposed (1:10-21), Esther stands before the king in all her splendor, desiring to impress him, so that he might choose her as the one to replace Vashti.

The author gives no indication as to how long or how often Esther visited the king. The king may have been so overwhelmed by Esther in that first night that he immediately cancelled the remainder of the competition and selected her to be queen. Perhaps, however, Esther may have been sent to the second harem for a period of time while the king called additional virgins to his bedchamber before calling Esther for a second opportunity. Still the possibility exists that the king kept Esther with him for the whole month of Teveth – hence, the specific notation of the month of her introduction into the king's palace.

Treasures from an Abandoned Mine

Many people might be tempted to pass quickly over 2:1-16, considering it to contain no lasting spiritual values. Yet, this passage offers up many gems of truth that have the potential for making a difference in the lives of modern readers who apply them to their own situations:

1. God does not always rescue his people from sinful situations. If they do not turn to him for help and guidance, he may allow them to go their own way, plunging deeper and deeper into trouble. Silence in Scripture, therefore, is not necessarily golden. It may spell God's "abandonment" of

56. The month of Teveth includes approximately the last two weeks of December and the first two weeks of January in the modern calendar.

his people to their own willfully disobedient or spiritually apathetic ways.
2. Wisdom for practical living may be gained from any wise source, even if that source is not a believer.
3. Submitting to those who are wiser than we are is commendable if we do not have to compromise our faith in the process:
   a. Esther's submission to Hegai is presented as being positive, for it does not directly compromise her faith (except in the possible matter of eating nonkosher foods, but this and related "faith matters" are the result of her submittal to Mordecai's commands, 2:8–9, 12–15).
   b. Esther's submission to Mordecai is portrayed as being negative since her submission involves a direct compromise of her faith (2:10; cf. 2:20).
4. Maintaining one's humble character when being praised and when being showered with an abundance of material goods may be difficult, but it is possible.
5. Pushing ourselves or others to succeed at any cost may warp our thinking and keep us or them away from the development of spiritual values that give eternal success.

"Beam Me Up, Scotty!"

One of the more popular television series of all time is the *Star Trek* series. These science fiction programs are set approximately two hundred to three hundred years in the future. Invariably, key members of the crew of the U.S.S. Enterprise (a galaxy-class starship) would find themselves on some newly discovered planet in one of the far reaches of the galaxy in situations of extreme danger. The captain, James T. Kirk, recognizing that the danger was imminent and that there was no hope for his or his crew's survival if they remained on the planet, would issue the order to his chief engineer, Mr. Scott: "Beam me up, Scotty!" Scotty then was to activate the transporter beam, which would disassemble the captain's body to its individual molecules and then reassemble them on the ship. Time after time Scotty transported the captain and his "away team" out of the danger and into the safety of the ship, from which point they would defeat the enemy and restore order to that part of the galaxy.

The end of this section of the Book of Esther leaves the heroine Esther facing an extremely dangerous situation. She is in a battle—not a physical battle, but a spiritual one. The next step, if she takes it, will transform her life forever. Will God "beam" her out of danger or will she take the plunge of committing adultery with the heathen king? In an ongoing television series, the hero or the heroine always escapes, but will the same hold true for the screenplay of the life and times of Esther? Stay tuned for part 2 of "Esther, the Harem Girl."

11

A Marriage Made in . . . Susa
(2:17–20)

Weddings are festive occasions—royal weddings particularly so. Esther's wedding to King Ahasuerus must have been a particularly spectacular event. All of the royal family would have been there, and so would the princes, government officials, and leading people throughout the great Medo-Persian empire.[1] Perhaps even foreign dignitaries would travel great distances with their entourages to be in attendance. Those who were responsible for managing all of the wedding arrangements would have spent much money on the facilities, decorations, clothing, and feasting. Nothing would have been left undone in the efforts to make the wedding of the king and the queen the most gala event the realm had ever known.

Undoubtedly the wedding was a time of joy for all who attended, yet there must have been a deep sense of sadness among those Jews in the empire who sought to maintain a purity of faith, for they would have recognized that Esther, a

1. In 2:18, the author stipulates that the king invited his princes and his servants to the banquet. The term *servants* is a reference not to slaves but rather to the government ministers and the special attendants of the king.

Jewess, was marrying Ahasuerus, a heathen.[2] Sadness also would exist because there would have been no traditional Jewish wedding ceremony—no symbolic article of value given to the bride's father for the "purchase" of his daughter, no *ketubah* (special written marriage document), and no *ḥuppa(h)* (wedding canopy).[3] Understandably, there would have been Persian equivalents to these Jewish traditions but they still would not have conveyed the same sense of cultural joy to the Jews who observed Esther's marriage as the Jewish practices would have done.

Esther 2:17–20 sets the stage for what is to come. Esther now is in a position of authority in the empire, but why that truth is important or how it will come into play in the future is not yet clear. Will the events of this royal banquet turn out in a similar fashion as those of the previous royal banquet (1:4–22) when Queen Vashti was deposed? Furthermore, what is the significance of the gathering of virgins a second time (v. 19)? Does this suggest that Queen Esther is on her way out now too? Finally, why should Esther still conceal her faith at a time when seemingly she could have revealed it without possible threat to her position? Although the author clearly indicates that the hiding of Esther's faith is crucial to the rest of the story, he does not at this point divulge how or why her secrecy will impact the events that are about to unfold—but he soon will.

2. Many Jews throughout the empire would not have known that Esther was a Jewess, for she had concealed her heritage (2:10). In all probability, however, some of the Jews (especially those in Susa, where she and Mordecai lived) would have known of Esther's background and thus must have wondered what Esther's wedding and elevation to the position of queen would mean to their state of affairs within the empire.

Although there may have been no direct command against a Jew in exile marrying a non-Jew, the declarations of Ezra 9:1–10:44 and Neh. 13:23–31 make clear that those who were righteous interpreted the command of Deut. 7:3 as applying to the Jew in exile. In other words, Jews were not to marry outside of their faith, for such a marriage constituted an abomination to God.

3. Very little is known of Jewish wedding customs at the time of Esther. Most of what we know today about those ancient customs dates back only to the first century a.d., although the Hebrew Scriptures do shed some insight on the practices of even earlier times. R. K. Bower and G. L. Knapp, "Marriage; Marry," *International Standard Bible Encyclopedia*, ed. Geoffrey W. Bromiley (Grand Rapids: Eerdmans, 1982), 3:261–66; Lilly S. Routtenberg and Ruth R. Seldin, *The Jewish Wedding Book: A Practical Guide to the Traditions and Social Customs of the Jewish Wedding* (New York: Schocken, 1968), 79–91.

Portents of Bigger Things to Come

There is a saying that good things come in small packages. Engagement rings, babies, and mint truffles all prove that rule. Esther 2:17–20 is another example.

This short, four-verse section (vv. 17–20) contains both straightforward and cryptic information. Verse 17 reveals that Esther wins the competition (vv. 1–4, 8–16) and becomes queen of the Medo-Persian empire. Verse 18 indicates that the king convenes a banquet on Esther's behalf and in various ways blesses his subjects. Verse 19 notes that virgins are gathered a second time and that Mordecai, Esther's adoptive father, has acquired a position of authority. Finally, verse 20 declares that Esther remains quiet about her Jewish heritage in obedience to Mordecai's wishes. Interestingly, despite its lack of size and the seemingly innocuous presentation of its contents, this section is explosive in relation to the thrust of the entire book.

These few verses signal the end of the beginning (vv. 17–18) and the beginning of the end (vv. 19–20) of the Book of Esther. The signal is, moreover, a transition from a focus on the Persian world to a focus on the Jewish world. From this point on, the king is no longer the prominent character in the book; non-Persians—Haman, Esther, and Mordecai—take over that role. Thus, if the Book of Esther were divided into three sections, these four verses would form the beginning of the second section. The three sections then would be as follows:

1. Persian control of the Persian empire (1:1–2:16)
2. Mixed control of the Persian empire—Haman (with actual power) and Esther (with position power) (2:17–7:10)[4]
3. Jewish control of the Persian empire—Mordecai (with actual power) and Esther (with position power) (8:1–10:3)

What makes such a structural analysis of the book so appealing is that each of the sections begins with a presentation of the

4. King Ahasuerus possesses the ultimate (human) power in the Medo-Persian empire in all three sections of this outline, yet the king (from 2:17 to the end of the book) appears to have delegated to these two prime ministers the power of running the day-to-day operations of the empire.

power player(s)—section 1 with King Ahasuerus, section 2 with Queen Esther and Prime Minister Haman, and section 3 with Prime Minister Mordecai. Each section also commences with a feast of celebration that in some way or another is empire-wide in its scope—in section 1 (1:1–9) the feast is at Susa, the capital, with people throughout the empire invited to go to Susa to celebrate there; in section 2 (2:18) the feast is at Susa with holidays of celebration taking place throughout the empire; in section 3 (8:17) the feasts take place in the various provinces of the empire.

Organized Chaos

Years ago, one of the biggest attractions at carnivals was the fun house—a place where kids could run though large revolving barrels, use burlap bags to slide down undulating wooden runways, and generally go wild and crazy. Invariably, either at the beginning or the end of the fun house was a hall of mirrors. Those mirrors seemingly had magical powers to make the person who looked into them appear warped in all different directions—tall or short, fat or skinny. Those mirrors quite obviously were not built the way normal mirrors are built; they were designed to shake the sensibilities.

Likewise, the author of the Book of Esther designed 2:17–20 to shake the sensibilities. The four verses do not naturally seem to flow together. Their contents seem to provide a jumbled view of reality—all true, but all mixed together, causing the reader to wonder why these four verses are placed side by side.

The mix of verses (vv. 17–20) seems incongruous at first, yet there is order to this chaos. The verses almost seem to say: "There is time for applause and time for pause." The joyous celebration of a wedding fades with the passage of time, and life goes on.

The contents of this section, therefore, may be divided as follows:

A. A Jewess is elevated (2:17)
B. A people are elated (2:18)
C. A Jew is elevated (2:19)
D. A faith is evaded (2:20)

The formulation of an outline for these verses is made particularly difficult by the twofold message of verse 19: the virgins are gathered and Mordecai is sitting in the gate. Yet the grammar of the passage emphasizes the information concerning Mordecai, while placing in a subordinate relationship the clause concerning the virgins. In other words, as used in verse 19, the function of the first clause of the sentence is to provide the time frame in which the second clause of the sentence takes place. Thus the preceding outline, taking into account that grammatical understanding of the verse, serves as an appropriate structural outline for verses 17–20.

A second assessment of this section produces the following summary:

A. A Jew is elevated and there is physical blessing (2:17–18)
B. A Jew is elevated and there is spiritual unrest (2:19–20)

With these various outlines in mind, the individual components of this section can now be studied in detail.

Love at First Night (2:17)

Esther 2:17 states that the king becomes enthralled with Esther and chooses her to take Vashti's place as queen. In what way, though, does the king "love" Esther? The author here uses the basic Hebrew term for love, *ʾāhab,* which generally means "to love" or "to like." This verb envisions some level of emotional interest that an individual has for another individual or for an object. The term, however, is used throughout Scripture to express a broad gamut of feelings ranging from the total loyal commitment that God has for his people to a passionate craving that a sinful individual has for something illicit.

Michael V. Fox advocates the position that "[t]his 'love' can only mean that he [the king] enjoyed the night with her" and that Ahasuerus's "feelings for both Vashti and Esther could hardly amount to more than pride of possession plus sexual arousal."[5] Fox's statement may be unduly harsh, for Ahasuerus, who like any individual who meets the "right one," could have

5. Michael V. Fox, *Character and Ideology in the Book of Esther* (Columbia, S.C.: University of South Carolina Press, 1991), 37–38.

"fallen in love" with Esther. Ahasuerus's actions in chapter 5, moreover, suggest that he has some affection (if not love) for her.[6] Yet Fox is probably correct in light of the fact that 2:17 states that the king loves Esther "more than (he loves) all the [other] women."[7] The more-ness implies that he has similar affections (although not to the same degree) for the other women as he does for Esther, the primary basis for those affections being, of course, sexual attraction.

Esther, however, does strike a chord of honest admiration, if not affection, within the king, for she, more than the other virgins,[8] secures his grace and lovingkindness. This passage (2:17) combines the use of two terms used previously by the author to describe Esther: *ḥēn* (grace, cf. 2:15)[9] and *ḥesed* (lovingkindness, cf. 2:9).[10] Defining these terms fully has proven somewhat elusive to scholars. Generally speaking, *ḥēn* (grace) conveys the idea of agreeableness, elegance, or charm, that is, a sense of attractiveness.[11] By contrast, *ḥesed* (lovingkindness) suggests a relationship that one has toward another person, a relationship that expresses itself through loyalty, kindness, affection, or mercy toward that person.[12]

6. Esther 2:1 seems to suggest that the king also had had some degree of affection for the former Queen Vashti whom he foolishly deposed when he was drunk.

7. The term *women* here refers to those who were virgins before the competition started but who now are concubines in the king's harem.

8. Whereas the term *women* refers to the status of those who appeared before the king after they left the king's presence, the term *virgins* as used here refers to the status of those who appeared before the king at the time of their entrance into his presence. The two terms refer to one and the same group. The author merely uses the term *virgins* here to ensure that there is no confusion as to which group of women he is referring, that is, that group of women who as virgins participated in the contest.

9. The term *ḥēn* (grace) is found in four other verses in the Book of Esther: 5:2, 8; 7:3; and 8:5.

10. The term *ḥesed* (lovingkindness) is found in the Book of Esther only in 2:9 and 17.

11. Francis Brown, S. R. Driver, and Charles A. Briggs, *A Hebrew and English Lexicon of the Old Testament with an Appendix Containing the Biblical Aramaic* (reprint; Oxford: Clarendon, 1968), 336; Ludwig Koehler and Walter Baumgartner, eds., *Lexicon in Veteris Testementi Libros* (Leiden: Brill, 1985), 314.

12. Brown, Driver, and Briggs, *A Hebrew and English Lexicon*, 338; Koehler and Baumgartner, *Lexicon in Veteris Testementi Libros*, 318.

The result of the king's affection for Esther is that he chooses her to be queen. The crown that he places on her head is called the "royal crown" *(keter malkût),* the same crown Vashti was to have worn but refused to wear to the king's banquet (1:11). Thus a process that begins in chapter 1 with the removal of Queen Vashti now ends with the coronation of Esther to that same position.[13]

Celebration of Love (2:18)

Partying apparently is one of the great pleasures of the Medo-Persian empire during King Ahasuerus's reign. Nearly one-half of all the scriptural uses of the term *mište(h)* (banquet or feast) are found in the ten chapters of the Book of Esther—twenty out of a total of forty-five occurrences. Sandra Beth Berg notes that throughout the Scripture this term "is used almost exclusively to indicate the concepts of eating and drinking on special occasions."[14] The author, by calling this banquet "great," implies that the banquet is spectacular, lavish beyond normal expectations.

The king wisely holds only one feast, and that feast is called "Esther's feast." By doing so, he does not risk a repeat of the debacle with Vashti (1:10–12), since Esther would be present (and visible to all) at all times during this celebration. Furthermore, he limits the guest list to a select but prestigious group of people: the princes and the servants of the king. Even though the king limits the number who attend Esther's banquet, he makes certain that all throughout the empire rejoice with him in the celebration of the coronation of Esther as queen.

First, the king offers the provinces "a release" (lit., "a rest"). The question is a release or rest from what. Various views have been advanced including a release from taxes, work (i.e., a holi-

13. Pierce rightly reminds us, however, that what seems so good (i.e., the promotion of Esther to the position of queen) is in fact a further testimony to the spiritual poverty of the Jews in exile: "Indeed, Esther's marriage to Ahasuerus tragically mimics one of the key failures of the Jewish people that resulted in her family being brought to Susa in the first place." Ronald W. Pierce, "Purim: A Time to Mourn or a Time to Dance?" Ms. presented to the Evangelical Theological Society in San Diego, Calif., 18 November 1989, 9.

14. Sandra Beth Berg, *The Book of Esther: Motifs, Themes and Structure* (Missoula, Mont.: Scholars, 1979), 31.

day), military service, and prison.[15] Although all four options are possible, either one or the other of the first two views are favored by most commentators. Joyce G. Baldwin argues in favor of the tax release by noting that the granting of a remission of taxes (alone of the four options) is "well attested in ancient Persia."[16] The singularly curious statement of Esther 10:1 regarding the king's initiation of a tax burden may also support the tax view since, by that news item, the author may have intended to indicate that what begins here in 2:18 at Esther's wedding concludes there in 10:1. C. F. Keil, however, argues that the verb *ʿāśā(h)* (to do or to effect) favors the establishment of a holiday,[17] yet he does not indicate in what way the verb supports such a position.

The second means by which the king encourages celebrating is by his giving of gifts. He distributes these gifts out of his abundant wealth, which suggests that the gifts would be "plentiful in quantity and worthy in quality."[18] This generosity reflects the pouring of drinks at the seven-day feast in 1:7, where the same phrase—"according to the hand of the king"—is recorded. Thus, the author seems to be saying that as freely as the drinks flowed at that earlier banquet, so the gifts flow forth freely here.

Something Old, Something New (2:19)

Unlike the wedding tradition of "something old, something new, something borrowed, something blue," verse 19, a post-wedding verse, concerns itself only with the old and the new. The first part of the verse (the old)—the gathering of the virgins

15. Joyce G. Baldwin, *Esther: An Introduction and Commentary*, Tyndale Old Testament Commentaries, ed. D. J. Wiseman (Downers Grove: InterVarsity, 1984), 69; Paulus Cassel, *An Explanatory Commentary on Esther*, trans. Aaron Bernstein (Edinburgh: T. and T. Clark, 1888), 76; Fox, *Character and Ideology in the Book of Esther*, 38; C. F. Keil, *The Books of Ezra, Nehemiah, and Esther*, Biblical Commentary on the Old Testament, trans. Sophia Taylor (Grand Rapids: Eerdmans, n.d.), 339; Lewis Bayles Paton, *The Book of Esther*, International Critical Commentary, ed. Samuel Rolles Driver, Alfred Plummer, and Charles Augustus Briggs (Edinburgh: T. and T. Clark, 1908), 185.

16. Baldwin, *Esther: An Introduction and Commentary*, 69.

17. Keil, *The Books of Ezra, Nehemiah, and Esther*, 339.

18. Cassel, *An Explanatory Commentary on Esther*, 76.

a second time[19]—functions to establish the time frame for the second part (the new)—Mordecai's activities at the king's gate—and thus, for the events of verses 21–23.[20]

Who[21] specifically these virgins are or when[22] they are gathered is unknown. The lack of the definite article preceding the noun *virgins,* however, suggests that the group of virgins gathered here is different from that of which Esther had been a part. Moreover, the term translated here as "gathering" is the same word as that which is used in verse 8 to indicate the general bringing together of virgins, that is, the term as used here does not convey the concept of a regathering.

Paulus Cassel capsulizes the significance of the first half of verse 19 when he notes: "the power of the new queen had already begun to decline."[23] This verse, therefore, may indicate

19. The Hebrew here merely says "a second," and does not specify whether that term refers to a second "place" or a second "time." If "place" is intended, then the verse harkens back to the second harem (v. 14). The difficulty with such a view, however, is that at this point in the story, Esther is already queen (cf. vv. 17, 22). Furthermore, the reference cannot be to the gathering of the women (note that v. 19 actually says "virgins") to the second harem as described in verse 14, since in that verse the women went in turn, one at a time (not as a group), after each individually spent the night with the king. Thus the term *second* is better understood as a reference to time than to place—a view that most commentators advocate. Cassel, *An Explanatory Commentary on Esther*, 77–78; Keil, *The Books of Ezra, Nehemiah, and Esther*, 340–41; Paton, *The Book of Esther*, 187–88.

20. Keil, *The Books of Ezra, Nehemiah, and Esther*, 340.

21. Several views have been posited as to who these women are: a group of virgins who arrived from a long distance but after the contest was over, additional virgins whom the king desired to have at the palace for his personal sexual enjoyment even after he married Esther, other virgins whom the courtiers tried to use to influence the king to select someone other than Esther, an additional pool of virgins from which the king would choose another queen, or even virgins used by the king to make Esther jealous and to get her to tell him her racial heritage. Paton, *The Book of Esther*, 187–88.

22. The difficulty of determining the exact timing of this event is exacerbated by the lack of specificity of the phrase *after these events* in 3:1. If that phrase implies "immediately after," then the gathering of the virgins a second time takes place probably near the end of the eleventh year or during the beginning of the twelfth year of Ahasuerus's reign (cf. 3:7), approximately four years after Esther becomes queen (cf. 2:16). If, however, the phrase *after these events* suggests some passage of time, then this gathering of the virgins occurs at some time closer to Esther's coronation than the previous statement suggests.

23. Cassel, *An Explanatory Commentary on Esther*, 78.

that the king's relationship with Esther is at this time less than perfect, especially in light of 4:11, in which she remarks that she has not been summoned to the king for a period of thirty days.

In contrast to the many views regarding the meaning of the first half of 2:19, there are essentially only two different positions that commentators advocate regarding the meaning of the second half of the verse in which Mordecai is said to be sitting at the king's gate. The lesser defended of the two views is that Mordecai is one of the idle rich of the capital city of Susa who enjoys being where the significant governmental rulings of the city and of the empire most frequently (outside of the palace) are made.[24] The second and more widely held view is that Mordecai is at this time a royal official, probably possessing a minor level of authority.[25] The weight of argument in favor of this second position is the idiomatic use throughout Scripture of the phrase *sitting at the gate* to indicate those who are "elders and leading, respected citizens who settled disputes that were brought to them."[26] The author's inclusion of the fact that Mordecai is at the king's gate (apparently on a regular basis) gains meaning in light of 2:21–23 and in 3:1–6.[27] Furthermore, the introduction of this fact at this time suggests that Mordecai has been promoted to some official position subsequent to Esther's coronation.

24. Cassel, *An Explanatory Commentary on Esther,* 79; Paton, *The Book of Esther*, 188. Paton notes that Haupt believes that Mordecai was perhaps a moneychanger who worked his trade there.

25. Fox, *Character and Ideology in the Book of Esther,* 38–39; F. B. Huey, Jr., "Esther," *Expositor's Bible Commentary,* ed. Frank E. Gaebelein, 12 vols. (Grand Rapids: Zondervan, 1988), 4:810; Howard F. Vos, *Ezra, Nehemiah, and Esther*, Bible Study Commentary (Grand Rapids: Lamplighter, 1987), 154. Baldwin, however, contends that Mordecai may have been a high official, perhaps holding the trusted position of gatekeeper. She bases her argument on "[a] cuneiform tablet from Borsippa, near Babylon, [that] mentions Marduka [Mordecai?] as a high official at the court of Susa during the early years of the reign of Xerxes, under Uštannu, satrap of Babylon and 'Beyond the River'." Joyce G. Baldwin, *Esther,* The New Bible Commentary, 3d ed., ed. D. Guthrie and J. A. Motyer (Grand Rapids: Eerdmans, 1970), 413.

26. Huey, "Esther," 810.

27. The author also notes Mordecai's presence at the king's gate in 5:9 and 6:12.

What a Tangled Web We Weave . . . (2:20)

Sir Walter Scott perhaps said it best in the narrative poem *Marmion* (canto 4, stanza 17) in that oft-quoted lament: "Oh! what a tangled web we weave / When first we practise to deceive!" Marmion rued the deceptive events that he had set in motion, events whose consequences he was quickly learning to regret.

Likewise, once more (cf. v. 10), Mordecai and Esther play a dangerous game of deception. As happened to Marmion, so Mordecai and Esther one day mourn the consequences that arise, in part, as a result of their deception (4:1–17).

Breaking again the flow of the passage (as in v. 10) by altering the normal Hebrew sentence pattern, the author of the Book of Esther seizes his readers' attention, forcing them to consider carefully the stark reality of the antideclaration pact that Mordecai and Esther make. The web of deception spun in verse 10, prior to Esther's wedding, continues strong even after the wedding.

What motivates Mordecai to command Esther to keep her faith hidden at this point, however, is certainly a mystery. If at any time he should have felt comfortable allowing her to reveal her heritage, surely now that she has become queen would seem to be the most likely time of all. Such a time, in fact, might even be potentially a propitious time because the king "loved" Esther greatly and the social and political status of the Jews within the realm could do nothing but be elevated by having as queen one who is identified as being one of their own.

Mordecai's unwillingness[28] to "risk" having Esther cease in her deception paves, as it were, the path to the potential ruin of those who might otherwise rest securely under the protection of the queen. The fact that Esther, in obedience to Mordecai, buries her background in secrecy later permits Haman, "the enemy of the Jews," the freedom to vent his fury against the Jews (3:6–15). Had Esther revealed her Jewish identity, Haman undoubtedly would have thought twice about issuing an edict to destroy

28. Mordecai's "unwillingness" lasts at a minimum for five years—for the year of the competition (and perhaps for some period of time before the competition as well) and for the first four years of Esther's marriage (cf. 2:16 and 3:7). Mordecai's unwillingness meant, therefore, that Esther did not openly (if at all) practice her faith for those five years.

the Jews, if from no other reason than the fear that in doing so, he would have been making an enemy of the queen.

Carey A. Moore points out that the words *her kindred* and *her people* in 2:20 are in reverse order from the order in which they are found in verse 10. He argues that this crisscrossed pattern (i.e., a chiasm) forms an *inclusio*[29] "to bind together the subject matter of v[erses] 10–20"[30] in order to frame the narrative of Esther's crisis. Quite definitely the two verses appear to be working together to make a strong statement. Whether that statement, however, is regarding Esther's "crisis" or regarding her total neglect of the faith, is a matter of debate. During the time between verse 10 and verse 20, Esther says nothing about her God, and as far as we know, nothing *to* her God. Furthermore, she would have spent no time in the study of God's Word, in the maintenance of divinely established days of worship (neither the regular Sabbath days nor the special feast days), or in the observance of Jewish dietary regulations. If by "crisis" Moore means "spiritual crisis" (or "spiritual disaster"), then Moore is correct.

Esther 2:20 also reveals that the bond between Esther the daughter and Mordecai the father remained intact even after Esther the daughter becomes Esther the wife of King Ahasuerus. Such an arrangement placed additional unbiblical constraints on an already unbiblical marriage. The postmarriage daughter-father relationship of Esther to Mordecai was potentially at odds with the mandate in Genesis 2:24 regarding the autonomy of the married couple. Yet, how extensively or how frequently Mordecai exercised direct control over Esther after her marriage is not stated. What the passage does imply, however, is that whatever Mordecai commanded, Esther did. Her loyalty thus remained with her father and not with her husband.

Human Odds and God's Ends

The setting of odds and the placing of bets has proliferated in recent years. Odds are set for and bets placed on almost anything from Super Bowl games to the outcome of crab races to the

29. See chap. 9 n. 45, for a definition of the term *inclusio*.

30. Carey A. Moore, *Esther*, The Anchor Bible, ed. William Foxwell Albright and David Noel Freedman (Garden City, N.Y.: Doubleday, 1971), 22.

time of day a child will be born to a royal family. If Las Vegas oddsmakers existed in the days of King Ahasuerus, they would have had a field day with the contest: setting odds on each virgin's chances of marrying the king based on her looks, grace, personality, family connections, and of course sensuality. What odds would the oddsmakers have given that an orphaned Jewish girl living in exile would one day sit on the throne as queen—one in a hundred, one in a thousand, one in a million? Few if any would have predicted victory for Esther (until they got to know her), but despite the odds and because of the grace of God, Esther became queen.

This section (2:17–20) of the Book of Esther reveals God's mercy that he may choose to extend to his people even when they go astray, even when they seek to join in a union with unbelievers. One wonders, however, if the real lesson is not one that parallels the statement of Psalm 106:15 regarding the post-exodus group of Israelites: "He [God] gave to them their request, but he sent a leanness[31] into their soul."

In addition, verses 17–20 reflect in part the promise that God made directly to Abraham (Gen. 12:3), through Isaac to Jacob (Gen. 27:29), and through Balaam to the nation of Israel: Those who bless Israel will be blessed, those who curse Israel will be cursed. In Esther 2:18 there is much rejoicing and the nation of Gentiles is greatly blessed because of the selection of Esther as queen. The Book of Esther as a whole, moreover, seems to be a record of the outworking of God's promise at a time when Israel had turned away from God. Certainly those in the Book of Esther who treated the Jews poorly experienced negative consequences; those who treated Israel well earned positive consequences of their actions. The most obvious examples are Haman and all those who were opposed to the Jews, who, while seeking to destroy the Jews, were themselves destroyed (7:10; 9:2, 5, 12, 15, 16). By contrast, those who showed an interest in or a concern for the Jews—the king and many of the people of the Medo-Persian empire—were ultimately and thoroughly blessed with material blessings (8:17; 10:2–3).

31. Koehler and Baumgartner use a more graphic term to translate the Hebrew *rāzôn*—"emaciation." Koehler and Baumgartner, *Lexicon in Veteris Testementi Libros*, 883.

This section of the Book of Esther also reminds us that there are mysteries in life that are not easily explained: in 2:17, the marriage of a Jewish girl to a pagan king (how would that work itself out in the events to follow?); in 2:19, the second gathering of virgins (was it part of some political intrigue to find another wife for the king?); again in 2:19, the appointment of Mordecai to a government position (did this keep him from being summarily executed by Haman in 3:6 and 5:9 for failing to show respect to Haman in 3:2-5,; 5:9); and in 2:20, the keeping secret of one's faith (was this a premonition of a future need to reveal one's faith or was this the result of the fear of losing the privileged position of a Jew in power?). Each of these seemingly isolated events appears to have played a role in the outcome of the story. Esther's marriage to the king places her in a position where she can act on behalf of her people in a way no other person in the empire could act (5:1ff.). The gathering of the virgins for the second time may be the cause for Esther's not being with the king for a period of thirty days, and hence a contributing factor that causes her to fear approaching the king publicly to intervene for the lives of her people (4:11). Mordecai's promotion places him physically at the king's gate, where he is observed not showing respect to the newly appointed prime minister, and hence becomes Haman's excuse for attempting to eradicate the Jews (3:6-15). Finally, Esther's failure to publicly observe her faith creates no obstacles for Haman to overcome when he determines to approach the king for permission to destroy a race of people who unknown to Haman or to the king are the queen's people (3:6-15; 7:3-6).

Amazingly, three significant lessons emerge from these few verses:

1. God's mercy toward and judgment of his people may be exhibited simultaneously.
2. God keeps his promises: If he says he will bless, he blesses; if he says he will curse, he curses.
3. The actions one takes today have consequences that will be forthcoming tomorrow – consequences that are not always what one anticipates them to be.

Just Ordinary Folk

Although obviously unique in many respects (e.g., becoming prime minister, cf. 8:1–10:3, and queen, cf. 2:17, respectively), Mordecai and Esther in many ways typify the average Jewish man and woman of the exile. They undoubtedly would have been categorized by their neighbors as "decent folk who did not cause any trouble," but Mordecai and Esther, like so many other of the Jews of the exile, were people who had lost their first love, their love for the one true, living God.

The exile was perhaps the lowest period in Israel's history as recorded in the Hebrew Scriptures. The temple had been destroyed, Jerusalem lay in ruins, and God's people were living outside the Promised Land. God's people, moreover, had adopted the customs and social conventions of the surrounding heathen nation. They blended in with their pagan neighbors to such an extent that, at least in the case of Mordecai and Esther, distinguishing them from their secular neighbors was virtually impossible.

Ironically, Isaiah the prophet, commenting on the reasons for the exile, declares (in Isa. 5:12–13) one reason why God originally sent his people Israel into exile: God's people had no knowledge of God and they did not care to know him or to recognize his works. Sadly, as we learn by reading the Book of Esther, even the judgment of the exile and the potential annihilation of their entire race did not shake the Jewish people back to a commitment to God. As we have seen before, not once in the Book of Esther do they turn to God for help, not once do they study his Word, not once do they worship him, and not once do they give thanks to him for the great deliverance that he gave them.

Perhaps Eisen sums up (from the perspective of a twentieth-century Jewish scholar) the attitude of the Jews regarding their deliverance in 8:1–9:19 from Haman's deadly clutches. He writes concerning their understanding of the meaning of Purim—the festival established by the Jews in 9:16–32 to celebrate their miraculous deliverance: "*This* is how we remember to forget Amalek's (a reference to Haman and his people) awful but all-too-normal behavior. We drown it out by screaming as loudly as we can. We celebrate the one time that we can remember when we, without God's direct aid, defeated Amalek at his own game."[32] Thus to the Jew of the twentieth century,[33] and apparently to the Jew of Ahasuerus's day, the victory reported later in the Book of Esther (8:1–9:19) was a self-made victory, a victory that had little or nothing to do with God. Tragically, even the judgment of the exile had not taught the people of God to discover the *God behind the seen.*

Esther 2:17–20 signals the transition for the Jews in the Medo-Persian empire from a generally idyllic period of life to a period of great anguish that later becomes one of rejoicing and peace. The remaining sections of the Book of Esther highlight both Mordecai's and Esther's roles through that transitional period.

32. Michael Strassfeld, *The Jewish Holidays: A Guide and Commentary* (New York: Harper and Row, 1985), 191.

33. Obviously, not all Jews today would agree with Eisen, but many if not most would.

12

The Stage Is Set
(2:21–23)

There is much debate in certain academic circles as to whether the essential nature of history is linear, circular, spiral, or some other shape. Yet history happens whether we fully understand its nature or not. Looking back in time we can see how various events, even some seemingly minor ones, were the spark for great conflagrations or scientific breakthroughs.

Likewise, when we look back on the history of our own lives, we see where an event here or there, one that seemed inconsequential at the time, now looms large as a shaper of our lives. When I was in college, I had the opportunity to study in Japan for part of one summer. When it was time to return to the United States, for a number of reasons I nearly missed my plane. Had I missed that plane and arrived home a day later, I might not have met the girl who later would become my wife.[1] We met the night I returned from Japan in the church that I regularly attended but to which she had been invited as a guest speaker to give her testimony for that one night. My life has never been the same since.

1. Since the Book of Esther deals with the providence of God, I am "compelled" to say that God in his providence might have still brought my wife and me together under different circumstances. In that case there probably would be another event in my life to which I could point to indicate that that specific event played a major role in bringing the two of us together.

The events of the Book of Esther might have been significantly different had Esther not become queen and, subsequently, had Mordecai not been promoted to a government position. He then would probably have not been sitting at the king's gate, and thus might not have learned of the plot to assassinate King Ahasuerus (2:21–23). Mordecai's knowledge and reporting of the plot give rise to a significant turn of events later in the story (6:1–13).

Proper Security Clearance

When I was employed in the defense industry, I became aware that a certain level of security clearance was required to read certain documents or to attend certain meetings. One day I found myself being barred from a technology briefing because attendance at that meeting required a higher security clearance than I held at that time. My paperwork for that higher security clearance level had previously been submitted, but the actual clearance did not come through from the appropriate government agency until a few weeks later. At that later date, meetings like the one to which I rightly had been barred became open to me, and documents upon which I was not allowed to look before became documents to which I had free and open access.

The author of the Book of Esther treats this section (2:21–23) much like a classified document. He permits his readers to know only as much as their security clearance at this point will allow. He reserves comment on the operational aspects of these materials until chapter 6, by which time his readers have gained a higher security clearance level through the study of the intervening chapters.

Furthermore, 2:21–23 appears as a strange interlude in the flow of the story. Unlike 2:5–7 (the introduction of Mordecai and Esther), which also initially seems out of place but is quickly interwoven into the events that immediately follow it, the author does not provide an immediate answer to the question of why 2:21–23 is included at this point. His failure to address those issues generates a sense of unresolved tension that he maintains until chapter 6. Only then does he, by means of hilarious irony, declassify the text and thereby allow us, his readers, insight into data that previously had been "for his eyes only."

The information that the writer allows us to study at this point, however, is quite straightforward and easily understood. He depicts an antigovernment activity (v. 21) being defused by a pro-government reaction (vv. 22–23). In essence, these three verses unfold as follows:

A. A plot against the king is designed (2:21)
B. A plot against the king is detected (2:22)
C. A plot against the king is defeated (2:23)

Thus the author reveals the instigation of a conspiracy (v. 21), followed by the communication of information about that conspiracy (v. 22), and finally a statement regarding the investigation of that conspiracy (v. 23).

Politics as Usual

Political intrigue was abundant in most ancient royal courts. The court of the Medo-Persian empire in Ahasuerus's day was no exception. Apart from presenting the display of royal wealth and the apparent buying of political favors in chapter 1 of the Book of Esther, the author presents seven other potentially politically charged land mines around which political pundits of Ahasuerus's day had to step carefully:

1. (?)*Vashti's refusal to obey the king (1:12);
2. (?)Memucan's proposal to remove Queen Vashti and to find a replacement for her (1:15–20);
3. (?)The king's attendants' suggestion to have beautiful, young virgins brought so that one might be chosen by the king to be queen to replace Vashti (2:1–4);
4. (?)Hegai's favoring of Esther within the harem (2:9);
5. (?)The gathering of a second group of virgins (2:19);
6. The plot of the eunuchs against the king (2:21)—this is the only easily demonstrable political plot in the early portion of the book; and

* The question mark placed at the beginning of a given situation indicates that the event described thereafter may or may not have been politically motivated, the author having provided insufficient data to make an accurate assessment.

7. Esther's and Mordecai's plot to overthrow Haman the prime minister—this is the only successful political coup in the Book of Esther that may be directly demonstrated to be politically motivated (4:1–7:10).

The information that follows looks closely at the data recorded about the unsuccessful cabal noted in 2:21–23.

Danger Lurking in the Palace (2:21)

Boss-subordinate relations are often fragile at best. Some bosses, on the one hand, do not express a high degree of trust in their subordinates' abilities or desires to achieve the company's goals. Some subordinates, on the other hand, constantly complain about their bosses' unreasonableness, incompetence, or lack of sensitivity. Generally, however, bosses and subordinates work well together. Yet on occasion one or the other of the parties loses his or her self-control and expresses anger at the other. The confrontation at times turns violent, and on rare occasions (but sadly with increasing frequency) one of the individuals is injured or even killed.

The author of the Book of Esther informs us that, around the same time that Mordecai is sitting at the king's gate[2] and the virgins are gathered together a second time (v. 19), two disgruntled employees in King Ahasuerus's service—Bigthan and Teresh—plot the king's overthrow (2:21). Little is known of these schemers other than that they are not high government

2. "Sitting at the king's gate" implies that Mordecai was a royal official of some stature, most likely a minor official. One can surmise that if he were a highly placed official, he would have gone directly to the king with such highly sensitive information (and thus would have avoided any risk of exposing Esther's connection to him and, hence, to her Jewish heritage, cf. vv. 20, 22). Furthermore, if Mordecai had been a highly placed official, the king most likely would have made a special effort to reward Mordecai immediately for exposing the plot. Being an official, Mordecai probably would have had far more access to information about the activities on the street than would someone who was an outsider to the politics of the day. Paulus Cassel, *An Explanatory Commentary on Esther*, trans. Aaron Bernstein (Edinburgh: T. and T. Clark, 1888), 79; Lewis Bayles Paton, *The Book of Esther*, International Critical Commentary, ed. Samuel Rolles Driver, Alfred Plummer, and Charles Augustus Briggs (Edinburgh: T. and T. Clark, 1908), 188.

officials[3] but that they play an important role in ensuring the king's physical welfare.[4] Lewis Bayles Paton notes the high degree of volatility of this plot because of the proximity to the king that these guards enjoyed: "The *threshold* which these eunuchs guarded was presumably the entrance to the King's private apartments. They were the most trusted watchmen; and, therefore, their treason was doubly dangerous."[5]

The reason for the anger of the eunuchs is not clear; the fact that they are outraged, however, is clear. The author chooses a term *(qāṣap)* that signifies an extremely intense anger—a "burning and consuming wrath." This term, according to Gerard Van Gronigen, "refers to the relationship developed, held or expressed in various ways when there is anger, heat, displeasure held or felt within one because of what another has said or done."[6] The author uses this term on two other occasions: of the king's anger against Vashti while he is drunk (1:12), and of the hypothetical anger of the wives of the princes or of the princes themselves (or of some other unnamed group or individual) that would ensue if Vashti were not dealt with properly (1:18). Seen in this light, and recognizing that the author employs different terms to express anger in 3:5; 5:19; and 7:7 (i.e., in places where the anger is held in check for a period of time and does not immediately issue forth into action), the use of this term here (and in 1:12, 18) suggests that the anger is the type of emotion that issues into action soon after that feeling is experienced. In this case, the action that is forthcoming is seeking to assassinate (lit., to send out / stretch forth a hand against) King Aha-

3. The author does not call these two individuals "officials" but instead uses the term *eunuchs*. Throughout the Book of Esther (1:10, 12, 15; 2:3, 15; 4:4, 5; 6:2, 14; 7:9), however, the term *eunuch* is used consistently as a designation of certain physically so-qualified individuals who hold positions of responsibility in Ahasuerus's government, or in his or his royal court's service. Thus, here in 2:21, "officials" is an acceptable understanding of the functions that these two individuals exercise.

4. Cassel, *An Explanatory Commentary on Esther*, 80–81.

5. Paton, *The Book of Esther*, 190. See also Howard F. Vos, *Ezra, Nehemiah, and Esther*, Bible Study Commentary (Grand Rapids: Lamplighter, 1987), 156.

6. Gerard Van Gronigen, "2085. . . *(qāṣap)*," *Theological Wordbook of the Old Testament*, ed. R. Laird Harris, Gleason L. Archer, Jr., and Bruce K. Waltke (Chicago: Moody, 1980), 2:808.

suerus. The sense conveyed is that the assassination attempt will take place immediately and, hence, immediate action needs to be taken to thwart it.

A Snitch in Time Saves Mine (2:22)

"A bird in the hand is worth two in the bush." "Early to bed, early to rise, makes a man healthy, wealthy, and wise." "A watched pot never boils." "Red sky at night, sailors' delight; red sky in morning, sailors take warning."

Probably all languages have pithy sayings to express folk wisdom. Most of those sayings arise from common daily events, some perhaps from the activities of famous people or from natural phenomena. If the Jews in Mordecai's day had coined a special saying based on Mordecai's actions in verse 22, they might have expressed the folk wisdom arising from Mordecai's actions as "a snitch in time saves mine." Such a saying would have developed because Mordecai snitched on the two eunuchs who were plotting against the king. The result of his informing against the eunuchs was not only the sparing of the life of the king but also quite probably sparing the life (or at least the position) of the queen—from Mordecai's vantage point: "mine."

The author does not consider the motivation of Bigthan and Teresh to be of sufficient importance to record. What is important to the author is that Mordecai acts swiftly in order to protect the king (and that Mordecai is unrewarded for his efforts).

How Mordecai learns of the plot in 2:22 is also shrouded in mystery. Michael V. Fox notes that the Hebrew "*wayyiwwada'*, 'became known,' suggests that Mordecai did not simply overhear the conspirators speaking . . . , but somehow learned of it from an unnamed source."[7] Paton concurs, arguing that the king's gate "would not be a likely place for the concocting of a plot"[8] because of the ease at which a conversation held there might be overheard.

The author also leaves unexpressed the details of how Mordecai passes the information on to Esther. Mordecai undoubtedly uses a trusted servant to transmit the information to Esther. In

7. Michael V. Fox, *Character and Ideology in the Book of Esther* (Columbia, S.C.: University of South Carolina Press, 1991), 39.

8. Paton, *The Book of Esther*, 191.

doing so he would bypass the palace guard—the people to whom he would normally turn because of their responsibility to protect the king, but the people whom he now could not trust since he might not be certain of the extent to which the plot had pervaded the guard. All of this, however, is again mere speculation.

Esther relays to the king the information she received from Mordecai and credits Mordecai as being the source of that information. She does not, however, disclose her relationship to Mordecai, for that would unmask her Jewish heritage.[9]

Despite the debate as to whether Mordecai should or should not have acted to spare the life of a heathen king, Mordecai's motives should not be impugned. He undoubtedly acts from a concern for the need to stop the assassination of the king. In doing so, he at the same time protects his interests in helping to maintain Esther's position within the palace.

Yehuda T. Radday points out the irony of this situation when he states: "The only loyal subject the king possesses is—unknown to him—one of those whom he is soon to condemn to death."[10] As the next chapter in the Book of Esther reveals, Mordecai, along with the rest of the Jews of the Medo-Persian empire (Esther included), is sentenced to be killed because of an act of disrespect shown to the king's second in command, Haman the Agagite (3:1–15).

Judicial Sentences and Historical Sentences (2:23)

"The plot was investigated"—how strange. Curiously enough, this is the only instance in the entire book where the king takes any time to investigate the facts of the matter. It is also the only time when his life is directly threatened. No investigation takes place regarding Vashti's refusal to obey the king's command, regarding Haman's desire to annihilate a race of people, or

9. Mordecai's ethnic background is apparently known by certain court officials (and by perhaps even the king) at this time. This awareness is evidenced by the fact that immediately following the reading to the king of the record of the account of these events in 6:1–2, the king declares his intention to reward Mordecai whom he (the king) identifies as being a Jew (6:10).

10. Yehuda T. Radday, "Esther with Humor," in *On Humor and the Comic in the Hebrew Bible,* ed. Yehuda T. Radday and Athalya Brenner (Sheffield: Almond, 1990), 301.

regarding Esther's claim that Haman is a traitor to her and to her people (note: not a traitor to the king). Perhaps, lesser important matters could be dismissed summarily, whereas those that were life-threatening to the king had to be investigated.

In any case, the details of the matter are sought out and found to be exactly as Mordecai had reported. The guilty officials then are summarily executed. The specific method of execution has been a matter of some question throughout history. Three different possibilities have been suggested: impaling, crucifixion, and hanging. The term *wayyittālû* clearly means "they were hanged,"[11] yet specifically how that hanging occurred is not easily determined since the term often translated "gallows" is simply the term *tree (ʿēs)*. Unfortunately, this lack of clarity is not resolved by turning to 5:14; 6:4; 7:9–10; or 9:14—the other passages in the Book of Esther where the same form of execution is mentioned in reference to other individuals. Paton's argument in favor of hanging (as opposed to impaling or crucifixion) accords with the Jewish tradition regarding the "hanging" of the ten sons of Haman in 9:14 and provides perhaps the most logical explanation in light of the gallows that Haman constructs (5:14; cf. 7:9) on which he hopes to execute Mordecai. Paton states that "both these methods of execution [impaling and crucifixion] seem to be precluded by the fact that *the tree* of 5[14] is 50 cubits [i.e., seventy-five feet] high. This can only have been a gallows."[12]

The entire incident is written "in the book of the matters of the days," that is, placed in the official court records, or the historical annals of the Medo-Persian empire.[13] This recording, moreover, takes place "in the presence of the king." Why Ahasuerus failed to reward Mordecai is not stated. To conclude that Ahasuerus did not consider rewarding his benefactor to be important, however, would be inaccurate in light of his immediate reaction in 6:1–10. In that passage, upon learning of the oversight, the king takes immediate steps to rectify his mistake.[14]

11. Ludwig Koehler and Walter Baumgartner, eds., *Lexicon in Veteris Testementi Libros* (Leiden: Brill, 1985), 1029.

12. Paton, *The Book of Esther*, 191.

13. See also 6:1 and 10:2. Compare 9:20, 32.

14. Note how God providentially uses even the oversight of a heathen to accomplish his wondrous ends (cf. 6:1–13).

Golden Threads

Although verses 21–23 of chapter 2 are not a major portion of the tapestry of the Book of Esther, they are golden threads that the author uses to lace the work together.

Looking to the past, 2:21–23 reestablishes the fact that Mordecai has access to the inner workings of the palace via Esther, who is now queen. The communication link that Mordecai set up in 2:11 in relation to the harem is reconfirmed in 2:22 in relation to the residence of the queen. That link, moreover, performs a vital function in 4:4–16 for the ultimate deliverance of the Jews.

Looking to the future, 2:21–23 demonstrates Mordecai's loyalty to the king and to legal authority in general. Without this act of rescuing the king from an attempted assassination plot, Mordecai's actions in 3:2–4 and 5:9 could easily be interpreted as acts of disloyalty to the crown.

Still again looking to the future, 2:21–23 introduces a history book—*The Book of the Chronicles*[15] of Medo-Persia—that becomes highly significant later in the story (6:1–11). By means of that secular history book, God works providentially behind the scenes to bring about a significant reversal in the fortunes of one member of the nation of Israel. The feeling that the author thus conveys is that if God can bring about such a dramatic shift for one Israelite, he can and will do it for all of the Israelites in exile.

A Man of Character and a Man of Character Flaws

Sales training consultants suggest that one method for helping customers to determine whether or not to buy a given product is to draw up a "strengths and weaknesses" chart for that product. The theory is that if customers see more strengths than weakness in the product being assessed, they then will be favorably disposed toward that product.

Perhaps now would be a good time to analyze the character of Mordecai, the Jewish hero in the story of the Book of Esther, to determine what type of image the author of the Book of Esther up to this point portrays Mordecai to be. Does the author view Mordecai as a spiritual giant, as a morally upstanding person,

15. The term *Chronicles* is a translation of the Hebrew *dibrê hayyāmîm* (lit., the words [or matters] of the days).

as a shaper of his own destiny (or one shaped by his circumstances), as a man possessing a less than admirable character, or as an individual who exhibits a combination of these or still other character traits? The following list reviews the strengths and weaknesses of Mordecai as suggested in chapter 2 by the author of the Book of Esther:

Strengths	*Weaknesses*
He possesses an excellent lineage through the line of Benjamin (v. 5).	He remains in exile rather than returning to the Promised Land (v. 6).
He willingly takes care of his orphaned cousin, raising her as his own daughter rather than abandoning her to her own fate (v. 7).	He fails to protest Esther's participation in the bride-search contest even through she at best would be married to a heathen, and at worst, become a concubine.
He demonstrates an ongoing concern for Esther's welfare while she is in the harem (v. 10).	He commands Esther to keep her heritage (i.e., faith) a secret while she is in the harem (v. 11).
He exhibits some level of administrative ability (i.e., is sitting at the king's gate) (v. 19).	He requires Esther to maintain silence about her faith even after she is married (v. 20).
He reveals a loyalty to the king (or at least to Esther's husband) (v. 22).	He does not acknowledge his relationship to his own daughter.
He displays a willingness not to demand recognition for work well done.	He maintains a position of dominance in Esther's life, even after she has married and left home (v. 20).

So far, the verdict on the character of Mordecai is still pending. He appears to be a man of solid character, but also a man with no visible concern for spiritual matters. Overall judgment, therefore, must be suspended until his performance in other situations can be evaluated.

Today's Headlines Influence Tomorrow's Views

In 2:21-23, the author expresses a key component of his overall thesis regarding God's providential care of his people. By presenting an isolated act of good citizenship that appears to be incongruous to the perceived movement of his story, the author reveals that seemingly unrelated events fit together in God's providential plans for his people. No event, therefore, should be deemed as being insignificant, for no one knows how God may choose to use that event to secure his aims and to ensure the welfare of his people.

Three additional principles, although less central to the author's thesis, emerge from this passage:

1. Nothing done for good is ever ultimately left unrewarded. Goods deeds should be done without consideration of immediate reward, yet the doer of those deeds should never forget that God will ultimately reward those acts. Mordecai's reward for rescuing the king's life is delayed possibly several years after he acted, but Mordecai receives that reward at the most propitious time – in God's perfect timing (6:1-11).
2. God's people must act responsibly in relation to the government under which they live, even if that government is controlled by unbelievers. Clear examples of this principle are found in the lives of Joseph, who served the Pharaoh in Egypt, and Daniel, who served heathen kings in Babylon. Ezra and Nehemiah, among others, could also be cited as those who acted honourably in the midst of pagan empires.
3. Anger often is a self-defeating force, as the two officials discover at the price of their lives. Anger is also self-defeating for King Ahasuerus in 1:12, and his anger cost him his most beautiful wife. Anger, moreover, plays a role in Haman's downfall (3:5; 5:9; 7:10), with the result that his family and more than seventy-five thousand people lose their lives.

All of these principles suggest that individuals should live wisely for God, since they do not know when their sin might bring their downfall or when their righteous acts will be used of God to accomplish his purpose and their own eternal good.

Interconnections

This section (2:21–23) contributes important data on two different themes that the author develops throughout the Book of Esther. The first theme encompasses the concepts of hiddenness and revelation. The second theme encompasses the idea of plotting or scheming to achieve one's ends.

The interplay between hiddenness and revelation serves as a linchpin to lock 2:21–23 perfectly in its place in the flow of the Book of Esther. Hiddenness and revelation occur in almost a leapfrog fashion beginning in 2:10 and extending until 7:4:

A Heritage hidden (2:10, 20)
  B Hatred hidden (2:21)
  B′ Hatred revealed (2:22–23)
    C Helpfulness hidden (2:23)
    C′ Helpfulness revealed (6:1–3)
A′ Heritage revealed (7:4)

In each of these dyads, the motif of hiddenness signifies that all is not as it should be. By contrast, the motif of revelation indicates a restoration of order to the world found in the text of the Book of Esther. In each case, the restoration of order either directly or indirectly benefits the Jews. Thus, each restoration provides the vehicle by which a reversal of fortunes takes place.

In A (2:10, 20), Esther conceals her faith and acts in complete disregard for—in direct disobedience to—the laws of God. In B (2:21), the eunuchs secretly, in anger, plot the overthrow of the regime, and in C (2:23), the king's scribes, at the king's order, relegate Mordecai's heroism merely to a few lines in a history book that few if any would ever read. None of these incidents should have occurred. Esther should not have obscured the reality of her Jewish beliefs, the eunuchs should not have harbored hate in their hearts, and the king should not have forgotten to demonstrate tangible gratitude to Mordecai for Mordecai's loyal action that led to the defeat of the enemies of the king.

Although the hiddenness of these events suggested less than positive results, its counterpart (i.e., the revelation of what had been hidden) generated highly favorable results. The revelation of the eunuchs' assassination plot preserved the king's life and preserved Esther's position within the palace (2:22–23). The revelation of Mordecai's lack of reward for stopping the eunuchs' attempt to kill the king brought with it both the honoring of Mordecai and the humiliation of Haman (6:1–3). Finally, the revelation of Esther's ethnic background (7:4) secured the death of Haman (7:10) and paved the way for the deliverance of the Jews from the sentence of death (8:7–14).

Along with the hiddenness-revelation motif, the author presents an example of a second theme—the theme of plotting or scheming to secure one's advantage. The example that he records in 2:21 is but one of five examples in the book of readily discernible maneuverings motivated by personal or political gain:

1. by Mordecai and Esther—to secure victory and to maintain a position of authority over the women of the king, that is, over Esther's rivals both before and after her marriage to the king (2:10, 20);
2. by Bigthan and Teresh—to secure victory over the king (2:21);
3. by Haman—to secure victory over a personal enemy (i.e., Mordecai, the Jew) and the enemies of his (Haman's) people (i.e., the Jews, 3:5–15);
4. by Mordecai and Esther—to secure victory over their enemy (i.e., Haman, the Agagite, 4:4–17); and
5. by Haman, together with his wife and friends—to secure victory over a personal enemy (i.e., Mordecai, the Jew, 5:10–14).

In each instance, Jewish plotting succeeds, whereas Gentile plotting fails. The Jews, Mordecai and Esther, successfully ensconce Esther in the role of queen and successfully bring the downfall of their hated enemy, Haman. The Gentiles, Bigthan and Teresh, lose their lives, as do Haman, his wife, and his friends.[16]

16. The Scripture does not state directly that the Jews killed Haman's wife or his friends (9:1–15). In all probability they did. The Scripture, however, does note that the Jews killed Haman's ten sons (9:7–10).

A Forward Look

What follows 2:21–23 is a movement into the heart of the drama of the story of the lives of Mordecai and Esther. What came before—Esther's rise to the throne, her secrecy about her faith—and what happens here—Mordecai's acts to protect the throne—come together at critical points later in the story to permit a dramatic reversal of the anti-Jewish actions of Haman, the enemy of the Jews. The next section (3:1–15) introduces Haman, the antagonist, and pits him against Mordecai, the protagonist. The hatred that develops between these two enemies makes the anger of Bigthan and Teresh toward the king pale by comparison. The Mordecai-Haman feud almost costs the lives of one entire ethnic population of the Medo-Persian empire, and does bring about the deaths of more than seventy-five thousand people. Yet, this section (2:21–23), despite its brevity, contributes necessary and vital information regarding the overall thesis of the Book of Esther, that is, regarding God's providential guidance of his people irrespective of their interest in or service to him. Without this section, valuable insight into that theme would otherwise be missing.

13

A Death Warrant
(3:1–15)

Life for the Jews in exile could not have been much better. One of their own was queen (although most would not have been aware of that fact, cf. 2:10, 20) and one of their own had just rescued the king and was certain to be rewarded for that heroic act. Humanly speaking, they were as secure as any exiled people possibly could be. All of that, however, would quickly change. The Jewish stock on the Susa Board of Exchange, which in chapter 2 reaches all-time highs, plummets in chapter 3 to all-time lows.

Chapter 3 begins innocuously enough—a promotion of one individual and a seemingly insignificant act of defiance on the part of another. The chapter ends, however, with the shocking revelation of an entire nation of people being placed under a sentence of death. The Jews are made to pay for a crime committed by one of their own. Ironically, the same individual who in chapter 2 is instrumental in bringing about the meteoric rise in the Jewish stock now becomes the reason for its dramatic drop.

Power Play

One of the most exciting and dynamic of sports is professional ice hockey. The speed, the agility, the raw power, the hard-hitting body checks, together with the artistry of stick handling, the perfectly timed passes, and the implementation of team strategy, all accentuate the clash of wills as two teams do battle to drive the puck into the other team's net and grab victory. In the process of the combat, emotions run high. Players at times go beyond the rules of the game and end up tripping, slashing, high-sticking, or fighting their opponents. For a minor infraction, a player is penalized by being sent to a penalty box for a period of two minutes; major infractions involve other penalties. As a result, the team of the penalized player plays short-handed; the other team has a power play advantage. During the next two minutes, the team with the advantage does everything it can to score against its weaker opponent.

In life outside of sports, people who secure positions of authority over others at times attempt to exert their authority to their own advantage and to the detriment of others. Leaders who press their advantage simply because they have the power to do so, however, may, if they are not careful, work to the detriment of the people whom they are supposed to serve.

In chapter 3, a man named Haman is given power. Along with that power come certain rights and privileges. Most, but not all, of the people respond in an expected manner toward Haman in his new role as prime minister. Haman himself acts within the limits of his power—until his authority is challenged. He then shifts to an abusive mode of action. He presses his power advantage not only to the detriment of the offender, but also to the detriment of the ethnic group of that offender, and eventually to the detriment of the entire Medo-Persian empire.

In order to accentuate the power play taking place, the author develops this chapter by adhering to a chiastic pattern of presentation, but with a double center: ABCC′B′A′. He uses a doubled center to emphasize the fact that Haman's abuse of power is neither an accidental nor an unwitting occurrence, but is the result of a well thought out plan.

A Sitting in a position of authority (3:1)
- B Disobeying the commands of authority (3:2–4)
  - C Preparing a plan for the abuse of authority (3:5–7)
  - C′ Presenting a plan for the abuse of authority (3:8–11)
- B′ Obeying the commands of authority (3:12–14)

A′ Sitting in a position of authority (3:15)

Thus, in a few short verses, the author of the Book of Esther depicts one individual who defies power (Mordecai), another who abdicates power (Ahasuerus), and still another who abuses power (Haman). The author does not represent any of these main characters as operating in a proper relationship to power. At the end of the chapter, moreover, the brunt of the judgment falls on the one who has no power but who has unsuccessfully attempted to defy certain powers that be. Innocent bystanders also get caught in the fallout from this political struggle.

Career Advancement (3:1)

A promotion is cause for celebration. If the promotion is the result of a wise decision, then both the individual and the company benefit.

In Esther 3:1, King Ahasuerus promotes an individual named Haman to a position that might be equivalent to that of prime minister today. Yet, unlike that of a modern prime minister, the position Haman acquires contains much authority to rule but without the burden of having to justify his actions to a duly elected legislative body. The chain of command for this prime minister consists of a single, direct link to a king who has full authority in the empire.[1]

Three Hebrew terms or phrases describe the reality of Haman's promotion. First, the king makes Haman great or important, that is, magnifies Haman's position in the kingdom.[2] Second, King Ahasuerus lifts up or raises up Haman, that is, honors or exalts him.[3] Third, the king establishes Haman's seat above those of all the princes who were with him.[4] Paulus Cas-

1. As a result of his promotion, Haman would have been one of the most powerful people in the world in his day.

2. Ludwig Koehler and Walter Baumgartner, eds., *Lexicon in Veteris Testementi Libros* (Leiden: Brill, 1985), 171.

3. Francis Brown, S. R. Driver, and Charles A. Briggs, *A Hebrew and English Lexicon of the Old Testament with an Appendix Containing the Biblical Aramaic* (reprint; Oxford: Clarendon, 1968), 669–72.

4. The grammar of the passage identifies the princes in relationship to Haman rather than to the king (i.e., the word *Haman* is a closer grammatical antecedent to the pronoun *him* than is the word *king*). Thus Haman is pictured as already holding a high office before he is appointed prime minister.

sel notes: "The elevation of a man at court was figuratively represented by the elevation of his seat in the presence of the king. The highest seat was occupied by the king, and the one who sat the nearest to him was the most honoured and distinguished."[5] Thus the author clearly records that Haman was in fact promoted, and that he acquired the position of prime minister as a consequence of the actions of the king.

The author, however, offers no special reason for Haman's promotion, nor does the author suggest that Haman secured the position of prime minister by any means other than legitimate ones. There is no reason, therefore, to assume, as Carey A. Moore does, that "[t]his verse sets up a sharp contrast between the unrewarded merit of Mordecai and Haman's unmerited rewards."[6] Although Mordecai should have been rewarded in some way for his actions that saved the life of the king (2:21–23), there is no reason to believe that Haman's promotion was not merited or that he received the promotion that Mordecai deserved. Haman may have done something significant to capture the king's favor, or he may have been promoted merely to maintain a balance of power within the government. The author of the Book of Esther apparently does not consider the reasons for Haman's promotion to be as important for his readers to know as the fact that Haman is promoted and that a critical sequence of events flows from that promotion that has a direct bearing on the welfare of the Jewish people.

At some unspecified time after Esther becomes queen (2:17), the virgins are gathered a second time (2:19), Mordecai averts a plot against the king (2:21–23), and King Ahasuerus promotes Haman (3:1). The date for this promotion can be narrowed somewhat by examining the events of chapters 2 and 3. Esther becomes queen in the tenth month of the seventh year of Ahasuerus's reign (2:16) and, in the first month of the twelfth year of Ahasuerus's reign, Haman establishes a date for the implementation of an edict calling for the destruction of the Jews (3:7). Some time—a period of months (but probably not as much

5. Paulus Cassel, *An Explanatory Commentary on Esther*, trans. Aaron Bernstein (Edinburgh: T. and T. Clark, 1888), 90.

6. Carey A. Moore, *Esther*, The Anchor Bible, ed. William Foxwell Albright and David Noel Freedman (Garden City, N.Y.: Doubleday, 1971), 35.

as a year)—may have elapsed from the time of Haman's promotion to the time when Mordecai's disobedience is discovered (3:2–5). Thus Haman's promotion probably occurs during the eleventh year of Ahasuerus's reign, some three to four years after Esther becomes queen.[7]

After setting the general time frame for the promotion, the author of the Book of Esther introduces the person who receives the promotion, Haman, the antagonist in the book. In doing so, the author makes a special effort to identify Haman's ancestral heritage—the son of Hammedatha,[8] an Agagite—an effort that he does not make even in relation to the king's lineage. The author appears to use Haman's ancestry to provide an informative contrast between Haman's background and that of the protagonist of the story, Mordecai.[9]

Haman was an Agagite, Mordecai an Israelite. Many scholars believe that the contrast between these two ancestries highlights the reason for Mordecai's unwillingness to bow down in respect to Haman and for Haman's seemingly irrational desire to eliminate the Jewish people.[10] In short, a family feud existed between the Agagites and the Israelites that dated back at least to the time of King Saul, the first king of Israel (1 Sam. 15),[11] and quite possibly back to the time of the exodus of the nation of Israel from the land of Egypt (Exod. 17:8–16), more than nine hundred years before the events recorded in the Book of Esther take place.[12]

7. This dating assumes that the king's command in 3:2 (i.e., that the people bow down in respect to Haman) is issued at the time of Haman's promotion and not at some later date.

8. Nothing is known regarding who Hammedatha was.

9. The argument favoring the existence of a tribal enmity between Haman and Mordecai gains support in part by the fact that the author makes frequent reference to Mordecai's background as a Jew (of the tribe of Benjamin; 2:5; 3:4, 6; 6:10; 8:7; 9:29; 10:3) and to Haman's as an Agagite (the son of Hammedatha; 3:1, 10; 5:13; 8:3, 5; 9:10, 24).

10. Moore, *Esther*, 35.

11. See 2:5–7 regarding the animosity between Mordecai's people and Haman's people.

12. The Amalekites fought against and were defeated by the Israelites at Rephidim soon after Israel, under Moses' leadership, had departed from Egypt. In King Saul's day, Agag was the king of the Amalekites. Hence, the fact that Haman is identified as an Agagite would link him directly to the ongoing feud.

Stubborn Refusal (3:2–4)

Why is it that children very early on in life learn that they "better not tattle" on other people who have done something wrong? Sometimes that attitude is carried over into adulthood, and grown men and women choose not to report the offenses, even the crimes, committed by others.

The people in King Ahasuerus's day faced the same choice. Mordecai (2:21–23) has to make that decision, and so do the king's servants (3:2–4). In both cases the individuals who are faced with that dilemma take the offense to the proper authorities. Mordecai informs the king (via Esther, the queen) of a plot against the king's life; the servants inform the prime minister, Haman, about Mordecai's disobedience to the king's command.

The particulars of 3:2–4 reveal the following concerning Mordecai's actions:

A. Disobedience observed (3:2)
B. Disobedience questioned (3:3)
C. Disobedience reported (3:4)

In 3:2, the king's servants act in obedience to the king's command, whereas Mordecai does not. These individuals may be Mordecai's equals in social status in the realm, being those who are together with Mordecai in the gate. They apparently are his friends (or at least his good acquaintances), because when they discover that he is acting in disobedience to the king's command, they do not immediately report him to the higher authorities, but first question him regarding his actions (3:3–4).

Several reasons have been offered in explanation for Mordecai's repeated acts of disobedience. Michael V. Fox summarizes the four most frequently suggested reasons as arrogance, monotheism, God's dignity, and tribal enmity.[13] The first suggestion (arrogance, the view advanced by Lewis Bayles Paton)[14] is always a possibility in any direct affront to authority, yet the

13. Michael V. Fox, *Character and Ideology in the Book of Esther* (Columbia, S.C.: University of South Carolina Press, 1991), 43-45.

14. Lewis Bayles Paton, *The Book of Esther*, International Critical Commentary, ed. Samuel Rolles Driver, Alfred Plummer, and Charles Augustus Briggs (Edinburgh: T. and T. Clark, 1908), 195.

text of Esther does not intimate such an attitude to be the case. The text shows Mordecai to be a loyal subject of the king, one who in fact protects the king's life (2:21–23). The text also reveals Mordecai's stated reason for his refusal to bow to Haman, namely, that he (Mordecai) is a Jew.

The text, moreover, holds out no support for the second reason that some offer to explain Mordecai's disobedience, that is, that Mordecai could not worship any god other than Yahweh and thus did not bow down to Haman.[15] In the first place, Yahweh is nowhere mentioned in the text of Esther, nor is there any indication that the Jewish people engaged in any worship practices during the events recorded in the Book of Esther. In the second place, ancient Persian kings did not claim for themselves the status of divinity, and hence did not grant such a status to their subordinates. Thus the king's command in 3:1 does not demand that his subjects bow down in worship to Haman.

The next argument—that bowing down to humans in some way is an affront to God's dignity—does not accord either with the text of Esther or with Jewish practices as recorded elsewhere in Scripture. Esther prostrates herself before the king in 8:3,[16] and there is no indication from the author of the Book of Esther that by doing so, Esther in any way compromises the dignity of Yahweh. Joyce G. Baldwin notes that "part of eastern courtesy [is] to bow in recognition of age and honour, and there is evidence that Israelite culture was no exception."[17] Fox concurs and points out the fact that "Mordecai was an official ('sitting in the King's Gate') for some time before Haman was

15. Keil advocates this position and argues that Mordecai could not bow down to Haman "without a denial of his [Mordecai's] religious faith." C. F. Keil, *The Books of Ezra, Nehemiah, and Esther*, Biblical Commentary on the Old Testament, trans. Sophia Taylor (Grand Rapids: Eerdmans, n.d.), 344. If Keil is correct, then Mordecai is seen here as taking a step of faith. Yet, such a step of faith seems to be out of character for Mordecai in light of the rest of his conduct in the Book of Esther. Furthermore, even Jewish commentators find Mordecai's refusal to bow very difficult to explain.

16. The Hebrew verb used in 8:3 is different from either of the verbs used in 3:2, 5 to indicate bowing down, but as Fox states, Esther's "act can hardly be distinguished from prostration." Fox, *Character and Ideology in the Book of Esther*, 44.

17. Joyce G. Baldwin, *Esther: An Introduction and Commentary*, Tyndale Old Testament Commentaries, ed. D. J. Wiseman (Downers Grove: InterVarsity, 1984), 72. See also Paton, *The Book of Esther*, 196.

promoted, and if he had all along been declining on principle to bow to all humans, his fellow officers would have noticed long ago. And as vizier, Mordecai could hardly avoid bowing to his king."[18]

Although both *kāra*ᶜ (to bow down) and *šāḥā(h)* (to prostrate oneself) in 3:2, 5, are used at times in connection with the worship of either the true God or false gods, both terms also occur in a variety of nonreligious settings. Often they depict bowing down in respect of one person to another. The context in which they are found dictates the specifics of how each is to be interpreted.

Thus without any direct indication in Esther 3:2, 5, that the bowing down (or lack thereof) is being done in regard to someone claiming to be a god, the proper interpretation of the king's command is that the bowing down or prostrating of oneself is to be done merely out of respect for the individual (not the god) Haman, who is now prime minister of the empire.

Having eliminated three arguments as to why Mordecai refuses to pay respect to Haman, the fourth view must now be considered. That position advances the theory of a family feud as the basis for Mordecai's refusal to bow to Haman. Of all the views, the text lends greatest support to this view. As noted, the author of the Book of Esther presents the genealogies of Mordecai and Haman in a way that he does not do for any of the other characters in the book. By so doing, he highlights the differences in the lineages of both men and identifies them as being born into families (nations) that had been at odds with each other for centuries. Thus, from the standpoint of the literary components of the Book of Esther, from the history of Israel, from the weakness of the other arguments, and from the intensity of the animosity that exists between Mordecai and Haman, the view of tribal enmity appears to be the strongest contender of the four views.

In 3:3, the servants or officials of the king who work with Mordecai question him as to why he does not obey the king's command. In fact, they question him at length, daily[19] seeking to

18. Fox, *Character and Ideology in the Book of Esther*, 44.

19. The text (3:4) does not indicate how long these officials actually question Mordecai before making Haman aware of Mordecai's misdemeanor. The same idiom for "daily" (*yôm wāyôm*) is used in 2:11 to denote a period of time that extends for a minimum of one year. We therefore should not assume that the servants necessarily acted quickly.

understand his reasoning. Their questioning, moreover, turns into advice giving in 3:4, but Mordecai does not heed their words. He remains adamant in his refusal to bow down to Haman, merely asserting that he would not bow down to Haman because he, Mordecai, was a Jew.

Interestingly, the king's officials do not appear to report Mordecai's conduct to Haman for the purpose of seeing Mordecai punished for his refusal to obey the king's command. Rather, they are curious to discover whether being Jewish does or does not exclude an individual from adherence to a given law of the land.

Fox points out an irony in these verses: Haman's "haughtiness" causes him only to see the adulation being poured out on him and prevents him from noticing what "everyone else sees," that is, the one person who "remains unbowed and thus most conspicuous."[20]

One for All and All for One (3:5–7)

If you have ever purchased an automobile, you have probably experienced what Haman experiences here and throughout the rest of the book, namely, selective perception. Prior to buying your car, you may not have paid much attention to that particular make and model when you saw it on the road. After buying it, however, you notice cars just like yours almost every time you go for a drive.

Haman does not notice Mordecai, probably does not even know that he exists—until the king's servants point out to Haman the fact that Mordecai refuses to show any respect to Haman. Then, as if by selective perception, Haman sees Mordecai everywhere. Haman becomes consumed with getting even with Mordecai. Even later, at a time when Haman could be expected to think of nothing but a great honor that he had recently received (5:1–8), he focuses his attention on Mordecai's failure to show respect to him (5:9). As a consequence, Haman becomes so incensed with Mordecai that he (Haman) cannot enjoy his cause for celebration (5:11–13).

The author notes in 3:5 that, as a consequence of Mordecai's defiance, Haman is "filled with anger." The Hebrew word

20. Fox, *Character and Ideology in the Book of Esther*, 45.

hāmā(h) (anger) is a very strong term referring to "an inner and emotional heat which rises and is fanned to varying degrees" – to "a burning and consuming wrath."[21] Within the Book of Esther the term is used six times: four times of the king (1:12; 2:1; 7:7, 10) and twice of Haman (3:5; 5:9). In reference to the king, anger is seen to arise quickly and then to subside. In regards to Haman, however, anger likewise bursts into existence, but there is no specific mention of it ever subsiding. In 3:5, Haman's anger rages because of Mordecai's direct affront.

Although Mordecai is legally in the wrong and Haman is legally both in the right and in a position of power, Haman cannot tolerate Mordecai's disrespect, particularly when it comes from a Jew. In 3:6, however, Haman controls his emotions and directs them at a larger target. He determines to press his advantage of power and to secure something far better to him than the mere elimination of one Jew – the eradication of all Jews.

The initial words of 3:6 reveal Haman's ability to keep his emotions in check: "He despised in his eyes [i.e., he would think contemptuously himself, cf. 1:17] to send out a hand against [i.e., lay his hands on] Mordecai alone." The operative term is "alone." In essence, Haman could not live with himself if he did not make full use of this once-in-a-lifetime opportunity to wreak havoc on all of the Jews.

At first glance, this verse does not make a great deal of sense. Why would Haman suddenly determine to destroy all of the Jews for the actions of one man? Does he fear, as Lewis Bayles Paton contends, that "other Jews might be expected to act similarly"?[22] Does he perhaps, Paulus Cassel's words, regard Mordecai's act as "not . . . merely . . . an offence against the majesty of the king, but also against the established religion of the country, and hence his great wrath"?[23] Still further, does Haman, as Howard F. Vos suggests, see this as an opportunity to rid the empire of these

21. Gerard Van Groningen, "860 . . . (*yāhām*)," *Theological Wordbook of the Old Testament*, ed. R. Laird Harris, Gleason L. Archer, Jr., and Bruce K. Waltke (Chicago: Moody, 1980), 1:374; Gerard Van Groningen, "2058 . . . (qasap)," *Theological Wordbook of the Old Testament*, 2:808.

22. Paton, *The Book of Esther*, 200.

23. Cassel, *An Explanatory Commentary on Esther*, 99.

Jewish "troublemakers" and, at the same time, to secure "great wealth in the operation"?[24] The author of the text does not openly describe Haman's innermost thoughts regarding the matter. Perhaps there exists in Haman some part or all of each of the reasons offered by these commentators.

The author does offer, however, what appears to be likely the foundational component underlying Haman's reasoning: the Agag-Saul family feud. The author's frequent identification of Haman as an Agagite and of Mordecai as a Jew (or Benjamite) suggests that the author desires his readers to recognize the Agag-Saul confrontation to be at work within the events portrayed in the book.

Regardless of his motivation, Haman proceeds with his plan to eradicate the Jews. He does so by having lots cast in his presence. Lots were specially marked stones or sticks that were placed into a jar or the fold of a garment and shaken until one fell out, that one providing the "divinely approved" answer to the question being posed. From the wording of the verse, Haman[25] apparently has lots cast for each day of the month, one day at a time, until the most auspicious day of the month is determined. He then follows the same method to identify the correct month of the year in which he is to carry out his plan for the destruction of the Jews. With each casting of the lots, the favored month of the year is pushed further and further away from the first month of the year,[26] the month of Nisan, the

24. Vos, *Ezra, Nehemiah, and Esther,* 160. Although Haman may have desired to increase his already enormous wealth (see 3:9; 5:11), the motivation for his actions appears to go beyond a mere desire for money. Esther 3:13 (which speaks of plundering the Jews' possessions) may intimate that the desire for money played some part in Haman's thinking. Yet, Haman was willing to spend a considerable sum of his own money to bear the expenses of a military action against the Jews (3:9).

25. Esther 3:7 literally reads "he cast pur, that is the lot, before Haman." To whom specifically the "he" refers is not clear. Quite probably Keil and Vos are correct in their independent assessments that either an astrologer or a magician performed the actual task of casing the lots. Keil, *The Books of Ezra, Nehemiah, and Esther*, 345; Vos, *Ezra, Nehemiah, and Esther*, 160–61. Compare, however, 9:24 which leaves open the possibility that Haman casts some or all of the lots himself.

26. The author of the Book of Esther adheres to a Babylonian order of the months of the calendar year, rather than to a Hebrew order.

month in which the lots were cast. Ultimately, the lots point to the thirteenth day of the twelfth month as being the ideal time for the eradication of Mordecai's people.

By casting lots, Haman seeks guidance from his gods as to the most propitious time in which to destroy the Jews. Ironically, of all the characters in the book, the most despicable one, Haman, is the only one who seeks some sort of help from a higher being. That higher power, however, is not the true God of the universe, but the false gods or demons of either (or both) the Amalekite or Medo-Persian religions.

A Silver-Tongued Orator (3:8–11)

Credit must be given where credit is due: Haman is a skilled persuader. Like any good orator, he knows his audience; he also knows what to say, when to say it, and how it should be said.

Haman creates within his speech a sense of urgency—a problem that needs to be resolved, and resolved immediately. Such a problem, Haman declares, is empire-wide and therefore worthy of the king's utmost attention. In Haman's estimation, however, the problem can be resolved by a few simple acts—the creation of a royal decree and the payment of money by Haman so that the king incurs no financial burden by the implementation of that decree (3:9).

Not once in his brief speech does Haman identify who is causing the problem.[27] Yet in 3:8 he establishes three reasons why those problem people should be destroyed:

1. they have infiltrated all regions of the empire;
2. they are unlike all of the other (law-abiding) people of the empire; and
3. they are rebels who defy the king's laws.

Those unnamed people, therefore, are not worthy to continue their current practices.

27. Haman's tactic of keeping hidden the identity of those troublesome people allows him to observe the king's reactions before he (Haman) proceeds. Logically, Haman at some later time would have to divulge the identity of those people, but now is not the time.

Haman begins by decrying the antisocial character of the king's enemies. They are "scattered and separated." Moore comments on these two terms: "The first participle refers to the Jews' being scattered throughout the hundred and twenty-seven provinces of the empire, while the second participle refers to their self-imposed separateness, or exclusiveness. . . ."[28] Those people, therefore, surround the king and, failing to be assimilated into the natural flow of the empire, pose a direct threat to him.

Continuing his speech, Haman builds his argument by declaring that those isolationists have established their own laws by which to govern themselves. Those laws, moreover, do not coincide with any other known laws (and thus they do not work for the good of the empire). The adherence to such unnatural laws, therefore, "amounted to a passive disloyalty to the king."[29]

Haman now brings forth his final argument: "they [the king's enemies] do not observe the king's laws." This final argument is the one that seals the fate of the rebels, because King Ahasuerus cannot conscience any potential rebellion in the land. Within painfully recent memory, he has experienced the rebellion of his wife the queen, two military defeats at the hands of the Greeks, and an attempted palace coup by two of his trusted officers. Further rebellion, no matter how remote, cannot be tolerated.

Haman now subtly shifts into his proposal: The king must take action; the rebels cannot be allowed to remain as they are. What Haman means by the use of the term *remain* he does not clarify. His edict in 3:13 makes his intentions clear, but at this point they are ambiguous. His choice of words leaves room for anything from a mild, general punishment to a stronger act of banishment from the empire to the ultimate judgment of annihilation. Haman's words allow him to protect himself and to "negotiate" with the king should the king not respond as enthusiastically as Haman would like. The king, however, responds favorably, apparently without questioning Haman in any way (vv. 10–11). Thus, Haman is free to define his terms to his fullest advantage.

28. Moore, *Esther*, 39.

29. Cassel, *An Explanatory Commentary on Esther*, 112.

In 3:9, Haman submits a formal verbal petition[30] to King Ahasuerus for the destruction of the enemies of the state.[31] Haman then immediately moves on to highlight the financial benefits that would accrue to the king should he choose to enact Haman's proposal. He promises to pay the king ten thousand talents of silver, that is, approximately 60 percent of the annual revenue of Ahasuerus's kingdom.[32] Although the offer seems incredibly large, it is within the bounds of reality in the ancient world.[33] Baldwin underscores the need for Haman's offer of the silver to be genuine: "the sum he promises is a vast fortune, and while it is probable that he was planning to take over the property of the Jewish families he annihilated, his proposition would have been ludicrous if he had not had money already at his disposal."[34] Haman's personal position also would have been extremely tenuous if the king had accepted the offer and Haman had not been able to produce the money he had promised.

The king responds by giving Haman not only his request, but also (by giving him the king's own signet ring)[35] the authority needed to implement that request in any way that Haman deems appropriate.

At this point, the author registers his utter distaste for Haman. First, the author calls Haman the son of Hammedatha. Who Hammedatha was is unknown; how the ancient Jews would have reacted to hearing his name is equally unknown.

30. The clause, "if it is pleasing to the king," is a standard means by which individuals in ancient times appealed to a king for his favor in granting a request (see also 5:4, 7–8; 7:3–4; 8:5–6; 9:13).

31. Despite the king's seeming ignorance of the existence of the death warrant (in 7:5), Haman's statement in 3:9 clearly indicates that the king is without excuse. He knows that he is consenting to annihilation of some group of individuals throughout his kingdom. Evidently, however, as 7:5 combined with 9:12 suggest, he is not aware of the full ramifications of that consent.

32. Fox, *Character and Ideology in the Book of Esther*, 51–52.

33. Paton, *The Book of Esther*, 206.

34. Baldwin, *Esther: An Introduction and Commentary*, 74.

35. Regarding the signet ring, the official seal of the king, Cassel writes: "The seal of the king included all his power. A document which bore the impression of the royal seal *(sigillum)* demanded unhesitating obedience. It was considered divine law, and irrevocable (see chap. viii. 8). Therefore with the king's great seal was transferred royal power." Cassel, *An Explanatory Commentary on Esther*, 118.

Second, the author identifies Haman as being an Agagite, a people hated by the Jews from the time of King Saul, over five hundred years earlier. Finally, the author declares that Haman is *ṭôrēr hayy^{e}hûdîm,* i.e., "the enemy of the Jews." Interestingly, the author uses this final designator for the first time (cf. 3:1).

Whereas verse 10 reveals the king's physical response to Haman's request, verse 11 denotes the king's verbal confirmation, seemingly refusing Haman's financial offer and then placing the rebels into his hands. The king, however, may have in fact taken Haman's money since, in 7:4, Esther declares that she and her people had been "sold." Such a statement implies a transfer of money (or barter) from one person to another, and thus suggests that Haman purchased the rights to destroy the Jews.[36]

Express Mail Delivery (3:12–14)

The famous Pony Express of the American west ran some twenty-one hundred miles from St. Louis, Missouri, to San Francisco, California. This high-speed mail delivery system utilizing relay teams of horses and riders epitomized the rugged, individualistic spirit of the old west. Ironically, it lasted only one and a half years, from April 1860, to November 1861,[37] but in that brief time it provided the fodder for the feeding of legends.

A similar pony express system existed in the Medo-Persian empire some twenty-three hundred years earlier. That system lasted considerably longer and provided a mail service for a region extending from Pakistan to northern Sudan. Haman makes use of that mail system in 3:13, as does the king in 1:22, Mordecai in 8:14 and in 9:20, and Esther in 9:29.

Haman does not waste any time in drafting or disseminating the edict of death. On the thirteenth day of the first month, the month of Nisan, the same month in which he had the lots cast before him to determine the most auspicious time for the destruction of the Jews (3:7), Haman summons the royal scribes

36. If the king does accept Haman's financial offer, then Moore may be correct when he interprets the king's statement, "the silver is given to you," to mean "if you want to spend it that way, its all right with me." Moore, *Esther,* 40.

37. Although there were several minor Pony Express companies prior to 1860, the most famous was that operated by Russell, Majors, and Waddell, which began its operations on 3 April 1860.

to write the edict in the various languages of the people of the empire (v. 12). Haman's timing could not have been any more devastating to the Jews; the next day, the day when the edict would first reach the Jews by way of the royal courier service, would be the first day of the Jewish holiday of Passover.[38] During Passover, the Jews were to celebrate their miraculous deliverance by God from bondage in Egypt more than nine hundred years earlier. During that first night of Passover, moreover, the heads of the Jewish households, in conjunction with God's command (Exod. 13:1–16), were to tell their children the story of that earlier redemption of Israel from Egypt. This Passover holiday, however, would be marked by the announcement, not of a joyous or miraculous liberation from bondage in Medo-Persia, but of a scheduled annihilation at the hands of their captors.

The edict (Esther 3:12) was addressed specifically to the three echelons of officials who would have the responsibility for implementing it. The first group, the satraps, ruled over the 20 major divisions of the empire. The second group, the governors, managed the 127 provinces mentioned in 1:1; whereas the third group, the princes,[39] "served under the governors and were perhaps chiefs of the conquered peoples."[40] The edict was sealed with the king's signet ring signifying that no one, not even the king himself, could alter its contents. The edict was now an official law of the Medes and the Persians.

Esther 3:13 provides the contents of the newly established law: all Jews—men, women, and children—are to be destroyed, killed, and annihilated on Adar 13, and their possessions are to be seized. By piling on the verbs of destruction as well as describing in detail those who are to be exterminated, the author conveys to his readers the utter seriousness and the

38. Pierce notes: "Almost as interesting is the fact that the actual deliverance comes on the thirteenth of Adar, one month prior to the next Passover [8:12]. Unfortunately, it is consistent with the secular mood of the people and tone of the book that no mention is made of the observance of either Passover by the exiles in Susa." Pierce, "The Politics of Esther and Mordecai: Courage or Compromise?" 86.

39. The term *śar* (prince) does not imply that these individual are of royal birth. It also may be used to designate one who is a leader or a commander.

40. F. B. Huey, Jr., "Esther," *Expositor's Bible Commentary*, ed. Frank E. Gaebelein, 12 vols. (Grand Rapids: Zondervan, 1988), 4:814.

utter totality of the events that the Jews of the Book of Esther anticipate will soon take place.[41] No Jew is to be left alive. No trace of the Jews is to remain. Their goods, as well as their lives, are to be plundered mercilessly.

At this stage in the Book of Esther, between verses 13 and 14, the Septuagint adds a purported text of Haman's edict ordering the destruction of the Jews. There is, however, no Hebrew manuscript evidence to support that addition being part of the original text of the Book of Esther. Thus, although such an addition may provide an interesting curiosity, there is no need to assess its contents at this point.[42]

The contents of the edict, however, were published. Their publication, according to 3:14, was designed to ensure that all non-Jews would be prepared to take action against the Jews on the appointed day. As Cassel notes: "[t]hese were no private instructions to the authorities, but rather open orders to the people."[43] Thus, all non-Jews, not merely the magistrates or

41. Baldwin finds threefold expressions such as those found here and throughout the Book of Esther to be "a stylistic feature of legal documents." Baldwin, *Esther: An Introduction and Commentary*, 75.

42. In an apparent attempt to cast a spiritual character on the contents of the Book of Esther and to fill in what some may consider to be gaps in the story line, the Septuagint adds six major sections (all without ancient Hebrew manuscript support) to the Book of Esther. Those additions are as follows:

1. prior to 1:1—a purported dream / vision that came to Mordecai regarding a battle between a wicked but more powerful nation and a righteous nation, with the righteous nation ultimately winning, and a fuller account of Mordecai's thwarting of the plot against the king than is recorded in 2:21–23;
2. between 3:13 and 3:14—a supposed text of Haman's edict against the Jews;
3. following 4:17—a purported prayer by Mordecai followed by a purported prayer by Esther;
4. part of the beginning of chapter 5—a supposed detailing of Esther's approach to the king as her first step toward securing the deliverance of the Jews from the death warrant written by Haman;
5. between 8:12 and 8:13—a purported text of Mordecai's edict identifying the Jews as a righteous people and condemning to death the enemies of the Jews; and
6. following 10:3—a supposed text of Mordecai's recollection of his earlier dream / vision (recorded prior to 1:1) and his newly-discovered understanding of the meaning of that dream / vision.

43. Cassel, *An Explanatory Commentary on Esther*, 135.

even the avowed enemies of the Jews, but all non-Jews, were to take whatever steps were necessary to ready themselves for that day. The Jews, therefore, could expect to find no help from either government officials or friends; humanly speaking, they were on their own.

Fiddling While Susa "Burns" (3:15)

The riders spread the news throughout the Persian countryside. Death warrants are posted in the capital city, and the king and his prime minister, Haman, sit down to drink.[44] How aware the king is of what is happening in his kingdom is unclear. Quite probably, he is oblivious to what is going on around him. Haman has taken charge and has orchestrated the anti-Jewish pogrom. As he celebrates with the king, Haman undoubtedly relishes within himself every thought of the terror that he has caused among the Jews.

The act of feasting and partying apparently were a frequent occurrence in the Medo-Persian empire. Thus, the author of the Book of Esther strategically places five feasts into the literary structure of the book to key the reader to the flow of the story:

1. Chapter 1—feasting that ends in tragedy for a pagan;
2. Chapter 2—feasting that celebrates joy because of a Jewess;
3. Chapter 3—feasting that celebrates the destruction of the Jews;
4. Chapters 5–7—feasting that ends in tragedy for a pagan; and
5. Chapter 9—feasting that celebrates the triumph of the Jews.

Interestingly, the drinking party in 3:15 breaks the pattern of (A) pagan tragedy—chapter 1, (B) Jewish success—chapter 2, (A′) pagan tragedy—chapters 5–7, (B′) Jewish success—9. The

44. In view of the frequency of feasts and drinking bouts, Paton is probably correct when he states that "as in 7[1], we should translate *banquet* instead of *drink,* regarding the verb as a denominative from the word 'banquet,' lit. 'drinking.'" Paton, *The Book of Esther,* 211.

drinking here is out of kilter with the flow of the story because the story itself has gone out of kilter with what one would expect to happen to the people of God. The Jews are devastated; even the pagans are confused.

Note that there is no specific purpose given for this feast, as well as no specific outcome mentioned for it. In essence, it is a "meaningless" feast – a meaningless feast, however, that speaks volumes regarding the situation the Jews are facing. This verse (3:15), therefore, may be considered a low point or a critical juncture of the story – to a large part because it shows confusion with no resolution.

What adds to this sense of a world turned upside down is the fact that in this verse a flurry of action takes place. Riders hurry in all directions in order to post the edict of death. The people of Susa rush mentally in all directions, attempting to make sense of the edict. Yet, in the midst of all this activity, much like the calm in the eye of a storm, the king and Haman feast with no thought about the edict and seemingly unconcerned with the maelstrom swirling around them that soon will change their world.

Furthermore, the author portrays the people of Susa as being confused or bewildered. The noun he uses to describe this confusion, *nābôkā(h)*, conveys the sense of wandering in perplexity.[45] Such an emotion would be a natural reaction, irrespective of how the people of Susa felt about the Jews in particular. Their consternation would be as much for themselves as for the Jews, perhaps worrying that the same or worse would happen to them.

Yet, far worse than the worry that filled the minds of the non-Jews is the seemingly hopeless state in which the Jews find themselves. As Cassel writes: "The condition of Israel was sad in the extreme. Their annihilation was impending – their enemies were drinking – and their neighbors were gossiping. Where else were they to seek help, but in repentance towards the living God!"[46] Yes, where else could they turn? Yet, nowhere in the Book of Esther does the author depict the Jews as turning visibly or openly to God.

45. William Gesenius, *Hebrew and Chaldee Lexicon to the Old Testament Scriptures*, trans. Samuel Prideaux Tregelles (reprint; Grand Rapids: Eerdmans, 1967), 107-8.

46. Cassel, *An Explanatory Commentary on Esther*, 138.

A Terrible Way to Learn Life's Lessons

In practical terms, what did the Jews learn from the fifteen verses of chapter 3? Very simply, they learned, if nothing else, that life is precarious. Reversals in life's fortunes can come quickly and unexpectedly. At the end of chapter 2, life is good for the Jews. By the end of chapter 3, however, life had turned sour. The pall of death had wrapped its dead weight around them and was suffocating the life out of them.

Other lessons, important but less central to the thrust of 3:1–15, are as follows:

1. The consequences of self-serving acts may have wide-ranging effects. Mordecai's decision to claim his Jewishness as a reason for not bowing down to Haman gave Haman an excuse for seeking the extermination of the entire race of the Jews.
2. Pride leaves a path of folly and destruction behind it. Haman's pride kept him from being satisfied with 99 percent of the population bowing down to him; he wanted 100 percent. His pride left a nation in an uproar and a people in fear for their lives. Mordecai's pride kept him from being obedient to the law, with the result that he put the lives of his people into jeopardy.
3. Being part of God's chosen people does not guarantee that an individual will never face difficulties or life-threatening crises. This theme, which recurs throughout the Book of Esther, shows itself particularly strong here. The people of God have no special claim to peace and prosperity in this life, especially if they are out of God's will.
4. The actions of one individual can affect an entire nation. One man, Mordecai, chooses not to act responsibly, and a whole race of people is threatened with annihilation. Another man, Haman, oversteps his responsibility, and an ethnic minority writhes in anguish. Still another man, Ahasuerus, abdicates his responsibility and confusion reigns throughout his empire.
5. Improper governing leaves the people in a shambles. This lesson, a subset of the previous lesson, captures the essence of

King Ahasuerus's failure to examine the facts of the situation before he gives free reign to Haman to act on such a serious matter as the annihilation of a group of people.

Compared, But No Comparison

One important way to study Scripture is to compare one Scripture with another, or one biblical character with another. By noting the similarities and differences and by observing the comments of the authors of the parallel passages, we can gain insight into what God considers to be pleasing to him or not so pleasing to him.

In an earlier chapter, we briefly compared the life of Esther to the lives of Daniel, Shadrach, Meshach, and Abednego, four other Jews (nearly contemporary with Esther) who find themselves in exile and yet who are able to serve God faithfully. We noted that Esther does not compare favourably in declaring her faith or in following certain laws that God had established for the welfare of his people.

We now briefly list the similarities and differences between the lives of Mordecai and Joseph, a hero of the Jewish faith (see Gen. 37ff.). Let us first look at several key similarities.

1. Both men face a life-and-death situation – Joseph's is created by his brothers, whereas Mordecai's is created by a non-Jew, Haman.
2. After creating the problem for Joseph and for Mordecai, Joseph's brothers and Haman, respectively, sit down to eat or drink, seemingly caring little about the distress of the one whose life they have put in jeopardy.
3. Both men are left in a quandary as to what to do to rectify the situation.
4. Both men at some time interact meaningfully with their respective king's servants.
5. Both men rise to the position of prime minister, Joseph in Egypt and Mordecai in Medo-Persia.
6. Both men, after rising to the position of prime minister, help their people, the people of God.

Despite these similarities, there are several differences between the two men:

1. Joseph is young and inexperienced when his story begins; Mordecai is older.
2. Joseph is taken into exile against his will; Mordecai remains in exile by choice, failing to return to Jerusalem even though that option may have been open to him.
3. Joseph faces opposition from his own people (his own brothers), Mordecai faces opposition from an individual who is not one of his people.
4. Joseph shuns sexual relations with someone in authority who potentially could advance his career; Mordecai encourages the use of sexual relations – those of his adopted daughter with the king in hopes of advancing her career (and his own as well?).
5. Joseph shows compassion for non-Jews; Mordecai does not directly show compassion for non-Jews (although his work as prime minister appears to have been such that the non-Jews would have benefited by his administrative acts).
6. Joseph turns to God in his difficulty and openly gives God credit for his success; Mordecai neither turns to God in his difficulty nor openly (if ever at all) gives God credit for his success.
7. Joseph's story is concluded both with a positive feeling regarding the situation of the Jews and with a belief in a better tomorrow for the people of God; Mordecai's story ends with only a view that all is well at present for the Jews – there is no forward look or prophetic vision to suggest that God has great plans for Israel's future.[47]

Where are the heroes in the Book of Esther? Look no further than Mordecai and Esther. They are the ones who take the necessary risks to secure the deliverance of their people.

Where are the spiritual heroes in the Book of Esther? Look elsewhere; there are none to be found in this book.

47. This last category – future hope – also differentiates between the lives of Ruth and Esther. The story of Ruth concludes with her giving birth to a son who would become the grandfather of arguably the greatest human king of Israel, King David, and who thus would ultimately become a human ancestor of the Messiah of Israel. The end of the Book of Esther concludes, however, with no mention of any offspring for Esther, much less one who would provide Israel a measure of comfort or deliverance.

14

Woebegone Days
(4:1–17)

Have you ever had one of those days when everything seemed to go wrong? You woke up late. The clothes you wanted to wear were either in the laundry or not ironed. No matter how you combed your hair, it went in all directions. Your toast burned. Your car took forever to start. The traffic was horrendous, and your boss was waiting for you with fire in his eyes because you missed an important meeting.

The thirteenth of Nisan was one of those days for Mordecai. He woke up in the morning quite possibly thinking of some aspect of the Passover celebration that would soon take place,[1] only to discover that he and all of his Jewish friends had been sentenced to die. The rope of bondage of the exile with which he had become so comfortable had now become a noose around his neck, and was being tightened to squeeze the life out of him. His life would never be the same.

In chapter 4 the author portrays Mordecai's response to what undoubtedly was the worst day of his life. Only the day before

1. The assumption is that Mordecai and the other Jews with him would celebrate Passover (beginning on Nisan 15) in one fashion or another, yet that assumption may be unfounded since there is no record of any Passover remembrance anywhere within the Book of Esther.

(3:2–5), Mordecai seemed to be in complete control of his life; now he must expend every effort to stay alive.

Chapters 3 and 4 are chapters of contrast. In chapter 3 the author of the Book of Esther reveals how non-Jews react to a threatening situation, that is, to the "rebellion" of Mordecai. In chapter 4, the author displays the ways in which the Jews react to a life-threatening situation. Chapter 3 focuses on the plans and actions of non-Jews, chapter 4 on the plans and actions of Jews. Chapter 3 indicates a reaction to a "good" law, chapter 4 to a "bad" law. Chapter 3 concludes with a commitment to drinking, chapter 4 with a commitment to fasting.

Chapters 3 and 4, however, are also chapters of similarity. In both chapters, the main action begins at the king's gate and ends in the corridors of imperial power. In both chapters the king's servants are involved in questioning Mordecai's actions as well as in functioning as conduits of information to a royally chosen power. In both chapters the leading figures (Haman in 3, Mordecai in 4) seek royal assistance and dictate to royalty what that assistance should be. Both leading figures, furthermore, present their cases before royalty as involving situations that threaten the well-being of royalty, and both are successful in securing their desired response.

Esther 4:1–17, moreover, contains a jumble of similarities and differences between the two main Jewish figures, Mordecai and Esther. Mordecai agonizes over the facts of the situation. Esther expresses anguish out of sympathy for Mordecai's agony before she learns the facts of the situation. Esther wants to smooth over the trappings of the situation; Mordecai wants the world to see those trappings. Mordecai expects Esther to face reality; Esther wants to avoid it altogether. Thus 4:1–17 provides an interesting study in human relations under fire.

Excuses, Excuses, Excuses

The author of the Book of Esther interweaves the various components of the book to drive the story forward in order to accomplish his intended purpose. Esther 1:1–9 focuses on the hollow opulence of a heathen kingdom; 1:10–22 highlights the foolishness of the pagan leaders. Chapter 2 emphasizes the extent to which seemingly good people go to succeed in the midst of corruption; chapter 3 stresses the tragedy of an abuse of power. Now, chapter 4 presents the upheaval that results from an ineptly run government. The upside-down world of chapter 4 may be outlined as follows:

A A command that causes mourning and fasting (4:1–3)
  B An explanation of the situation and a call to action (4:4–8)
    C An excuse for not taking action to resolve the situation (4:9–12)
  B′ An explanation of the situation and a call to action (4:13–14)
A′ A command that causes mourning and fasting (4:15–17)

By structuring the passage in this way, the author of the Book of Esther does not make the focus of this passage Esther's supposed statement of faith in verse 16 ("if I perish, I perish"). Furthermore, he does not make Mordecai's supposed declaration of reliance on the providence of God in verse 14 ("relief and deliverance will arise for the Jews from some other place") the central point. Instead he zeros in on Esther's excuse for not taking action. In other words, the central thrust of this passage is human failure, not human faith.

Reliance on God is nowhere to be seen. In fact, Esther's excuse in verse 11—her failure to trust God in this situation—is sandwiched between Mordecai's own twofold failure: his failure to turn to God personally for help (vv. 7–8) and his failure to instruct Esther to turn to God for help (vv. 13–14).

We now need to draw our attention to the details of this chapter to observe how the author continues to unfold his overall purpose in writing the Book of Esther: to show that God accomplishes his plan for his people despite their lack of commitment to him.

A Wake-Up Call (4:1–3)

Excellent communicators generally begin their presentations by using some form of an attention-getter, be it a story, an illustration, a significant statistic, or a reference to someone or something with which the audience is familiar. Mordecai is no exception.

In Esther 4:1–2, he uses a public act of mourning and a near-breach of the king's gate—an offense punishable by death—to motivate Esther to act. His methods work. He gains Esther's complete attention, as is evidenced by her immediate action in an effort to assist him (vv. 4–5).

Some scholars have questioned whether Mordecai's grief in verses 1–2 is genuine or staged.[2] Interestingly, the words of the text seem to suggest both. The actual words of the text are the standard Hebrew words for the tearing (*qāraᶜ*—cf. Gen. 37:29, 34; Num. 14:6; 2 Sam. 1:11) of clothes and the wailing (*zāᶜaq*—cf. Exod. 2:23; 1 Sam. 28:12; Ezek. 21:12) of a person who truly is in mourning. Yet, both the grammar of the text and the actions described by the text suggest that Mordecai controlled the timing of the outward expression of his grief in order to achieve certain ends.

The author joins 4:1 to 3:15 by means of a *wāw* connective rather than a *wāw* consecutive, thereby allowing for the possibility that any number of events intervened between the two verses. Thus he implies that Mordecai's actions do not follow immediately on the heels of the events of 3:15.

In addition, the author suggests that Mordecai does not immediately tear his clothes, put on sackcloth and ashes, or wail loudly and bitterly upon learning of the edict of death. Furthermore, the author notes that Mordecai (between his initial awareness of the death warrant and his actions described in 4:1) takes some period of time to discover the detailed sequence of events (lit., "all that had been done") leading to the current situation (see vv. 7–8).

Moreover, the author nowhere points to any private mourning on the part of Mordecai. Mordecai's wailing takes place in the open, in the midst of the capital city of Susa (4:1). Still further, and conspicuous by its absence, the author makes no mention of Mordecai sending any private communiqué to Esther as he had done in the past (see 2:10–11, 20, 22).

Mordecai's expression of grief, therefore, is a sign of both personal and public mourning,[3] with emphasis on the public exhibition. In the ultimate sense, his actions seem calculated to

2. See Michael V. Fox, *Character and Ideology in the Book of Esther* (Columbia, S.C.: University of South Carolina Press, 1991), 57–58.

3. Paulus Cassel, *An Explanatory Commentary on Esther*, trans. Aaron Bernstein (Edinburgh: T. and T. Clark, 1888), 140.

secure the greatest impact on Esther, not merely to express his own personal grief or even to make Esther aware of the facts. Once Mordecai achieves his goals, he quickly returns to sitting as before in the king's gate (5:9) rather than continuing to express his mourning.

Thus, generally speaking, Mordecai's actions seem to be calculated, not spontaneous. Being human, he undoubtedly feels grief, even extreme anguish, over the entire situation. Yet he appears to be an extremely practical person who does whatever it takes to gain the greatest advantage from a given situation.

Do the actions of Mordecai in particular (4:1) and of the Jews in general (4:3), however, say anything concerning their spiritual demeanor? Are they actions that reflect either a depth of spirituality or, if not that, at least a recognition of the need to rely on God in a crisis situation?

The actions of tearing one's clothes (*qāraᶜ*—by Mordecai in 4:1) and of wailing (*zāᶜaq*—also by Mordecai in 4:1) are not necessarily indicators in Scripture of a spiritual activity. For those actions to be regarded as such, the context in which they occur must depict them to be so. So too is the case for the wearing (*lābaš*—by Mordecai in 4:1) or the laying upon[4] (*yāṣaᶜ*—by the Jews in 4:3) of sackcloth and ashes. In Scripture, when sackcloth and ashes denote an act of humbling by individuals or the turning of those individuals to God, direct textual indicators specify that those individuals who are wearing sackcloth do so because of a desire to secure a right relationship with God (cf. 2 Kings 19:1–2; 1 Chron. 21:16; Neh. 9:1). The wearing of sackcloth and ashes, however, does not always imply a humbling of oneself or a turning to God, but may simply be an outward expression of a deep inward grief (cf. Gen. 37:34; 2 Sam. 3:31).[5] Still other examples exist which the wearing of sackcloth and ashes is anything but an indicator of spirituality (1 Kings 20:31–32; 2 Kings 6:30).

4. Nothing of significance should be made of the fact that the people "lay down upon" rather than clothe themselves in sackcloth and ashes. Isaiah makes clear that such a practice existed among the Jews, when he speaks of the "spreading out" of sackcloth and ashes "as a bed."

5. C. F. Keil, *The Books of Ezra, Nehemiah, and Esther*, Biblical Commentary on the Old Testament, trans. Sophia Taylor (Grand Rapids: Eerdmans, n.d.), 350.

Thus, in Esther 4:1–3, because there is no direct scriptural statement revealing a spiritual component in conjunction with the presence of sackcloth and ashes, we should not assume that either Mordecai or the Jews are engaged in spiritual acts before God.

Nevertheless, Esther 4:3 presents what may be the nearest statement to an expression of a sense of spirituality in the Book of Esther. The Jews fast *(ṣôm)*, weep *[bākā(h)]*, and wail *(sāpad)*. Their actions parallel what the Lord declares through the prophet Joel that a wayward and devastated Israel should do (Joel 2:12): "Return to Me with all your heart, with fasting, with weeping, and with wailing." Their actions are the right actions, but the question remains: Are their hearts (their lives) right with God? There is no mention in the Book of Esther of the people performing the first component of that command in Joel, that is, returning to God with all their hearts.[6]

Still further, the Lord through Joel (2:13a) demands torn or broken hearts, not merely torn garments. In the Book of Esther, however, although the Jewish people tear their garments, they do not repent. They give no indication of a desire to be reconciled to God, to rely on God for deliverance, or even to give God credit for their ultimate deliverance (Esther 8:16–17; 9:17–19). All of these realities when taken together lead us to conclude that the author of the Book of Esther records that the Jews expressed a deep personal grief, but not a deep spiritual repentance.

Panic in the Palace (4:4–6)

When a bomb explodes, people even at a great distance from it are often impacted by it. They may be deafened by its sound or knocked over by its percussion. Frequently, they are unaware

6. The Hebrew of Joel 2:12 is unclear as to whether there are four separate actions—turning, fasting, weeping, and mourning—or only one action (turning), which being internal to the individual is manifested by the other three (external) actions (fasting, weeping, and mourning). If the former is the correct rendering of Joel 2:12, then the Jews of Esther's day most certainly did not fulfill all that they are required to fulfill in order for us to be able to recognize them as being truly spiritual. If the latter is true, then the Jews of the Book of Esther may be exhibiting a spiritual repentance. Yet, the remainder of the Book of Esther does not portray them to be committed to God. Furthermore, the grammar of Joel 2:12 favors the four-action position over the one-demonstrated-by-three-action view.

of what hit them. In 4:4–6, the shock waves of the king's edict (3:12–15) that burst forth upon the empire finally reverberate within the walls of the palace, and ultimately Esther is bowled over by them.

In verse 4, Esther's maidens and eunuchs bring news to her—news ostensibly of Mordecai's current actions. The news that they bring apparently focuses on Mordecai's predicament rather than on the edict;[7] it is information regarding the status of one they assume to be a close personal friend[8] of their queen.

Esther reacts to the news about Mordecai with a paroxysm of agony. She convulses in a genuine fit of anguish,[9] either out of sympathy for Mordecai (even though she does not comprehend the reason behind Mordecai's own wailing) or out of fear for Mordecai's life should he attempt to breach the king's gate dressed in sackcloth (v. 2). The latter seems to be the more likely view, since her first action toward Mordecai is not that of seeking to discover the reasons for his suffering but rather is an attempt to clothe him properly. Only later (v. 5) does she send messengers to learn the whys and wherefores of Mordecai's sorrow.

Despite Esther's concern for his well-being, Mordecai refuses her gift of clothing; yet he offers no explanation for his acts of mourning or even for his rejection of her offer. The author apparently does not consider Mordecai's motives to be as important to the development of the plot of the book as are his actions.

Moreover, structurally, such a side trip into Mordecai's reasonings would disrupt the flow of the story at this point. These three verses (vv. 4–6) function as a means of shifting the story from a description of the Jewish reaction to the edict of death (vv. 1–3) to a presentation of the need for Esther herself to react to that same edict (vv. 7–16). In doing so, these verses in high-speed fashion pile action upon action with little extraneous descriptive material: servants come and speak to Esther, Esther

7. Esther's immediate reaction in 4:4 (directed solely toward Mordecai) and her seeming lack of knowledge of the contents of the edict in verses 5–9 suggest that she is unaware of the predicament of her people, the Jews.

8. The assumption is made that Esther has not yet revealed her heritage (2:10, 20; 4:8), and thus her maidens and eunuchs do not know of her direct family connection to Mordecai, a Jew.

9. The Hebrew term *tithalḥal* is an intensive form of *ḥûl*, meaning "to be seized with painful grief." Keil, *The Books of Ezra, Nehemiah, and Esther*, 350.

writhes in anguish, Esther sends clothes to Mordecai, Mordecai refuses the clothes, Esther summons another servant and orders him to go to Mordecai, and the servant goes to Mordecai. In a few brief strokes of the quill, the author has captured a fast-paced, highly charged sequence of events. Furthermore, he has brought the story to still another, and an even more significant, crisis point, that is, whether Esther (who has kept secret her heritage) will or will not now intervene on behalf of her people.

Insider Information (4:7–8)

On Wall Street, where various stock exchanges and brokerage houses exist, use of insider information to improve one's stock portfolio is considered illegal. Severe fines, perhaps even prison sentences, are levied against those who take advantage of privileged company information to buy or sell stocks at a profit. The actions of those who have access to such insider information are often carefully monitored by government agencies or stock market personnel to ensure that insiders do not misuse that vital information for their own advantage or for the private advantage of others.

Mordecai (4:7–8) quite obviously possesses insider information. In fact, he possesses two crucial pieces of insider information—one regarding the king's business, the other regarding the queen's background. He attempts to use that insider information, moreover, to secure his own advantage. The question is whether he will be able to parlay his knowledge into a permanent advantage before the government authorities move in and shut down his operation (i.e., his life) permanently.

Being previously acquainted with the queen's background (2:5–7), Mordecai now secures a second piece of insider information. Somehow he has developed a conduit to what may have been some of the more closely guarded secrets of the palace[10]—secrets of which even the queen herself is unaware (4:5). Since Mordecai would not under normal circumstances have had direct access to

10. More than simply having access to information regarding the edict once it is published, Mordecai is aware of the critical details of the private conversation that occurred between the king and his prime minister regarding the establishment of the edict.

the meeting between Ahasuerus and Haman (3:8–11), he needed someone on the inside who could acquire such sensitive data. Who his conduit was, however, we are not told. Most likely, the individual was one of the servants who served in the king's inner circle and whose friendship Mordecai had cultivated.

Regardless of who that trusted informer was, Mordecai chooses to place his trust in still another individual, Hathach, a non-Jew and a servant whom Esther sends to Mordecai to discover the reason for Mordecai's suffering.[11] Mordecai risks placing himself in further jeopardy by revealing his possession of certain confidential government information; he also risks both Esther's position as queen and her life by exposing her as being a member of the Jewish people, a people under an imperial warrant of death.

Mordecai (4:7–8) conveys three crucial pieces of information to Hathach that he expects Hathach to relay to Esther the queen: background data regarding Mordecai's own situation, secret details regarding the formation of the death warrant, and a copy of the death warrant itself. The background data undoubtedly refers to the events of 3:1–6, that is, Mordecai's refusal to bow down to Haman and Haman's subsequent reaction. The secret details are specifically noted as being a precise accounting of the financial arrangements for the destruction of the Jews agreed upon between Haman and the king. Finally, the copy of the death warrant appears to be one of the official government documents distributed throughout Susa rather than merely a summary or privately made copy.[12] Thus Mordecai transmits to Esther what he believes to be irrefutable and over-

11. Cassel notes that "Mordecai understood that Esther had full confidence in her messenger, and so he communicated to him everything. Mordecai's message in return was surely not without danger, for it contained an accusation against the powerful Haman. It revealed Esther's Jewish origin, and it demanded from the queen something which might seriously affect her." Cassel, *An Explanatory Commentary on Esther*, 156.

12. The term *copy (pātšegen)* is ambiguous and may refer either to an original (i.e., official) copy or to a secondarily made copy. Two points, however, lend credence to the "official document" view: the use of the term elsewhere in Esther (3:14 and 8:13) to indicate an official document (the term is used nowhere else in Scripture; hence we cannot draw on other biblical passages for insight into its meaning) and the position of the term at the beginning of the verse suggests that the author gives special emphasis to this word.

whelming evidence (personal, private, and public) of treachery being perpetrated against the Jews – evidence upon which she must act.

The author uses his personal literary skills to convey the urgency and importance of what Mordecai is here demanding. The author, as Sandra Beth Berg notes, "structures the command on the pattern of 3 + 3. The initial set of three infinitives presents the grounds for Esther's expected actions, the latter [i.e., the actions themselves] suggested by the second set of infinitives."[13] Interestingly, the author records the infinitives according to a pattern that suggests ever-increasing difficulty of fulfillment:

Expected of the Servant	Expected of the Queen
1. to show (*rā'āh*)	to go (*bô'*)
2. to report (*nāgad*)	to seek favor (*ḥānan*)
3. to command (*ṣiwwāh*)	to plead or to seek (*biqqēš*)

With the declaration of Mordecai's final expectation (i.e., that Esther must plead before the king on behalf of her people), Esther's security behind the palace walls is jeopardized. No longer can she function as a member of Mordecai's protective witness program. Hathach now knows – Esther is a Jewess.

You Think You've Got Problems (4:9-12)

Have you ever started to tell somebody about a problem you were having, only to have that person interrupt you by saying "you think you've got problems; you should hear what I have to put up with" and then he or she would go on to explain in detail some minor problem he or she was facing? If so, then you can easily recognize what is happening in 4:9-12.

In 4:5, Esther asks Mordecai what seems to be the wrong in his life. When Mordecai responds by telling her that his problem is a life-threatening one, not only for himself but also for the entire Jewish population of Medo-Persia, and that Esther has

13. Sandra Beth Berg, *The Book of Esther: Motifs, Themes and Structures* (Missoula, Mont: Scholars, 1979), 90 n. 69.

the responsibility to do something about it (vv. 7-8), she immediately reacts by saying by saying, "you think you've got problems" (v.11). Esther does not now[14] express any conern for Mordecai's or her fellow Jews' plight; rather, she worries because she might personally have to risk incurring the wrath of governmental authority and that such an act would put her own life in jeopardy. Furthermore, she engages in one-upsmanship by slipping in the fact that, on top of all else, her marriage had not been going to well lately. Oh, woe is me!

This section (4:9-12) begins (vv. 9-10) and ends (v. 12) with a reminder of the physical seperation that exists between Esther and Mordecai, and the consequent process by which they are forced to communicate. They must rely on trusted intermediaries to carry their messages.

Verse 9 presents an example of a wise subordinate who does what he is ordered to do and who does it in such a way as not to offend others. Hathach proves himself to be not only a trusted servant, but also a prudent servant who recognizes his place in the chain of command. Specifically, when Mordecai wants him to show (*rā'āh*), report (*nāgad*), and command (*siwwāh*) Esther certain things (v.8), Hathach wisely only fulfilles the first two of Mordecai's desires (v.9).[15] Hathach, a servant, does not presume to overstep his position as a servant by attempting to command (*siwwāh*) the queen. Any commanding of the queen would have to be done by Mordecai himself.

Unlike Hathach, however, Esther does not immediately act as Mordecai would have her to do. Although she accepts Mordecai's explanation of the situation to be accurate, she questions his interpretation of how those facts are to have application in her life. She reacts with extreme reluctance, citing legal and personal excuses as justification for not fulfilling Mordecai's command to approach the king on behalf of her people.

14. Earliers (v.4) Esther writhed in anguish when she learned that Mordecai was wearing sackcloth and ashes. Now her focus in on her own problems, not on the suffering of others. As Huey states: "It appears that initially [upon learning of the edict] Esther was more concerned about her own welfare than about her people." F. B. Huey,Jr., "Esther," Expositor's Bible Commentary, ed. Frank E. Gaebelein, 12 vols. (Grand Rapids: Zondervan, 1988), 4:817.

15. Technically, the text records only that Hathach reported (*nāgad*) to Esther the words of Mordecai. The tenor of the text, however, suggests that Hathach also showed her the copy of the edict given to him by Mordecai.

Some commentators have understood Esther's reluctance to be parallel to Moses' hesitancy to accept God's call to action in Exodus 3:11; 4:10, 13; 6:12, 30. Michael V. Fox, however, puts Esther's protestation in its proper perspective: "This comparison is, however, instructive rather for the contrast it offers: Moses—like Gideon (Judg. 6:15), Saul (1 Sam. 9:21), and Jeremiah (Jer. 1:6)—hesitates out of feelings of personal unworthiness, whereas Esther is simply concerned for her personal safety."[16] Thus, nothing heroic can be seen in Esther's statements in 4:11. She expresses rational and logical fears—fears that she overcomes when she realizes she has no real alternative but to do so (4:15–16; 5:1–4; 7:2–6).

As previously noted, in 4:11 Esther offers two excuses—one on legal grounds, the other on personal grounds. By the choice of her words and the patterning of her response, Esther chides Mordecai for failing to grasp the seriousness of the legal predicament in which he is placing her. She emphasizes the fact that everybody—from the individual who directly serves the king in the palace to the least educated peasant in the far regions of the empire—knows the law regarding the procedure for approaching the king.[17] Mordecai, she believes, could not be ignorant of those facts; he certainly must be aware of the extreme danger that would face her if she carried out his commands. To Esther's way of thinking, there is a strong likelihood that she will be executed if she approaches the king uninvited.

Esther, however, fails to mention a second legal provision—one that would allow her to avoid any and all of this danger. That provision permitted an individual to make a formal petition for an audience with the king.[18] Approaching the king in that way (assuming that the king granted the request) reduced the risk of having to face the wrath of a king whose domain had been disturbed. Esther conveniently forgets this provision in her plea to Mordecai to allow her to be absolved from this burden of being a representative on behalf of her people, the Jews.

16. Fox, *Character and Ideology in the Book of Esther*, 61–62.

17. Fox notes that "[t]here is a touch of reproach in her [Esther's] words." Ibid., 61.

18. Herodotus 3.72, 77, 84, 118, 140. See also Berg, *The Book of Esther,* 90 n. 70; Huey, "Esther," 817.

In addition, Esther presents a second excuse, a personal one. She cannot be certain that the king would respond favorably to her anymore, for she and her husband, the king, have not had any physical contact for the past thirty days (4:11).[19] They no longer are the intimate lovers they once were (2:17). As far as Esther is concerned, the timing could not be any worse.

Perhaps now, Esther is finally beginning to realize the truth of words that much later would be penned by a wise Puritan author: "If you marry a child of the devil you can expect to have trouble with your father-in-law."[20]

This section closes with an unnamed group of servants, not simply Hathach, whom Esther has commanded (4:10), transmitting Esther's words to Mordecai (v. 12). Why Hathach himself does not perform this task (or at least does not perform it alone) is a mystery.

Déjà Vu—All Over Again (4:13–14)

Former professional baseball player and manager Yogi Berra has been credited for the origination of numerous statements that cause his listeners to do double takes, such as: "It's not over until it's over," "I didn't say everything I said," and "It's déjà vu all over again."

Mordecai in 4:13–14 seems to adopt Yogi Berra's "déjà vu" statement for his own use. He argues that the Jews are survivors—they have been in difficult situations before and they have always managed to escape. This time would be no different; they would be delivered once more. His words are words of boldness and confidence.

Concerning these words of Mordecai, Paulus Cassel pens the following sentiment—a sentiment that sounds so good and uplifting, that I almost wish it were true: "His [Mordecai's] chief design was to plant in her [Esther's] heart faith in an overruling Providence, and then she would have nothing to fear.—He was the right man to do this, because she knew how very much he

19. Esther emphasizes her point by adding the unneeded personal pronoun *I* to the beginning of this clause: "and I, I have not been called to come unto the king. . . ."

20. Cited in H. A. Ironside, *Notes on the Book of Esther*, 1905, *Notes on the Books of Ezra, Nehemiah, and Esther* (New York: Loizeaux, 1960), 110.

loved her. He would not advise her to sacrifice her life needlessly."[21] Unfortunately, Cassel's perspective on the passage does not match that of the author of the Book of Esther for at least three reasons: Mordecai never mentions God in these verses or intimates that God would be the one who delivers Israel; Mordecai does everything he can here to instill, not alleviate, fear in Esther; and although Mordecai may not desire Esther to "sacrifice her life needlessly," he does threaten her with the certainty of death and the subsequent destruction of her family. Such a threat seems strange coming from one of whom Cassel writes, "she knew how very much he loved her."[22]

In 4:13, Mordecai counters Esther's reluctance to act by rifling back a negative command: "do not think you will escape." He reads into her reaction of verse 11 a strong orientation to self-preservation; she wants first and foremost to save her own life. Mordecai, however, warns her against, not merely having the thought cross her mind, but dwelling on, even planning,[23] how she will remain safe and secure within the palace.

Mordecai makes certain that Esther realizes she has no better chance of surviving than does any other Jew in the empire.[24] In fact, in verse 14, he guarantees that she will die—"actually threatens Esther's life"[25]—if she does not do what he tells her to

21. Cassel, *An Explanatory Commentary on Esther*, 164.

22. Mordecai undoubtedly loved Esther very much (2:11), but at times he had a strange way of showing it: encouraging her to marry a heathen and commanding her to keep her faith hidden (2:10, 20).

23. Literally, Mordecai says, "do not form (devise) an idea in your soul" *(ʾal-tᵉdammî ḇᵉnapšēḵ)*.

24. Paton points out that Mordecai makes "[n]o allowance . . . for the possibility that the King may make an exception in Esther's favour." Lewis Bayles Paton, *The Book of Esther*, International Critical Commentary, ed. Samuel Rolles Driver, Alfred Plummer, and Charles Augustus Briggs (Edinburgh: T. and T. Clark, 1908), 222. Mordecai did not make an allowance, because Mordecai could not. The law of the Medes and Persians was inviolable, even by a king (1:19; 8:8).

25. Ronald W. Pierce, "The Politics of Esther and Mordecai: Courage or Compromise?" *Bulletin for Biblical Research* 2 (1992): 87. Pierce further argues that there is a sinister side to this threat that most people fail to see or choose to overlook. He concludes that "it seems that he [Mordecai] was prepared to take matters into his own hands if she refused to help. And, if it became necessary, he would make sure that she paid the price for her disloyalty to her people." Without a doubt, Mordecai does threaten Esther with the certainty of

do. Her chance of survival should she fail even to attempt to do what Mordecai says would be worse than that of the rest of the Jews, because somehow they or at least a remnant of them would avoid annihilation, but she most certainly would die.

Fox assesses Esther's predicament in light of the debacle with Vashti in chapter 1: "It is dangerous for her [Esther] to stay out of the king's presence as well as to enter into it, as Vashti discovered when she was called to him. . . . Esther, however, would be hazarding death, not banishment."[26] Fox's connection of Esther's situation to Vashti's is instructive and brings to light two important considerations. First, the situations are not directly parallel to one another. Vashti encountered the king's wrath for not entering the king's presence when he summoned her; Esther, however, may get into trouble if she does. She also may or may not (irrespective of Mordecai's threat in 4:14) face death if she does not enter into the king's presence. Second, Vashti did not know what the penalty would be for her disobedience; Esther, however, knows full well what penalty (if any) might be meted out against her.

Mordecai, moreover, goes one step further in his threat to Esther. Not only will she die (if she maintains her silence),[27] but her father's house[28] also will face extinction (based also on

---

her death and the end of her father's line in history. The Scripture, however, does not provide sufficient information to corroborate or refute Pierce's contention that Mordecai intends "to take matters into his own hands."

26. Fox, *Character and Ideology in the Book of Esther*, 62. Clines concurs and, in light of verse 14, adds that "whereas Vashti had risked only the wrath of the king Esther risks the king's sentence of death or else a divine punishment on her and her family." David J. A. Clines, "The Esther Scroll: The Story of the Story," *Journal for the Study of the Old Testament: Supplement* 30 (Sheffield: University of Sheffield, 1984), 35. Clines's reference to "divine punishment," however, goes beyond what the text states. Mordecai makes no suggestion as to the origin of the potential judgment on Esther and her family.

27. Cassel notes that the use of the infinitive here conveys the idea of a "continuance of silence." Cassel, *An Explanatory Commentary on Esther*, 165. In other words, Mordecai warns Esther against maintaining the status quo of hiding her ancestral background—something she has been doing faithfully at Mordecai's command for the past five years.

28. The Scripture does not indicate that Esther is the sole child born to her father, Abihail. Conceivably, she may have brothers and sisters who also are adopted (by Mordecai or others) or who at this time either are single adults or have established their own families.

Esther's unwillingness to act appropriately in this situation). Mordecai's threat is serious. To have one's family eternally cut off was a terrifying prospect to the ancient Israelite who, in part, understood his or her life in some way bound up in the preservation of his or her line. Esther, therefore, certainly could not afford to take Mordecai's challenge lightly.

Mordecai, however, is not a prophet of doom. Curiously, in the midst of his threat to Esther, he expresses confidence that the Jews would not be eradicated, but would be delivered. Ironically, he does not say how or by whom, merely that deliverance would come "from another place."

Some commentators have incorrectly assumed that the phrase *from another place* is an indirect reference to God.[29] They base their assumption either on logic ("whom or what else could Mordecai mean?") or on the use of the Hebrew term *māqôm* (place) in later Hebrew history as a reference to God.[30] Yet, neither argument fits the facts. First, the context of the Book of Esther reveals that Mordecai nowhere makes any reference, direct or indirect, to God. In fact, in this passage, Mordecai seems to go out of his way to avoid any reference to God. Second, the use of *māqôm* (place) to refer to God does not come into vogue until rabbinic times, hundreds of years after the writing of the Book of Esther.[31] Furthermore, the author of the Book of Esther records Mordecai as juxtaposing the adjective *ʾaḥēr* (another) to the noun *māqôm.* If *māqôm* functions as a surrogate for the term *God,* then who is the other god to whom Mordecai is referring?[32] The grammar as well as the logic of this passage dictates that deliver-

29. Meir Zlotowitz, trans. and comp., *The Megillah: The Book of Esther: A New Translation with a Commentary Anthologized from Talmudic, Midrashic and Rabbinic Sources* (Brooklyn: Mesorah, 1981), 80.

30. Ackroyd notes that "[t]he use of surrogates for the name of God is well-known from later Jewish practice. מָקוֹם; *[māqôm]* was one of these surrogates. . . ." Peter R. Ackroyd, "Two Hebrew Notes," *Annual of the Swedish Theological Institute* 5 (1967): 82.

31. Fox explains this rabbinic sense as follows: "In rabbinic Hebrew, God is called 'the Place' because (according to the most likely explanation) he is the place in which the world exists (Genesis Rabba §68)." Fox, *Character and Ideology in the Book of Esther*, 63.

32. As Ackroyd points out, "[n]o such rendering is admissible." Ackroyd, "Two Hebrew Notes," 83.

ance for the Jews would come from some unspecified source other than God.[33] Mordecai's failure here to credit God for Israel's anticipated deliverance is one more confirmation of his lack of spiritual depth.

Interestingly, Mordecai concludes his reproof of Esther in 4:14 with a remarkable statement: "Who knows if for a time such as this you have attained to royalty?" Does Mordecai hint at God's providential care here? Sadly, there is nothing in the passage to suggest that Mordecai's words mean anything different than what he is proposing may be Esther's destiny to do, that is, her ultimate purpose for having become queen.

Expecting the Worst (4:15–17)

Verses 15–17, in particular verse 16, have been used in many ways by many people to justify a wide variety of positions regarding Esther's state of mind, ranging anywhere from a strong commitment to God, to a sense of resignation, to a nonspiritual this-is-the-only-option-I-have-left mentality, to a belief that by going to the king voluntarily she would no longer be able to consider Mordecai as her legal husband.[34] The logic used to support some of these views is in many ways similar to that found in that old poem, "Why Are Fire Engines Red?"

> They have four wheels and eight men;
> four plus eight is twelve;
> twelve inches make a ruler;
> a ruler is Queen Elizabeth;
> Queen Elizabeth sails the seven seas;
> the seven seas have fish;
> the fish have fins;

33. Berg, *The Book of Esther,* 76; Clines, "The Esther Scroll," 36; Fox, *Character and Ideology in the Book of Esther*, 63.

34. Yes, you read that last phrase correctly. According to the *Megillah*, 15a n. 12, "[b]y submitting voluntarily to Ahasuerus she [Esther] would be for ever forbidden to Mordecai who was . . . her legitimate husband, according to the law which forbids a wife to her husband where she had relations of her own free will with another man." Rabbah b. Lema "determined" that Esther was Mordecai's wife by interpreting the words "as she had done when under his care" in Esther 2:20 to mean "that she used to rise up from the lap of Ahasuerus and bathe and sit in the lap of Mordecai [as wife]." *Megillah*, 13b and 13b n. 5.

the Finns hate the Russians;
the Russians are red;[35]
fire engines are always rushin';
so they're red.[36]

We need to be careful that we too do not misuse logic in our attempts to justify a given position. We must draw from the Scripture the truths that are contained therein and, at the same time, make certain that we do not read our own ideas (i.e., biases) into the text or intentionally omit text-truths in order to skew the data to suit our purposes.

In 4:15, Esther sends her reply to Mordecai's challenge. There is no indication as to how long she took to respond; there is also no information regarding the mental state of either Esther, the sender, or Mordecai, the receiver.

Whereas little controversy surrounds 4:15 (apart from the inability to determine precisely whom Esther entrusts to carry her message to Mordecai), there is much debate regarding 4:16. Several issues take center stage: the significance of fasting relative to the spiritual condition of Esther, Mordecai, and the Jews; the purpose of Esther's maids fasting; the function of Esther's comment regarding the law; and the meaning of Esther's declaration: "If I perish, I perish."

First, Esther commands a three-day fast[37] that Mordecai and the rest of the Jews in Susa are to observe. She, with her maidservants, would do likewise. Is this a spiritual act that Esther is calling for? Not necessarily. As we have seen (4:1–3), fasting does not constitute a proof of the spirituality of the practitioner. Unbelievers fast[38] and so do the people of God who are not in

35. The word *red* is used as a reference to the time when Russia (i.e., the Union of Soviet Socialist Republics) was under communist domination, red being the color used in a derogatory manner by noncommunist countries to describe communists: e.g., "the Red Menace."

36. D. A. Carson, *Exegetical Fallacies* (Grand Rapids: Baker, 1984), 91.

37. Keil calculates that this fast would last approximately forty to forty-five hours, not seventy-two as we might initially suppose. He states: "The fasting . . . would not begin till midday; and on the third day Esther went to the king to invite him on that day to a banquet, which would surely take place in the forenoon. Thus the three days' fast would last from the afternoon of the first to the forenoon of the third day, *i.e.* from 40 to 45 hours." Keil, *The Books of Ezra, Nehemiah, and Esther*, 355.

proper fellowship with God (e.g., Isa. 58:3–5; Zech. 7:5), as well as do those believers who are in (or desirous of being in) a right relationship with God (e.g., 2 Sam. 12:22; Neh. 9:1).

What may be more telling, however, is the surprising lack of any mention of prayer in this context where one would rightly expect to find it. As F. B. Huey points out, "[p]rayer and fasting before God were customary concurrent practices in times of sorrow, anxiety, or penitence (cf. 1 Sam. 1:7–10; 2 Sam. 12:16–17; Ezra 8:23; Isa. 58:2–5; Jer. 14:12; Dan. 9:3; Zech. 7:3–5)."[39] Yet, to assume that prayer it to be considered as a component of fasting in Esther 4:16, as some suggest,[40] "is not only to beg the question," but also, as Ronald W. Pierce cautions us, "to ignore the possibility that the very point the writer wishes to make is that, in fact, prayer was absent in the case of Esther and Mordecai."[41]

A further indictment associated with Esther's fast is the failure of the Jews to observe the feast of the Passover. Esther's command to fast for three days would preclude any Jew from partaking in the Passover feast since the fast would include the fifteenth of Nisan, the first day of the Passover celebration. Thus all Jews who fasted in accordance with Esther's dictates would violate God's law—a law that was to be celebrated for all generations (Exod. 12:14).

Whereas Esther's call to fast is the first controversial issue in Esther 4:16, the second is her statement that her maidens would also fast. What was the purpose of having heathen maidens fast? Their prayers, if they offered any, would not be directed to the true God, but to the gods of Medo-Persia. Fur-

38. The practice of fasting is a common religious practice found in various religions throughout the world. J. Behm, "νῆστις, νηστεύω, νηστεία," *Theological Dictionary of the New Testament*, ed. Gerhard Kittel, trans. and ed. Geoffrey W. Bromiley (Grand Rapids: Eerdmans, 1967), 4:926; Berg, *The Book of Esther*, 91 n. 76.

39. Huey, "Esther," 817. Technically speaking, 1 Sam. 1:7–10 and Zech. 7:3–5 may not precisely support Huey's statement of "concurrent practices."

40. Joyce G. Baldwin, *Esther: An Introduction and Commentary*, Tyndale Old Testament Commentaries, ed. D. J. Wiseman (Downers Grove: InterVarsity, 1984), 80; Paton, *The Book of Esther*, 169.

41. Pierce, "The Politics of Esther and Mordecai: Courage or Compromise?" 88. Huey also highlights the fact that "[t]he author of Esther is careful . . . to avoid the mention of God or that prayer was made to him." Huey, "Esther," 817.

thermore, it also is very unlikely that Esther had converted her maidservants to Judaism (as some suggest),[42] since she had not yet made known her Jewish heritage to those in the palace (2:20). Most likely she had them fast since they were her property and they were to do whatever she commanded them to do. The fact that the author mentions Esther's inclusion of her heathen maidservants here speaks volumes regarding her spiritual condition (or lack thereof).

The third controversy (albeit less significant than the other three) of 4:16 concerns Esther's reminder to Mordecai of the supposed illegality of the action which he is proposing that she undertake. This statement is controversial for three reasons: Esther does not need to break any law to accomplish Mordecai's dictate;[43] Esther demonstrates a greater concern for the human-generated laws of the land than for the laws of God;[44] and Esther seems to use the law as a slap in Mordecai's face—having made mention of the law earlier, there does not appear to be any need for her to bring it up again, other than to remind Mordecai of what it is that he is asking her to do.

The fourth and most controversial issue of 4:16 revolves around Esther's statement: "If I perish, I perish." Many scholars have argued that Esther's declaration displays courage, others that it expresses a sense of resignation. The arguments are varied, dealing with issues of grammar, with Genesis 43:14 as a parallel passage, and with the immediate context of the passage.

Focusing on the grammar of 4:16, Cassel argues that Esther shows courage. He states: "The whole force of these thoughts lies in the repetition of the verb. She [Esther] gives by this expression free vent to her pent-up feelings of misery and woe, and to her determination, what ever may come, to submit to the will of God."[45] Cassel's argument, however, is weak. The mere

42. See Paton, *The Book of Esther*, 226.

43. Two ways existed by which Esther could avoid the consequences of the current law: she could formally petition an audience with the king, or the king could extend his scepter to her and thereby allow her to come freely into his presence. See the discussion of these options in 4:11.

44. Ironically, after all these years of being disobedient to the laws of God regarding dietary requirements, religious rites and festivals, and open worship of the true God of heaven, Esther shows great concern for adhering to human-generated laws.

repetition of a Hebrew verb does not constitute proof of either forcefulness or determination.[46]

By contrast, Ludwig Koehler and Walter Baumgartner argue for resignation. They do so because of the use of the conjunction *wᵉḵaʾăšer* (and if) which they identify as being that which is found *"in [a] formula of resignation."*[47] They cite only two examples: Genesis 43:14 and Esther 4:16. The interpretation of those verses, however, is greatly debated.

Despite the weakness of the Koehler-Baumgartner argument, the grammar of the statement ("and if I perish, I perish") lends support to their position. Interestingly, that support comes not from the conjunction but from the verbs (despite Cassel). The author uses the perfect rather than the imperfect verb form, suggesting a completed action or state of affairs, rather than an incompleted one. William Gesenius identifies the sense of the perfects being used here as that which is used "[t]o express actions or facts, which are meant to be indicated as existing in the future in a completed state."[48] Thus, by using the perfect, Esther declares her demise to be, in essence, a *fait accompli*.

Along with the grammar, both positions (i.e., courage vs. resignation) contend that Genesis 43:14 (with its sentence pattern[49] similar to that found in Esther 4:16—"if I am bereaved of my children, I am bereaved") supports their individual viewpoints.

In Genesis 42, Jacob sends ten of his sons (keeping his youngest son, Benjamin, with him) to Egypt to buy food so that they could survive a famine. Joseph, the twelfth son and the one

45. Cassel, *An Explanatory Commentary on Esther*, 172.

46. There is a grammatical pattern in which an infinitive absolute verb form followed by a finite verb form of the same stem is used to show emphasis. Bruce K. Waltke and M. O'Connor, *An Introduction to Biblical Hebrew Syntax* (Winona Lake, Ind.: Eisenbrauns, 1990), §35.2.1.c. That grammatical rule, however, does not apply here since neither verb is an infinitive absolute.

47. Ludwig Koehler and Walter Baumgartner, eds., *Lexicon in Veteris Testamenti Libros* (Leiden: Brill, 1985), 418.

48. William Gesenius, *Hebrew Grammar*, ed. E. Kautzsch and A. E. Cowley (1910, 2d ed.; Oxford: Clarendon, 1966), §106.o. Gesenius labels Gen. 43:14 specifically as "an expression of despairing resignation," and cites Esther 4:16 as a cross-reference of this use of the perfect.

49. Jacob uses the same *ḵaʾăšer* conjunction as found in Esther 4:16 to introduce the two verbs of his declaration, which again, as is the case for the verbs in Esther 4:16, are both in the perfect form.

whom Jacob presumes had died many years earlier, has risen to the second most powerful position in Egypt and is in charge of the distribution of food. He recognizes his brothers but dos not initially reveal himself to them. When his brothers return to their father with the food, Joseph warns them not to return to Egypt again unless they bring with them their youngest brother. Joseph then imprisons one of the brothers, Simeon, to ensure that the other brothers will bring their youngest brother with them the next time they come to Egypt. The nine brothers return to their father who is distraught at their news.

In Genesis 42:36, Jacob assumes the worst – Joseph is lost to him, so is Simeon, and so will be Benjamin if Benjamin goes down to Egypt. Thus Jacob takes no action until the food supplies are once again depleted (43:1-2). He finally relents and allow his sons to take Benjamin with them. Jacob hopes that God will be compassionate but, in 43:14, he concludes, "as for me, if I am bereaved of my children, I am bereaved."

None of the events of Genesis 42-43 suggests that Jacob's statement of 43:14 is one of courage. Quite the opposite, Jacob appears to be forced into his decision. Thus, the evidence seems to suggest that, if Genesis 43:14 is a legitimate parallel passage to Esther 4:16, it argues for Esther's statement as being one of resignation rather than one of courage.

One further argument in the resignation-courage debate concerns the immediate context of Esther 4:16. Everything seems to suggest that Esther has no expectation of success. She is fighting two imperial laws and a serious threat issued by her adopted father. The first inviolable law (4:11, 16) proclaims death to any who enter the king's presence uninvited. Esther, according to 4:11, has not been invited into the king's presence for a period of thirty days. Consequently, she has no confidence that he will extend to her the sceptre of permission. Thus she can only anticipate the worst, that is, immediate death, if she proceeds with Mordecai's plan. Finally, in 4:13-14, Mordecai pronounces a death sentence for Esther if she does not act according to his will. Esther realizes that Mordecai's threat is not issued with a wink of the eye, but with the full seriousness of the reality of its being carried out. Thus, in Esther's mind, she can expect nothing but death whether she acts or does not act.

Esther realizes that she has no viable option but to do what Mordecai commands. His plan offers the only hope of changing her fate. Yet, even that plan holds no guarantees of success, since the king has no power to change the official law of the Medes and Persians that has been enacted against the Jews. Furthermore, the king may side with Haman against Esther, or the king may, for some unknown reason, have lost all interest in Esther and thus not care whether she or her people live or die. Thus, as Lewis Bayles Paton writes: "No religious enthusiasm lights up Esther's resolve. She goes [to the king], as one would submit to an operation, because there is a chance of escaping death in that way."[50] All other options have been taken away from her, and what is left seemingly forces her into her worst nightmare. All things considered, Esther's declaration is an expression of resignation, not of courage.

Esther 4:17 concludes a highly controversial section of the Book of Esther. Even this seemingly straightforward statement of Mordecai's departure to carry out Esther's commands has become the center of some minor debate. The focus of attention is on the interpretation of the initial verb of the verse, *wayyaʿăbōr*, which may convey legitimately the meaning of either "and he transgressed" or "and he crossed over."

Those who favor the "transgression" view assume that the author alludes to Mordecai's failure to keep the feast of Passover in accordance with Exodus 12. As is noted, Esther's commandment in 4:16 to fast for three days would not have permitted the Jews to celebrate the first day of Passover; thus they (and here in particular, Mordecai) would be "transgressing" the law.[51] Despite this argument, the translation of *wayyaʿăbōr* as "and he transgressed" is not widely held.

Most commentators render *wayyaʿăbōr* to express a directional sense of Mordecai's departure ("and he went away") from where he was to where the Jews of the city of Susa lived. That interpretation is drawn from the fact that the palace of Susa was located on one side of the Ulai (or Choaspes) River (see Dan.

50. Paton, *The Book of Esther*, 226.
51. Ibid., 226–27; Zlotowitz, *The Megillah*, 82.

8:2), whereas the citizenry of the city of Susa were situated on the other.[52] Thus Mordecai would have had to have crossed over the river in order to do what Esther had commanded him to do.

The directional interpretation appears to be preferable to the transgression view, since the directional view fits better with the context and the structure of the chapter than does the transgression view. If the directional meaning is correct, then 4:17 forms a type of *inclusio* with 4:1–2. Thus, whereas in 4:1–2, Mordecai crosses over to the entrance of the palace, in verse 17 he crosses back over to the city from the entrance of the palace. By use of this *inclusio,* the author suggests that he has completed his discussion about the events that took place in front of the palace gate. He can now move the story on to its next critical juncture.[53]

Tracking the Truths

Like building blocks, the truths of Esther 4 build on those of previous chapters. Not only is the storyline moved forward, but so also are the lessons that God is teaching his people.

An analysis of the actions of Mordecai and Esther in chapter 4 leads to the discovery of several valuable truths:

1. God's people need to step up to the responsibility given to them. Mordecai had a job to do: convince Esther to approach the king on behalf of the Jews. Esther, in turn, had a job to do: approach the king on behalf of the Jews. Each had a task for which he or she was responsible,[54] and ultimately each did what he or she had to do. Had either of

52. Cassel, *An Explanatory Commentary on Esther*, 173–74; Paton, *The Book of Esther*, 226–27.

53. As noted (discussion of Esther 3:12–14), various ancient translations insert between 4:17 and 5:1 two prayers, one purportedly offered by Mordecai, the other by Esther. There is, however, no Hebrew manuscript evidence to suggest that either of those prayers is part of the original text of the Scripture.

54. Mordecai's question to Esther in 4:14—"Who knows if for a time such as this you have attained to royalty?"—suggests a principle that each person has a specific purpose for his or her life. The author could easily have left that question out of the story with little change to the overall storyline. The fact that he includes it implies that the idea does carry some weight with him. The author, however, does not appear to be making a major point of this principle, since 4:14 is the only place in the book where he suggests such a concept.

them chosen to act otherwise, the events and subsequent outcomes might have turned out differently for the Jews of Medo-Persia than those that are recorded in the Book of Esther.

2. Crisis situations, real or perceived, often bring out the true character of people. The reader of the Book of Esther can find numerous examples of this truth not only in chapter 4 but also throughout the book:
   a. Mordecai is seen as a strong-willed, very determined individual (cf. 2:22; 3:2–4; 4:1–4, 13–14).
   b. Esther begins to develop into a person who is willing to take responsibility and to act responsibly (4:15–16).
   c. Ahasuerus elsewhere (1:12–21; 2:1–4) shows a lack of control and a dependence on others to make decisions for him.
   d. Haman elsewhere (in the face of a perceived crisis) loses his temper but maintains his self-control (3:5–15; 5:9–14), or (in the face of more a significant crisis) breaks under the pressure and loses self-control (6:10–13; 7:3–8).
3. You can run but you cannot hide. If Esther the queen (protected by her position, power, wealth, and fame) could not escape the fate of the Jews, what hope does any member of the family of God have for escaping the attacks of the enemy?
4. Circumstances do not in and of themselves necessarily drive people to God. Despite any number of different types of circumstances, people may choose to live as though God does not exist. In Esther's case, neither a life of luxury nor the threat of annihilation was sufficient to cause her to seek God's help openly.

Transitions and Trauma

Fox identifies Esther 4:13–17 as the turning point in Esther's process of maturation: "She moves from being a dependent of others (all of them men) to an independent operator who, whatever the objective restrictions on her freedom, will work out her own plans and execute them in order to manipulate one man and break another."[55] Without a doubt, Esther does seem to come into her

55. Fox, *Character and Ideology in the Book of Esther*, 66.

own at the end of chapter 4. She now dictates to Mordecai what he and the Jews must do, and he and (presumably) they obey.

Up to this point Mordecai has dominated the relationship. He has functioned in the role of Esther's father (2:7), and in so doing has given orders that she has obeyed, whether under his care (2:10) or married to the king (2:20). Even in chapter 4, until the end of the chapter, Mordecai controls the relationship. From this point on, however, Esther and Mordecai appear to function generally as equals—Esther as queen and Mordecai as prime minister. Only in the final chapter does Esther fade from prominence and Mordecai comes to the fore again (10:2–3).

The changes of chapter 4 portend even greater changes. Yet, for the moment, the trauma of the crisis remains unabated. The Jews still face mass execution with no foreseeable possibility of their deliverance. Ironically, as Fox comments, the sole hope for the Jews lies in the hands of "a young lady whose life has hitherto been devoted to beauty treatments and the royal bed."[56]

Whether Esther is up to the challenge placed before her remains to be seen.

56. Ibid., 67.

15

A Little Gallows Humor
(5:1–14)

What makes for a good joke or for humor in general? The answer to that question depends, of course, on who is doing the answering, and whether the humor is visual or verbal. Visual humor includes situation comedy, pranks, sleight-of-hand, pratfalls, and slapstick—everything from the sublime to the ridiculous. Verbal humor finds acceptance among different people for a variety of reasons. Some people prefer jokes told as long and involved stories; others prefer word plays; still others favor ridiculous exaggeration, insult, or general absurdity. Verbal humor also includes puns, one-liners, riddles, parodies, or satires.

In chapter 5, the author begins to lay the foundation for a much needed comic relief in this potentially tragic story. He sets the stage that later allows him to describe certain ironic twists in the fortunes of three of the main characters—twists that will produce joyful laughter among his readers. He lays this foundation by juxtaposing two similar yet diametrically opposed events: a royal banquet and a gathering of family and friends.

These two events parallel one another on several notable counts. The main characters in each situation (i.e., Esther at the royal banquet and Haman at the gathering of family and friends)

1. encounter a personal crisis that they want resolved;
2. approach their respective spouses for encouragement;
3. function within the same time frame
   a. appeal to spouse "today";
   b. act to set a trap "today"; and
   c. determine to approach the king for a resolution "tomorrow."

The writing of chapter 5 is incredibly intricate. The author interweaves not only these parallel events but also the following highly contrasting actions of Jewish and Gentile machinations that eventually lead to a volatile conclusion:

	Jewish Plotting (Esther) (5:1–8)	*Gentile Plotting (Haman) (5:9–14)*
1.	does not exhibit any emotion	exhibits a variety of emotions
2.	approaches spouse cautiously	approaches spouse confidently
3.	is controlled by the proceedings	controls the proceedings
4.	speaks humbly as a servant	speaks boldly as a braggart
5.	fails to secure guidance from spouse	secures guidance from spouse
6.	keeps plot secret	develops plot openly

Furthermore, the events described in chapter 5 are written in such a way as to keep readers on the edges of their collective seats:

1. Esther curiously fails to ask immediately for her request that the king presumably would have granted.
2. Esther, in a surprising move, invites her archenemy to a banquet (twice).
3. Esther is ambiguous when she invites the king and Haman to the first banquet, saying that the banquet is for "him." To which "him" is she referring—to the king or to Haman? She

seems to be setting up a condition of doubt in the mind of the king to whom she must make her appeal.

4. Esther risks angering the king (by failing to respond as he expects) when she hesitates to reveal her petition when given a second opportunity to do so.
5. Both Esther and Haman set into motion their diametrically opposed strategies without either being aware of the scheming of the other.
6. Although the plans of Esther and Haman follow a similar time frame, Haman's are designed to come to fruition sooner than are Esther's. Her plans therefore appear to be headed for a critical setback that could jeopardize their desired outcome.

Tension runs high. The two leading Jews place themselves in precarious positions, Esther testing the patience of the Gentile king, Mordecai the patience of the Gentile prime minister. Gentiles look forward to a wonderful tomorrow, a day that is expected to bring much personal gratification. Nothing seems to be working right for the Jews. Their world is completely out of kilter.

Parallel Battle Plans

The author designs the contents of 5:1–14 according to a parallel literary structure. He does so in order to emphasize the contrastive nature of the battle plans being implemented by a Jew (i.e., Esther) on the one hand (vv. 1–8) and by a Gentile (i.e., Haman) on the other (vv. 9–14). The antagonists—Jew first, then Gentile—are seen to act as follows:

A Approaches spouse regarding the problem of the enemy (5:1–2)
 B Interacts with people in a festive but tainted atmosphere (5:3–6)
  C Establishes a framework to meet the crisis head-on, tomorrow (5:7–8)
A′ Approaches spouse regarding the problem of the enemy (5:9–10)
 B′ Interacts with people in a festive but tainted atmosphere (5:11–12)
  C′ Establishes a framework to meet the crisis head-on, tomorrow (5:13–14)

The literary structure as well as the contents of the chapter reveal what appears to be the superseding of a Jewish plan by the ascendancy of a Gentile plan. What was a desperate situation for the Jews (3:13) now looks even more hopeless.

Crossing the Rubicon (5:1–2)

History records that on 10 January 49 B.C., Julius Caesar, who by the Senate of Rome had been declared an enemy of the Roman state, took a step that forever changed the course of history—he crossed the Rubicon. By leaving his home province and crossing that shallow river with his army, Caesar in effect had declared war on the Roman Empire: *Alea jacta est*—"The die is cast."

Caesar risked his all and succeeded as perhaps no one else could. Will the same be true for Esther when she takes that one small step across the threshold to the king's royal hall?

Unlike what one might anticipate, the author at this point (5:1) does not discuss the possible outcomes of Esther's actions. Instead, he focuses the readers' attention directly on that Caesar-like move that Esther takes. Significantly, he presents that move almost as an everyday event, with no special fanfare.

Interestingly, the author does not build the tension surrounding Esther's approach to the king, but immediately reveals that the king graciously welcomes Esther into his presence. Thus the author does not suggest that Esther's actions are anything other than to be expected. He does not paint her as a heroine of superhuman proportions, but merely as someone who has a task to do (albeit difficult) and who does it calmly and efficiently.[1]

The events of chapter 5 take place "on the third day," that is, the day the fast that Esther instituted was to end (4:16). Esther wisely sheds the remnants of her fasting and then dresses herself appropriately to meet the king. Literally, she puts on royalty *(malk̲ût)*, a reference to royal robes.

1. The Septuagint inserts a significant amount of text at this point in an attempt to explain Esther's appearance and feelings, as well as the king's reaction to seeing her. The Septuagint pictures Esther fainting, God transforming the king's heart so that the king comforts Esther, and Esther fainting once again. The actions depicted by the Septuagint, however, are not included in the Hebrew manuscripts and thus must be relegated to the status of interesting speculation.

Esther now (5:2) makes her approach to the king who is seated on his throne in the throne room (lit., in the royal house). Immediately upon being seen (by the king) standing in the court, Esther secures the king's good pleasure. Michael V. Fox astutely points out that, when reference is made to Esther acquiring the king's favor, two distinct patterns of verb usage occur that suggest that Esther downplays her influence over the king. The first is used consistently (2:9, 15, 17; 5:2) by the narrator who, by use of the verb *nāśāʾ* (to gain), projects Esther as aggressively gaining the king's favor. The second, which implies passivity on Esther's part and initiative on the king's, is to be found coming from Esther's lips (5:8; 7:3; 8:5) when she expresses the hope that she has found *(māṣāʾ)* favor in the king's eyes.[2] Thus, in 5:2, the author wants his readers to realize that Esther's actions and appearance function in such a way as to effect a positive influence over the king.

Having been won over by Esther's charms, King Ahasuerus does not hesitate to hold out his golden scepter to her, thereby indicating that she is free to enter his presence without fear of death (see 4:11). Esther may now safely approach the king, which she does.

Clever Cleaver (5:3–8)

There is nothing quite like a good meal to get a group of people in a good mood. Esther recognizes the value of using a feast as a means to establish a congenial atmosphere—one in which she later would set forth her concerns before the king. In this section (5:3–8), Esther avoids responding directly to the king's question regarding her desires and instead invites the king, together with Haman, to a banquet that she has prepared. The king eagerly accepts her invitation and then commands that Haman be brought quickly to join them at the feast. At the banquet, Esther repeats herself, avoiding the king's query and extending an invitation to both the king and Haman to attend another feast to be held the next day. By holding two feasts in two days, Esther prepares the ground to lay out her troubles

2. Michael V. Fox, *Character and Ideology in the Book of Esther* (Columbia, S.C.: University of South Carolina Press, 1991), 68.

and accusations before the king. She seems to believe in the old adage that the way to a man's heart is through his stomach.

Because of Esther's actions, 5:3–8 might easily be titled "Unanswered Questions." Yet, because of the way the author structures these verses, a better title might be "An Ironic Summoning," for the author organizes the passage to highlight what is the beginning of the end for Haman. The author sandwiches the summoning of the enemy of the Jews to a feast prepared by a Jewess between the peculiar dialogues that take place between the king and Esther—peculiar because, as previously noted, Esther does not respond to the ruler of the Medo-Persian empire as might be expected:

A Avoiding the question (vv. 3–4)
    B Calling the adversary (v. 5)
A′ Avoiding the question (vv. 6–8)

In 5:3, the king asks Esther two questions to learn why she risked coming before him. In colloquial terms, he says: "What is troubling you, Queen Esther? And what is your request?" These appear to be standard questions used in the Scriptures. They do not suggest either that the king is bothered by Esther's intrusion to his throne room or that he is responding with a special sensitivity to her plight.

The king then magnanimously offers Esther essentially everything she could possibly want, "even to half of the kingdom." Joyce G. Baldwin correctly notes, however, that the expression does not imply any great extravagance on the part of the king; in light of its repetition in verse 6, it is merely a conventional phrase used by kings in ancient times.[3]

At this point, the reader naturally expects Esther to pour out her soul to the king, exposing Haman's heinous deed and begging for the deliverance of her people. Such, however, is not the case. Surprisingly, even though she appears to have gained the advantage, Esther fails to press her cause before the king at this time. In fact, she avoids making any reference to her true intentions. What is

3. Joyce G. Baldwin, *Esther: An Introduction and Commentary*, Tyndale Old Testament Commentaries, ed. D. J. Wiseman (Downers Grove: InterVarsity, 1984), 86.

more, she specifically requests that Haman, the enemy of her people, be permitted to join the king at a banquet that she has prepared.

Why Esther chooses not to intercede for her people at this time has been a matter of much speculation. Some argue that she does not consider the time to be psychologically propitious, others that her courage fails her, and still others that she feels that the banquet hall would be a more appropriate place than the throne room in which to make her request.[4] The Scripture, however, provides no information as to which view, if any, is correct.

The Scripture is also silent regarding Esther's motivation in inviting Haman to the banquet. Again, numerous commentators have offered a wide range of suggestions: to set a trap for Haman; to keep Haman from becoming suspicious; to keep Haman from forming a conspiracy against her; to make the king jealous; and to arouse fear in the Jews that she was catering to Haman and thereby to stimulate them to put their trust in God rather than in their queen.[5] Since the Scripture is silent on this matter, dogmatic positions regarding Esther's purposes need to be avoided.

There is a curious grammatical ambiguity in Esther's statement in 5:4 that causes people to wonder whether Esther intentionally spoke in such a manner so as to generate a feeling of tension within the king. That ambiguity arises from Esther's use of the pronoun *him* at the conclusion of her declaration that she has prepared the banquet "for him" *(lô)*. What is difficult to determine is the antecedent to this pronoun. In other words, for whom does Esther suggest that her feast is specially prepared—for the king or for Haman?

The context suggests that the pronoun *him* refers to the king; the grammar, however, points to Haman (i.e., the closest antecedent to the pronoun *him*). The author, moreover, does not clear up the ambiguity but allows it to stand, thereby sus-

4. Carey A. Moore, *Esther*, The Anchor Bible, ed. William Foxwell Albright and David Noel Freedman (Garden City, N.Y.: Doubleday, 1971), 56.

5. Paulus Cassel, *An Explanatory Commentary on Esther*, trans. Aaron Bernstein (Edinburgh: T. and T. Clark, 1888), 180; Moore, *Esther*, 56; Meir Zlotowitz, trans. and comp., *The Megillah: The Book of Esther: A New Translation Anthologized from Talmudic, Midrashic and Rabbinic Sources* (Brooklyn: Mesorah, 1981), 85.

taining the already high level of tension that exists in this portion of the story. Once again, we wonder what Esther is trying to do.

An additional curiosity with potentially greater ramifications than the ambiguity surrounding either Haman's invitation to the banquet or the antecedent to the pronoun *him* is also found in verse 4. It revolves around the question of why God is nowhere directly mentioned in the Book of Esther.

In the thirteenth century, Rabbi Bachya ben Asher first identified what he believed to be the presence of the divine name (YHWH)[6] in four different places in the Book of Esther.[7] He noted its existence in 5:4 in the form of an acrostic drawn from the first letters (read forward)[8] of the Hebrew words *Yāḇôʾ Hammelek Wᵉhāmān Hay yôm*[9] translated "and may the king and Haman come today." He also identified three other examples in the Book of Esther: 1:20, first letters read backward, *Hîʾ Wᵉkāl Hannāšîm Yittᵉnû* (it, and all the women will give); 5:13, last letters read backward, *zH ʾynnW šurH lY* (this does not give satisfaction to me); and 7:7, last letters read forward, *kY kltH ʾlyW hrʿH* (that harm was determined against him).

Ever since Rabbi ben Asher's day, a debate has raged as to the validity and significance of such a finding. Those who seek to find a spiritual character in the people of Israel make much of these acronyms. Those who maintain Israel's lack of spirituality at this time in history view these acrostics either as random coincidences or as the author's way of intimating that God is working behind the events of the book.

Each of the acrostic passages needs to be evaluated to determine the probability of its being intentionally generated by the author. Four criteria may be of help in identifying the possible existence of an intentional acrostic:

6. The divine name in Hebrew consists of four consonants (often referred to as the Tetragrammaton), which when written in English are YHWH and are usually pronounced "Yahweh" (the pronunciation *Jehovah* originates from German).

7. Rachel B. K. Sabua, "The Hidden Hand of God," *Bible Review* 8 (1992): 31–32.

8. "Forward" means right to left, following the Hebrew pattern of writing. In transliteration into English, the English sequencing of words converts "forward" into a left-to-right format.

9. The capitalization for emphasis in this and the following three examples is mine.

1. the acrostic exists within a grouping of words that reflects some alteration to the normally expected grammatical pattern for such words;
2. the acrostic occurs at a critical juncture of the text;
3. one or more of the words in which the acrostic is found are infrequently used terms for which more frequently used terminology is available; and
4. the acrostic is visible in a repetitive grammatical pattern or in a component that breaks up a repetitive grammatical pattern.

These criteria, of course, are not foolproof. Apart from an author's declaration of his intent to include an acrostic (something which does not happen in Scripture), we do not have any guaranteed method by which to ascertain the validity of our declaration of certain acrostics to be intentional. Each acrostic, therefore, needs to be evaluated in light of its function within its contextual environment.

None of the four acrostics under consideration (i.e., Esther 1:20; 5:4, 13; 7:7) exists on the basis of the standards set forth in either criterion 3 or criterion 4. The following analysis, therefore, focuses on the four acrostics in light of the first two criteria cited.

To establish the YHWH-acrostic in 1:20 demands that the acrostic be made from two separate clauses, using the last word from the first clause and the first three words from the second clause. This requirement does not in and of itself invalidate the acrostic as being intentional, since the author may have sought to link together two specially significant components. Yet, in 1:20 such a linkage does not appear to be the case.

What lends credibility to the acrostic of 1:20 being intentional, however, is the placement of the subject (*w^{e}kāl hannāšîm*—all the women) before the verb (*yitt^{e}nû*—will give), which falls outside the standard Hebrew sentence pattern of the verb preceding the subject. This altered order gives emphasis to the subject of the clause, an emphasis that fits well with Memucan's attempts to persuade the king.

The mention of Memucan's name in connection with the acrostic presents one other issue to be considered: Should an acrostic of the divine name rightly be expected to come forth intentionally from the mouth of a pagan? The natural response to this question is no, but if the author of the Book of Esther is paraphrasing rather than quoting, then the author's intent may come to the foreground.

Finally, the acrostic of 1:20 occurs at an important crossroads in the text—the ousting of Vashti (which then paves the way for Esther to become queen). Yet, one wonders whether God desires to receive credit for working providentially to separate Vashti from her husband or to support Memucan's need to suppress a potential feminine uprising. Thus, at best, only a weak case can be made for the acrostic of 1:20 being intentional.

In similar fashion to that which is found for the YHWH-acrostic in 1:20, both criteria 1 and 2—an altered grammatical pattern and existence at a critical juncture—potentially lend credence to the argument that the author intentionally hid the divine name in 5:4 (*Yāḇô' Hammelek Wᵉhāmān Hayyôm*—and may the king and Haman come today).

First, the word order in 5:4 may possibly have been altered slightly to form the YHWH-acrostic. In 5:4 the temporal adverb *hayyôm* (today) is at the end of the clause *may the king and Haman come* rather than at the beginning of the clause where, according to Bruce K. Waltke and M. O'Connor, temporal adverbs are more normally found.[10] Yet, an analysis of the use of the unmodified Hebrew temporal adverb *hayyôm* (today) in postexilic biblical books reveals no one location favored over any other within a given clause for the placement of the term *hayyôm*. In other words, the placement of *hayyôm* in 5:4 at the end of the clause suggests nothing unusual. Hence, the grammar of this passage does not offer conclusive proof that Esther spoke these words in 5:4 intentionally to camouflage the YHWH-acrostic.

Second, the YHWH-acrostic in 5:4 exists at a critical juncture in the text. Barry J. Beitzel notes that "the heroine has just risked her life to plead the case of her betrayed people. The dramatic suspense reaches a climax when, in response to the king's query, Esther's first sentence of intercession includes the words *y[ābô'] h[ammelek] w[ĕhāmān] h[ayyôm]*, 'let the king and

10. Bruce K. Waltke and M. O'Connor, *An Introduction to Biblical Hebrew Syntax* (Winona Lake, Ind.: Eisenbrauns, 1990), §39n38.

Haman come today.'"[11] Ironically, if Esther is consciously calling upon God's help in this situation by means of an acrostic, she fails to rely on him at this time even though the king is willing to fulfill her request (5:3, 6). Once again, the acrostic in 5:4 does not appear to be intentional.

Neither is the argument very strong for the YHWH-acrostic in 5:13 (*zH ʾynnW šwH lY*—this does not give satisfaction to me). The grammar only hints at a possible reworking of the sentence order. Specifically, *ʾynnw* (does not) might normally be expected to occur at the beginning of its clause, but there are sufficient examples of *ʾynnw* outside of the initial position to suggest that this expectation is not based on a hard-and-fast rule of Hebrew grammar. Although the acrostic is buried at an important juncture in the text, it comes from the mouth of an avowed enemy of the Jews. Thus the YHWH-acrostic in 5:13 (final characters read backward) has little to commend it as having been generated intentionally.

The final YHWH-acrostic (in 7:7—cf. *kY kltH ʾlyW hrʿH*—that harm was determined against him), receives no special support from its grammatical construction, but finds significant support from its context. Haman, the enemy of the Jews, who has condemned the Jews to destruction, now recognizes that he too is doomed. Who else but YHWH could accomplish such an amazing feat? This YHWH-acrostic, therefore, has potential for being an intentional acrostic.

The overall assessment of these four YHWH-acrostics is that they do not appear to have been intentionally designed.

Returning to the unhidden text of Esther, we discover in 5:5 that the king, despite Esther's having sidestepped his direct question (v. 4), willingly accepts her invitation to a banquet that she has prepared. He also accepts on behalf of Haman and gives orders (probably to his servants)[12] to bring Haman quickly to the banquet.

At this point the author reveals a second forward movement in Esther's progress toward gaining some measure of control

11. Barry J. Beitzel, "Exodus 3:14 and the Divine Name: A Case of Biblical Paronomasia," *Trinity Journal* 1, n.s. (1980): 7.

12. The king uses the second person masculine plural imperatival form of the verb *māhar* (to hurry).

over her life. The first occurs in 4:16–17, when Esther gives orders to Mordecai and he responds affirmatively. The second takes place here, when the king, responding to Esther's request, issues a command that Haman be hastened to the banquet to fulfill Esther's desire.[13] Thus, once more, what Esther said is being not only received positively, but also acted upon—both the king and Haman attend Esther's banquet.

Esther 5:5 also marks a subtle turning point in Haman's life—a turning point of which he undoubtedly is unaware. Unlike Esther, who is beginning to exert her will, Haman from this point on will be more and more propelled by external forces over which he seemingly has no control. In 5:5, he is hurried by the king. In 5:9, he is enraged by Mordecai but must rely on the advice of his own wife and friends (5:14) to solve his problem. Furthermore, the next day, Haman finds himself being ordered by the king to give special public honors to his own worst enemy, Mordecai (6:10). Disgraced, Haman returns home, only to hear his wife pronounce a sentence of "doom" on him (6:13). Immediately, the king's servants arrive at Haman's house to rush him to Esther's second banquet (6:14), where he is accused of planned genocide against Queen Esther and her people (7:6). Haman then hears the king order his execution (7:9), following which he is hanged (7:10). In a matter of one twenty-four-hour period, Haman plunges from being at the top of his career—second in command in the Medo-Persian empire—to the depths of humiliation and ultimately to his death.

The scene (5:6) shifts to the banquet hall where, in the midst of drinking wine, the king once again asks Esther to reveal what she wants. He queries: "What is your petition *[šᵉʾēlātēk]* and it will be given to you. And what is your request *[baqqāšātēk]*? Even as far as half the kingdom, and it will be done." The words translated "petition" and "request," when used in parallel, are essentially the same in content and, as Siegfried Wagner states, are "part of a fixed form in the ceremonial of the court."[14] Certainly, the phrase "even as far as half the kingdom" functions as

13. Lit., "to do the word of Esther."

14. Siegfried Wagner, "בִּקֵּשׁ *biqqēsh;* בַּקָּשָׁה *baqqāshāh,*" *Theological Dictionary of the Old Testament*, ed. G. Johannes Botterweck and Helmer Ringgren, trans. John T. Willis (Grand Rapids: Eerdmans, 1975), 2:241.

a fixed ceremonial phrase during ancient times.[15] Courtiers would have recognized in it an expression of the king's willingness to assist the petitioner, not a statement that was to be taken at face value.

Esther once again has an open invitation to place her desires before the king. Yet, in 5:7–8, she, as before, chooses not to broach the subject at this time. In verse 7 she seemingly begins to entreat the king, yet in verse 8 she stops herself in midsentence and asks to be allowed to present her concerns the following day.[16]

The Scripture does not indicate why Esther fails to press her case before the king in verses 7–8. Some commentators feel that Esther planned it that way. Others assume that she recognized she had committed a breach of protocol, was concerned about the king's affections toward her, developed a case of the nerves, or was hesitant about where to place her loyalty. Yet there is insufficient support to accept any of these reasons dogmatically. The Scripture does not portray Esther as seeking God's guidance in the matter of when or how she should approach the king. Her unwillingness to present her case here and in 5:4 appears to have been self-generated and not based on divine instruction.

Esther's postponement, as Carey A. Moore notes, may have been defensible the first time in verse 4, but was "tempting fate" in verse 8: "any number of things could go wrong in the interval between the two dinners: the king's benevolent mood could change, for example, or Haman could learn of Esther's true feelings toward him and of her relationship to Mordecai."[17] Whatever her reasoning for postponing the declaration of her petition one more time, "[t]he greater importunity and humility in the request" for the postponement in 5:8, Fox surmises, "suggest that she is worried about testing the king's patience."[18]

Esther in verse 8 invites both the king and Haman to a banquet that she has, this time, prepared for "them." The most logical explanation for the change from "him" in verse 4 to "them" in verse 8 is

15. Even the dreaded King Herod in the first century A.D. made use of this ceremonial phrase in his courtroom. See Mark 6:23.

16. Although some English translations smooth over the transition between verses 7 and 8, the Hebrew reveals an abrupt break between them.

17. Moore, *Esther*, 57–58.

18. Fox, *Character and Ideology in the Book of Esther*, 69.

that both the king and Haman are present before Esther the second time (v. 8), whereas only the king was present the first time (v. 4).

In 5:8, Esther concludes her invitation to the king by declaring that she would make her request known to the king at the banquet the next day. By so doing, Esther lets the king know that her delaying tactics would not continue forever. This declaration would placate the king and reduce the risk of his becoming impatient with her.

Interestingly, although Esther undoubtedly experiences a great deal of anxiety between the two banquets, the author does not focus on her feelings at all. Instead, he interposes between the two banquets a chapter and a half of discussion regarding selected, crucial actions that take place among the three leading males of this story—Haman, Mordecai, and the king.

Eat, Drink, and Be Merry, for Tomorrow *He* Dies (5:9–14)

The scene abruptly changes from one of Jewish orientation (5:1–8) to one focused on Gentile matters (vv. 9–14). No longer does it concern a Jewess who hesitatingly approaches her spouse in an attempt to deal with a Gentile-generated problem. Now it zeros in on a Gentile leader who boldly approaches his spouse in order to eliminate a problem brought on by a particularly recalcitrant Jew.

Although the thematic structure of verses 9–14 parallels that of verses 1–8 (see the introduction to this chapter), the literary development of verses 9–14 reveals a stand-alone chiastic structure:

- A Haman is pleased (5:9a)
  - B Mordecai is the source of Haman's problems (5:9b–10)
    - C Haman boasts of having the greatest life possible (5:11–12)
  - B′ Mordecai is the source of Haman's problems (5:13–14a)
- A′ Haman is pleased (5:14b)

What makes this chiastic structure particularly informative is that these verses form the central point of the chiastic structure of the entire book (see the final chapter). Thus the crucial issue that the author highlights in the Book of Esther is the boasting of a Gentile who believes that he is on top of the world and that his enemies, the Jews, and one in particular, Mordecai, are about to die. Thus the high point for Haman is the low point for the people of God.

Nothing in these verses is very promising for the people of God. In fact, the one hope that they could hold on to now appears to be slipping through their fingers—Esther's scheme will come to fruition too late to do any good. Her banquet will take place after Haman has executed judgment against his enemy, Mordecai.

In 5:9, the author reveals a dramatic mood swing that will be characteristic of Haman's emotional state over the next few chapters. In the short span of this verse, Haman changes from joyful exuberance to out-and-out anger.

In order to capture the extent of Haman's ecstasy at being invited by the queen to another banquet, the author uses not one but two different expressions. Haman is *śāmē(a)ḥ,* that is, glad, joyful, merry. He is also *ṭôb lēḇ,* that is, happy or pleased of heart (lit., "good of heart"). The combination of these two expressions suggests that Haman's excitement is what might be called pure joy. Ironically, this combination of expressions would drive the Jewish reader well versed in Scripture back to one of the most joyful events in all of Israel's history—the dedication of the Solomonic temple, when the glory of God descended and filled the sanctuary (1 Kings 8:66; 2 Chron. 7:10). At that time, the Jews were at their greatest. They were "glad and pleased of heart." Here in Esther, however, the archenemy of the Jews experiences a similar ecstasy. He too is at his greatest, whereas (by contrast) the Jews are mourning their impending doom.

Yet the instant Haman sees his nemesis, Mordecai, Haman reacts violently. Mordecai refuses to show Haman any respect, choosing not to stand or tremble in Haman's presence. Haman becomes enraged (lit., filled with anger), and an enraged Haman is an extremely dangerous Haman. The previous time Haman was filled with anger is in 3:5, and the outcome of his anger at that time was the edict to condemn to death not merely Mordecai but all of the Jewish people in the Medo-Persian empire. What will be the horrifying consequence of his anger this time?

Of all the characters in the Book of Esther, Haman is portrayed most vividly by the author as possessing a full range of emotions. Only rarely does the author provide insight into the feelings of the other personalities. Yet the author shows Haman at different times as being enraged (3:5; 5:9), ecstatic (5:9), dissatisfied (5:13), pleased (5:14), anguished (6:12), and terrified (7:6).

The author, however, does not depict Haman as an emotional basket case. Just the opposite; the author points out on two important occasions (3:6; 5:10) that Haman is able to gain control over his emotions and to function rationally. Both situations arise because Mordecai fails to extend to Haman the proper respect due to him as required by the law of the empire.

Much like the giant redwood trees of northern California that survive lightning bolts, floods, fire, and earthquake but are destroyed by the persistence of tiny termites, so too Haman (5:9) finds himself being eaten away by the insidious gnawing of Mordecai's rebellion. Yet, unlike the redwoods, Haman takes steps to overcome the attack of his antagonist. In verse 10, he begins by first taking charge of his own emotions; later (5:14; 6:4) he implements a plan to eradicate that much-despised nemesis.

The Scripture notes that Haman "restrained himself" (*wayyitʾappaq*) rather than let his own anger toward Mordecai get the best of him. The use of this verb in Scripture generally suggests a sense of struggle, an overcoming of what might naturally be expected to happen in a particular situation.[19] Cassel indicates that this term may even convey the idea of wrestling with something, in this case, oneself.[20] Haman thus finds his emotions more difficult to control here than he did in 3:6. This increased difficulty may account for Haman's readiness to act immediately (5:14) to eliminate his problem, whereas previously (3:6, 7, 12) he had been willing to delay the initiation of his revenge.

Having gained control of his emotions, Haman summons his friends and his wife to join him. He then details his greatness (5:11–12) as seen in his riches,[21] his large family (cf. 9:7–

19. See Gen. 43:31; 45:1; 1 Sam. 13:12; Isa. 42:14; 63:15; 64:12 (Heb. v. 11) for the remaining instances of *ʾāpaq* in Scripture.

20. Cassel, *An Explanatory Commentary on Esther*, 187 n. 1.

21. Haman is extremely wealthy, as 3:9 reveals.

10),[22] his royal decorations, his promotions (cf. 3:1), and even [23] his latest honor of an invitation to a special banquet prepared by the queen herself for both him and the king.. Humanly speaking, Haman had every right to boast of his accomplishments. There was probably no one in the empire, except the king, who had more than Haman had. Yet because of one insignificant problem, he could not fully enjoy his treasures. He needed that troublesome irritant to be removed before he could find contentment.

Curiously a Hebrew idiom crops up in 5:13 that occurs in two other highly charged times of Haman's life. That idiom is *šēwe(h) le / be. . .*, variously translated "adequate for," "suitable for," "equivalent for," "commensurate for." In 3:8, Haman indicates to the king that allowing the continued existence of a certain troublesome people (i.e., the Jews) is a matter that is not *suitable for* bringing before the king, but is a matter for which he, Haman, has a final solution. Ironically, Esther parrots the same basic idiom to the king in 7:4, when she declares that had her people, the Jews, merely been sold into slavery rather than been condemned to death, she would not consider their predicament to be *equivalent* to the annoyance that she has caused the king by bringing the matter to his attention. In 5:13, Haman cries out that all his achievements are not enough – literally, "yet in all this there is not sufficiency for me"[24] – because his enemy, Mordecai the Jew, still lives. Thus at three crucial points, mistaken notions regarding the significance of the Jews ultimately affect Haman's life. In 3:8, his political life is affected as he initiates what later turns out to be unsound governmental policy. In 5:13, his personal life is impacted negatively and, in 7:4, his very existence is compromised.

22.Herodotus records that to possess a large family was of special significance to the ancient Persians. Herodotus 1.136. The Scripture indicates that Haman had ten sons (9:7-10).

23. Keil indicates that the use of the adverb *ʾap* (even) indicates, in Haman's mind, the importance of this invitation to the banquet by the queen. C.F. Keil, *The Books of Ezra, Nehemiah, and Esther*, Biblical Commentary on the Old Testament, trans. Sophia Taylor (Grand Rapids: Eerdmans, n.d.), 357.

24. The final consonants of each of the Hebrew words of this clause, when read backward as an acrostic, spell out the proper name of God, YHWH. See 5:4 for a discussion of the significance of such a finding.

Instructively in 5:13, Haman refers to Mordecai as "the Jew." Apparently much of the bitterness that Haman harbors toward Mordecai arises from the ancient antipathies that existed between the Agagites and the Jews (see 3:1). In 5:14, however, Haman's wife and all his friends provide a way for him to escape from his debilitating fixation on Mordecai. They recommend to Haman that he build a gallows[25] on which to hang Mordecai, and then secure permission from the king to carry out the proposed execution. Doing these things, they affirm, would allow Haman to enjoy life again. Haman concurs.

Esther 5:14 concludes with Haman constructing the gallows on which to hang Mordecai. H. A. Ironside reminds us that while all of this work is going on, Mordecai is oblivious to the "fate which is to be meted out to him on the morrow." Ironside then poses the question that would strike many readers at this point: "Hath God forgotten to be gracious?"[26] The people of God stand condemned to death. Mordecai, a leader among the people of God, faces imminent death. Yet God remains silent. Perhaps God truly has forgotten his people. The next few chapters will tell.

Lessons Learned from the Midst of a Hopeless Situation

Contrasted to Esther 4, which begins with despair but concludes with some promise, chapter 5 opens in an atmosphere of guarded hope but ends with the anticipation of another setback for the people of God.

The primary thrust of this chapter is to show the tenuous position in which the people of God find themselves. Their hope for deliverance is placed in a woman who is inexperienced in politics and in leadership. This woman, Esther, seemingly does not even have the wisdom to press her advantageous position on behalf of her people when her husband, the king, presents her an open door to do so (5:3–8). Worse still, her failure to act immediately allows her enemy time to devise a plan of his own that, if implemented, may upset any hope for her to succeed in her plans

25. See 2:23 for a discussion of the form of execution being proposed.

26. H. A. Ironside, *Notes on the Book of Esther*, 1905, *Notes on Ezra Nehemiah and Esther* (New York: Loizeaux, 1960), 65.

(v. 14). The wisdom of Esther's delay must now be severely questioned. Her people depend on her, yet she seems unwilling to act.

Studying this less than desirable position from a comfortable distance, the reader discovers several principles that are subtly being conveyed by the author:

1. Believers should never let their guard down, because the people of God and the enemies of God's people are at direct cross-purposes to each other. Both Esther and Mordecai assume that all is progressing well with Esther's plan, yet their enemy has a different plan in mind.
2. Failing to follow through on what one is supposed to do leaves that individual vulnerable to potential dangers of which he or she may not be aware. Esther's request to hold a second banquet rather than to press for the deliverance of her people gives Haman time to prepare the means for Mordecai's early demise.
3. Focusing on a negative situation may rob one of the joy of life. Haman lets one small event (Mordecai's refusal to honor him) ruin what should have been the most wonderful time of his life.
4. Securing advice from family and friends can be a strong antidote to discouragement. Haman's joy returns after he listens to the counsel of his wife and friends.

Everything's *Kapakahi*

Hawaiians have a word that best describes this chapter: *kapakahi.* That means that everything is all lopsided. Everything in this chapter is topsy-turvy. At the beginning we are concerned about what will happen when Esther approaches the king. Our fears, however, are quickly dispelled when the king warmly welcomes her. We then anticipate a swift victory for Esther; yet, without warning, she falters and fails to press her advantage. Thus what early on looked as though it would soon produce great success, now appears to be in a holding pattern with dark storm clouds on the horizon. What is more, the very person whom Esther apparently could have defeated by merely presenting her requests to the king is now preparing to exterminate Esther's adoptive father. Haman, the enemy of the Jews, who should be defeated, is very much alive and very much in power. Something is drastically wrong.

This chapter leaves us with many unanswered questions. How well thought through is Esther's plan, and will it work? Can anything be done to alter the irrevocable law of the Medes and Persians that decrees the annihilation of the Jews? What can be done to keep Haman from hanging Mordecai on the gallows tomorrow?

Seemingly nothing short of a miracle will prevent Mordecai's death.

Strangely, by the end of the chapter, we are in the dark regarding the plans of the children of light, but very much in the light regarding the plans of the children of darkness. Fortunately, the next few chapters will restore our joy and laughter. God in his providence will deliver his people.

16

Egg on the Face
(6:1–14)

There is nothing quite like lacing up gym shoes or tennis shoes or track shoes in anticipation of an upcoming sporting event. Each side of the lace sits intertwined in the shoe waiting to be pulled ever tighter, one over the other, until the laces are tied together. This lacing process requires a mental effort that subconsciously anticipates the struggle that is about to take place in the sporting world.

The interweaving of the threads of a story is much like the lacing of gym shoes—the threads that at the beginning seem to work at cross purposes to each other are finally laced together. The author of the Book of Esther has allowed the threads of the stories of the antagonist, Haman, and the protagonists, Mordecai and Esther, to run at direct cross purposes to each other for several chapters. He now pulls them together for the final cross-over lacing—the antagonist's thread being bent toward defeat and destruction, the protagonists' toward victory and jubilation.

Merely Coincidences—Oh, Really?

Chapter 6 is about reversal: about honor and dishonor, about hope and dashed hopes. More significantly, it is about the providential work of God.

There are far more "coincidences" in this chapter than in any other; far too many to be accounted for as mere chance. The following list identifies tend of the more significant coincidences that occur in the fourteen verses of this chapter:

1. the timing of the events such that they occur the same night as Haman's building a gallows on which to hang Mordecai (5:1; cf.5:14);
2. the king's inability to sleep (6:1);
3. the king's decision to read the chronicles rather than to find some other means by which either to amuse himself or to lull himself to sleep (v.1);
4. the reading of the specific story about Mordecai's actions that avoided a palace coup and the discovery that he had never been rewarded (vv. 2-3);
5. Haman's eagerness to hang Mordecai that drives Haman to be at the king's courtyard early in the morning (v.4);
6. Haman being identified as the only one in the courtyard at that time (v. 5);
7. Haman misinterpreting the king's question (v. 6);
8. Haman being required to honor the man whom he most hates, Mordecai the Jew (vv.10-11);
9. Haman's wife and friends, who had supported his efforts only a few hours earlier, now predict his doom (v. 13); and
10. the servants' arrival when Haman is at his lowest to hasten him to the queen's banquet where (in the next chapter) he will be brought even lower (v. 14).

These "coincidences" interject a glimmer of hope that somehow – despite the seeming impossibility of the situation – God will work all things for good in the end.

No Excess Baggage

My wife and I enjoy going to the airport to meet people or to watch people depart. We enjoy even more going to the airport so that we ourselves can fly somewhere. One of the things that we have learned – and it is not too profound – is that the more luggage we take with us on a trip, the more time it takes for us to get in and out of an airport. A carry-on bag works best for us. We avoid having to check our luggage and having to wait for it at the baggage claim area.

The author has designed chapter 6 to move quickly through an amazing sequence of events. There is no excess baggage in this chapter. The author drives the reader quickly—much like Haman is driven quickly—through a period of high intensity and anxiety. The author moves us from Haman's greatest hour (chap. 5) to Haman's ignominious defeat and death (chap. 7), not allowing us to linger long over the doom of the Jews.

In line with the author's concern for speed and efficiency, he presses through the chapter in straight-line fashion:

A. The record of the empire (6:1–3)
B. The request of the emperor (6:4–6)
C. The recklessness of the enemy (6:7–9)
D. The reward of the exemplar (6:10–11)
E. The remorse of the enemy (6:12–14)

The author's purpose for this chapter appears to be to lead the reader rapidly through some amazing coincidences in order to see even greater works that God will perform. His use of a straight-line structure best accomplishes that goal.

Got Insomnia? Read a Book (6:1–3)

Many people today, for one reason or another, have difficulty sleeping. In their attempt to get that desired sleep, they willingly try all sorts of remedies, everything from sleeping pills to blindfolds to lying down on a hard surface to hugging a pillow to listening to quiet music to drinking warm milk to counting sheep (or blessings) to reading a book. Many of these supposed remedies are not new. At least one of them is quite old—that of reading a book.

More than twenty-four hundred years ago, King Ahasuerus (for some unspecified reason) could not fall asleep during the night between the two banquets that Queen Esther had prepared for his pleasure. He decided therefore to have a book containing the history of the Medo-Persian empire read to him. Although this remedy did not work for the king's insomnia, it set into motion a series of events that ended with the humiliation of a prime minister of the Medo-Persian empire (vv. 6–12) and with the replacement of that prime minister by another individual (8:1–2).

In 6:1, by means of a temporal clause, the author signals a break in the action (actually a change in venue). This suggests that the story will take a direction different from that in which it has been moving.

In introducing this chapter, the author highlights the immediacy of the coincidences that are about to take place. He identifies the events as taking place "that night." The recording of time is vital to the author. He portrays it in a funnel-like fashion, narrowing in focus, throughout the book. At times he uses a broad brush: in the days of Ahasuerus (1:1), in those days (1:2; 2:21), in the third year (1:3), after these things or events (2:1; 3:1), and in such and such a month (2:16; 3:7). At times he paints with greater precision: on the seventh day (1:10), on the thirteenth day of the first month (3:12), and on the thirteenth day of the twelfth month (3:13). Still, at other times and particularly now as he highlights the rapidity of events, the author draws his picture of time with the sharpest of calligraphy brushes: that day (i.e., a reference to the daylight hours—5:9), that night (6:1), and while they were still talking (6:14). There is no question that the author wants his readers to understand the ever-increasing speed at which events are taking place—a pace that seems to be out of the control of the characters in the story, and thus a speed that God alone can control.

That night begins badly for the king. He is unable to sleep (lit., "the sleep of the king fled"). That sleep "fled" or "departed" from someone is a standard Hebrew idiom used for communicating the concept of a person having difficulty sleeping (cf. Gen. 31:40). As such, this idiomatic expression does not suggest that any special connotation (e.g., moral or political) should be attached to King Ahasuerus's insomnia. As Paulus Cassel reminds us, "[n]o one has command over sleep,"[1] not even kings.

Because the king cannot sleep, he gives an order that *The Book of the Remembrances, the Chronicles*[2] (i.e., the historical

1. Paulus Cassel, *An Explanatory Commentary on Esther*, trans. Aaron Bernstein (Edinburgh: T. and T. Clark, 1888), 192.

2. See Ezra 4:15 and Mal. 3:16 for other examples of similar historical record books.

records of the kingdom) be brought to him. The contents then are read to him. Apparently, the reading of these books does not put the king to sleep, for the Hebrew niphal participle form of the verb used here (*niqrāʾîm*—were read) denotes "an action in process,"[3] that is, "the long continuance of this reading."[4]

God's providence is definitely at work! The king who cannot sleep has many optional activities by which to amuse himself during this restless night, yet he chooses to read the chronicles of the empire. Perhaps he believes that the reading of the history books would be sufficiently boring to lull him to sleep. More likely, since these records contain accounts of his own great exploits, he desires to have them read so that his spirits would be lifted in order to counteract the miserable mood that a sleepless night might otherwise bring. God's providence, however, is at work. In the midst of all that King Ahasuerus had read to him, one story in particular catches his attention: the story of how Mordecai rescued the king by reporting a plot by two of the king's eunuchs, Bigthana[5] and Teresh, against the king's life (6:2; cf. 2:21–23).

What intrigues the king about the story is that there is no indication that any reward was given to his benefactor, Mordecai. The king becomes genuinely concerned. He questions his servants as to what "honor or dignity" [y^e*qār û*g^e*dûllā(h)*][6] had been extended to Mordecai. On learning that nothing had been done to show the king's gratitude to Mordecai, the king sets about to rectify that oversight (6:6–10).

Correcting the deficiency is of great importance to the king, the concepts of honor (particularly) and dignity (generally) being considered highly significant at this period in history. The

3. Paul S. J. Joüon, *A Grammar of Biblical Hebrew,* trans. and rev. T. Muraoka, 2 vols. (Rome: Editrice Pontificio Instituto Biblico, 1991), §121q.

4. C. F. Keil, *The Books of Ezra, Nehemiah, and Esther,* Biblical Commentary on the Old Testament, trans. Sophia Taylor (Grand Rapids: Eerdmans, n.d.), 359.

5. The first eunuch's name in 2:21 is Bigthan *(bigtān),* whereas in 6:2 it is Bigthana *(bigtānā').* The different spelling is merely a variant.

6. Huey postulates that the terms *yeqār* (honor) and g^e*dûllā(h)* (dignity), as used in Esther 6:3, "may be a hendiadys for 'great honor.'" F. B. Huey, Jr., "Esther," *Expositor's Bible Commentary,* ed. Frank E. Gaebelein, 12 vols. (Grand Rapids: Zondervan, 1988), 4:822.

term y^e*qār* (honor) occurs seventeen times in the Hebrew Scriptures.[7] Ten of those occurrences are found in the Book of Esther.[8] Furthermore, the word g^e*dûllā(h)* (dignity, greatness) finds its way into twelve verses of the Scripture, three of which are in the Book of Esther (1:4; 6:3; 10:2). Thus, during the Medo-Persian era, the failure to extend honor and dignity to a deserving benefactor is an affront to what is proper and socially correct. King Ahasuerus, therefore, now must act to rectify with magnanimous benevolence this morally offensive situation.

Crossed Signals (6:4–6)

When Muhammad Ali was the heavyweight boxing champion of the world (1964–1967, 1974–1978, and 1978–1979), he proved to be as great a promoter of his career as he was a boxer. Oftentimes, to the ire of those who hated him and the admiration of his supporters, he would boast: "I am the greatest!"

Haman, during the Medo-Persian era, would have disputed Muhammad Ali's claim. As Esther 6:6 records, Haman considers himself to be the greatest: "To whom would the king desire to show honor more than to me?" In making that statement, however, Haman misreads the king's intention to reward Mordecai as a desire to reward Haman himself (cf. vv. 7–10). The events leading up to that misunderstanding are interesting in their own right; they are presented in verses 4–6.

The king begins verse 4 with a question: "Who is in the court?" This seems to be a strange question, especially in light of the king's concern about the failure to reward Mordecai (v. 3). Does this question have anything to do with the situation with Mordecai? Perhaps—perhaps not. Has the king merely heard a sound in the outer court and wondered who was there? The reader does not yet know the significance of the king's question and the ironic turn of events that will radiate from it. The author continues by noting that Haman is the one who has entered the outer court, and that he is determined to ask the

7. The word *honor (yeqār)* also occurs seven times in the Aramaic portion of the Book of Daniel (2:6, 37; 4:27, 33; 5:18, 20; 7:14), a book written during the early portion of the Medo-Persian captivity.

8. Esther 1:4, 20; 6:3, 6 (2x), 7, 9 (2x), 11; 8:16.

king's permission to kill Mordecai. The king's servants then announce Haman's presence to the king (v. 5).[9]

At this point, the king commands that Haman be allowed to enter the inner court. The author keeps the tension level high. The reader (and not the king) knows of Haman's devious plans and wonders whether he will be able to carry them out. One quick word from Haman to the king and Mordecai is potentially dead. Even though the king is favorably disposed toward Mordecai—a fact of which Haman is unaware—Haman might still secure the king's permission to kill Mordecai. Haman might convince the king that, despite Mordecai's former heroics, he now is a rebel who willfully breaks the king's law (3:2–5; 5:9). Haman then could suggest that Mordecai be made an example of before he contaminates the empire with his seditious attitudes and acts. Far better, the reader believes, that Haman not be allowed to enter the inner court—but the king has spoken.

Haman enters and the king speaks (6:6). If the first words out of the king's mouth are similar words to those that he spoke when Esther approached him "illegally" in 5:3,[10] then Mordecai conceivably will die. Instead the king asks Haman what he would recommend to be done for the man whom the king desires[11] to honor.

The irony of what is about to happen hits the reader. The king is asking Haman—the avowed enemy of Mordecai—what he (the king) should do to honor Mordecai. Haman, moreover, has been ushered in, as far as he knows, to present his business to the king, that is, arguments designed to secure Mordecai's death. God, however, has different plans for Mordecai and Haman, and thus providentially guides the king to work at cross purposes to Haman, ultimately compelling Haman to honor rather than destroy Mordecai. H. A. Ironside writes that despite the fact that Haman "has reached the highest pinnacle of

9. The author uses the active participial form of the verb *ʿōmed* (standing, waiting) here to indicate that Haman has been waiting continually for some period of time, rather than having just walked in to the outer court at the precise time the king asks his question.

10. "What is troubling you . . .? And what is your request? Even to half of the kingdom, it will be given to you."

11. The term *ḥāpēṣ* indicates a special delight or pleasure (cf. 2:14). The author uses this verb consistently throughout the present passage (i.e., in 6:6 [2x], 7, 9 [2x], 11).

earthly glory to which he can lawfully aspire[,] . . . [h]e is about to be hurled into the lowest depths of shame and ignominy."[12]

Egotistically, Haman misinterprets the king's question, assuming that he himself is the one to be honored. Haman is in the dark about the king's request, but not so the reader. The irony of Haman's situation is delightful. It will soon become uproariously funny when, in verses 10–11, the king commands Haman to honor Mordecai publicly in the exact way that Haman anticipated would be done by others to himself.

Answering the Magic Wand Question (6:7–9)

Sales is a challenging business, and the sales process can be fascinating to observe. Several years ago when I was part of the electronics distribution industry, I had the opportunity to train my company's national sales force to develop a win-win relationship with our customers. During those training sessions we focused on ways to gain insight into our customers' problems and desires. One method we discussed is known as "the magic wand question." This question allows the customer to dream about what he or she would like under ideal conditions. The question is: "Assuming that you did not need to worry about money and that you had all the control that you needed, if you had a magic wand and could wave it over this situation, what would you like to have?"

In essence, King Ahasuerus asks Haman a magic wand question in 6:6. In verses 7–9, Haman answers that question by expressing his wildest dreams as to how he would like to be honored by the king. In verse 7 Haman begins to respond, and then stops. He pauses, almost as if he is mulling over the amazing words of the king: "for the man whom the king desires to honor." This break in Haman's speech, according to Michael V. Fox, "suggests that Haman is pausing to savor the phrase, which he applies to himself."[13] In fact, Haman is so enamored with the phrase that he uses it three different times in this short speech.

12. H. A. Ironside, *Notes on the Book of Esther,* 1905, in *Notes on the Books of Ezra, Nehemiah, and Esther* (New York: Loizeaux, 1960), 70–71.

13. Michael V. Fox, *Character and Ideology in the Book of Esther* (Columbia, S.C.: University of South Carolina Press, 1991), 76. Fox continues by observing that Haman, in his eagerness to reply to the king, forgets the standard court protocol of beginning a speech before a king "with a courtesy formula such as 'if it please the king' . . ."

Haman wants two things to be given to and four things to be done for "the man whom the king desires to honor." In verse 8 he describes what the honoree should receive, in verse 9 what should be done for the honoree. The two items that should be made available to the honoree are a royal robe and a royal horse. The robe must be one that the king already has worn.[14] Furthermore, the horse must be one on which the king previously has ridden, not just any royal horse. This horse now must be bedecked by having a royal crown placed on its head.[15]

Herodotus records that in Persian culture the giving of royal garments signaled that the recipients were deserving of special favor and respect.[16] Such garments, moreover, were assumed to possess a magical power that conveyed to the wearer a status of royalty.[17]

In verse 9 the author lists the four actions that Haman states should be done "for the man whom the king desires to honor." First, the responsibility for properly handling the royal robe and the royal horse should be given over to one of the most highly positioned individuals in the land. Second, the nobles should dress the honoree in the royal garment. Third, they should march the honoree (who now is seated on the horse) through the city square. Finally, they should go before the honoree and declare that those whom the king chooses to honor receive this type of royal treatment.

Haman's request that the honoree be rewarded by these various means rather than by having riches and property lavished upon that individual makes logical sense in light of the fact that Haman (who assumes that he is the one to be honored) is already fabulously wealthy (3:9; 5;11). Cohen believes that Haman is laying the foundation for a coup against the king.[18]

14. Keil, *The Books of Ezra, Nehemiah, and Esther,* 360.

15. There is much debate as to whether the crown is worn by the horse or by the person being honored. The positioning of the clause immediately after the discussion of the royal horse as well as the historical record show that Persian horses sometimes wore crowns.

16. *Herodotus,* trans. A. D. Godley (Cambridge: Harvard University Press, 1990), 3:84.

17. Sandra Beth Berg, *The Book of Esther: Motifs, Themes and Structure* (Missoula, Mont.: Scholars, 1979), 77.

18. Abraham D. Cohen, "'Hu Ha-goral': The Religious Significance of Esther," *Judaism* 23 (winter 1974): 93.

The Scripture, however, does not shed any light on Haman's motivation nor does it ever present Haman as being less than loyal to the king.

The reader soon learns that no matter what Haman's motivation is, it is of no consequence whatsoever. God has sealed Haman's downfall already and will bring it about shortly.

A Crushing Defeat (6:10–12)

For many people, the most terrifying thing that they could ever imagine happening to them would be to have their worst nightmares turn into realities. Fortunately, few people ever have to face situations that even approximate their horrifying dreams.

Haman, however, experiences something that to him is undoubtedly worse than his most frightening nightmare. He is commanded by the king to honor one whom Haman considers to be the most despicable creature in the world. Worse still, he is required to honor that enemy of his in full view of the inhabitants of the city of Susa.

The king hurries Haman to fulfill all that Haman has just said should be done "for the man whom the king desires to honor." This is the second of three times that Haman finds himself being hurried (cf. 5:5; 6:14).

Each time that Haman is hurried, his hurrying has some relationship to a Jew. In 5:5 and in 6:14, he is rushed off to a banquet being given by Queen Esther, a Jewess. In both of those situations, Haman is ignorant of Esther's ethnic background. He experiences pleasure throughout the first banquet (5:6, 9). He even experiences pleasure at the second banquet (7:1–2), until he learns of Esther's Jewish origins (7:4). Thereafter he only knows terror (7:6–10). In 6:10, by contrast, Haman is fully aware that the person for whom he must make all haste to honor is a Jew. Thus Haman's hurrying plunges him into the whirlpool of his worst nightmare, a whirlpool of humiliation because of a Jew (6:12–13). In 6:10, the king commands Haman to do what he (Haman) suggested should be done (leaving nothing out) to honor the king's favored one and to initiate that honoring process quickly. The king orders Haman to take the robe and the horse and to use them to honor not Haman himself but his worst enemy, Mordecai.

In order to ensure that Haman understands specifically whom the king means, the king identifies Mordecai as "the Jew" and as the one "who is sitting at the gate of the king." These descriptors are simply that, descriptors. The king does not appear to use them pejoratively against Mordecai or with any intent of humiliating Haman. King Ahasuerus simply wants to make certain that Haman honors the right man, the name *Mordecai* being a not uncommon name in the Medo-Persian empire.

What the king does not realize is that he, in essence, strikes three hard blows in Haman's face: the name *Mordecai*—the same name as the name of the one Haman hated most (5:9, 13); the identification of this Mordecai as being a Jew—a race of people detested for centuries by Haman's own people (cf. 3:1); and the designation of this Mordecai as being one who is "sitting" at the king's gate—the word *sitting* meaning in Haman's mind more than that Mordecai is an official but also that Mordecai "sits" defiantly rather than stands and bows out of respect to Haman (3:2–5; 5:9, 13).

Adding further irony is the fact that the responsibility for holding the bridle of the horse on which an honored man rides is considered an honor in itself.[19] The king would have assumed that Haman would feel honored to have the privilege of leading Mordecai throughout the city square.[20] Yet, for Haman, this honor is his shame. As Cassel states, Haman "is singled out to attend upon the man whom he abhorred from the bottom of his heart, words cannot describe this galling annoyance which this command caused him."[21]

In 6:11, Haman honors Mordecai according to the command of the king and in accord with all that Haman earlier declared should be done "for the man whom the king desires to honor." Nothing of special significance is recorded in this verse other than that Haman obediently does what the king expects him to do. Haman

19. Cassel, *An Explanatory Commentary on Esther,* 201.

20. In 6:11 the Hebrew term *r^{e}ḥôb,* translated "square," signifies "an open square, the place of public assemblage, the forum, or a collective signifying the wide streets of the city." Keil, *The Books of Ezra, Nehemiah, and Esther,* 361.

21. Cassel, *An Explanatory Commentary on Esther,* 201. In addition, the king unknowingly strikes one further blow against Haman. The king reminds Haman on two occasions that Haman himself provided the specifics of what should be done to honor Mordecai.

recognizes that discretion is the better part of valor. Never does he openly question the king's command to honor Mordecai and, just as wisely, never does Haman mention to the king what he (Haman) actually desires to do "for the man whom the king desires to honor," that is, to hang Mordecai from a seventy-five-foot high gallows.[22]

At least three points, however, are instructive about 6:11. The author does not

1. record any dialogue between the two antagonists, Mordecai and Haman;
2. divulge either man's emotional state at this time; or
3. dwell at length on the honoring of Mordecai.

On the first point, Fox writes that "the silence itself speaks, leaving the impression that nothing was said. Haman gritted his teeth and did what he had to, while Mordecai taciturnly accepted the honor."[23] The lack of dialogue seems reasonable. Any conversation at all between the two principals—beyond what is required to honor Mordecai—is unlikely due to their mutual hatred.

Point 2 is consistent with the author's commitment to presenting in rapid fashion the events that take place in this chapter. Presenting the emotional state of the two men would merely slow that pace and would add little to the story.

Point 3—the decision not to dwell at length on the honoring of Mordecai—suggests that the main point of this chapter is not the honoring of a Jew but the humiliation of a Gentile who desires the destruction of God's people. Everything in this chapter in some way contributes to Haman's downfall and moves the story closer to the ultimate defeat of the enemy of the Jews.

Verse 12 declares that, after Haman fulfills the command to honor Mordecai, both men go their separate ways. Mordecai returns to his duties at the king's gate (seemingly as if nothing out of the ordinary had happened).[24] By contrast, Haman

22. Ironside notes that "[t]he gallows stand like a monument to folly and vanity, still towering up to heaven, casting a shadow that speaks of approaching disaster." *Notes on the Book of Esther,* 74.

23. Fox, *Character and Ideology in the Book of Esther,* 78.

returns to his home with his head covered[25] to commiserate with his family and friends.

Kick Him While He's Down (6:13–14)

Many years ago there was a Broadway musical and then a movie titled *How to Succeed in Business Without Really Trying.* The lead character, Ponty, is a window washer who secures a job in the mail room of a large corporation and within only a few days rises in comedic fashion to the position of vice president of marketing. He is told by the president of the company to develop a full-blown advertising campaign over the weekend or be fired. Ponty panics and borrows an idea of a "buried treasure" television game show from the president's nephew, Bud Frump. The game show becomes a disaster because of the president's secret girlfriend, a dim-witted model on the show. Ponty, however, is held responsible and is brought by all of the top brass of the company to face the chairman of the board. The chairman demands to know whose idea the game show was. Ponty points to Bud Frump. The instant that Bud Frump's name is mentioned, all those standing around him quickly move away. The chairman then asks whose idea it was to use the scatterbrained model. Ponty motions in the president's direction, and those standing around the president immediately desert him as well.[26]

In the same way that Bud Frump's and the president's friends leave them like people fleeing a burning building, so too in 6:13, when Haman's family and friends hear of his humiliation, they leave him "hanging" all by himself. Instead of giving

24. In fact, for Mordecai, nothing has changed. The gallows still stand. Furthermore, he still remains under the edict of death that hangs as a pall over the Jews (3:13).

25. In ancient times (among both the Hebrews and the Persians) the covering of one's head in a situation such as this was an outward sign of the grief that a person was experiencing internally. Carey A. Moore, *Esther,* The Anchor Bible, ed. William Foxwell Albright and David Noel Freedman (Garden City, N.Y.: Doubleday, 1971), 66; Lewis Bayles Paton, *The Book of Esther,* International Critical Commentary, ed. Samuel Rolles Driver, Alfred Plummer, and Charles Augustus Briggs (Edinburgh: T. and T. Clark, 1908), 255.

26. The musical ends happily. No one is fired, a few are even promoted, and Ponty becomes the new chairman of the board when the former chairman retires and marries the scatterbrained model.

him comfort in his darkest hour, they offer him only words of discouragement: "you will not overcome him [Mordecai] but you will certainly fall before him."

Verse 13 begins with Haman pouring out to his wife and friends the horror of what has just happened to him. The *Midrash Lekach Tov* and Malbim separately argue that this verse reveals that Haman has not been fully dissuaded by his experience from seeking to take Mordecai's life. They base their argument on the verb *qārā(h)* (to happen) which "implies a *coincidental* happening." Thus they say that Haman views his situation as follows: "*It was just a matter of bad luck* in my going to the King to hang Mordechai on the day the King decided to repay Mordechai some old debt of gratitude. Now that the debt has been paid, I am sure the King will listen to my advice and hang Mordechai."[27] Their position makes sense since the verb *qārā(h)* carries, at times, the connotation of a chance occurrence, something beyond human control.[28] Interestingly, the author uses this verb only here and in 4:7. In 4:7, the author records that Mordecai details all that had "happened" to him in relationship to Haman. Thus in 4:7 and here in 6:13, the characters understand the events that happened to them as being beyond their control, yet not so large as to overwhelm them completely.

In the midst of unfolding the interaction among Haman, his wife, and his friends, the author indicates that those who respond to Haman are "his wise men and Zeresh, his wife." The group designated "his wise men" conceivably could refer to a previously unidentified group or could merely be another title for "his friends." The context seems to favor the latter, that is, that there are only three distinctions being made (i.e., Haman, his wife, and his friends / his wise men), not four.

27. Meir Zlotowitz, trans. and comp., *The Megillah: The Book of Esther: A New Translation Anthologized from Talmudic, Midrashic and Rabbinic Sources* (Brooklyn: Mesorah, 1981), 98.

28. Francis Brown, S. R. Driver, and Charles A. Briggs, *A Hebrew and English Lexicon of the Old Testament with an Appendix Containing the Biblical Aramaic* (reprint; Oxford: Clarendon, 1968), 899; Leonard J. Coppes, "2068. . .; *(qārâ),*" *Theological Wordbook of the Old Testament,* ed. R. Laird Harris, Gleason L. Archer Jr., and Bruce K. Waltke (Chicago: Moody, 1980), 2:813–14; Ludwig Koehler and Walter Baumgartner, eds., *Lexicon in Veteris Testementi Libros* (Leiden: Brill, 1985), 853–54.

Why the author has chosen to denote Haman's friends as his wise men is not stated. Perhaps the author wants to indicate that the response they give to Haman this time is superior to the advice they gave him previously (5:14). Here these wise men and Zeresh predict Haman's ultimate downfall.[29] Curiously, they offer only one explanation as to why Haman cannot possibly succeed: Mordecai is a Jew![30]

What do Haman's friends sense about Mordecai's Jewishness that they believe will cause Haman's downfall? Do they recognize the hand of God in the honoring and subsequent preservation of Mordecai? If so, they are the only ones in the story who seem even to hint at his existence.

As indicated earlier (cf. 6:1–3), the author makes special mention in 6:14 of the timing of the arrival of the king's eunuchs at Haman's home to escort him to the second banquet. They arrive in the midst of Haman's discussion with his wife and friends, at a time when he is at his lowest point emotionally. The timing provides an ironic twist—Haman, being demoralized, quite probably thinks that life could not get any worse for him, yet, as he soon learns (7:6–10), life can and will take one final turn for the worst.

The author also indicates in 6:14 that the eunuchs "hurried" to take Haman to the banquet. This "hurrying" is one more reminder that events are moving rapidly—too rapidly for Haman ever again to gain control of his destiny.

Important Lessons from Seemingly Insignificant Events

Chapter 6 begins and ends with a Gentile in a disturbed state of mind. In 6:1, the king cannot sleep. Haman probably

29. The grammatical construction used here—an infinitive absolute followed immediately by a finite verb of the same root—emphasizes the force of the verb in its context. C[hoon]. L[eong]. Seow, *A Grammar for Biblical Hebrew* (Nashville: Abingdon, 1987), 182. Bruce K. Waltke and M. O'Connor, *An Introduction to Biblical Hebrew Syntax* (Winona Lake, Ind.: Eisenbrauns, 1990), §35.3.1b.

30. Beginning a clause with the particle *ʾim* (if) (as is the case here) is the most frequent way in Scripture of indicating that the supposition which follows is "real" as opposed to "unreal." Thus Haman's wise men and his wife are well aware of Mordecai's ethnic background. In essence they are saying, "if Mordecai is a Jew (and he is), then . . ." or "since Mordecai is a Jew, then. . . ." Joüon, *A Grammar of Biblical Hebrew*, §167; Fox, *Character and Ideology in the Book of Esther*, 79.

wishes that he had slept late that day. Had either man slept through the entire night, and if God were not providentially guiding all life as he always does, the events of this chapter would have taken a significantly different turn than they in fact did: Mordecai would not have been honored; Haman would not have been humiliated; and Mordecai, most likely, would have been hanged.

Interestingly, Mordecai's sleep, or lack thereof, apparently makes no difference to the events of the day. He appears for but a brief moment between these two Gentiles who do not sleep the whole night through. He receives their accolades for having earlier rescued the king from disaster, after which he returns to his civil-service job (6:10–12). His honoring is almost incidental to the chapter. It occurs there to show that God can accomplish his goals despite seemingly insurmountable odds.

This fact that God is actively at work even when everything seems to be bleak and hopeless is the first of two main principles being taught in the chapter. The author wants his readers to recognize that God alone rescues Mordecai and that Mordecai has no hand whatsoever in his own deliverance. If God can rescue Mordecai after Haman has sounded Mordecai's death knell, then there is hope that God will do the same for the rest of the Jews under a similar edict of death.

The second key principle of this chapter is that God works providentially through even the day-to-day circumstances of life. He works through such human events as insomnia, the reading of a specific text of a specific book, the anger of a man, the timing of events, the words of unbelievers, and the actions of people doing their jobs. Nothing in life is too small or insignificant for God to oversee or use to ensure the good of his people or the downfall of their enemies.

Two additional principles present themselves in chapter 6, though they do not form the main purpose around which the author designs this chapter: pride can be dangerous and circumstances reveal character.

First, pride blinds Haman to the truth. He assumes that his plans cannot be thwarted so he rushes headlong into a given situation without first learning what forces are shaping that situation. His pride, therefore, precedes his fall (Prov. 11:2; 16:18; 28:14; 29:23).

Second, difficult situations shed the veneer of superficial character traits. Haman's wife and friends surround him with encouraging advice when he is at the peak of his power (5:9–14). When he is disgraced, however, they offer him only negative words that neither comfort nor guide (6:13). The friendship they show him in chapter 5 quickly vanishes in chapter 6 when he experiences a setback.

The presence of these four principles in chapter 6 suggests that the author wrote this chapter not merely to retell the story of Haman's humiliation, but also to give words both of hope and of caution. Hope exists because God exists and cares for his people. Caution needs to be exercised because God expects everyone—believer and unbeliever alike—to serve him faithfully in accordance with the truth of his word.

A Crack in the Levee

In the summer of 1993, the Mississippi River overflowed its banks in one of the worst floods in American history. Thousands of people heroically labored to build and shore up the sandbag levees. Tragically, at certain places, a crack would develop in one of the levees and water would begin to trickle through. If the workers were unable to repair it quickly enough, the pressure of the water would rupture the entire levee and the countryside would be almost instantly submerged under several feet of water.

Likewise, in Esther 6 a crack develops in Haman's seemingly impregnable position. On the surface all appears to be as it was before—Haman is still prime minister and Mordecai is still under the edict of death. Underneath the surface, however, the structural integrity of Haman's political levee has been weakened. Mordecai rather than Haman has been honored; Haman, by contrast, writhes in humiliation. His plans have been shattered.

Whereas thousands came to the rescue of those who lived along the Mississippi River, no one comes to Haman's rescue when his world begins to crumble around him. He alone must fight back the destructive forces. The question is whether he will be able to work quickly enough to preserve his dignity, his position, and his life. Esther 7 provides some amazing and totally unexpected answers.

17

The Death of Despair
(7:1–10)

One of the most explosive rollercoaster rides is found at Knott's Berry Farm in Southern California—Montezuma's Revenge. It is not a long ride—it has only one loop—but once the ride begins it combines sheer terror with two very short respites in which impending terror is anticipated with exhilaration. The ride begins when you are strapped into a rollercoaster car and it is shot forward into the loop. Whipping through the loop, you hang upside down at one point. Immediately upon exiting the loop, the car follows the track upward until gravity slows it to a dead stop. At that point you attempt to catch your breath until reality sets in—you realize you are going to rocket through that terrifying loop *backward*. Instantly the car drops back down the track, gaining momentum with every split second. Almost before you know what is happening, the car has gone ballistic through the loop (upside down again) until it again begins to climb up another incline, slowing to a complete halt—another respite—HA! At that instant when you hope to catch your breath, you find yourself looking almost straight down, down that track where you once more are compelled to hurtle. The car picks up speed again until it nears the bottom of the track where it is brought to an abrupt halt. The ride is over, and you stagger shakily out of the car, glad to be alive (and, depending on your mental age, eager to go on the ride again).

Delving into chapter 7 of the Book of Esther is much like buckling into a rollercoaster car on Montezuma's Revenge. There is a sense of anticipation at first, followed by the explosive acceleration of Esther's accusation. This leads to a momentary respite as the king leaves the room. Immediately thereafter, the terror returns as Haman "attacks" the queen and the king catches Haman in the act. Once more for a few short seconds a lull in the action occurs during which the king's servant mentions the gallows that Haman has built. The action quickly resumes when the king commands that Haman be hanged and Haman is executed. The chapter then comes to an abrupt halt, and everyone except Haman seemingly breathes a sigh of relief. The "ride" is over.

Questions, Questions, Questions

Chapter 7 is built around a series of questions posed by the king—"What do you desire?" (v. 2), "Who did it and where is he?" (v. 5), and "How can he do what he is doing?" (v. 8—and are answered by either verbal (vv. 3–4, 6) or physical responses (v. 8). The questions signal, in order, an open door to speak, a freedom to confront, and an end to the conflict.

The king, queen, and prime minister are feasting together when the first question shifts the reader's attention to the business of the day (vv. 1–2). The king graciously expresses a willingness to fulfill Queen Esther's desire (v. 2). She responds initially by submitting herself to the king's good graces (v. 3). Then she fires her first salvo by announcing that she and her people have been condemned to die (v. 4). The king interrupts with the second set of questions, demanding to know who would dare to issue such an order and where that person is (v. 5). Esther finally unloads her rifle—Haman is the guilty one (v. 6). The king, troubled by what he hears, leaves the banquet hall for a while, only to return to find Haman falling down upon Esther's couch pleading for his life (vv. 7–8). Mistaking Haman's actions for an attack on the queen, the king utters a rhetorical question that challenges Haman's audacity (v. 8). The servants respond by preparing Haman for death and then by hanging him (vv. 9–10).

Chapter 7 therefore may be understood to flow in accordance with the questions of the king. The following three-point outline reflects such a perspective:

A. Explaining a problem (7:1–4)
B. Exposing a person (7:5–6)
C. Eliminating a person (7:7–10)

Chapter 7 may also be viewed from the standpoint of the five major blocks of action:

A. The calm before the storm (7:1–2)
B. The crux of the storm (7:3–4)
C. The crisis of the storm (7:5–6)
D. The calamity of the storm (7:7–8)
E. The calm after the storm (7:9–10)

This chapter is a fast-paced, action-packed passage that quickly eliminates a major barrier inhibiting the deliverance of the Jews from their predicament.

An Emotional Upheaval

From the beginning of Esther 7 to its end, the Jews go from the depths of despair to seeing the death of despair—Haman, their enemy, is dead! The Jews can celebrate! Yet, all is not as it should be. Just as in *The Wizard of Oz,* when the Munchkins sing "Ding dong, the witch is dead," the viewer soon realizes that the killing of the witch (or of Haman) does not resolve all of the problems presented in the story. Much more needs to happen, yet there is hope that the story will turn out well. In the same way, the death of Haman in chapter 7 excites a sense of hope in the Jews. That which at the beginning of the chapter is the seemingly impossible becomes by the end of the chapter the potentially achievable. Guarded hope exists that deliverance for the Jews may actually arise from Esther's efforts on their behalf. The initial toppling of Gentile antagonistic domination over the Jews has begun.

One More Time, for the Record (7:1–2)

Second chances in life are often rare. How often do we find ourselves saying, "If only I had said or done such and such"? Frequently we walk away kicking ourselves in the proverbial seat of the pants, wishing that we had acted differently or had made better use of our opportunities.

At the beginning of Esther 7, Esther seems to have pressed her "luck" too far. She has failed to respond to the king as he expected her to do on two earlier occasions (5:3–4, 6–8). Now she is hoping for another chance. Has she perhaps tried the king's patience beyond the breaking point? If not, will he be amenable to her requests?

Amazingly, in 7:1–2 we discover that Esther receives a second chance—actually, a third chance—to make the king aware of her problems and to plead for his help. Even more amazingly, he grants all of her requests fully (7:9; 8:8).

God seemingly is working overtime to ensure the deliverance of his people. He works behind the scenes to make the king receptive to Esther as a person (5:2). God also maneuvers the king to develop a positive feeling toward Mordecai (6:1–3, 10). Furthermore, God keeps the king favorably disposed to Queen Esther, despite her tactical delays on two different occasions (5:3–4, 6–8).

Esther 7:1 declares that the king and Haman join Esther for the drinking portion[1] of the second banquet that she has prepared for them (cf. 5:8; 7:2, 14). At that time, the king once again makes the formulaic but magnanimous gesture of promising to fulfill any of Esther's desires, up to half of the kingdom (cf. 5:3, 6). Whether the king deigns to grant Esther her request remains to be seen. Yet, as Carey A. Moore states, "having offered such emphatic assurances on three separate occasions, he [the king] could hardly deny that he had really made such a promise. Thus the king had painted himself in a corner."[2]

Let My People Go (7:3–4)

An old-time spiritual, "Go Down, Moses," has the familiar refrain: "Go down Moses, 'way down in Egypt's land. Tell ol' Pharaoh, let my people go." Esther in 7:3–4 repeats the sentiment

1. Paton notes that the drinking of wine took place after the food had been served. Lewis Bayles Paton, *The Book of Esther*, International Critical Commentary, ed. Samuel Rolles Driver, Alfred Plummer, and Charles Augustus Briggs (Edinburgh: T. and T. Clark, 1908), 257.

2. Carey A. Moore, *Esther*, The Anchor Bible, ed. William Foxwell Albright and David Noel Freedman (Garden City, N.Y.: Doubleday, 1971), 73.

of such a song, appealing to the king of the Medo-Persian empire to free her people from the bondage of the edict of death imposed on them by their enemy, Prime Minister Haman.[3]

Esther remains composed, despite having to face the incredible pressure of petitioning the most powerful human being of her day, an individual who was easily persuaded to depose the previous queen (1:10–22) and to issue a death warrant against Esther's people (3:8–11). Esther's composure is manifest in 7:3, when she remembers to introduce her plea using the ceremonial language of the court. In fact, she begins with two such statements of humble servitude: "If I have found favor in your eyes, O king"[4] and "if unto the king it *seems* good."

Esther's calmness under fire in 7:3–4 is remarkable. Is it the result of a well choreographed plan either laid out for her by Mordecai or developed by herself? The Scripture seems to suggest that Mordecai and Esther have no interpersonal communications from the end of chapter 4 to the beginning of chapter 8. No mention is made of them either being at the same place at the same time or transmitting any messages via servants. In addition, Esther 4:17 argues against Mordecai's involvement in the development of Esther's plans since he leaves his normal position (i.e., the king's gate) in order to act in accord with Esther's wishes. Although Esther previously followed Mordecai's orders (2:10, 20), after 4:17 she no longer is portrayed as doing so. Mordecai's involvement in any plan by which Esther is to approach the king thus seems to be minimal or nonexistent.

Furthermore, 5:4 leaves open the possibility that Esther choreographed the entire sequence of events. That verse indicates that she had prepared her first banquet before approaching the king. Such a fact suggests that she had planned to delay broaching the subject of the death edict on her first encounter with him. There is no indication, however, whether prior to her

3. Unlike Moses, who seeks to have his people leave their bondage in Egypt and return to the Promised Land, Esther expresses no similar interest to have her people return to the Promised Land.

4. Note that Esther's calmness is coupled with a sense of intimacy. She includes as part of her ceremonial address to the king the second person singular pronoun *you*. Her use of this personal pronoun is a calculated risk. Such a breach of formal courtroom language would invite disaster if the king became offended by its lack of formality.

approaching the king in the inner court (5:2) she had designed into her plan a second banquet to be held the following day.

If Esther has planned out the entire sequence of events (5:1–8; 7:1–4), then she most definitely qualifies as one of the master politicians of all time. Few before or since her time have been able to do so much with so little hope of success. She approaches the negotiating table with little or no experience in the political arena, yet she accomplishes the seemingly impossible, that is, the sidestepping of an irreversible law.

Most likely, Esther's delays—definitely the first and quite possibly the second—are a programmed part of her plan. The delays (i.e., banquets) function in such a way as to lubricate the social relationship between Esther and the king, thereby reducing any tension that may exist between them (cf. 4:11). They place the king in a jovial and receptive mood, almost guaranteeing that he will be amenable to Esther's requests.[5]

In 7:3, after adhering to court formalities, Esther arrests the king's attention: "Let it be given to me, my life as my petition and my people as my request." The terseness of these words cut to the heart of her concerns.[6] She wants the king to recognize immediately the seriousness of her problem. She does not want some trinket or bauble, not even property. She wants life itself—for herself and for her people.[7]

Esther continues her persuasive speech in 7:4 by explaining her situation, stressing the importance of her plea, and flattering the king. Wisely, she avoids any remarks that might directly implicate the king as being a perpetrator of the problem that she and her people face.

5. The relaxed atmosphere of the two banquets, moreover, would work to put Haman off his guard. He would assume that all is well with his world (cf. 5:12).

6. The brevity of Esther's speech may be better attributed to her desire to gain the king's attention than to her emotional state (against Cassel and Moore). Paulus Cassel, *An Explanatory Commentary on Esther*, trans. Aaron Bernstein (Edinburgh: T. and T. Clark, 1888), 211; Moore, *Esther*, 70.

7. Esther pleads for her own life before that of her people. Fox writes that she does so because she realizes "that the king will be ready to save his wife but will show less vigor in acting on behalf of her people." Michael V. Fox, *Character and Ideology in the Book of Esther* (Columbia, S.C.: University of South Carolina Press, 1991), 83. Fox's observation proves to be true (note that Esther must make a second plea to the king for her people's lives—8:5–6).

Esther fleshes out the "my life" and "my people" of verse 3 by declaring in verse 4 that she and her people have been sold in order to be eradicated from the face of the earth. The fact that she uses the term *sold (nimkarnû)*[8] indicates her belief that a monetary transaction actually took place (3:8–11), despite the king's gracious refusal of Haman's offer of money (3:11).[9]

Next, Esther parrots to the king the language of the edict itself. In fact, the terms *to be destroyed, to be killed,* and *to be annihilated* are word-for-word replications[10] in the exact order of their counterparts in the death warrant previously issued by Haman (cf. 3:13). The king, however, shows no recognition that he is aware of the recently issued edict. By contrast, Haman undoubtedly is well aware of the significance of Esther's words. Interestingly, the Scripture remains silent regarding Haman's reaction until after Esther points the finger of condemnation at him (7:6).

Esther continues by calling attention to the significance of what she is saying. She declares that she would not have brought the matter before the king—she would have kept silent[11]—if it had not truly been a matter of life and death. She introduces this declaration by means of the conditional particle *ʾillû* (if), which signifies that the conditional clause that follows

8. By presenting the verb *sold* in a passive form (i.e., "we have been sold"), Esther avoids identifying those who are guilty of attacking the king's wife and her people. Thus she skirts mentioning the king's involvement in the plot. Fox also notes that "Esther does not name Haman yet, for she seeks to point the king's anger at a nameless perpetrator, before the king starts fretting about harming his vizier and favorite, and before he recalls how the 'sale' came about. Once his ire is provoked, Esther will give it a target." Fox, *Character and Ideology in the Book of Esther*, 84.

9. Some commentators advance the idea that Esther uses the term *sold* as an idiomatic expression to mean "delivered over to" (cf. Deut. 32:30; Judg. 2:14; 4:2, 9; 10:7) rather than to suggest that any monetary transaction took place. This view is tenuous in light of Mordecai's reference in Esther 4:7 to the exact amount of money that Haman promises the king.

10. There is one spelling variation of the verb *hārag* (to kill) to be noted: *lahărōg* occurs in 3:13; whereas *lahărôg* occurs in 7:4. This difference, however, does not affect the meaning of the words.

11. One wonders if Esther truly would have remained silent or if she is merely using the polite language of the royal court that has nothing whatsoever to do with reality.

the particle refers to that which is unreal.[12] Thus the meaning of the first half of Esther's statement here is to be understood as "if we had only been sold as male slaves and female slaves (but we were not sold as slaves at all)." These words, therefore, act as a broad marking pen to underline the reality of the destruction, killing, and annihilation that awaits Esther and her people.

Esther concludes her brief plea by subtly flattering the king. She states that, had reality been different, the condemnation of a man who would enslave a whole race of people would have been too minor a problem to bring before the king. In essence, Esther declares that she would rather allow that enslaver go free and her own people be enslaved than to trouble the king with such a petty problem.

To convey such a message to the king, Esther uses six Hebrew words: *kî ʾên haṣṣār šowe(h) b^e^nēzeq hammelek*—"because the adversary would not equate (in value) with the annoyance of the king." The precise meaning of three of those six words, however, is a matter of some discussion.

The first difficult word is *haṣṣar*. Technically, *haṣṣar* should be rendered "the enemy" or "the adversary," yet many commentaries translate it as "the adversity" or "the calamity." Paulus Cassel, who favors the latter rendering, sums up the argument: "True, צר *[ṣr]* means 'enemy,' but in the abstract also 'distress,' 'tribulation,' 'misfortune;' and even if it is insisted that the article points to the enemy, still it must be conceded that the emphasis cannot be on the person, but . . . upon the act of the enemy."[13]

The context favors repointing *haṣṣār* as *haṣṣar* that is, "the adversity" or "the trouble," focusing attention on the concept of slavery and supporting the idea that the slavery of Esther's people would be considered to be a minor problem in comparison to their being slaughtered. The Hebrew manuscripts, however, consistently record this term as *haṣṣār*, and the ancient translations concur.[14] Thus, because of the overwhelming textual evi-

12. Ronald J. Williams, *Hebrew Syntax: An Outline* (reprint; Toronto: University of Toronto Press, 1986), 86, §516.

13. Cassel, *An Explanatory Commentary on Esther*, 213.

14. The Septuagint, Vulgate, and Syriac (Peshitta) texts agree with the Masoretic Text position that an individual, an adversary, is in view here. Fox, *Character and Ideology in the Book of Esther*, 282.

dence and because the translation *the adversary* can be shown to fit easily with the context, Esther should be understood to be declaring that the culprit, the guilty party, the unnamed Haman, that is, the enemy, is not worth the annoyance (or damage) of the king.[15]

The second word under the microscope in 7:4 is *šowe(h)*, variously translated as "commensurate," "equal," "worth," "worthwhile," "value," or "justify." In the Book of Esther the term occurs only in 3:8; 5:13; and here. In all three verses, the speaker uses *šowe(h)* to reveal that an imbalanced equation exists (3:8; 5:13) or would exist (7:4) in a given situation. Thus Esther seems to be suggesting in 7:4 that the value of the adversary in no way approaches the value that she places on the king's well-being.

The third word whose meanings is contested is *nēzeq,* which occurs only here in the Hebrew Scriptures. The term, however, does appear later in history in rabbinic Hebrew where it means "damage" or "loss."[16] Fox understands *nēzeq* to refer "to the financial loss that cancelling the sale would cause to the seller,"[17] whereas Paton contends that it means "injury."[18] Haupt views *nēzeq* as meaning "annoyance"[19]—a view that is most widely accepted today, and one that fits the context well.[20]

Despite the disparate views, an analysis of the text and the context of the clause *kî ʾên haṣṣār šowe(h) b^{e}nēzeq hammelek* suggests that the preferred English translation of the clause should closely approximate the following: "because the adversary would not equate (in value) with the annoyance of the king."

15. C. F. Keil, *The Books of Ezra, Nehemiah, and Esther*, Biblical Commentary on the Old Testament, trans. Sophia Taylor (Grand Rapids: Eerdmans, n.d.), 364.

16. Joyce G. Baldwin, *Esther: An Introduction and Commentary*, Tyndale Old Testament Commentaries, ed. D. J. Wiseman (Downers Grove: InterVarsity, 1984), 92.

17. Fox, *Character and Ideology in the Book of Esther*, 84. Huey also advocates the financial-loss position. F. B. Huey, Jr., "Esther," *Expositor's Bible Commentary*, ed. Frank E. Gaebelein, 12 vols. (Grand Rapids: Zondervan, 1988), 4:825–26.

18. Paton, *The Book of Esther*, 261.

19. Paul Haupt, "Critical Notes on Esther," *American Journal of Semitic Languages and Literature* 24 (1907–1908): 147, reprint in *Studies in the Book of Esther*, ed. Carey A. Moore (New York: KTAV, 1982), 1–90.

20. See Robert Gordis, "Studies in the Esther Narrative," *Journal of Biblical Literature* 95 (March 1976): 56; Moore, *Esther*, 70–71.

Rage Unfurled (7:5–6)

For most people, rage naturally explodes when a prized possession is damaged or when a loved one is hurt by someone else. That rage often flares like a wildfire during the hot dry season, consuming everything that crosses its path.

King Ahasuerus, upon hearing Esther's plaintive plea in 7:3–4, becomes concerned, even outraged that some unnamed assailant would mount an attack against his wife. He demands to know who and where that assailant is (v. 5).

The author introduces the king's questions with the following words: *wayyoʾmer hammelek ʾăḥašwērôš wayyoʾmer leʾestēr hammalkā(h)* (lit., "and King Ahasuerus said and he said to Queen Esther"). In so doing, the author uses an idiomatic expression consisting of the Qal imperfect form of the verb *to say* being repeated (*wayyoʾmer . . . wayyoʾmer*—and he said . . . and he said) with reference to the same speaker and in relation to the same words about to be quoted by the author.

Some commentators have assumed incorrectly that the repetition of *wayyoʾmer* in 7:5 is the narrator's way of revealing the anger or agitation that the king feels as a result of the attack by the unnamed assailant on his wife.[21] Michael V. Fox, however, provides an explanation that comes closer to the sense of the grammatical construction being used. He states that the repetition of *wayyoʾmer* is "an acceptable idiom, whose effect may have been to control the pacing of the verse."[22] Further research may prove that the authors of Scripture utilize this idiomatic expression when they desire to indicate that a speaker exhibits a measure of self-control in his or her manner of speech.[23] The beginning clause of 7:5 then would imply that the king is attempting to keep his anger in check until he learns the name of the person who initiated the assault against Esther and her people.

Keeping the reins on his anger, the king asks Esther two questions in quick succession: "who is this and where is he who

21. See Cassel, *An Explanatory Commentary on Esther*, 213; Keil, *The Books of Ezra, Nehemiah, and Esther*, 365.

22. Fox, *Character and Ideology in the Book of Esther*, 283.

23. See Gen. 22:7; 1 Kings 20:28; and Ezek. 10:2.

has filled his heart[24] to do thus?" These are logical questions, since Esther has aroused his anger but has not shown him where it should be directed. He needs to know, and he needs to know now.

Even though Esther has the king where she wants him (i.e., willing to act on her behalf against her enemy), she does not blurt out the name of her adversary. Instead, she remains the consummate communicator. She builds suspense by making certain that the king understands that the name she names is the name of someone who is totally committed to her destruction. Such an individual understandably deserves to be struck down by the full brunt of the king's wrath. Interestingly, however, Esther never once asks for Haman to be killed. The king assumes that Haman's death is what Esther seeks.[25]

Esther in 7:5 announces who that despicable one is: "a man, an adversary, and an enemy—Haman is this evil one!"

Haman reacts immediately. He is terrified at what he hears. He has been named the guilty one toward whom Queen Esther wants the king to direct the fury of his anger.

The Hebrew word order in the final sentence of verse 6 indicates that the person of Haman, rather than the terror of Haman, is being held forth as the most important component. Thus the author wants to impress upon the reader that Haman himself, the enemy of the Jews who condemned the Jews to death, cringes in fear before not only the king, but also the queen, a Jewess.[26]

Yet, will the king side with Haman, his well liked and recently promoted prime minister, or with Esther, his wife? As Lewis Bayles Paton states: "The fatal word is now spoken which will decide whether Haman or Esther has the greater influence with the King."[27]

24. Moore paraphrases "who has filled his heart" as "who has the nerve?" Moore, *Esther*, 71. Note that the verb *m*ᵉ*lāʾō* (who has filled) is an active rather than a passive form. The king, therefore, is not asking Esther whether some outside being or force has put these terrible ideas into her enemy's mind, but rather who the individual is who filled his own mind with such plans against her.

25. In Esther 8:1–8, Esther needs to approach the king a second time before he acts upon her request for the deliverance of her people.

26. The reversal of the good fortune of the enemy of the Jews continues. In 6:10–12, Haman was embarrassed before Mordecai. Now, in 7:6, he is terrified before Esther. Soon, in 7:10, he will be dead before all of Susa.

27. Paton, *The Book of Esther*, 259–60.

A Chicken with Its Head Cut Off (7:7–8)

Much like a chicken with its head cut off, Haman runs in all directions in 7:7–8. He turns first to the king, but the king walks away from him. Haman then turns to the queen, but she who has condemned him remains silent. His life then turns into a tragic farce. Haman, who is in the midst of petitioning the queen for his life, is accused by the king of assaulting her and as a result is condemned to death. Then the king's servants cover Haman's face and cart him off to be executed (v. 10) on the very gallows that he had prepared for his enemy, Queen Esther's adoptive father, a Jew, Mordecai.

Specifically in verse 7, both the king and Haman stand up—the king to leave the room, Haman to stay to plead for his life.

Even at this stage in the story, the author maintains a high level of tension. He records that the king arises in anger, but anger against whom—Haman or Esther—the author does not explicitly say. Haman is the king's hand-picked prime minister, his second in command for the ruling of the empire (3:1; 5:11). Esther is the king's hand-picked wife for the bedroom and, most likely, for official functions to show off as his prized jewel (2:17). The king is angry at one of them—but which one?

This is the second time that the king becomes angry at a drinking party (cf. 1:10–12). On each occasion his anger arises in connection with his wife, the queen. At the previous banquet he unleashed his anger in the direction of the queen for the "good" of the empire. Will he do the same here? Curiously, the author uses one of the same terms for anger *[ḥēmā(h)]*[28] that he records in 1:12. Whether he has done so intentionally in order to suggest an emotional connection between the two events is unclear. The reader, however, is left wondering if the outcome of the current situation might be similar to that of the earlier one. If so, Esther is in grave danger.

28. There are, at a minimum, twelve Hebrew words available to the author of the Book of Esther by which he could describe the king's anger. Those twelve words are *ʾap, zaʿam, zaʿap, ḥārôn, ḥēmā(h), ḥŏrî, kaʿas, ʿebrā(h), pānîm, qeṣep, rogez,* and *rûah,* and are variously translated (in alphabetical order) as anger, fury, heat, hot displeasure, indignation, poison, rage, or wrath. The word that the author chooses here, however, is one of the more frequently used of those twelve terms in Scripture. It is, moreover, the word most often used by the author (1:12; 2:1; 3:5; 5:9; 7:7, 10) to describe the emotion categorized as anger or wrath.

The king storms out of the banquet hall and quickly enters the palace garden (7:7). By omitting an expected verb, the author captures the king's frenzied pace. The literal translation of the king's action reads: "And the king arose in his anger from drinking wine into the palace garden." The fact that the words *and went* are missing suggests speed—"the king arose into the garden"—almost as if no time elapsed between his leaving the dining hall and his entering the garden.

Whereas the king hurries out of the banquet room, Haman remains there to beg for his life from Queen Esther. He turns to her rather than to the king for help because he believes "that harm was determined against him by the king."[29] The verb *kāl-tā(h)* (was determined) conveys the idea of completion, "something that is fully settled in a person's mind."[30] When its context indicates that a sense of "determination" is meant, the verb always suggests the negative side of determination and may, at times, be translated "plotted."[31] In 7:7, the Scripture indicates that Haman definitely accords a negative sense to the events that are happening. He does not anticipate that he will find the king in a favorable mood when he returns from the garden. In fact, Haman expects the worst possible scenario to play out, that is, his death.

Ironically, in 7:8, no matter what the king is planning to do to Haman, Haman seals his own fate. At the exact moment King Ahasuerus returns from the palace garden, Haman is in the act of falling[32] on the couch where Queen Esther is reclining. He does so in order to plead for his life; yet the king grossly misinterprets Haman's intentions: "Will he even assault the queen with me in the house?" The king assumes that Haman is attack-

29. The final consonants of the four consecutive Hebrew words translated "that harm was determined against him" when read backward as an acrostic spell out the proper name of God, YHWH. See 5:4 for a discussion of the significance of such a finding.

30. Paton, *The Book of Esther*, 263.

31. Francis Brown, S. R. Driver, and Charles A. Briggs, *A Hebrew and English Lexicon of the Old Testament with an Appendix Containing the Biblical Aramaic* (reprint; Oxford: Clarendon, 1968), 477.

32. The verb form used here is the participial form, which implies an ongoing process. In other words, when the king reenters the banquet hall Haman is caught in the very act of falling—somewhere between standing upright and lying on Queen Esther's couch.

ing the queen either to take her life violently or to rape her.[33] Immediately, unnamed servants cover Haman's face, symbolically indicating that the sentence of death now hangs over Haman's head.[34]

The covering of Haman's face continues the downward spiral of Haman's fortunes. Much like a person who drives a car on a mountain road when a thunderstorm strikes, Haman is overwhelmed by events outside of his control. At first, before the storm hits, the sun is shining and "all is well with the world." All is well in Haman's life when he becomes prime minister (3:1) and writes a death warrant against his enemies (3:8–15). Then, suddenly and seemingly without warning, a cloud covers the mountain road, engulfing the car, and an eerie, foreboding darkness settles in, chilling the bones. Tragedy first sets in for Haman when, after receiving pleasing advice from family and friends (5:14), he is commanded to honor publicly his most despised enemy, Mordecai (6:10–13). Finally, the terrifying torrential rains, together with the lightning flashes, crash down all around the car—disaster has struck. Disaster strikes Haman when Queen Esther exposes his involvement in a crime against her and her people (7:6) and when (7:8) the king catches Haman "assaulting" Queen Esther in the royal banquet hall. The sentence of death now rains down on Haman.

Tragically for Haman, and humorously for the reader, what brings Haman's world crashing down is not his irresponsible edict of death against the Jews, but his kneeling before a Jewish woman. Haman is declared guilty of a crime that he neither commits nor intends to commit—the attempted murder or rape of Queen Esther.[35]

33. Brown, Driver, and Briggs, *A Hebrew and English Lexicon*, 461; Cassel, *An Explanatory Commentary on Esther*, 218–19; John N. Oswalt, "951. . . *(kābash)*," *Theological Wordbook of the Old Testament*, ed. R. Laird Harris, Gleason L. Archer, Jr., Bruce K. Waltke (Chicago: Moody, 1980), 1:430.

34. This instance is the only record in Persian history (so far discovered) of an individual's head being covered to indicate a sentence of death. Such a practice, however, has been attested in the ancient Greek and Roman cultures. Fox, *Character and Ideology in the Book of Esther*, 87, 283–84.

35. Yehuda T. Radday, "Esther with Humor," in *On Humor and the Comic in the Hebrew Bible*, ed. Yehuda T. Radday and Athalya Brenner (Sheffield: Almond 1990), 295–313, quote on 312.

The End Justifies the Beams (7:9–10)

Junior high and high schools are filled with all different kinds of kids. Some are teachers' pets, others the class bullies, and still others the strong silent types. Other children would be labeled as wallflowers, others as class clowns, and still others as tattletales. Some of these are well-liked people, whereas others are universally disliked.

In the Book of Esther, these same types of people exist. Esther might qualify as the teacher's (king's) pet, Haman as the bully, and Mordecai as the strong silent type. Vashti would perhaps be classified as the beauty queen, the author as the clown, and Harbonah, one of the king's eunuchs, as the tattletale.

Haman definitely wishes he had never met or heard of the all-too-talkative tattletale Harbonah (7:9). The king asks for no information, but (naturally) Harbonah offers some, and it is information that Haman prefers would not be brought to the king's attention. Harbonah's manner of slipping this information to the king must also be extremely pernicious to Haman. In essence, Harbonah openly declares to anyone who might be in earshot in an offhanded fashion that a gallows exists—a seventy-five-foot high gallows that is close at hand, in fact, at Haman's house. What is more, this untested gallows was designed to expedite the death of Mordecai, who (as you, O king, know) is the king's protector. At this point, Harbonah, the tattletale, becomes curiously mute, not daring to suggest (although definitely intimating) that the king make use of Haman's own gallows to dispose of Haman. Quickly, the king seizes on Harbonah's "ramblings" and orders Haman to be hung on the very gallows that graces Haman's yard.

Harbonah's information provides the king with an extra, and perhaps clinching, incentive that he needs to unleash the full fury of his wrath against Haman. The king may have felt constricted by Persian law, which prevented him from executing an individual for having committed only a single offense. Herodotus writes: "This is a law which I praise; and it is a praiseworthy law too which suffers not the king himself to slay any man for one offence, nor any other Persian for one offence to do incurable hurt to one of his servants."[36]

36. *Herodotus,* trans. A. D. Godley (Cambridge: Harvard University Press, 1990), 1:137.

Thus, assuming the accuracy of Herodotus' statement, the king requires at least two serious accusations against Haman that would stand up in a court of law[37] in order to justify executing Haman. The first irrefutable accusation of which Haman has been found guilty is that of his assault on the queen and her people via the edict of death (3:12–13). The second accusation is that of his attack on Esther in an attempt either to force her sexually or to kill her (7:8). This accusation is shaky,[38] but the servants at least believe it is sufficient to mark Haman as a condemned man by covering his head. The mention in 7:9 of Haman's plot to kill the man whom the king had only recently honored for his loyalty to the throne most certainly tips the legal scales against Haman. The king is now free to proceed with Haman's execution without fear of repercussion.

The king orders his servants to hang Haman on the gallows that Haman had prepared for Mordecai. In 7:10, the king's servants carry out that order and hang Haman. Thereafter, the king's anger[39] subsides.[40] The tension breaks, and all can breathe a sigh of relief. The enemy of the Jews is dead!

37. Kings, of course, could exercise much power outside of the law, and King Ahasuerus easily may have been able to maneuver around the law to which Herodotus alludes. Yet, Ahasuerus appears to desire to work within the confines of the Medo-Persian law. His consulting of the legal minds in 1:15 regarding what was to be done to Queen Vashti for her act of disobedience is one example of the king's willingness to comply with the law of the land. Another example is his acquiescence to the law of nonreversal, which prevented the disregarding of laws to which the royal seal had been affixed (1:19–21; 8:8).

38. Despite his accusation against Haman in 7:8, the king may subconsciously have been aware that, in reality, Haman had not been attacking the queen but had been pleading for his life.

39. Interestingly, whereas the king's anger plays a role in the downfall of Gentiles—Queen Vashti's removal from power in 1:12, and Prime Minister Haman's demise in 7:7—the subsiding of that anger paves the way for the reversal of fortunes of the Jews—Esther is made queen in 2:1ff., and Mordecai is elevated to the position of prime minister in 8:2 (cf. 10:2–3). Had King Ahasuerus been able to control his temper and had he responded to various situations with a level-headed rationality, the story of the Book of Esther undoubtedly would have been written differently (if at all).

40. See the discussion of *šākah* (to subside) in 2:1.

The Ups and Downs of Life

Being on top and staying on top of one's profession is a difficult task at best. Invariably, someone comes along seeking that top position—sometimes with the right motives, sometimes not. Maintaining that level of success, moreover, is particularly difficult if the individual has made enemies along the way to the top. The fall from the top, especially when it comes at the hands of one's enemies, can be very hard and have lasting consequences.

In the Book of Esther, Prime Minister Haman discovers the truth about the difficulty of being preeminent. Only he discovers it too late to do himself any good. The author of the Book of Esther has designed chapter 7 to convey the truth that there is no security in being at the top if God is one's enemy. The end is always nearer for the enemies of God then they might think. Conversely, no matter how low, discouraged, or out of power one may seem to be, that person can suddenly and dramatically be elevated to a position of success if God desires him or her to succeed.

In Esther 7, God causes Haman's world to come crashing in on him. In chapters 8 and 9, he also causes Haman's well-laid plans to "come to naught." Even more wonderfully, in the process of ending Haman's career and life, God raises up Mordecai, a Jew, to the position of second in command in the Gentile-dominated Medo-Persian empire (8:2; 10:3).

In addition to presenting God's often hidden role in shaping the destinies of people, chapter 7 reveals several other valuable principles for living.

First, assuming that all is well in life may be dangerous for the person who has enemies, no matter how weak those enemies may appear to be. Little did Haman know that making an enemy of one so "insignificant" as Mordecai would have catastrophic consequences.

Second, and conversely, being at odds with those who hold positions of power in an organization can be hazardous to one's career (or, as in Haman's case, to one's life). Proverbs 20:2 makes this principle very clear: "The terror of a king is like the growling of a young lion [while devouring its prey]; the one who incites him to fury forfeits [or errs against] his own life." Haman immediately recognized the dangerous situation into which he had stumbled. Yet, foolishly he turned to Esther for help, rather than attempting to carry out the truth taught in Proverbs 16:14: "The anger of a king is a messenger of death; but a wise man will pacify it." Haman did not even attempt to appease the king's anger and so paid the consequences of his failure.

Third, a well-designed communication approach can be an effective means by which to achieve one's goals. Esther did not possess sufficient power to accomplish what she hoped would happen. She therefore needed to gain compliance from the one person who did have the power to stop Haman and the edict that he had promulgated. Creating a positive climate in which the king would be receptive to her plea, Esther won the king to her side, not by force but by words.

Life is tenuous at best. Those who are down one moment may be on the top the next moment, and those on top may instantaneously become as those on the bottom. Securing the good favor of people in positions of power may help to allay a potential fall and to assist a hoped-for rise. Being in God's good graces, however, is far better.

A One-Way Street into a Dead End

Near to where my wife works, the city is constructing a new road. At the entrance to the construction area is a sign announcing the road currently is a dead end. Should people drive down that street, they would discover that at some point they would have to turn around and travel on the other side of the road to return to their starting point.

Haman's life is much like that road under construction, with one major difference. The street on which he is traveling is a one-way street to a dead end. Haman unknowingly begins moving down that one-way street almost from the moment he becomes prime minister. Tragically for him and happily for the Jews, the road on which he is traveling is filled with potholes and the further he travels down it the more dangerous it becomes.

For Haman there are four major potholes or crises in his life:

1. Mordecai's refusal to bow down to Haman after Haman has been promoted to the position of prime minister (3:1–15).

2. Mordecai's refusal to bow down to Haman after Haman has left a banquet in which Queen Esther appears to have honored him (i.e., Haman) (5:9–14).
3. Haman's need to honor his enemy (i.e., Mordecai) publicly in accordance with the king's command at a time when Haman had already made preparations to have that enemy executed (6:4–13).
4. Haman's realization that the queen, Esther, and perhaps, though not necessarily, Ahasuerus want Haman dead for having sentenced Esther and her people to death (7:3–8).

With each new crisis, Haman becomes less and less able to handle the situation. Ultimately, he crumbles under the strain.

Although chapter 7 of the Book of Esther signals the end of the person of Haman, it does not announce the end of the influence of Haman over the Jews. At this stage, any Jewish euphoria over the death of Haman must be tempered by the realization that the death warrant that he wrote against the Jews is still in effect. Haman seemingly reaches out from the grave and pulls them down with him.

Yet, God makes certain that Haman does not have the last laugh. By having the king hang Haman publicly, God does more than merely eliminate an enemy of the Jews. He sends a forceful message throughout the empire that the Jews are a people to be feared. Such a message plays itself out in the many conversions to Judaism in 8:17, and in the destruction of the enemies of the Jews in chapter 9.

The Jews only begin to taste victory in chapter 7. In the upcoming chapters, they will experience even greater victories that will transform their social and political status, but that transformation will have little or no impact on their spiritual condition.

18

Break Out the Manischewitz
(8:1–17)

Animals secure their food in a variety of ways. Some forage for it; others just chew on leaves. Some attack with speed and savage ferocity, and some use stealth. Other animals pursue their intended victims and keep pursuing until their prey is worn down and helpless. The wolverine is one such animal.

Wolverines are built with powerful legs that propel them mile after mile in search of food. They possess a tremendous strength and determination. Once they set their mind on their target they press on despite all odds, seemingly never giving up until they achieve their goal.

Queen Esther is much like the wolverine. Once she makes up her mind to secure the deliverance of her people (4:16), she tenaciously presses forward until she achieves that end (8:3–8). Even after that victory is secured, she forges ahead to ensure that the enemies of her people are thoroughly defeated (9:13) and that her own people establish a permanent means by which to remember their amazing victory (9:29–32).

Variations on a Theme

The events of chapter 8 parallel those of chapter 3, yet with several significant differences. As the following outline reveals, the similarities between the two chapters are evident in the structural development of the passages:

A. Promotion of a non-Persian to a position of leadership (3:1 and 8:1–2)
B. Problem with an enemy requiring action to be taken (3:2–6 and 8:3–6)
C. Publication of an edict by which to eliminate the enemy (3:7–15b and 8:7–14)
D. Presentation of an emotional response in reaction to the edict (3:15c and 8:15–17)

Numerous other similarities occur at the level of details, including the parallel actions of the two main characters, the contents of the edict, and the manner in which the edict is disseminated throughout the empire.

Apart from the naturally expected differences between the two chapters (e.g., different characters and different outcomes), there are a host of minor differences. These dissimilarities, however, do not cloud the parallels in content, general structure, and literary development between the two passages.

Yet because these two chapters function differently within the story, they are outlined somewhat differently. Whereas chapter 3 flows naturally according to a chiastic structure, chapter 8 does not. Chapter 8 drives the storyline forward, on into chapter 9, which continues the portrayal of the Jews in a dominant role. The following outline reflects the Jewish focus of chapter 8:

A. Elevation of a Jew (8:1–2)
B. Expectation of another Jew (8:3–6)
C. Explanation to two Jews (8:7–8)
D. Edict of a Jew (8:9–14)
E. Elation of all Jews (8:15–17)

Although chapters 3 and 8 are parallel in many ways, they present contrastive images of the Jews. In chapter 3, the Jews are seemingly helpless; in chapter 8, they are seemingly invincible. Thus the two chapters form an *inclusio* that establishes the literary boundaries of the Jews' desperate situation under an anti-Jewish rule.

Before and After Pictures

Many advertisements today depend on "before" and "after" photographs to convey their message. Esther 8:1–17 also presents a before and after picture. The "before" is a Jewish woman weeping at a tragedy facing her and her people. The "after" is the Jewish people joyfully celebrating *en masse.* What makes the difference is the development by a newly promoted Jewish prime minister, Mordecai, of a countermeasure that effectively overrides the irrevocable anti-Jewish death warrant of chapter 3.

Chapter 8 portrays Mordecai's edict as being no less harsh than Haman's original edict. Mordecai's edict gives the Jews the right to annihilate without mercy all of their enemies who had found inspiration and encouragement in Haman's edict. Such an irrevocable edict understandably is the cause of the "after" picture of Jewish rejoicing.

A Power Broker in Action (8:1–2)

Years ago there was a popular weekly television drama called *The Millionaire.* The basic premise of the program was that a wealthy, but unnamed, person gave an unsuspecting individual a million dollars, tax free, with no strings attached. The program then followed the new millionaire to see how that individual's life would change. Many who watched the show wondered what it would be like to be given a million dollars, tax free. As I reflect on that television program now, however, I wonder instead what it would be like to be rich enough to be able to give away one million dollars, tax free, over and over again.

In Esther 8:1–2, an extremely wealthy man, King Ahasuerus, gives away, seemingly without a second thought, considerably more money than a million dollars. Esther, the person who receives that enormous sum, in turn gives away to still a third person, Mordecai, the power of attorney to exercise full control over it. Unlike the television program, however, the Scripture does not focus on the impact that money has on people's lives.

Instead, as it follows those lives, it does so without any apparent concern for the monetary fortunes they have acquired.

The author notes (8:1) that the same day Haman's treachery is exposed and he is hanged the king gives to Esther Haman's *bayit* (house).[1] The term *bayit* here includes not only the walled building in which Haman lived, but also all of his possessions.[2] Thus Esther gains Haman's physical house, his property, his servants, and his vast financial treasures (see 3:9).

Curiously, even though Haman is dead, the author still identifies him as the enemy *(ṣorēr)* of the Jews. The author uses the phrase *the enemy of the Jews* (or "the enemy of all the Jews") only once prior to Haman's death (in 3:10) but three times after his death (in 9:10, 24, and here in 8:1). Seemingly, the antipathy between the Jews and Haman remains as strong after his death as before.[3] In part, that feeling is understandable since the effects of Haman's actions continue unabated after his death.

Next (8:1), Mordecai appears before the king in a formal audience.[4] The Hebrew word order places emphasis on Mordecai rather than on either the king or Esther. Yet, the author indicates that Mordecai is able to approach the king only because Esther discloses (contrast 2:10, 20) to the king her relationship to Mordecai. Hereafter, the author portrays Mordecai and Esther as working in tandem to secure the deliverance and the prosperity of the Jews. At times Esther has the leading role (8:2, 3–6; 9:12–13, 32), at times Mordecai (8:9–10, 15; 9:3, 20–23; 10:2–3), and at times both share the limelight (9:29, 31). Thus, the author suggests that Esther no longer functions under the control or author-

1. Herodotus notes that a Medo-Persian king could seize the property of an executed criminal. *Herodotus,* trans. A. D. Godley (Cambridge: Harvard University Press, 1990), 3:128–29.

2. Lewis Bayles Paton, *The Book of Esther*, International Critical Commentary, ed. Samuel Rolles Driver, Alfred Plummer, and Charles Augustus Briggs (Edinburgh: T. and T. Clark, 1908), 267.

3. Even today, during the festival of Purim, as the scroll of Esther is read in Jewish synagogues, "[w]henever Haman's name is read, everyone breaks out in loud noise to literally fulfill the curse *Yimah shmo*—May his name be erased (or in this case drowned out)." Michael Strassfeld, *The Jewish Holidays: A Guide and Commentary* (New York: Harper and Row, 1985), 190.

4. The Hebrew is not clear here as to whether Mordecai comes before the king on the same day as the events just described or at a later time. Most likely he does so on the same day.

ity of Mordecai; but likewise, neither does she dominate him. In fact, the author concludes the book by focusing on Mordecai and his greatness, rather than on Esther and her position of power.

Amazingly (8:2), the king makes Mordecai prime minister,[5] by transferring to Mordecai the king's own signet ring—the symbol of royal authority (cf. 3:10). Thus Jews now occupy two extremely powerful positions within the Medo-Persian empire.[6] They soon will begin to exercise that power.

Upon receiving Haman's possessions (8:2), Esther places them in Mordecai's care to manage them for her as he deems best. She, however, retains full ownership of them.[7] The author is very clear concerning this last point. Whereas King Ahasuerus "gives" (*nātan*) Esther Haman's *bayit,* Esther only "places" (*wattāśem,* from *śûm*) Mordecai "over Haman's house" (*ʿal-bêt hāmān*).[8] Thus, Esther makes Mordecai her agent in regard to the disposition of Haman's property and wealth.

We've Only Just Begun (8:3–6)

Like an athlete who knows the game is not over until the final gun sounds, Esther in 8:3–6 reveals that she understands the principle of doing everything possible—of never quitting—until

5. Mordecai is not the only person of Jewish heritage to become a high official in a Gentile-dominated government in ancient times (cf. Joseph in Gen. 41:41–45; Daniel and his friends in Dan. 2:48–49; and Nehemiah in Neh. 1:11). Baldwin notes that, outside of Scripture, "[i]n a collection of tablets from the reigns of Artaxerxes I and Darius II more than a hundred Jewish names occur in connection with important positions in the realm." Joyce G. Baldwin, *Esther,* The New Bible Commentary, 3d ed., ed. D. Guthrie and J. A. Motyer (Grand Rapids: Eerdmans, 1970), 413.

6. Huey states that "[t]he most impressive evidence for Mordecai's rise to power was the discovery of the name Marduka (= Mordecai) on a cuneiform tablet from Borsippa. He is identified as a high official in the royal court at Susa during the early years of Xerxes' reign." F. B. Huey, Jr., "Esther," *Expositor's Bible Commentary,* ed. Frank E. Gaebelein, 12 vols. (Grand Rapids: Zondervan, 1988), 4:790–91.

7. Herodotus notes that Medo-Persian women could own wealth in their own right. Herodotus 9:109.

8. Michael V. Fox, *Character and Ideology in the Book of Esther* (Columbia, S.C.: University of South Carolina Press, 1991), 90. See 1 Sam. 18:5 and 2 Sam. 17:25, where *śûm ʿal* is used to depict a king entrusting his soldiers into the hands of a qualified leader.

the final victory is secured. Although the king assumes that the death of Esther's enemy, Haman, resolves Esther's problems, Esther does not. She knows that as long as the edict of death against the Jews remains in place, the victory has not been won. Settling simply for the death of Haman means achieving a hollow victory, so Esther presses the king for further concessions.[9]

Although Esther is in the king's good graces (as evidenced by his willingness to act on her behalf against her enemy), she does not presume upon his graciousness. Instead, in 8:3, she humbles herself before him, falling at his feet and weeping. Previously when Esther brought her petitions before the king, she had been either standing (5:2) or sitting (5:6–8[?]; 7:3–6, 8). Now she makes an extra effort to impress upon the king the seriousness of her request and the desperateness of the situation in which she and her people find themselves.

Esther seeks the king's favor to overcome the tragedy perpetrated by Haman against the Jews. Wisely she avoids reminding the king of his complicity in these evil schemes—never mentioning him by name nor even identifying her problem as a matter of Medo-Persian law. Haman alone is to bear the guilt. The king alone, however, can put an end to[10] Haman's evil plot against Esther's people.

In 8:4, the king once again (cf. 5:2) extends his golden scepter to Esther. He may have done this to permit Esther back into his presence if she has left and then returned uninvited. He may also have extended his scepter to encourage her "to rise from her prostrate position before continuing to speak"[11] or to reassure her that he does not find her tears to be offensive.[12]

9. According to Fox, "in the absence of a new time indicator it is natural to read this scene as a continuation of the previous one. This is not a new audience with the king, for Esther is said to 'speak' again rather than to 'come' again." Fox, *Character and Ideology in the Book of Esther*, 91–92. Fox is most likely correct in his assessment of the general time frame in which Esther's second plea takes place. One potential difficulty exists, however: 8:4 pictures the king extending his golden scepter to Esther. There would be no need for him to do so, if she has not departed from his presence. This suggests that Esther leaves the banquet hall (perhaps to bring Mordecai to the king), probably after 7:10, and then returns in 8:4.

10. Literally, "to cause to pass over," that is, "to turn away from."

11. Huey, "Esther," 829.

12. If people are not permitted to enter the king's gate clothed in sackcloth (a sign of mourning, cf. 4:2), they are less likely to be allowed to exhibit emotional outbursts of mourning in the king's presence.

Once the golden scepter has been extended, Esther composes herself and demonstrates the height of court etiquette. On previous occasions she began her requests before the king with formulaic statements of politeness.[13] Now (8:5), at the point when she places her most important petitions before King Ahasuerus, Esther maximizes her degree of politeness. She utilizes four distinct ritualistic statements, shifting back and forth between impersonal and personal appeals:

Impersonal:	"If unto the king *it seems* good"
Personal:	"And if I have found favor before him"
Impersonal:	"And *if* the matter *seems* proper[14] to the king"
Personal:[15]	"And *if* I am pleasing[16] in his eyes."

Esther continues her impassioned plea, taking care on the one hand not to offend the king and on the other hand to emphasize her personal and enduring relationship to her people, her life being bound up in their destiny. She avoids any direct accusation that the king in any way participated in the heinous deeds of Haman (cf. v. 3). She also skirts the issue that what Haman did is now the law of the land,[17] for even that would indi-

13. In 5:4, Esther begins her petition with the statement: "If unto the king it *seems* good." In 5:8, she uses two introductory statements: "If I have found favor in the eyes of the king," and "If unto the king it *seems* good." Likewise, in 7:3, she prefaces her requests with two similar conventional sentences: "If I have found favor in your eyes, O king," and "If unto the king it *seems* good."

14. The word *kāšer* (proper) also conveys the idea of being "advantageous" or bringing "success." Francis Brown, S. R. Driver, and Charles A. Briggs, *A Hebrew and English Lexicon of the Old Testament with an Appendix Containing the Biblical Aramaic* (reprint; Oxford: Clarendon, 1968), 506.

15. Contrary to Haupt, this is not "a coquettish climax, equivalent to our *If you really care for me a little*." Paul Haupt, "Critical Notes on Esther," *American Journal of Semitic Languages and Literature* 24 (1907–1908): 154, reprint in *Studies in the Book of Esther,* ed. Carey A. Moore (New York: KTAV, 1982), 1–90. The structure and the lexical content of the sentence argue against Haupt's position.

16. The term *tôbā(h)* (pleasing) expresses, among other concepts, the notions of happiness and agreeability. Brown, Driver, and Briggs, *A Hebrew and English Lexicon of the Old Testament*, 373–75.

17. Esther pleads that "the letters" (*hass^{e}pārîm*), not "the laws" (*hadātîm*), be revoked.

rectly implicate the king. Furthermore, by mentioning Haman's full name—Haman, the son of Hammedatha the Agagite[18]—Esther stresses the fact that all of the blame should fall on him.

Continuing her speech, Esther wisely avoids harping on known facts. She does not oversell her point by repeating (as she does in 7:4) all three requirements of the edict—"to destroy, to kill, and to annihilate." In 8:5, she only cites the last—"to annihilate"—as a reminder of the entire tragic situation she and her people face.[19]

Esther presses forward, concluding her appeal in verse 6 by emphasizing her personal relationship to the tragedy that will take place if the king does not act. She is intimately and inextricably connected to her people. She utters two pleading rhetorical questions that are semantically parallel to each other and thus emphasize the same point:

For how	could I endure if I saw	the evil which will befall	my people?
And how	could I endure if I saw	the annihilation of	my kindred?

Esther does not say that she too would die in Haman's planned pogrom. She does, however, suggest that her life would come to an end, at least psychologically, for she personally would not have the will or desire to continue living.

It's Not My Problem (8:7–8)

How often do we hear someone say: "Don't look at me, it's not my problem"? King Ahasuerus, in 8:7–8, responds to Esther and Mordecai in that same way. His response both saddens and encourages them. Whereas they hope that he will tackle their problem, he in essence says: "I've already done all that I'm going

18. See 3:1 for a discussion of Haman's ancestry.

19. Esther's communication strategy here is flawless. In 7:4 she engages in a meaningful "data dump" of all three provisions of the edict in order to enrage the king and to tighten the noose around Haman's neck. In 8:5, however, she is seeking further help from someone already on her side, someone who has the power to rectify the potentially cataclysmic situation that soon may befall her people.

to do. If you can figure out how to handle this impossible problem, then I'll support you."

Rather than responding with sympathy, the king seems to be somewhat perturbed with Esther's impassioned plea. As Michael V. Fox states, the king's "eagerness to get the whole messy business off his hands makes the latter attitude [i.e., the attitude of annoyance] seem the more likely."[20] As far as the king is concerned, he has done more than his share in resolving their problem. He has made Esther wealthy beyond comprehension; he has destroyed their enemy; and he has elevated Mordecai to the position of prime minister. The king therefore has done all that he intends to do. He now leaves to Esther and Mordecai any additional work that needs to be done to circumvent the edict of Haman.

Thus, the king once more (8:8; cf. 3:10–11) abdicates his responsibility to take direct control over the management of his empire, especially on a matter so grave as this.[21] He commands Esther and Mordecai to write a document on the king's own authority which they are to seal with the king's own signet ring. He gives them, as Meir Zlotowitz states, "*carte blanche* permission not to annul, but to override Haman's decree by wording a new decree in any manner they thought effective."[22] What is ironic is that even though the king knows what he is saying to them—that is, "if you can figure out a way to get around the law, go do it"—he makes certain, for the record, that all who are present know that a law of the king cannot be revoked (cf. 1:19). Thus, no matter what they write, Haman's edict will still remain in effect. They cannot abrogate it; they might be able to neutralize it.

A Method to the Madness (8:9–14)

For the most part, the Book of Esther flows with smooth chronological regularity. Esther 8:9–17, however, does not.[23] At first

20. Fox, *Character and Ideology in the Book of Esther*, 94.

21. Only nine months later, when seventy-five thousand of his subjects are killed in two days (9:5–10, 12, 15–16), does the king finally realize the full impact of his relinquishing his power to Mordecai and Esther in 8:8.

22. Meir Zlotowitz, trans. and comp., *The Megillah: The Book of Esther: A New Translation with a Commentary Anthologized from Talmudic, Midrashic and Rabbinic Sources* (Brooklyn: Mesorah, 1981), 110.

23. Interestingly, there is a similar choppiness in 3:12–15, the parallel passage to 8:9–17.

(vv. 9–10), the chronological flow continues that of verses 1–8, albeit jumping ahead two months and six days to the designing and distributing of Mordecai's edict. Then the flow is interrupted to provide information concerning the edict itself (vv. 11–12). When the passage resumes in verses 13–14, it recapitulates the events of verses 9–10. By contrast, verses 15–16 shift the action back to a time before the events of verses 9–10 (i.e., to the time immediately following Mordecai's promotion to prime minister), or to the time immediately after the issuing of the edict, or both. Thereafter, verse 17 leapfrogs over all the events of verses 1–16 to chronicle the reactions of the people throughout the empire when they at last receive Mordecai's edict.

The beginning of 8:9 echoes the beginning of 3:12, the verse that describes the writing of Haman's edict against the Jews. Both verses begin: "So the scribes of the king were called." Both verses, moreover, describe the similar process by which the two opposing edicts are developed.

The scribes in 8:9 are summoned the twenty-third day of Sivan, that is, two months and six days after Mordecai's promotion to prime minister, or two months and ten days after the writing of Haman's edict. Why Mordecai delays so long is a mystery.[24] A host of reasons may be posited, but the Scripture is silent as to the reason(s) for the delay. It simply relates the details of the events as they actually happened.

The rest of 8:9 closely parallels 3:12 in many aspects, but 8:9 differs on three points: the originator of the edict (Mordecai vs. Haman), a special emphasis on the Jews receiving the royal law and receiving it in their own script and language, and a reminder of how extensive the empire is throughout which the edict is to be promulgated (i.e., ranging from Pakistan to northen Sudan, with a total of 127 provinces).

Mordecai, in 8:10, writes the authorized version of the edict which, like Haman's earlier one, is produced "in the name of King Ahasuerus." Thus it carries the full weight of the throne behind it; it is not merely a document issued by a prime minis-

24. The Septuagint resolves the "problem" of the delay by making the date Nisan 23 rather than Sivan 23, thereby shortening the delay to only five or possibly six days. There is, however, no Hebrew manuscript evidence to support the Septuagint's rendering of this date.

ter, as significant as that would be. Mordecai, moreover, seals the law with the signet ring of the king, thereby officially making the edict an irrevocable law of the Medes and the Persians.

Mordecai next sends out the royal letters (i.e., the edicts) in the care of the royal messengers. Up to this point in 8:10, everything matches with what Haman did in 3:12–13. Unlike the couriers sent out in 3:13, Mordecai's couriers in 8:10 ride on a special breed of horses, which Lewis Bayles Paton believes "are granted as a special favour to Mordecai, in order that the news of their deliverance may reach the Jews more speedily."[25]

The author in 8:11–12 presents an overview of the contents of Mordecai's edict. Although there are similarities to Haman's edict in 3:13, there are also a number of significant differences.

First, even though both edicts are sent out under the king's seal, Mordecai's edict alone makes special mention of the direct imprimatur of the king—the king grants the Jews the right to act.

Second, whereas both edicts affect all Jews throughout the Medo-Persian empire, Mordecai's edict focuses on the Jews in every city, the assumption being that Jews outside of the cities would gather together with the Jews in the cities for an effective mutual defense. Whether Mordecai's edict specifies defense-only tactics or whether it permits offensive action as well is a matter of debate. The Hebrew *w^ela^cămod ^cal-napšām* translates literally as "and to stand on account of their soul." The basic idiomatic expression occurs only here in 8:11 and in 9:16 in the Scripture. The verb *^cămad* (to stand) when used by itself functions at times idiomatically to express the concept of "standing one's ground" (2 Kings 10:4; Amos 2:15; Mal. 3:2). When the verb occurs in conjunction with the preposition *^cal* (against), however, the expression on occasion may indicate "the rising up *as an enemy* against" someone else (1 Chron. 21:1; 2 Chron. 20:23; Dan. 8:25; 11:14). Understandably, the fact that the Hebrew clause *w^ela^cămod ^cal-napšām* exists in only two places in the Book of Esther (and in reference to the same event) makes translating it difficult. Yet, the presence of the term *napšām* (their soul, i.e., their lives) as the object of the preposition *^cal* tips the balance of the scales in favor of the clause allow-

25. Paton, *The Book of Esther*, 273.

ing the Jews only to defend themselves. There does not appear to be any suggestion in the clause that offensive aggression is intended (though it is not directly ruled out). This position, moreover, makes the most sense in view of the remainder of 8:11, in which the edict grants to the Jews the right to destroy, to kill, and to annihilate any who attack them.[26]

Third, the two edicts naturally differ as to who is to be destroyed, killed, and annihilated. Haman's edict decrees that all Jews, both young and old, including children and women, are to die; Mordecai's edict declares that all the members of any army[27] that attacks, as well as children and women, are to be killed.

Some have argued that Mordecai does not command the destruction of children and women but intends the phrase *children and women* to refer to Jews who are under attack.[28] According to this view, the royal decree permits the Jews to destroy those who "attack them, their children, and their women." For this view to be correct, however, the Hebrew text would need to be emended to join the possessive pronoun *their* to the two nouns so that the resultant translation would read: "their children and their women." There is, however, no textual support for such a reading.

Fourth, both edicts allow for the taking of spoil and both laws cite the same day for their respective killings to take place—the thirteenth day of Adar (i.e., the twelfth month). The edicts, however, present these two similar points in reverse order: Haman listing the date before the right to plunder, Mordecai the right to plunder before the date.

26. How then do we account for more than seventy-five thousand people in the Medo-Persian empire dying at the hands of the Jews (9:5–10, 12, 15–16)? The Scripture does not provide an explanation. The Jews, however, apparently interpreted the edict according to the spirit of the law rather than according to the letter of the law.

27. Esther 9:2 interprets the edict to allow for the slaughter of "those who sought their [i.e., the Jews'] harm," and thus does not limit the scope of the edict merely to those who are soldiers.

28. Joyce G. Baldwin, *Esther: An Introduction and Commentary* Tyndale Old Testament Commentaries, ed. D. J. Wiseman (Downers Grove: InterVarsity, 1984), 97–98; Robert Gordis, "Studies in the Esther Narrative," *Journal of Biblical Literature* 95 (March 1976): 49–53.

Continuing on,[29] the author records in verse 13 that "all of the peoples" are to receive a copy of Mordecai's edict. Interestingly, they are to be given a copy of the newly created royal law "so that the Jews [not themselves] would be ready for this day." Mordecai undoubtedly distributes the edict in this manner in order to counteract Haman's edict, which also was sent out to "all of the peoples" (3:14). The impact of such a distribution pattern would strike fear in the hearts of the enemies of the Jews (8:17; 9:2), encourage Gentiles to stand with the Jews against those who are determined to attack the Jews (8:17), and ensure that all government officials and military leaders understood their need to work on behalf of, and not against, the Jews (9:3).

Interestingly, 8:13 records that the Jews are given the right "to avenge themselves on their enemies." Fox notes that the term *nāqam* (to avenge) "refers to the legitimate exercise of power outside a judicial context . . . [but] never refers to a simple defense or rescue, but everywhere designates a punitive action and presupposes a prior wrong, that is, some offense to which the avenging party is responding."[30] The prior wrong in this case would be specifically the attack of the Gentiles on the Jews on Adar 13, but also may include other acts of hatred or violence perpetrated by the Gentiles against the Jews prior to that time.

As soon as Mordecai's edict is drafted and published, the official couriers ride out of the capital city to all of the cities of all of the provinces of the Medo-Persian empire (8:14; cf. 3:13). They ride on the royal horses (cf. 8:10), "hastened and impelled[31] by the command of the king" (8:14). In addition, the edict is given out in Susa, the capital—an action that parallels that which was done for Haman's edict in 3:15.

29. Between 8:12 and 8:13, the Septuagint interjects a purported text of Mordecai's edict in which he depicts the arrogance of the enemies of the people of God, the evil acts of Haman, the goodness of the Jewish people, the right of those people to defend themselves against their enemies, and a charge to all peoples to come to the aid of the Jews. This addition, however, is not supported by the Hebrew text.

30. Fox, *Character and Ideology in the Book of Esther*, 100–101.

31. The words *hastened* and *impelled* may function as a hendiadys for "spurred on" (cf. NIV).

It's Party Time (8:15–17)

One of the great traditions that seems to cross all cultural boundaries is the celebration of a victory, particularly the victory of someone who has just won an important political office. Such is the case in ancient Medo-Persia when Mordecai becomes prime minister. Celebrations spontaneously break out in the capital city and ultimately throughout the empire.

Esther 8:15–17 depicts Mordecai going forth from the palace in triumph, the city of Susa in celebration, the elation of the Jews, and the reaction of the people in the provinces upon receipt of Mordecai's edict. The timing of these events, however, is unclear. Some or all of the events of verses 15–16 may have transpired before the issuing of the edict or all of the events of verses 15–17 may have taken place after Mordecai publishes it. The author does not provide a detailed chronology.

By contrast, the author is very concerned with presenting (in v. 15) the way in which Mordecai is honored. The author states that Mordecai departs from the king's presence wearing royal robes of blue (or violet) and white coloring. Cassel notes that these colors are the official colors of the ancient Persian society and that they also carry significance within Persian religious practices as being symbolic of light (white), sky (blue), and sun (purple).[32] The wearing of these colors by Mordecai, however, should not be construed as suggesting that he at this point has become involved in the religion of the Persians. Rather, the colors imply that the king specially honors Mordecai in a way that only the king of the Medo-Persian empire has the right to honor someone.

Mordecai also wears a great crown of gold. This crown *[ʿătārā(h)]* differs from that *(keter)* worn by Queen Vashti (1:11), Queen Esther (2:17), and the royal horse (6:8). Those crowns are designated as being royal crowns. Here, Mordecai's crown is identified as being both large and gold. The size of the crown and the material from which it is made again suggest that great honor is being heaped upon Mordecai by the king.

32. Paulus Cassel, *An Explanatory Commentary on Esther*, trans. Aaron Bernstein (Edinburgh: T. and T. Clark, 1888), 239.

Finally, Mordecai goes out from the king's presence dressed in another unique garment—this one purple in color and woven from fine linen (cf. 1:6).[33]

No one else in the Book of Esther—not the seven eunuchs (1:10), not Queen Vashti (1:11), not the royal wise men (1:13–14), not Queen Esther (2:17), and not even Haman (3:1; 5:11; cf. 6:8–9)—receives these various honors that the king extends to Mordecai (8:15). These royal garments present quite a contrast from the sackcloth and ashes that Mordecai wore only a short while earlier (4:1).

Further (8:15), the people of Susa cry with high-pitched sounds in praise *[ṣāhălā(h)]* and rejoice *[śāmēḥā(h)]*. The mood of the city has changed. Whereas earlier, after the issuing of Haman's edict, the city was bewildered (3:15), now it is caught up in a festive atmosphere (8:15).

Understandably the Jews celebrate their new found hope. Their excitement is so rich and overflowing that the author uses four words in his attempt to capture their feeling of jubilation—the Jews are *light* and *gladness* and *joy* and *honor.*[34] This experience undoubtedly is like an oasis in the desert for the Jews. Life under Haman's edict must have felt like a living oppressive torture. Now, if even for a short while, exuberant joy appears. The contrast must have almost been unbearable for the Jews.

Chapter 8 concludes (v. 17) with a triumphal statement of how complete the reversal of the situation of the Jews had been. Now is the time when the Jews throughout the Medo-Persian empire break out the good wines and celebrate wholeheartedly. The psychological climate is one of gladness and joy. The people engage in drinking parties and consider the day as a holiday.[35]

At the end of verse 17, the author records an amazing event: "many among the peoples of the land became Jews, because the

33. This type of linen cloth is used in Israel's religious practices as part of the veil of the holy of holies (2 Chron. 3:14) and in the clothing of the priests (2 Chron. 5:12). Understandably, this linen was a much sought-after article of trade in the ancient Middle East (Ezek. 27:16).

34. The exact sense of each of these terms is a matter of much discussion. See Cassel, *An Explanatory Commentary on Esther*, 241; Paton, *The Book of Esther*, 280; Zlotowitz, *The Megillah*, 115. Suffice to say, the terms when taken together in 8:16 express exhilaration.

35. Literally, a good day.

dread of the Jews had fallen upon them." As Stan Goldman observes, "[t]he ultimate irony is that Haman's attempted genocide brings about a Persian religious conversion. . . ."[36] Whether the conversions to Judaism are genuine is unclear. The term the author uses here *(mityahădîm)* may refer either to true proselytism to Judaism or to a pretense at being Jewish. Undoubtedly, some of these conversions to Judaism in 8:17 are true; others would be false.[37] The Book of Esther makes room for the possibility that some if not all of the conversions may have been valid. In 9:27 provision is granted for proselytes (i.e., "all those who joined themselves with [the Jews]") to participate in the Purim celebrations at that time and in the future.

The reason for these individuals converting to Judaism is because the terror of the Jews had fallen on them. Despite what some argue, this fear is not a fear of God but, as the author of the Book of Esther clearly declares, a fear of the Jews. The Jews are now in the position of power, and within a few short months would decide who lives and who dies. The fear of becoming a target of the Jewish attack apparently is sufficient motivation for many Persians to identify themselves with the Jews.

The transformation of the Jews from a discouraged, dejected, and defeated people to a people filled with joy, gladness, and power is nothing short of miraculous. The author, however, does not record any of the Jews praising God for delivering them from the edict of death or for allowing them to gain the advantage over their enemies.

Neutralize Problems—Press On for Victory

During the time when I was working on this book I had a bicycle accident. As I neared the end of my ride, my front wheel hit a rut in the road and veered sharply to the right, and the

36. Stan Goldman, "Narrative and Ethical Ironies in Esther," *Journal for the Study of the Old Testament* 47 (June 1990): 24.

37. For a presentation of the various positions on this subject see Zlotowitz, *The Megillah*, 116 (false conversion); and Fox, *Character and Ideology in the Book of Esther*, 285 (genuine conversion). Cassel offers a third view: "What the passage means in all probability is this—that many Persians made common cause with the Jews . . . and united with them in hostility against the party of Haman . . . ." Cassel, *An Explanatory Commentary on Esther*, 242.

next thing I knew I was flying through the air. In midair, I intentionally twisted my body to avoid hitting my head and landed squarely on my shoulder. Pain rocketed through my body. At the hospital, my problem was diagnosed as being a broken collarbone. The doctor then administered pills to neutralize the pain that I was experiencing. When my pain was at its greatest, I needed something equally strong to neutralize it. The pain pills made a world of difference. They allowed me to get through an excruciating time and helped my body to start its recovery.

Likewise, when the Jews in ancient Persia were crushed by the powerful weight of Haman's edict, they needed something equally powerful to counteract it. Mordecai's edict provided that much sought-after relief.

One of the key principles of chapter 8[38] arises from Mordecai's ability to craft an edict that neutralizes Haman's irrevocable edict: power used wisely can rectify wrongs and achieve significant results. Prior to Mordecai's elevation to the office of prime minister, he had neither the power nor the authority to counteract Haman's edict against the Jews. After being promoted, Mordecai needed to exercise his power and authority wisely and expeditiously in order to protect his wrongfully condemned people.

A second principle flows from the first: one's focus should be on the welfare of God's people and not merely on one's own well-being. In chapter 8, both Mordecai and Esther find themselves in fairly secure positions. Despite Haman's edict, the king is unlikely to allow the enemies of the Jews to attack his beloved queen and his newly appointed prime minister, especially within the palace complex. Yet neither Esther nor Mordecai rests easy until the counter edict is written, sealed with the royal seal, and distributed throughout the empire. They feel compelled to act on behalf of the people of God to ensure that all of the Jews (not merely themselves) are empowered for success.

A third and related principle is the importance of pressing on to secure a complete victory, especially when the circumstances are in your favor. Although the king feels comfortable with the situation as it stands at the beginning of chapter 8, having no personal involvement in the problems of the Jews, Esther feels

38. As with all chapters in the Book of Esther, the overriding principle is that of God's providence.

otherwise. Recognizing that she is in his good graces, Esther skillfully presents her case before the king. She therefore uses the tactics of humbling herself (and thus flattering the king), of weeping, of politically correct language, of presenting the salient points succinctly,[39] and of showing personal involvement in the problem. Thus she relentlessly presses her case before the king until he yields to her wishes.

Two additional principles may be drawn from chapter 8 when it is viewed in light of the previous chapters.

Fourth, never give up if you are in the right, because your sorrow may be turned to joy in an instant. Mordecai's (4:1), Esther's (4:4; 8:3), and the Jews' (4:3) life-wrenching anguish becomes exuberant joy almost overnight.

Fifth, human power structures may change quickly; they are not permanent fixtures no matter how secure they may seem to be at any given moment. Haman is at the peak of his power in chapters 5 and 6. In chapter 7, he is dead. In chapter 8, a completely different political faction (i.e., the Jews) is thrust into political prominence and quickly moves to solidify its gains, to eliminate its opponents, and to establish a stable government (8:3–5, 9–17; 9:1–16; 10:2–3).

Success—The Best Way?

When Mordecai becomes prime minister in chapter 8, he is faced with an irrevocable edict—an edict, moreover, that requires the annihilation of the entire Jewish population living within the Medo-Persian empire. He does not have the luxury of dismissing it, nor can he be careless in the development of any countermeasures to neutralize its effect. As a consequence, with much wisdom, Mordecai produces a second edict that effectively countermands the first.

Humanly speaking, Mordecai's tactic is a brilliant success. Spiritually speaking, however, his actions are flawed. Scripture, over and over, jolts our earth-focus sensibilities, teaching us

39. Some people prefer to hear all of the details of a situation before making a decision; others prefer the basic facts, nothing more, nothing less. King Ahasuerus appears to fall in the latter group, as the well-received speeches of Memucan (1:16–20), Haman (3:8–9), and Esther (7:3–4; 8:5–6) reveal.

that earthly success is not the basis on which the eternal character of an act is to be evaluated (Num. 11:1–34; Ps. 73:1–20; Prov. 22:1; Eccles. 2:1–26).

Chapter 8 presents a document—Mordecai's edict. Chapter 9 portrays the implementation of that document. Chapter 8 depicts the ecstasy of the Jews when they learn of Mordecai's document. Chapter 9 pictures still more joy for the Jews when they enact the provisions of that document. Life for the Jews has changed dramatically and wonderfully. No longer do they weep and mourn. Joy and prosperity prevail, but. . . .

19

Hang 10 . . . or 75,000
(9:1–19)

Surfers are a wild breed. They live for the perfect wave. In between those perfect waves, they content themselves with shooting the curl, crashing down mountains of water at thirty-five miles per hour, and going crazy. Expert surfers work on special techniques such as one-footing, standing on their heads, or hanging 10. Hanging 10 in surfer parlance means surfing while curling all ten toes over the edge of the board. Obviously such techniques can be spectacular; they can also be dangerous. Although Queen Esther quite probably never surfed, she knew all about hanging 10. To her, hanging 10 did not mean curling her toes over the edge of a surfboard. It meant literally "hanging 10."

In Esther 9:1–19, Esther administers the final *coup de grace* against her enemy Haman. Not content with merely seeing his plans against her people thwarted, or even with learning that all of his sons had been killed, Esther wants to "hang 10," that is to say, to hang the bodies of all ten of Haman's sons on the very gallows on which their father had been hanged. She petitions King Ahasuerus and he consents to fulfill her request. Esther 9:1–19 contains the details of the events surrounding not only Esther's request, but also the Jews' victory over their enemies in ancient Medo-Persia.

The Right Perspective

The author of the Book of Esther is an artist in his own right, painting with words a picture of the events of ancient Medo-Persia. Much like an artist, he carefully picks and chooses what he will include and what he will exclude from his work. By skillfully working his craft, the author uses words, grammatical techniques, and structure to draw the reader's attention subtly and most certainly to the focus of his message. He accomplishes this feat throughout his work, and Esther 9:1–19 is no exception.

The author builds a chiastic structure into his presentation of the events pictured in 9:1–19. That structure flows as follows:

- A The timing of the victory (9:1)
  - B The extent of the victory throughout the empire (9:2–5)
    - C The victory in Susa (day 1) (9:6–10)
      - D The petition for more opportunity for victory (9:11–13)
    - C′ The victory in Susa (day 2) (9:14–15)
  - B′ The extent of the victory throughout the empire (9:16)
- A′ The timing of the victory (9:17–19)

By utilizing this structural pattern, the author intends his readers to focus their attention on Esther's petition to the king (vv. 11–13) as being the heart of the passage. In those few verses the Jews reach the pinnacle of their power in their battle against their enemies. Esther's petition is the capstone to an already successful day.

Up to this point in the book, the Jews have gone from fasting (4:3, 16) to feasting (8:17). They begin this section fighting (9:2, 5, 15–16); they end it feasting (9:17–19). Thus their sorrow turns to joy, their joy to determination, and their determination to elation.

An Upside-Down Cake (9:1–4)

Upside-down cakes are one of the enigmas of life. That which is normally expected to be on the top ends up on the bottom, and that which typically is found on the bottom rises to the top. Prior to Adar 13, the Medo-Persian empire was like an upside-down cake. The enemies of the people of God had hoped to gain victory over the people of God. Those enemies were like the batter of the upside-down cake that submerged and threatened to destroy tasty fruit (i.e., God's people). On Adar 13 and 14, however, the "baking" period was done and, like the cake, the empire was turned right side up to the enjoyment of all.

In Esther 3:12 the anti-Jewish forces in the Medo-Persian empire are empowered to inflict death on the Jews of the empire. For two months those who are opposed to the Jews have been able to anticipate, even to relish, the havoc they will inflict on the Jews. In 8:9, however, all of that delight suddenly evaporates. It is replaced by a dread of the very enemies they seek to destroy, that is, the Jews (8:17; 9:2–3). In 8:17, that terror becomes the impetus for many non-Jews to convert to Judaism. Here, in 9:1–4, that dread seemingly immobilizes (cf. Exod. 15:16) the enemies of God's people to such a degree that they are unable to defend themselves, and as a result fall in great numbers at the hands of the Jews (cf. Esther 9:6, 12, 14, 16).

Esther 9 presents an overview of the events of Adar 13 on which both Haman's and Mordecai's edicts come head to head. On that day, two diametrically opposed groups of people, on the basis of one or the other of those irrevocable edicts, seek to annihilate each other. As Lewis Bayles Paton remarks: "Lively times are to be anticipated."[1]

The enemies of the Jews set their sights on destroying the Jews. As 9:1 records, they "hoped *[śibbᵉru]* to gain the mastery *[lišlôṭ]* over" the Jews. The author uses two verbs rarely found in Scripture to express the tenor of the situation at this point.

The first verb, *śābar* (to hope), occurs only six times in the Scripture.[2] Each of those times, it conveys the idea of waiting expectantly or with great anticipation for something. In other words, in 9:1, the author notes that anti-Jewish forces have been eagerly looking forward to the time when they could slaughter the Jews with impunity.

The second verb, *šālaṭ* (to rule or to have dominion over) is found in eight places in the Scripture.[3] Of those eight occur-

1. Lewis Bayles Paton, *The Book of Esther*, International Critical Commentary, ed. Samuel Rolles Driver, Alfred Plummer, and Charles Augustus Briggs (Edinburgh: T. and T. Clark, 1908), 282.

2. Ruth 1:13; Esther 9:1; Ps. 104:27; 119:166; 145:15; Isa. 38:18.

3. Neh. 5:15; Esther 9:1(2x); Ps. 119:133; Eccles. 2:19; 5:19 (Heb. v. 18); 6:2; 8:9.

rences, only four (Neh. 5:15; Esther 9:1 [2x]; Eccles. 8:9) occur in the context of one human being exercising dominion over another.[4] In each of those cases, without exception, the interaction between the two human parties works to the detriment of the one who is in the subordinate position. Thus, in Esther 9:1, the author notes that the enemies of the Jews anxiously await the time when they could "exert mastery over" the Jews, that is, inflict the ultimate harm on them.

The situation, however, "has been changed" *(nahăpôk)*.[5] No longer are the enemies of the Jews in control; the Jews themselves[6] have come to power. Thus the author uses the verb *šālaṭ* in relation to the Jews who have become the dominant party. The fact that Mordecai, a Jew, is prime minister (and Haman, an enemy of the Jews, is dead), makes Mordecai's edict carry considerably more weight than Haman's. Mordecai's edict puts the Jews firmly in control. They now possess the power of life and death over those who hate them.

In accordance with Mordecai's edict, the Jews assemble together "in their cities" to fight any who seek their harm (9:2). The term *harm [rāʿā(h)]* is a generic term that expresses a range of meanings including distress, misery, injury, mischief, and evil.[7] In the present context, the sense of "injury (to death)" obviously is prominent. Yet, by using this term, the author leaves open the possibility that the Jews do not limit their killing solely to those who seek to destroy, kill, or annihilate them.

Although prior to 9:1 the outcome of the clash between these two opposing groups may not have been 100 percent certain in

4. The remaining four uses involve an abstract concept having dominion over a person (Ps. 119:133), a person controlling an inanimate object (Eccles. 2:19), or God ruling over a person (Eccles. 5:19 [Heb. v. 18]; 6:2).

5. The Niphal form of the verb *hāpak* means "to be reversed," "overturned," or "changed." Francis Brown, S. R. Driver, and Charles A. Briggs, *A Hebrew and English Lexicon of the Old Testament with an Appendix Containing the Biblical Aramaic* (reprint; Oxford: Clarendon, 1968), 245–46.

6. The Hebrew emphasizes the fact that the Jews "themselves" have gained control. William Gesenius, *Hebrew Grammar*, ed. E. Kautzsch and A. E. Cowley, 2d ed. (reprint; Oxford: Clarendon, 1966), §135aN; Paul S. J. Joüon, *A Grammar of Biblical Hebrew*, trans. and rev. T. Muraoka, 2 vols. (Rome: Editrice Pontificio Instituto Biblico, 1991), §146c.

7. Brown, Driver, and Briggs, *A Hebrew and English Lexicon of the Old Testament*, 949.

the reader's mind, the author, in 9:2–3, quickly dispels any suspense that might be lingering: the Jews score a complete victory. They win because the dread of the Jews falls on their enemies (9:2), and the government officials give their support to the Jews, rather than to the enemies of the Jews, because the dread of Mordecai falls on them (i.e., the leaders, 9:3).

What exactly is the dread of Mordecai? The next verse (v. 4) offers some insight into that question: Mordecai is powerful within the palace,[8] his reputation extends[9] throughout the empire, and his influence grows stronger and stronger.[10]

Ten Little Agagites, All in a Row (9:5–10)

The mystery writer Agatha Christie wrote a story entitled "Ten Little Indians," in which ten people find themselves being systematically murdered, each in a different way. Each death is "announced" by the destruction of a statue of an Indian on the mantelplace of the house where the murders take place. In the Agatha Christie mystery, however, not all ten are killed.

In the Book of Esther, by contrast, all ten sons of Haman are killed. All ten apparently are killed by the same means, the sword. Who specifically kills them is not revealed, although

8. Fox, following Gerleman, considers the statement in 9:4 that "Mordecai was great" "seems to be based on Exod 11:3, 'the man Moses was very great.'" Michael V. Fox, *Character and Ideology in the Book of Esther* (Columbia, S.C.: University of South Carolina Press, 1991), 109. There are interesting parallels between the situations faced by Moses and Mordecai, but the differences seem to outweigh the similarities. Both the content and the grammar of the two verses (Exod. 11:3 and Esther 9:4) vary too much to assume a direct borrowing by the author of the Book of Esther. Interestingly, in Exodus, the Lord *(YHWH)* is actively involved in causing the Jews to gain favor in the sight of the Egyptians. By contrast, nowhere in the Book of Esther is the Lord mentioned.

9. Literally, "his report was walking throughout all the provinces." Compare Josh. 6:27, where the same Hebrew word for "his fame" *(šāmᶜô)* is also used. Joshua's fame is also throughout all the land, but whereas the Lord *(YHWH)* is mentioned within the same verse as being "with Joshua," there is again (see previous note) no mention of the Lord in connection with Mordecai anywhere in the Book of Esther.

10. The literal Hebrew *hôlēk wᵉgādôl* (was walking and great) is an idiomatic expression meaning "to grow greater and greater." Bruce K. Waltke and M. O'Connor, *An Introduction to Biblical Hebrew Syntax* (Winona Lake, Ind.: Eisenbrauns, 1990), §37.6d.

their killer(s) is (are) of Jewish origin. What is more, not only ten are killed, but more than seventy-five thousand are slaughtered in a two-day period—all at the hands of the Jews.

Esther 9:5 presents the broad scope of the victory of the Jews. Specifically, verse 5 gives a summary overview of all the fighting that takes place. In verse 6, the Jews "kill" *(hārag)* and "annihilate" *(ʾābad)* five hundred in Susa. In verses 7–10, they slaughter the ten sons of Haman. Verses 11–14 reveal that when the king learns how many are killed in Susa alone, he accepts the results in a matter-of-fact manner and then willingly agrees to Esther's request both to continue the fighting in the capital for another day and to hang Haman's sons. In verse 15, the Jews kill another three hundred people in Susa, adding still more to the total of seventy-five thousand that they killed throughout the rest of the empire (v. 16). Yet, despite having destroyed their enemies, the Jews do not take any of the spoils of victory (vv. 10, 15, 16); instead, they celebrate their victory (vv. 17–19).

Thus the author portrays the fighting in three segments: verses 5–10—the battle taking place in Susa on Adar 13; verses 11–15—the activities leading up to the second day of killing in Susa and the actual slaughter of that day; and verse 16—the results of the action taken by the Jews throughout the rest of the empire. He marks off the conclusion of each of these segments (vv. 10, 15, 16) by declaring that the Jews do not plunder[11] the spoils of their enemies whom they have defeated.

The decision of all the Jews not to plunder the spoils runs counter to that which Mordecai's edict in 8:11 permits them to do. Curiously, the Scripture leaves shrouded in mystery the reason the Jews choose not to plunder their enemies' possessions.[12]

11. In the concluding clause of each of these three verses, the author emphasizes by means of word order "the plunder" that is not taken: literally, "but on the plunder they did not throw out their hand."

12. Much speculation abounds. See Joyce G. Baldwin, *Esther: An Introduction and Commentary*, Tyndale Old Testament Commentaries, ed. D. J. Wiseman (Downers Grove: InterVarsity, 1984), 105; Carey A. Moore, *Esther*, The Anchor Bible, ed. William Foxwell Albright and David Noel Freedman (Garden City, N.Y.: Doubleday, 1971), 87–88; Paton, *The Book of Esther*, 284; Meir Zlotowitz, trans. and comp., *The Megillah: The Book of Esther: A New Translation with a Commentary Anthologized from Talmudic, Midrashic and Rabbinic Sources* (Brooklyn: Mesorah, 1981), 121.

Returning now to 9:5—when Adar 13 arrives, the Jews strike down (killing and annihilating)[13] their enemies, literally, "with the stroke of a sword." The Jews also have free reign over those who hate them. Both halves of verse 5 stress the ease with which the Jews overpower those who are opposed to them. "Did what they pleased" in the second half of the verse expresses the same concept as "struck . . . with the sword, killing and annihilating" in the first half. Thus, the clause "did what they pleased" does not imply that the Jews act sadistically toward those who hate them, rather that the Jews have no difficulty in dispatching quickly their enemies.[14]

Esther 9:6–10 sets forth the results of the fighting within the city of Susa on Adar 13, the day of the implementation of both Haman's and Mordecai's edicts. In verse 6, the Jews kill five hundred of their enemies. No report is made of any Jews being killed. Verses 7–10 list, by name, ten additional individuals whom the Jews kill—the sons of Haman.

Outside of verses 7–10, the Scripture is silent regarding the ten sons of Haman.[15] Even though Haman is an Agagite, the names of all of his sons appear to be Persian names. The fact that the names are Persian should not be viewed by the reader as surprising. The practice of minority groups giving their children the names of the dominant group in a culture was quite common in ancient times. Even the Jews of Haman's day participated in such a practice, as the names *Mordecai* and *Esther* testify (2:5, 7).

In the Hebrew text the names of Haman's sons are aligned in two columns[16] (in similar fashion to the listing of the defeated kings of Canaan in Josh. 12:9–24). Why the Hebrew text lists

13. Obviously, even though the term *šāmad* (destroy) does not occur in 9:5, the Jews "destroy" their enemies as well as "kill" *(hārag)* and "annihilate" *(ʾā-bad)* them. The three Hebrew terms appear to be used synonymously throughout the Book of Esther.

14. The phrases *b*^{e}*kol ʾoy*^{e}*bêhem* (all their enemies) and *b*^{e}*śōn*^{e}*ʾêhem* (with those who hated them) do not refer to two different groups but to the same group of people whom the Jews slaughter.

15. Research into the meanings of the names of the ten sons has generated results that are less than conclusive. Paulus Cassel, *An Explanatory Commentary on Esther*, trans. Aaron Bernstein (Edinburgh: T. and T. Clark, 1888), 247–49; Paton, *The Book of Esther*, 70–71.

16. The *Biblia Hebraica Stuttgartensia* Hebrew text arranges the names as follows (Hebrew reads from right to left): the far right column contains the name of one son; the second column from the right consists of the conjunction

the names in this way is unstated, but speculation naturally abounds. Michael V. Fox writes: "According to one midrashic explanation, the columns represent the gallows; according to another, they are stacked directly atop one another like an unstable row of bricks, rather than being securely staggered (j. Meg. 3:7; b. meg. 16b)." He continues: "More likely, this is simply a logical arrangement for a repetitive list. It also has the effect of keeping the names distinct and thus emphasizing the number of executed enemy, rather than letting the names be run together and de-emphasized as they would be if written continuously on the horizontal."[17] A further possible rationale for this alignment of names is that it functions as an aid for the oral reading of the text.[18]

Enough Is Not Enough (9:11–15)

Have you ever noticed how some people never seem satisfied with what they have, especially after they have had it for a short while and a more advanced model comes out on the market?

In 9:11–13, Queen Esther also exhibits a sense of dissatisfaction with her situation. Even though her situation far surpasses anything she could have imagined as few as eleven months earlier (3:13), she wants more. When she learns of the amazing results of the slaughter of her enemies in Susa on Adar 13, Esther petitions the king and secures his permission to allow the killing in Susa to continue for another day and to permit the public disgrace of her enemies (9:13).

On Adar 13, when King Ahasuerus learns that 510 die at the hands of the Jews in Susa (9:11), he casually comments to Esther about the slaughter. He then offers to fulfill any further request that she might have (9:12).

The attitude of the king in verse 12 is a matter of debate, even among the English translations. On the one hand, the Jerusalem Bible and the New American Standard Bible perceive the

---

and plus the marker of the direct object; the third column from the right lists the name of another son; and the far left-hand column once again includes the conjunction *and* plus the marker of the direct object

17. Fox, *Character and Ideology in the Book of Esther*, 110 n. 60.

18. The practice of chanting the ten names of Haman's sons in one breath during Purim services in the synagogue is a long-standing tradition. How soon that custom developed after the writing of the Book of Esther, however, is unknown. "Esther" [Megillah] *The Babylonian Talmud*, 16b.

king to be expressing amazement when he considers how many more people may have been killed in the provinces if more than five hundred have been killed in Susa alone. On the other hand, the Authorized Version, the New International Version, and the New Revised Standard Version translate the king's words to Queen Esther in the form of a question: "What have they done in the rest of the king's provinces?" The evidence weighs in favor of the latter view, suggesting that the king is unshaken by the mounting death toll. First, the Hebrew grammar of the passage, in particular the word order of the king's first two comments in verse 12, suggests that the king takes a matter-of-fact approach at this point.[19] Second, the king's willingness, as Paton states, "to grant Esther permission to massacre a few more thousand of his Persian subjects"[20] aligns more closely with the view that the king takes the slaughter in stride than with the view that he is shocked by what he hears.

Either out of the graciousness of his heart or because he senses that Esther is about to petition him for something else, the king offers to grant her whatever she asks (v. 12). He does so without waiting for her to bring a formal request before him.

When given this opportunity, Esther, apparently having already thought through what she desires, immediately brings her formal petition before the king (v. 13). Yet, once again (cf. 5:4, 8; 7:3; 8:5), Esther does not presume on his goodness, but prefaces her request with the polite language required by court protocol—"If unto the king *it seems* good." She continues with a two-part request: "Let also tomorrow be given to the Jews who are in Susa to do according to the law of today" and "the ten sons of Haman, let them be hanged on the gallows."

Thus, in the first half of her petition, Esther states that she wants the killing to continue in the capital city of Susa for one more day. Jonathan Magonet theorizes that the fighting in Susa on Adar 13 took place only within the confines of the palace citadel and that Esther is merely asking for permission to extend

19. Following the order of the text, the king's words may be translated as follows: "In Susa the capital, the Jews killed . . . . In the rest of the king's provinces, what have they done?" The emphasis is on what has happened "in Susa" and "in the rest of the king's provinces," and not on the number of people killed.

20. Paton, *The Book of Esther*, 286.

the fighting beyond the king's gate to the remainder of the city on Adar 14.[21] Magonet's view, however, does not square with the pan-empire provisions of Mordecai's edict nor with the death toll in Susa (cf. vv. 6–10, 15), which rightfully would be expected to be higher on day 2 than on day 1 if the killing were extended outside of the citadel to the more populous region of the city at large.

In the second half of her petition, Esther specifically requests that Haman's ten sons be hanged on "the gallows" *(hāʿēṣ)* rather than "a gallows." The use of the definite article *the* indicates that Esther is referring to the same gallows on which Haman was hanged eleven months earlier (7:10).

What motivates Esther to make her petition? Paton finds no justification for "this horrible request" but contends that she is motivated by "a malignant spirit of revenge."[22] Similarly Fox suggests that Esther's requests reflect a personality change that has taken place within her, that she has become "harder, blunter, even crueler."[23]

The Scripture neither commends nor condemns Esther. If anything, a case may be made that her actions are appropriate for the situation that she and her people face.

First, the results of the second day's fighting in Susa (300 additional people killed, 9:15) indicate that there are significant pockets of anti-Jewish resistance still remaining in the capital city after the first day's fighting is over. Thirty-seven percent of the total anti-Jewish population killed in Susa (i.e., 810) are not killed until the second day. If those 300 are allowed to live, there is the strong possibility that they would work within or even plot against the power structure of the central government to overthrow the Jews.

Second, throughout the remainder of the Book of Esther, the author nowhere expresses any trace of vengeance in Esther's character, mentioning her only in connection with the establishment of the festival of Purim (9:29–32). He pictures her there both as queen (vv. 29, 31) and as a Jewess (i.e., the daughter of Abihail, v. 29). By doing so, he may be suggesting that Esther

21. Jonathan Magonet, "The Liberal and the Lady: Esther Revisited," *Judaism* 29 (spring 1980): 174.

22. Paton, *The Book of Esther*, 287.

23. Fox, *Character and Ideology in the Book of Esther*, 115.

functions comfortably and successfully in both worlds—the world of the Gentiles and the world of the Jews.

Third, although the king presents Esther with the opportunity to ask for much more, she limits her request to one additional day of fighting that is to take place only in Susa,[24] and to the hanging of Haman's ten sons.[25] Her decision to limit her petition in this way suggests that she exhibits neither a streak of cruelty nor a "malignant spirit of revenge."

Yet, by petitioning for, receiving, and enacting her two requests, Esther transmits a message to all who live in the Medo-Persian empire that antigovernment rebellions (particularly anti-Jewish rebellions) would be crushed immediately and with extreme prejudice. There would, therefore, be no toleration of disobedience in the new regime of Esther and Mordecai—and, oh yes, of King Ahasuerus.

The king (9:14) grants Esther's requests. The law regarding the continuation of fighting in Susa is given out in Susa and the ten sons of Haman are hanged. On Adar 14, the Jews in Susa reassemble to kill their enemies, slaughtering an additional three hundred men, but, once again (cf. v. 10), refusing to plunder the spoil.

Dual-Barreled Celebration (9:16–19)

The Jews of the Medo-Persian empire, after successfully overcoming their enemies, hold spontaneous celebrations throughout the empire on the day following their victory. Yet, because the fighting occurs only on Adar 13 in the countryside but on both Adar 13 and 14 in the city of Susa, two different traditional dates for celebrating the victory develop. The Jews living outside of the capital celebrate on Adar 14, whereas the Jews living in Susa celebrate on Adar 15. Esther 9:16–19 discusses the origins of those two sequential festivals.

24. If the percentages of day-1 killed to day-2 killed (63 percent to 37 percent, respectively) in Susa hold true in the provinces as well, then after the first day's fighting in the provinces, there would be approximately forty-four thousand individuals left alive who opposed the Jews.

25. Disposing of the bodies of Haman's ten sons in this way would function as a deterrent to others who might be contemplating any course of action against the Jews.

In 9:16, the author remarks that the Jews outside of the capital assemble themselves together. This action is the same as that described in verse 2. By joining together in this way, in like manner as that established in the provisions of Mordecai's edict (8:11), the Jews gain strength by their numbers.

The Jews, according to 9:16, achieve three results: they defend themselves, they secure rest from their enemies, and they kill a substantial number of their enemies.

Four primary views have been advanced to explain the phrase *w*^{e}*nô(a)ḥ mēʾoy*^{e}*bêhem* (and to have rest from their enemies), which some individuals feel is out of sequence in the text, the sequence of the text being "defend—secure rest—kill":

1. a literal translation—"and to have rest from their enemies,"[26]
2. a revised translation—"and to rid themselves of their enemies,"[27]
3. an emended text reading *nḥwm* for *nwḥ* ("haplography of the *mem* and consequent adjustment of vowel letters"[28])—"to gain relief from their enemies,"[29] and
4. an emended text (same as previous emendation) but a revised translation—"to avenge themselves of their enemies."[30]

Although the desire to alter the phrase according to number 2, 3, or 4 is understandable, there is no need to depart from literal meaning of the text. The passage makes sense as it stands, if we do not presume that the author intends the three phrases to be understood chronologically.

26. The AV supports this translation. The Hebrew manuscripts support both the literal translation and the "defend—secure rest—kill" sequence, as does the Septuagint.

27. JB, NASB translate the text in this way. The NASB, however, recognizes in its marginal notes that the literal meaning is to "have rest from" their enemies.

28. Fox, *Character and Ideology in the Book of Esther*, 285.

29. NIV, NRSV, Fox, and Moore advance this view. Fox, *Character and Ideology in the Book of Esther*, 285; Moore, *Esther*, 89.

30. Driver and Rudolph adhere to this position. G. R. Driver, "Problems and Solutions," *Vetus Testamentum* 4 (1954): 237, reprint in *Studies in the Book of Esther*, ed. Carey A. Moore (New York: KTAV, 1982), 387–407; Rudolph cited in Fox, *Character and Ideology in the Book of Esther*, 285.

In 9:16, the author also records that the Jews in the countryside kill seventy-five thousand of their enemies. This fact seems somewhat startling at first.[31] Yet, as Paulus Cassel points out, seventy-five thousand people spread out over an empire the size of the Medo-Persian empire would mean that the number of dead in any one place would not be too excessive.[32] In addition, in verse 16, the author again (cf. vv. 10 and 15) notes that the Jews do not take any of the spoils of their enemies.

Verse 17 indicates that the Jews in the countryside do their fighting on the thirteenth of Adar and their resting, feasting,[33] and rejoicing on the fourteenth. By contrast, verse 18 records that the Jews of Susa assemble (and fight) on Adar 13 and 14, and thus rest, feast, and rejoice on Adar 15.

The author concludes this section (verse 19) by indicating that the previous verses give the reasons why there are two different days of celebration.[34] He also points out that the day of celebration has become a holiday (lit., "a good day"—cf. 8:17) and a day on which the Jews send gifts (lit., "portions")[35] to one another (lit., "a man to his friend [or possibly, his fellow citizen]").

Hang In, Hang On, But Never Hang Up

The Jews of Medo-Persia must have experienced a sense of euphoria when they learned of Haman's defeat and the issuing of Mordecai's edict that worked to neutralize Haman's edict (8:15–17). Yet, that euphoria undoubtedly was tempered by the

31. The Lucianic recension of the Septuagint records the number of dead as being 70,100. The Septuagint text without the Lucianic recension reduces that number still further, to only 15,000 killed. No ancient Hebrew texts, however, support these or any other reduced figures.

32. Cassel, *An Explanatory Commentary on Esther*, 251.

33. The term *mište(h)* (feasting) literally means "drinking" and is used throughout the Book of Esther to indicate both Gentile and Jewish parties (cf. 1:3; 2:18; 5:4; 7:8; 8:17; 9:18, 19, 22).

34. The author's need to explain why Purim (cf. 9:26) is celebrated on different days in Susa and in the countryside suggests that the Book of Esther was not written during the time of Mordecai and Esther.

35. Contained within this term is the idea of choice pieces of food. Thus the gifts that are being given undoubtedly consist of various food items, as well as perhaps nonfood items. Compare Exod. 29:26; Lev. 7:33; 8:29; 1 Sam. 1:4, 5; 2 Chron. 31:19; Neh. 8:10, 12; and Esther 2:9; 9:22.

realization that they were but a small race of people in the midst of a very large and potentially hostile Gentile empire. Many changes easily could have taken place between the issuing of Mordecai's edict and its implementation nine months later. Nothing was certain for the Jews until after they secured their victory. Once that victory had been won, and only after it had been won, could they celebrate freely and confidently.

In the midst of describing the great victory of the Jews and their subsequent euphoria in 9:1–19, the author of the Book of Esther incorporates four important principles.

Principle 1—Be prepared to seize the right opportunity when it is presented, and then go ahead and seize it.

At the heart of the chiastic structure of 9:1–19, and thus at the author's center of emphasis for this passage, the king offers Esther a tremendous opportunity. On the spur of the moment, he promises to fulfill any petition or request that she might have.[36] Esther does not hesitate even for a moment. Already prepared for such an occasion, Esther knows exactly what she wants the king to do on her behalf—extend the fighting in Susa for an additional day and hang Haman's ten sons on the gallows that stands before the house where Haman used to live. Thus Esther immediately grasps the king's offer and thereby helps to secure an additional victory for her people.

Principle 2—Justice can be achieved despite every outward appearance of the inflexibility or immutability of an unjust law or of an unjust action.

Haman's edict, which sentenced the Jews to death, was unjust at its core (3:13). It was designed to bring an undeserved punishment upon the Jews, not for their own sins but for the sins of only one of their members, that is, Mordecai (3:6). That edict, therefore, was the result of an improper use of the power vested in Haman by the king. Seemingly miraculously, however, Mordecai and Esther neutralize the effect of that edict by securing Haman's death (7:3–10) and counterbalancing the edict (8:9–13).

Principle 3—God's people should never give up when facing seemingly impossible odds, because God may work *behind the seen* to bring about an unexpected reversal in their situation.

36. He does not even qualify his declaration here by adding the words *even to half of the kingdom,* as he did on earlier occasions (5:3, 6; 7:2).

This principle flows from the previous one. When, humanly speaking, there is no hope, God can give hope and bring victory.

Principle 4—Political power used wisely may exert great control over those who are governed by it.

Throughout the Book of Esther, the author never shies away from a presentation of the positive and negative sides of political power. In every chapter (except perhaps chap. 4) he records either the wise or the foolish acts of those who rule the greatest empire of its day. In 9:1–19, he highlights the exercise of power by each of the three main characters still alive: Prime Minister Mordecai, Queen Esther, and King Ahasuerus. The author pictures Mordecai as using his power wisely to secure the allegiance of the government officials in every province of the empire (vv. 3–4). The author also depicts Esther as exercising her influence positively both to procure an extra opportunity for her people to extend their successes and to send a message to would-be opponents that the power of the throne would tolerate no dissent (v. 13). Finally, the author presents King Ahasuerus's demonstration of power as being less than wise by exposing the king's callousness regarding the loss of hundreds of his people and carelessness in offering to grant and then actually granting Esther whatever petition or request she might make, with no stipulations attached (vv. 12, 14).

Delivering the Goods

Every year for the past several years, MIT (Massachusetts Institute of Technology) has held a contest for the students in its engineering design class. The goal of the contest is simple: build a machine that, within a thirty-second time limit, can place more ping-pong balls into your side of the goal than your opponent's machine can deposit into its side. Each student is given a box full of parts and gadgets—all students receive the same materials—and six weeks in which to build and test their machines. The head-to-head competition is fast and furious. Some machines depend on speed, some on accuracy, some on volume, and some on power. The better machines incorporate some or all of these characteristics.

The winning machine this past year combined both offense and defense. It utilized a blocker to cover its opponent's goal before dropping its load of ping-pong balls into its own cylinder.

The Jews of the Medo-Persian empire also recognized the need to combine both offensive and defensive strategies to ensure victory against their opponents in a struggle for life and death.

In Esther 9:1–19, the author reveals how the Jews implement their strategies and how successful those strategies turn out to be. Those verses show that the Jews secure success (i.e., the defeat of their enemies) by scare tactics (vv. 2–3), by extending their political power (vv. 3–4), by being prepared for any eventuality (vv. 12–14), and by presenting a unified and aggressive front against their opponents (vv. 1–2, 5, 15–16). The verses also highlight the spontaneous celebrations that follow the Jews' victories (vv. 17–19).

Having completed his description in 9:1–19 of the fighting on Adar 13 and 14 and the subsequent celebrations that take place from Adar 14 to 15, the author of the Book of Esther shifts his presentation to the means by which those celebrations become permanent fixtures within Jewish society. He makes that shift of direction in the next section of the book, 9:20–32.

20

A Pur-fect Day
(9:20–32)

Many radio stations play records known as oldies but goodies. That music of a bygone era brings floods of memories back to people who lived through the days when that music was first recorded.

In Esther 9:20–32, Mordecai and Esther establish what they hope will become an oldie but goody. They formalize the traditions of Purim, a festival designed to help participants remember the reversal of fortunes for the Jews of Medo-Persia. In these verses, Mordecai and Esther also give general guidelines on how the days of Purim are to be celebrated in order to ensure that each future celebration of Purim would be as meaningful as the first.

Nothing Up His Sleeve

Partway through a recent New Year's Eve party at the house of some of our friends, our hosts decided to perform several magic tricks to keep the festive atmosphere of the evening high. For some of the tricks, the magic was obvious to all of us. One of the tricks, however, a card trick, was difficult to figure out. Finally, after watching the trick three or four times and being thoroughly amazed at the mental prowess of our hostess, we figured out how it worked.

In Esther 9:20–32, as in all other sections of the book, the author does not attempt to hide anything from his readers, as did our hostess from us. He conceals nothing up his sleeve, but reveals that he in fact has three decks of cards, that is, three different perspectives that he is going to use to explain the history behind and the practices associated with the days of Purim. Those three perspectives are as follows:

A. A sign of reversal (9:20–23)
B. A sign of remembrance (9:24–28)
C. A sign of regulation (9:29–32)

Reversal (vv. 20–23) is the basis on which Purim is built. The Jews secure rest from a tense, life-threatening situation; their sadness and misery changes into joy and celebration.

In verses 24–28, the author brings to remembrance both the terrors the Jews faced because of Haman's edict and the involvement of a Gentile king in their deliverance. Those verses highlight the naming of the holiday, the Jews' role in its establishment, and the importance of making it an annual tradition for all Jews everywhere in all times.

Finally, in verses 29–32, the author notes the legalization of the celebration and the regulations established for the times of fasting and lamentation to help Jews throughout the ages consider the terror of impending annihilation that those early Jews faced.

The author writes each of these three summary sections so that, in general, they parallel one another structurally. The third segment (verses 29–32), however, as the following shows, contains only A″ and C″ components because, unlike the other segments, its focus is on the confirmation of the Purim celebration and not on its origins:

A The powers that be create a document that impacts the Jews (9:20–21)
  B The fortunes of the Jews are reversed (9:22)
    C The tradition of Purim is established (9:23)
A′ The powers that be create a document that impacts the Jews (9:24)
  B′ The fortunes of the Jews are reversed (9:25)
    C′ The tradition of Purim is established (9:26–28)
A″ The powers that be create a document that impacts the Jews (9:29–30)
    C″ The tradition of Purim is established (9:31–32)

Thus the author uses these verses not only to recap the events surrounding the establishment of Purim but also to provide fresh insight into its customs.

Times Certainly Have Changed (9:20–23)

Most politicians would love to be in Mordecai's situation. He has just won a major military victory—suppressed an internal revolt—and has no major political opponent on the near horizon (7:10; 9:1, 5, 6–10, 15–16). His political influence is great and it is increasing (9:3–4). He is, however, faced with the need to deal with a potential rift among his own people before it develops beyond repair (vv. 18–19). Fortunately, he is able to enact a simple solution to his problem that is readily accepted by both groups (v. 23).

In 9:20, Mordecai details in writing the events that have recently transpired.[1] At a minimum, Mordecai would have recorded information surrounding the fighting of Adar 13 and 14, and the celebrations of Adar 14 and 15. Quite possibly, he may have written something about the events leading up to the fighting.

After recording the events surrounding Purim, Mordecai sends (v. 20) letters throughout the empire establishing Purim as an annual holiday to be celebrated[2] on both Adar 14 and 15

1. Quite probably, Mordecai records these events in the official records of the empire. Those records are identified in 2:23 (as *The Book of the Chronicles*), in 6:1 (as *The Book of the Remembrances, the Chronicles*), and in 10:2 (as *The Book of the Chronicles of the Kings of Media and Persia*). Generally speaking, modern scholars do not maintain that what Mordecai wrote here is the Book of Esther. Most also do not believe that he was the author of the Book of Esther. Michael V. Fox, *Character and Ideology in the Book of Esther* (Columbia, S.C.: University of South Carolina Press, 1991), 117; F. B. Huey, Jr., "Esther," *Expositor's Bible Commentary,* ed. Frank E. Gaebelein, 12 vols. (Grand Rapids: Zondervan, 1988), 4:836.

2. The author notes that Mordecai makes this celebration "binding" (*l^eqayyēm*) on all Jews. Fox writes: "The uses of *qayyem* [i.e., the Piel form of *qûm*] elsewhere show that it means 'validate' or 'confirm,' rather than 'command, demand.' . . . . In all cases, it refers to the formalization or fulfillment of a decision or a previously declared intention. Nowhere does it mean the imposition of one person's will on another. Mordecai is not *demanding* obedience." Fox, *Character and Ideology in the Book of Esther*, 118.

(v. 21).[3] He includes as part of these letters his reasons for officially establishing these dates for the festival as well as his explanation as to how the holiday is to be celebrated (v. 22).

In verse 22, Mordecai expresses two reasons as to why Purim is to be celebrated when it is. He cites as his two reasons that those were the days on which the Jews (no mention is made of God's role) secured rest[4] from their enemies, and that the month of Adar was a month of "turning" for the Jews—a turning from grief to gladness,[5] from mourning to a holiday.[6]

Continuing in verse 22, Mordecai outlines how the Jews are to celebrate those days. The people are to have feasts (i.e., drinking parties; see note on v. 17), to rejoice, and to send food (lit., portions; see v. 19) to friends and gifts to the poor.[7]

The Jews (v. 23) commit themselves to perpetuating the celebration of Purim in the way that they began it. At the same time, they elect to incorporate certain new ideas proposed by Mordecai. What those ideas are, the author does not state directly. A close reading of the text, however, does identify three possible additions to the activities of Purim practiced in verses 17–19: the sending of gifts to the poor (v. 22), times of fasting (v. 31), and times of lamentations (v. 31). Caution needs to be exercised regarding making a firm determination as to whether the Jews actually adopt the last two possibilities under the conditions of Mordecai's first letter

3. Whether Mordecai establishes both days for all Jews or merely allows them to continue celebrating as they began (i.e., rural Jews on Adar 14 and Susa Jews on Adar 15) is unclear at this point (cf. vv. 23, 27, 31). Verse 28, however, seems to indicate that Mordecai encourages a two-day celebration for all Jews.

4. Certain translators (JB, NASB) have rendered the verb *nāḥû* (lit., they rested) to indicate that the Jews "rid" themselves of their enemies, that is, indicating the process by which the Jews secured rest. The preferred translation, however, is "rested," as is suggested by the AV, NIV, and NRSV.

5. The term *śîmḥā(h)* (gladness) conveys the idea of a festive mirth, a feeling of extreme pleasure. Brown, Driver, and Briggs, *A Hebrew and English Lexicon of the Old Testament*, 970.

6. Literally, "a good day" (cf. v. 19).

7. The *Talmud* takes the words *mānôt* (portions), *mattānôt* (gifts), and *ʾebyônîm* (poor) literally as plurals, arguing that at the very least two portions should be given to one friend and, also at the very least, two gifts should be given to two poor men. Meir Zlotowitz, trans. and comp., *The Megillah: The Book of Esther: A New Translation with a Commentary Anthologized from Talmudic, Midrashic and Rabbinic Sources* (Brooklyn: Mesorah, 1981), 128.

since those proposals are noted only after mention is made of a second letter being sent out jointly by Esther and Mordecai (v. 29). In any event, all three of Mordecai's proposals ultimately are accepted and put into practice by the Jews (v. 32).

Memory Enhancers (9:24–28)

The modern practice of Purim is a curious acting out of the events of the first Purim celebration, but is based on a very loose reading of the text of the Book of Esther.[8]

The Purim celebration itself is preceded by Ta'anit Esther (i.e., the fast of Esther). This fast is practiced in remembrance of the three-day fast that Esther requested her fellow Jews undertake on her behalf (4:16). By contrast, the days of Purim involve much merriment, feasting and the sending of gifts to friends and to the poor.

Expressive of the many reversals that occur throughout the book, Jews during the days of Purim are permitted to wear various costumes that exhibit a role reversal of one nature or another. They dress in the clothes of a Gentile king (to represent Mordecai), in the clothes of the wife of a Gentile king (to represent Esther), and even in the clothes of Haman. Jewish men may wear women's clothes, Jewish women may wear men's clothes.

In addition, the drinking of alcoholic beverages, which takes place frequently in the book, is urged on modern Purim practitioners. They often are encouraged to drink so much that they are unable to distinguish between blessing and cursing, between the statements *blessed be Mordecai* and *cursed be Haman*.

During the days of Purim, the text of Esther is read aloud—the scroll being folded to read as a letter (representative of the many letters mentioned in the book) rather than rolled as with a

8. The following discussion of Purim customs is taken from Monford Harris, "Purim: The Celebration of Dis-Order," *Judaism* 26 (1977): 164–69; and Michael Strassfeld, *The Jewish Holidays: A Guide and Commentary* (New York: Harper and Row, 1985), 190–91. Note that not all of these activities are practiced by all Jews everywhere. Some actions may be emphasized in one locale, but deemphasized (or not practiced) in another. For example, certain groups of Eastern European Jews engage in snatching of food from one another and in hitting one another, whereas Jews elsewhere generally do not incorporate those activities into their traditions.

Torah scroll. Furthermore, while that text is being read, the congregation is permitted to make noises of all kinds (frequently with a grager [rattle]), particularly when Haman's name is read so that the sound of that name may be drowned out.

Generally speaking, Purim is a time of rejoicing. The various customs serve as memory enhancers to remind all Jews of a time when an upside-down world turned around, and to encourage them when they too find themselves in difficult circumstances.

Esther 9:24–28 reviews the events leading up to the establishment of Purim as a holiday to be celebrated by all Jews and by all who ally themselves with the Jews. Verses 24–25 chronicle Haman's anti-Jewish actions; these verses, moreover, highlight the king's role in the deliverance of the Jews, thereby reminding the readers of the strangeness of this book, that is, that a heathen has the "final" say over the destiny of the Jews. Verses 26–28 continue the summary by explaining the meaning of Purim and recounting the commitment of the Jews to making Purim a permanent time of remembrance.

In 9:24, the author recalls the role of Haman (the dreaded but now dead enemy of all Jews) in the development of Purim. While doing so, the author also reveals that Haman was more closely involved than previously noted (cf. 3:7)[9] in the casting of "pur," which the author explains as meaning "the lot."[10]

In addition, in 9:24, the author records the goals Haman hoped to achieve in his schemes against the Jews and in his casting of pur. Haman's intent was both to disturb and to annihilate them. The fact that Haman wanted "to annihilate them" (*lᵉʾabbedām)* has been recorded before (3:9, 13; 4:7; 7:4; 8:5, 6). The fact that he also hoped "to disturb them" *(lᵉhummām)*[11] is

9. In 3:7, lots are cast "before" Haman, seemingly by someone else. In 9:24, Haman is seen as taking an active role in the casting of the lots. The author, therefore, may be suggesting that Haman himself threw some or all of the lots.

10. The author's need to explain the meaning of *pûr* (pur) as *hagôrāl* (the lot) suggests that his readers do not have a first-hand knowledge of the events of the book. Hence, the book was probably written several generations after Esther's and Mordecai's time.

11. The author's choice to include the term *lᵉhummām* (to disturb) here may be an attempt at a play on Haman's name (*hāmān*). If it is a wordplay, then the pun suggests that "to disturb" the Jews is "to Haman" (*lᵉhāmān*) them, as if Haman's presence in and of itself disturbs them.

new information, not given in any previous passage in the book. What Haman specifically intends by disturbing the Jews is unclear. The term conveys the ideas of confusing, discomforting, or vexing someone, as well as making a noise or moving noisily.[12] Perhaps he felt that by making a big show of his casting of lots he would psychologically disturb the Jews, or perhaps he hoped to disrupt their Passover celebration on Nisan 14 (cf. 3:7, 12). Yet neither explanation seems fully satisfactory.

One possible resolution to this dilemma is to understand the author to be employing a figure of speech known as synecdoche, in which a part of a larger entity is written down to indicate the entire entity. Thus in this case the casting of pur (which is the initial component of Haman's work to annihilate the Jews) would be used to signify Haman's entire anti-Jewish effort. If the author is using the casting of pur to be a synecdoche (and there is a good probability that he is), then he may be implying that Haman intended to cause a complete upheaval within the Jewish community.

In 9:25, the author shifts his focus from Haman to the king, indicating that when the king learned of the plight of the Jews he took appropriate measures to rectify the potentially disastrous situation. The author, moreover, includes two ambiguous statements, one of which he resolves immediately within the verse. The other he leaves as a mystery.

Ambiguity arises in the first statement of verse 25, which reads *ûb^{e}boʾāh lipnê hammelek* ("but when [?] came before the king"). The Hebrew *ûb^{e}boʾāh* may be rendered either "but when it came" or "but when she came." The author never clearly defines whether the king takes action only when "the matter of the edict" (i.e., it) or when "Esther" (i.e., she) comes before him. If the author intends the former, then he downplays Esther's and Mordecai's role in the process by which Haman's edict is neutralized. If, however, the author intends the latter, then he may be suggesting that the king has no intention of doing anything to rectify a legal injustice until Esther "pesters" him about the problem.

Based on the grammar of the passage, "it" is to be preferred over "she," since there has been no reference to Esther for the past twelve verses (cf. v. 13). Based on the logic and flow of the

12. Brown, Driver, and Briggs, *A Hebrew and English Lexicon of the Old Testament*, 243.

story, however, "she" is to be preferred, since Esther personally brings the matter to the king's attention on two different occasions (7:3–4; 8:3, 5–6). Various English translations are divided on which is the preferred translation. The New American Standard Bible and the New International Version favor "it," whereas the Authorized Version and the New Revised Standard Version favor "she."[13] I prefer to render *ûbᵉbōʾāh* as "but when it came" for three reasons: the strength of the grammatical argument, the legitimacy of such a translation within the context of the book, and the author's general portrayal of the king as being one who often is unaware of what transpires around him.

The second ambiguity of 9:25 is the author's use of the pronouns *he, his,* and *him* throughout much of the verse, with their immediate antecedent in the first part of the verse being "the king." The portion of the verse under discussion reads: "he commanded by a letter *that* his evil plot which he plotted against the Jews should return on his own head and *that* they should hang him and his sons on the gallows." The first "he" (in "he commanded") refers to "the king" in the clause "but when it [or she] came before the king." Grammatically the third person masculine pronouns that follow should all refer to the same antecedent as the first "he," in other words, to the king. Thus according to the grammar, the wicked plot is the king's, the king does the plotting, the plot should return on the king's head, and the king and his sons should be hanged.

Obviously, the context of the Book of Esther dictates that all but the first of the third person masculine pronouns in 9:25 refer to Haman. Yet, the author may have intentionally written a subtle attack against King Ahasuerus. By leaving the antecedent to third person masculine pronouns ambiguous, the author may be condemning the king for the king's participation (knowingly or unknowingly) in Haman's edict against the Jews (3:8–11), or for the king's slowness or unwillingness to respond on behalf of the Jews even after Haman has been hanged (8:1–8).

In 9:26 the author suggests that there is a connection between the singular term *pûr* (pur) and its plural form *pûrîm* (Purim). This connection needs to be understood in light of 3:7

13. The JB, following the Septuagint, translates this portion of verse 25 as "[b]ut when he [i.e., Haman] went again to the king to ask him to order the hanging of Mordecai." No Hebrew manuscripts, however, support the Septuagint reading.

where Haman has *pûr* cast before him, not merely once but many times. He does so in order to determine the month and day for the initiation of the pogrom against the Jews. The casting of *pûr* many times leads to the possibility that more than one *pûr* was cast, hence the use of the plural term *pûrîm.*[14]

The remainder of 9:26 presents the basis on which the Jews (in v. 27) both establish and implement for themselves the days of Purim. Verse 26 identifies the foundation of the Jews' practice of Purim as consisting of two basic building blocks: the written words of Mordecai and the experience of all the Jews themselves. That experience, moreover, embodies both what they saw[15] and what happened[16] to them.

Verse 27 continues what was begun in verses 20–23 and what will be presented in verses 29–32—a discussion of the origins of the celebration of Purim without any mention of God.[17] Verses 20–23 state that Purim develops as a spontaneous act of the Jews and as a result of a letter by Mordecai. In verse 27 the Jews are identified as being involved in the construction of a permanent festival. Finally, in verses 29–32, Esther and Mordecai play a significant role in the initiation of Purim.

In verse 27, the Jews establish[18] and undertake[19] the practice of Purim not only for themselves and their descendants, but also

14. Caution needs to be exercised in drawing this conclusion, however, since, in 3:7, the term *pûr* occurs only in the singular form.

15. Paton may be correct when he suggests that the word *rā'û* (had seen) "is used in the sense of *experienced,* as in Ex. 10[6]." Lewis Bayles Paton, *The Book of Esther*, International Critical Commentary, ed. Samuel Rolles Driver, Alfred Plummer, and Charles Augustus Briggs (Edinburgh: T. and T. Clark, 1908), 297. Nothing in the book specifically points out what the Jews, as a group of people, "saw."

16. The Hebrew term *ngᶜ,* when used in its Hiphil form as is the case here *[higgî(a)ᶜ]* may be translated "befall." Brown, Driver, and Briggs, *A Hebrew and English Lexicon of the Old Testament,* 619.

17. Without God's involvement, the days of Purim technically are not holy days (holidays). Harris, "Purim: The Celebration of Dis-Order," 170. Purim therefore should be understood as having been created out of a secular event by secular people for secular purposes.

18. See discussion of "binding" *(lᵉqayyēm)* in verse 21 (note) for information on the term *qiyyᵉmû,* translated in verse 27 as "established."

19. The word *qibbᵉlu* as used in 9:23 and 9:27 indicates the acceptance or assumption of something (e.g., an obligation). Brown, Driver, and Briggs, *A Hebrew and English Lexicon of the Old Testament,* 867.

for those who align themselves with the Jews. This suggests that some, if not all, of those who converted to Judaism in 8:17 remained true to the Jewish religion.

The Jews of Medo-Persia intend the celebration of Purim to become a permanent and annual fixture in Jewish social life.[20] Thus, of all the feasts in the Book of Esther, the feast of Purim alone is to be a feast that continues throughout time. Furthermore, whereas the feasts of 1:1–9; 2:18; and 8:17 span one empire for one brief period of time, the feast of Purim crosses all borders in all ages.

Functioning as an emphatic summary to 9:26–27, verse 28 highlights the fact that the days of Purim are to be a part of every Jew's life everywhere, throughout all time.[21] They are days that are not ever to cease from being practiced by or to fade from the memory[22] of future generations of Jews.[23]

One More Time (9:29–32)

The author apparently understands two axioms of advertising: the importance of repetition and the power of product endorsement by celebrities. In 9:29–32 he presents for a third time (all within the brief span of thirteen verses) the key events surrounding the establishment of the days of Purim. He punctuates his message by highlighting the efforts of three famous people from different ethnic backgrounds, age and gender categories, and patterns of social success. He has two Jews and a Gentile; a senior citizen, a middle-aged person, and a young adult; male and

20. The Jews (v. 27) should not fail (lit., "pass over"—*yaʿăbôr*) to celebrate these two days "according to their regulation" (lit., "their writing," all that Mordecai and Esther write regarding Purim) and "according to their appointed time" (Adar 14 and 15).

21. Moore notes that "[t]he distributive use of the nouns here . . . emphasizes that there are to be *no exceptions:* all Jews must observe both days." Carey A. Moore, *Esther,* The Anchor Bible, ed. William Foxwell Albright and David Noel Freedman (Garden City, N.Y.: Doubleday, 1971), 95.

22. The Hebrew word *zikrām* (their memory) is emphasized by its position in the final clause of verse 28.

23. The Talmud understands the words *lōʾ yaʿab^{e}arû* (should not cease) and *lōʾ yāsûp* (should not come to an end) to be a prophetic promise rather than an admonition. Zlotowitz, *The Megillah,* 132. Cassel counters, however, by stating that although "the feast of Purim has never been forgotten by the Jews; nevertheless, they [i.e., the two verbs] were not spoken in prophetical, but in legislative language." Paulus Cassel, *An Explanatory Commentary on Esther*, trans. Aaron Bernstein (Edinburgh: T. and T. Clark, 1888), 255.

female; and one who was born into power, one who married into power, and one who was promoted to power.[24]

In 9:29, Esther and Mordecai draft[25] a second letter whereby they together both confirm the details surrounding the establishment of Purim and add still further instructions regarding the manner in which it is to be celebrated (cf. v. 31).[26]

The author begins verse 29 by identifying Queen Esther as the daughter of Abihail. He expresses no particular reason for reestablishing Esther's connection with her father a second time (cf. 2:15). Yet, by making that connection, he reminds the reader that even though Esther is the queen of a Gentile empire she has not forsaken her roots. When all is said and done, Esther is a Jewess.

By contrast to his paucity of reference to Esther's heritage, the author frequently cites Mordecai's Jewish origins: 2:5; 3:4; 5:13; 6:10; 8:7; 9:29, 31. In each verse the identification of Mordecai as a Jew is crucial to the events taking place. This current reference (9:29) is no exception—Mordecai is establishing an annual Jewish festival.

The author continues verse 29 by commenting that when Esther and Mordecai write their letter of confirmation, they do so "with full authority." What makes their authority "full" is the fact that Esther and Mordecai are extremely powerful people (queen and prime minister, respectively), and, perhaps more importantly, they both are Jews who have secured victory for their people.

Mordecai then (9:30) takes responsibility for the distribution of the letters,[27] which the author describes as "words of peace and truth."

24. The author's efforts are undeniably effective—the days of Purim are still being celebrated today nearly twenty-five hundred years after the events recorded by the author in the Book of Esther.

25. The Hebrew of the first half of verse 29 does not adhere to typical Hebrew grammar. Normally, when a male subject and a female subject do something together, the verb form of that action is written in the masculine form. Here, however, the verb form is feminine (*wattiktob*—and she wrote). Such an anomaly suggests that Esther takes the lead in the creation of this letter.

26. When this letter is written is not stated. As Moore notes: "it could have been ten days or ten years after Mordecai's." Moore, *Esther*, 95. Most likely it is published soon after Mordecai's letter (cf. 9:20).

27. The plural form probably does not refer to the two letters of verses 20 and 29, but to the copies of the second letter that would be sent to the various language groups of the empire.

Those letters again establish the holiday of Purim. Interestingly, they include information not identified before—information regarding fastings[28] and lamentations[29] that are required of all Purim participants. Those additions to Purim practices therefore wed sorrow to the already-mentioned joy (9:17–19, 22) of the days of Purim.

Chapter 9 concludes (v. 32) with the brief statement that the command of Esther establishes the various matters of the Purim celebration. Esther's command, moreover, is recorded in "the book" (i.e., probably the official Chronicles of the Medo-Persian empire; see 2:23; 6:1; 10:2).

Expert Advice

The author of the Book of Esther is an expert in his field. He knows what took place in the Medo-Persian world of Esther and Mordecai. He has studied thoroughly both the broad sweep of events and the minute details of the circumstances surrounding the key individuals. He also knows what pieces of information from that period of time need to be conveyed to his readers so that they (we) can live more effectively. By noting what he says and by observing how he communicates his message, we can learn some important guidelines for success.

The following principles are drawn not only from what the author actually writes (or chooses not to write) in 9:20–32, but also from the manner in which he conveys that truth:

1. Later generations need to be reminded of the deliverance experiences of previous generations (9:27–28, 31) so that,

28. This fasting should not be considered as a religious act (cf. 4:3. 16), since Purim is not considered by the Jews to be a sacred holiday.

29. Baldwin suggests that the term *zaʿăqātām* should be translated "their supplication" because the verbal form of this noun is often found in connection with prayer to God. Joyce G. Baldwin, *Esther: An Introduction and Commentary*, Tyndale Old Testament Commentaries, ed. D. J. Wiseman (Downers Grove: InterVarsity, 1984), 111. If Baldwin is correct then the days of Purim contain religious overtones and the Jews in the Book of Esther do in fact demonstrate a spiritual concern. The noun form of *zaʿaq,* however, is never used in connection with prayer throughout the rest of Scripture. Thus the translation *their supplication* seems inappropriate here. See Gen. 18:20; Neh. 5:6; 9:9; Esther 4:1; Job 16:18; Prov. 21:13; Eccles. 9:17; Isa. 15:5, 8; 65:19; Jer. 18:22; 20:16; 48:4, 34; 50:46; 51:54; Ezek. 27:28.

when those later generations face difficulties, they may realize that God is capable of enacting a similar deliverance for them.

2. Purim is to be observed by all Jews throughout all generations, with no exceptions (9:21, 27–28, 31). The holiday of Purim, however, is not ordained directly by God or by his divinely appointed representative. As such, it is technically a nonreligious holiday and does not attain to the status of those festivals designed by God. As a cultural festival, Purim helps in a positive way to bind the community together. Moreover, when the participants truly honor the One who delivered the Jews, they then celebrate the days of Purim more appropriately than did their ancestors.
3. Giving guidelines for the standardization of programs that begin spontaneously can help to ensure their continuation and their meaningful practice by all who participate in them, even by those who become involved at a later date (9:20–22, 26–31).
4. Written records assist one in remembering what God has done (9:20, 26, 29, 32). Furthermore, without the written record of the author of the Book of Esther, we today would not know that these events transpired as they did. We would perhaps have missed a great truth that God works providentially on behalf of his people even when they do not honor him as they should.

A Festival Not to Be "Pass(ed)over"

Each year, Jews around the world celebrate two festivals that remind them that God is more than sufficient enough to deliver his people from desperate situations. Those two festivals are Passover[30] and Purim.

There are many important similarities between those two celebrations. Both recall the deliverance of the Jews from the grasp of their enemies. Both are annual events at specific times of the year that were designed to be celebrated by all Jews and

30. The feast of Passover is also known as the Feast of Unleavened Bread. The events of the Passover deliverance of the Jews from their bondage in Egypt are recorded in Exod. 12–13.

by all converts to Judaism throughout all time. Both are to be joyous times and times for reflection.

The differences between Passover and Purim, however, are significant:

1. Passover was directly ordained by God; Purim was not.
2. The instructions given for the way in which Passover is to be celebrated require the participants to remember God and what he has done; those for Purim do not.
3. The actual events of the Passover recall the deliverance of the Jews out of exile; the events of Purim do not—Medo-Persian Jews remained under Gentile domination as they had been prior to the events of Adar 13–14.
4. God takes an open and active role in bringing about the events of the Passover; he is entirely hidden from view in the events surrounding Purim.

The festival of Purim, therefore, definitely does not attain to the stature of the feast of Passover.

Yet the author of the Book of Esther considers the origins of the official establishment of the days of Purim to be significant. In 9:20–32, he concludes his discussion of the events of Purim by recording the process by which Purim is recognized as having a permanent place on the Jewish calendar. In those verses, he presents guidelines by which Jews are to keep fresh in their memory their great victory over their enemies.

The victory has been won. The days of Purim have been instituted. Nothing more needs to be said . . . or does it? The author of the Book of Esther feels compelled to add three more verses regarding the situation of the Jews in ancient Medo-Persia. Those three verses bring closure to the message of the book and reinforce the author's message concerning the Jews and their lack of an active relationship to God. Thus those verses form the basis for the next chapter of this book.

21

Exit Stage (All) Right

(10:1–3)

Near the end of television programs, after the murder has been solved, the marriage has been restored, or the problem has been resolved, there is often a brief commercial break followed by a short segment that brings closure to the show. If we apply this analogy to the Book of Esther, we observe the major problem of the story being resolved by 9:19. We then watch the commercial break in 9:20–32—an infomercial about Purim holiday celebrations. Finally, we discover the last three verses of the book (10:1–3) wrapping up the story and leaving us with both a sense of completion and a realization that life goes on as before in the Medo-Persian empire.

The Book of Esther could comfortably end with Esther's command in 9:32 that establishes Purim as a legal holiday for the Jews. Yet the book is not simply a polemic for Purim; it is concerned about a much larger issue—the "hidden" work of God on behalf of his people despite their spiritual condition. Thus, to highlight that larger issue, the author adds three seemingly innocuous verses that zero in on a tax, a book, and a person:

10:1—King Ahasuerus places a tax burden on all of his subjects, from the center of the empire to its widest expanse;

10:2—Mordecai's great works as prime minister can be found in *The Book of the Chronicles of the Kings of Media and Persia*; and

10:3—Mordecai, the Jew, is both famous and well liked by his people. Furthermore, he openly engages in activities that benefit them.

These three verses, however, are anything but innocuous. They invite us to reevaluate the details of the book in light of the broad thematic scope of the book. If we see them as "only a historical postscript"[1] or "an inelegant and otiose conclusion,"[2] then we will miss the author's closing comments that give final definition to all that he has previously placed before our eyes.

A Tale of Two Men

Well-written political biographies can be enlightening. Those who write them often use a variety of communicative techniques to capture the essence of the personality of the political leader under consideration. One technique is to interject at an appropriate point data about a contrasting personality or idea. The author, without comment, allows that data to speak for itself, thereby making the contrast appear as a stark reality.

The author of the Book of Esther makes use of contrastive interposition in 10:1–3 to highlight the different natures of two powerful leaders of the Medo-Persian empire: King Ahasuerus and Prime Minister Mordecai. By doing so, the author stresses the different attitudes of the two men toward the people of the empire. He pictures the former as acting as if the welfare of his people is not a top priority, the latter as demonstrating a great concern for the well-being of those people. Thus in 10:1–3, the author concludes his work with a few brief statements (outlined as follows) that capture the essential character of these two men:

A. Ahasuerus—a burden on the people (10:1)
B. Mordecai—a blessing on the people (10:2–3)

Throughout much of the book, King Ahasuerus does not appear to govern his people well. In 1:1–9 he engages in a seem-

1. Paulus Cassel, *An Explanatory Commentary on Esther*, trans. Aaron Bernstein (Edinburgh: T. and T. Clark, 1888), 257.

2. David J. A. Clines, "The Esther Scroll: The Story of the Story," *Journal for the Study of the Old Testament: Supplement* 30 (Sheffield: University of Sheffield, 1984), 59.

ingly pointless display of wealth; in 1:10–22 he permits the debacle with Vashti. In chapter 2 he is self-indulgent (vv. 1–4) and fails to reward one of his subjects properly (vv. 21–23). In chapter 3, without justification, he condemns a race of people to death and then participates in a drinking party while his people panic. At times he is oblivious to what is going on around him (6:1–10) and is easily swayed (7:1–10). He also condemns to death a large portion of his subjects (8:1–8) and shows little remorse for what he has done (9:11–14).

The author makes no evaluative comments regarding the king's actions in any of those situations. Even in 10:1 the author presents a new tax enacted by the king as a *fait accompli* and offers no comment on it. Yet the fact that he juxtaposes the statement about taxation to his concluding approbation of Mordecai suggests that the author views the king's action as being another example of the king's inability to govern well.

By contrast, throughout the book, the author usually portrays Mordecai as working for the good of his people or for the well-being of the empire (cf. 2:5–7, 21–23; 4:1–17; 8:9–17; 9:20–31). In 10:2–3, the author continues to present Mordecai in a similar positive light.

By placing these two leaders together in this fashion, the author concludes his work on a humanistically upbeat note. Although the king still rules, all will be well for the Jews because Mordecai, a Jew, wields power that can counterbalance the capriciousness of the king and thereby ensure the wise governing of the empire.

A Very Taxing Situation (10:1)

The news of 10:1 comes as a surprise: King Ahasuerus taxes his people. What is a verse about taxation doing in a book about the deliverance of the Jews? Why would the author who has so carefully scripted his book make a "mistake" at this point and insert an "irrelevant" statement of this nature into his story?

Commentators have proposed a host of ideas in an attempt to explain the author's actions as the following list (with my comments in parentheses) reveals:[3]

3. Cassel, *An Explanatory Commentary on Esther*, 258; Michael V. Fox, *Character and Ideology in the Book of Esther* (Columbia, S.C.: University of

1. to show that the fortunes of the Jews have changed to such an extent that all except the Jews are taxed (there is no indication that the Jews are not taxed);
2. to reveal the power of Mordecai—that he helped to extend the king's power over other nations (the text does not connect Mordecai with the issuing of the tax);
3. to describe the power of the king (possibly, but the author already has done that throughout the book);
4. to indicate that the king, because of his actions on behalf of the Jews, deserves to have his treasures replenished (the verse, however, makes no direct connection to the king's previous actions);
5. to parallel the Joseph story in which Joseph, after delivering the Egyptians from death (by famine), institutes a tax (Gen. 47:13–26) (again, the author does not picture Mordecai as being responsible for the tax; also there are too many differences between Joseph and Mordecai to assume the comparison [see conclusion of chap. 6, "A Death Warrant"]); and
6. to demonstrate that those who treat the Jews well realize some benefit from having done so (the king has every right to levy this tax irrespective of his earlier actions toward the Jews).

In contrast to these ideas, there is an option I would like to propose: the author includes 10:1 (as well as vv. 2–3) to suggest that life in the Medo-Persian empire goes on as it did before, that is, that the events surrounding Purim make no eternally transforming difference in the lives of the people of that day, nor do those events offer any eschatological hope for eternal deliverance.

This view fits well with the author's overall portrayal of Medo-Persian Jews as lacking in spiritual depth. There is no spiritual revival among the Jews, as might normally be expected to occur after such a deliverance. No credit is given to God for his work in

South Carolina Press, 1991), 129–30; C. F. Keil, *The Books of Ezra, Nehemiah, and Esther*, Biblical Commentary on the Old Testament, trans. Sophia Taylor (Grand Rapids: Eerdmans, n.d.), 379–80. Clines argues that an editor added these verses at a later date, but there is no evidence to support his view. Clines, "The Esther Scroll: The Story of the Story," 59.

rescuing his people. No credit, moreover, is given to God even for the conversion of Gentiles to Judaism (8:17).

This position also agrees with the author's lack of expression of any future deliverance for the Jews. A Gentile king still rules the empire; the Jews are not free. There is, moreover, no indication here that any of the Jews return to the Promised Land. Furthermore, Mordecai's work (10:2–3) does not lead the Jews any closer to that goal, nor does it draw either Jews or Gentiles to a recognition of the one true God. There is also no mention of any hope for the coming Messiah or of the prophesied messianic kingdom.

Thus the author of the Book of Esther uses 10:1 to bring the reader full circle to 1:1, that is, back to the realization that a Gentile still rules. The author, therefore, leads the reader to conclude that no permanent changes occur as a result of the human efforts of the Jews of Mordecai's and Esther's day.

In 10:1, the author declares that King Ahasuerus places a *mas* (a tax or a tribute) on his empire (lit., "on the land and the coastlands [or islands[4]] of the sea"). The Hebrew term *mas* elsewhere in the Scripture consistently conveys the meaning of conscripted labor, that is, of people who are forced to work for their government or for the government of their conquerors. The use of *mas* in verse 1 may contain such a meaning, but, as Joyce G. Baldwin points out, by the time of the Medo-Persian era, "the use of money . . . made possible taxation in coinage as well as in kind."[5] Thus, quite probably, some of those being taxed in verse 1 would pay their required taxes by giving money or goods, while others would find it necessary to work on government labor gangs to meet the newly instituted demands of King Ahasuerus.

Esther 10:1 appears to signal a transition from the period of Jewish concerns (begun with the release from a tribute—or institution of a holiday—in 2:18) to the period of Persian-

4. Although "the islands of the sea" is a possible translation of the words *ʾiyyēy hayyām*, the equally legitimate translation of "the coastlands of the sea" is to be preferred because of the historical context of the passage. Since the term *islands* can only refer to the islands of the Aegean, which Ahasuerus lost in battles during the fourth and fifth years of his reign, they would not be within his power to tax at this time. Michael Heltzer, "The Book of Esther—Where Does Fiction Start and History End?" *Bible Review* 8 (February 1992): 30.

5. Joyce G. Baldwin, *Esther: An Introduction and Commentary*, Tyndale Old Testament Commentaries, ed. D. J. Wiseman (Downers Grove: InterVarsity, 1984), 114.

empire concerns, with the Jewish question being resolved. The time of "aberration" is over; the reality of day-to-day living is now back.

Official Documentation (10:2)

In recent years, there have been a number of television docudramas that deal with a variety of social issues. Often, at the conclusion of the show, one of the actors approaches the camera and makes an announcement about other sources where additional information about the same subject matter can be found.

Likewise, the author of the Book of Esther, at the conclusion of his work, approaches his readers and indicates where further information may be found about the administrative activities of Prime Minister Mordecai.

In 10:2, the author, posing a rhetorical question, declares the effectiveness of Mordecai's efforts as second in command of the Medo-Persian empire. By doing so, the author points his readers to a source containing data regarding the events of Mordecai's administration, *The Book of the Chronicles of the Kings of Media and Persia* (cf. 2:23; 6:1; and possibly in 9:20, 32).

By means of the rhetorical question, the author conveys three points about Mordecai: "his power" *(toqpô),*[6] "his strength" *(gᵉbûrātô),*[7] and his "greatness" *(gᵉdullat).*[8]

The first two terms are synonyms. In the present context, the former may indicate a force that is inherent in a given individual

6. The term *toqep* means power, strength, or energy. It is found in the Scripture only in Esther 9:29; 10:2; and Dan. 11:17. Francis Brown, S. R. Driver, and Charles A. Briggs, *A Hebrew and English Lexicon of the Old Testament with an Appendix Containing the Biblical Aramaic* (reprint; Oxford: Clarendon, 1968), 1076; Ludwig Koehler and Walter Baumgartner, eds., *Lexicon in Veteris Testementi Libros* (Leiden: Brill, 1985), 1040.

7. The Hebrew word *gᵉbûrā(h)* has been variously translated as strength, might, valor, force, mastery, power, wisdom, weight, strong determination, strong performance, and success. Brown, Driver, and Briggs, *A Hebrew and English Lexicon of the Old Testament*, 150; Robert Baker Girdlestone, *Synonyms of the Old Testament: Their Bearing on Christian Doctrine,* 2d ed. (reprint; Grand Rapids: Eerdmans, n.d.), 54; Koehler and Baumgartner, *Lexicon in Veteris Testementi Libros*, 165.

8. The lexical definition of *gᵉdûlla(h)* is simply "greatness." This is a generic term. Brown, Driver, and Briggs, *A Hebrew and English Lexicon of the Old Testament*, 153.

or in an individual's position in life; the latter may focus on the strength that an individual manifests through actions. If this distinction holds true, then the author indicates that contained in the official state records is information concerning Mordecai's accomplishments as a result of the authority he exercises as prime minister and as a result of his personal power.

The third point the author makes in this verse is that *The Book of the Chronicles of the Kings of Media and Persia* includes a full account (lit., an exact statement) of the greatness that Mordecai achieves as a result of being promoted[9] to the position of prime minister by the king. The author makes no attempt to identify specifically what Mordecai accomplishes, but leaves the impression that everything that the official documents contain regarding Mordecai's administration is positive.

The Power (of Concern) behind the Throne (10:3)

There is no pompous fanfare in 10:3 or anywhere in the Book of Esther regarding the exalted position to which Mordecai attains. He is declared simply to be "Mordecai the Jew" (a reference to his heritage) who is "second *in command* to King Ahasuerus" (a reference to his position).

Is Mordecai's promotion an indication of God's hand of blessing on his life as it was when other believers in various states of exile occupied positions of high command—for example, Joseph (Gen. 41:38–45), Nehemiah (Neh. 1:11–2:1), and Daniel (Dan. 2:46–49)? The significant difference between Mordecai and those other men is that those men praise God openly before heathen rulers and turn to God for guidance in their difficult situations, whereas Mordecai never does so in the records of Scripture. Mordecai's promotion, therefore, may be understood to be another act of God's kindness to his people, even when they are not boldly committed to serving him in public.

The author continues by recording that Mordecai both attains a high status among his people and gains their admiration: liter-

9. The precise phrase *ʾăšer gidd^elô hammelek* (to which the king advanced him [i.e., Mordecai]) also occurs in connection with Haman in 5:11. See also 3:1 for a similar expression.

ally, Mordecai "is great to [for] the Jews and he was favored by [acceptable to] the multitude of his kinsmen [brothers]."

In addition, the author portrays Mordecai as acting aggressively to ensure that his people, the Jews, experience the good things of life.[10] The author also notes that Mordecai speaks out for the *šālôm* of his entire nation. The term *šālôm*, often translated "peace," also contains within it the following positive traits that perhaps more accurately reflect the author's intent here in 10:3: wholeness, completeness, harmony, prosperity, health, welfare, security, fulfillment, material well-being, and good relationships.[11]

Curiously, when the author states that Mordecai "spoke for the welfare of his whole nation," the author records the term *zarʿô* (his seed). Thus the author suggests that the focus of Mordecai's interest is not primarily on the well-being of the empire, but on the well-being of those who are of his same bloodlines, the Jews.[12]

At this point, following the end of the Hebrew text, the Septuagint adds approximately ten verses. Those verses present Mordecai's supposed remembrance of the dream / vision that he supposedly had prior to 1:1 together with Mordecai's thoughts on the interpretation of that dream / vision.[13] The Greek translation also affixes to the end of the entire book a brief passage noting the date and identifying the translator of the Hebrew text into the Greek version. There are, however, no ancient Hebrew manuscripts that support either of those additions.

A Lot in a Little Space

Packing a suitcase is a skill—at least packing it so that everything fits tightly without the clothes being in a jumbled mess.

10. The author does not indicate that Mordecai in any way seeks self-aggrandizement. Mordecai's primary focus (and commendably so) is on the well-being of his people.

11. Baldwin, *Esther: An Introduction and Commentary*, 115; F. B. Huey, Jr., "Esther," *Expositor's Bible Commentary*, ed. Frank E. Gaebelein, 12 vols. (Grand Rapids: Zondervan, 1988), 4:839.

12. Technically, the term *zarʿô* (his seed) could refer to Mordecai's personal offspring, but the context of the passage drives the reader to the broader application of the term.

13. See the discussion of Esther 3:13 for a listing of the major additions to the Hebrew text of the Book of Esther as found in the Septuagint.

The author of the Book of Esther demonstrates his skill of content packing as he properly fits many important points into the final three verses of the book.

When we first step into 10:1–3 we do not expect much, but as we study them we realize that they convey a tremendous amount of information. Along with that information, we discover five principles for life—some of which are obvious, some of which require a little more digging:

1. God's people can work effectively in the world. There is not necessarily a conflict between being a child of God and doing excellent work in a secular position.
2. Promotions to positions of power do not necessarily cause individuals to forsake their roots. Individuals may exercise power wisely not only to accomplish their organization's goals but also to benefit their own people.
3. Powerful people are able to achieve much. In 10:1 the king affects the entire empire by exercising his power to levy a tax. In addition, Mordecai (10:2–3) and Haman (3:8–15) demonstrate this truth. Both make a major impact on the people of Medo-Persia. The former works for the good of the people, the latter for their detriment.
4. Being in power does not automatically or even necessarily corrupt one or make one proud. Power may have corrupted Haman (3:1–15; 5:9–14), but it does not appear to affect Mordecai adversely.
5. People recognize and appreciate true compassion in their leaders (10:3).

All's Well That Ends Well . . . Perhaps, Perhaps Not

In the theater, players come and go. They are on the stage for a short while and then they are gone. Few remain to the end of the play.

The end of the Book of Esther has come. Most of the players have already left the stage. Queen Vashti departs early, as do many other minor characters. Of the main characters (Ahasuerus, Mordecai, Esther, and Haman—listed in order of appearance), Haman exits first, leaving in dramatic fashion (7:10). Esther departs next, exiting after having issued a popular command (9:32). Nothing more of greatness is expected from her as she returns to her life as queen of the Medo-Persian empire. Finally, only King Ahasuerus and Prime Minister Mordecai remain on the stage. As the curtain closes on the Book of Esther, King Ahasuerus is pictured as levying a tax on his people. Mordecai, by contrast, is portrayed as serving his empire and particularly his own people very well.

The final three verses—in fact the final four verses (9:32–10:3)—are a fitting conclusion to the Book of Esther. The book reveals a Gentile-ruled, non-God-fearing empire in which the people of God, the Jews, live but on which they have little or no lasting impact. The book also presents Esther and Mordecai, the heroes of the Jewish people, as woefully lacking in any spiritual dynamic. The conclusion of the book does nothing to alter the portrait of the people of God painted by the author in the earlier portions of the book. Although the final verses end on an upbeat note by picturing the well-being of the people of God, they do not offer any suggestion of a spiritual transformation in the hearts and lives of those people. All is not well, because in the Book of Esther all does not end well. God's people are physically comfortable, but they are not spiritually committed.

The storybook of Esther is finished. Yet, there is one more chapter to this commentary—a chapter that is designed to provide basic answers to the following important questions concerning the Book of Esther:

1. If Esther, Mordecai, and the rest of the Jews are not serving God, then why was the Book of Esther written?
2. What is the overall assessment of the lives of Esther and Mordecai? In what ways should we emulate their lives?
3. What is the structure of the entire book? What does that structure contribute to an understanding of the Book of Esther?
4. What is the overall message of the Book of Esther and what are some of the key points that we can learn from the lives of the people that we encounter in it?
5. What comparisons can be made between Haman and Mordecai? If Mordecai is unspiritual, does he act any differently from Haman, who also lacks a spiritual dimension?

6. In what ways does the Book of Esther parallel or differ from the Book of Ruth—the only other book in Scripture named after a woman?
7. Why is God's name missing from the pages of the Book of Esther?

Thus the final chapter of this commentary—"The Choreography of the Creator"—looks at important issues that should be of interest to the reader of the Book of Esther.

22

The Choreography of the Creator

Historically accurate, the Book of Esther presents a brief look at a sometimes tense, sometimes humorous slice of Jewish life in ancient Medo-Persia. The author portrays the Jews, the people of God, in times of life-threatening crises and in times of joyful exuberance. Yet, never does he record that the people of God seek God's help in their difficulties and never once does he write that they praise him for delivering them from those difficulties. The existence of these anomalies, in light of the rest of Scripture, gives rise to a host of questions. Some of those questions are treated subsequently.

Question 1—If Esther, Mordecai, and the rest of the Jews are not serving God, then why was the Book of Esther written?

Three explanations are highlighted:

1. The book pictures God's providential care over those who exhibit no demonstrable interest in him and who thus are undeserving of his work on their behalf. The fact that God providentially acts to protect and deliver such undeserving people from their enemies makes his

actions appear to be far greater than they would appear if he were acting on behalf of those who served him faithfully.

2. The Word of God portrays the people of God in a wide variety of spiritual conditions—everything from godliness to open sinfulness to apathy. In the scheme of the Scripture, the Book of Esther focuses its attention on one slice of that spiritual spectrum. It shows the depth of the spiritual morass into which the Jews had stumbled. The book paints no spiritual ideal; it does, however, picture one way that God deals with his people when they are not in a right relationship with him.
3. Some people suggest that the book should not be included in the Scripture because it portrays the people of God in a less-than-perfect spiritual condition. If such a standard were the criterion for inclusion or exclusion from the Scripture, then the entirety of the Scriptures would be shortened dramatically. Every place in Scripture in which people sinned intentionally, allied themselves with the enemies of God out of fear, fell short of God's standards, acted sinfully because of improper habits, insulated themselves from the will of God, or were apathetic toward God would be expunged as being unworthy of inclusion. Yet, God has chosen to draw in the Scripture an accurate picture of the history of his people by portraying both their faithful and their unfaithful acts—the Book of Esther being an extended example of the latter.

Question 2—What is the overall assessment of the lives of Esther and Mordecai? In what ways should we emulate their lives?

Both Esther and Mordecai should be considered as heroes of the Jewish people. They responded to the needs of their brothers and sisters who were facing extinction and worked carefully, boldly, wisely (shrewdly) to achieve their liberation and advancement. Esther and Mordecai were tenacious in these efforts, placing the needs of others before their own needs. Furthermore, with certain caveats, Esther and Mordecai demonstrated good family relations. Thus in these and in certain other areas Esther and Mordecai should be emulated.

Should Mordecai and Esther, however, be considered spiritual giants of the faith? Probably not. Too many elements of the story show that they do not appear to be taking a strong stand for God. The author, in fact, presents a complete absence of spiritual terms and practices in conjunction with either Mordecai or Esther. Their spirituality, if it existed at all, was well hidden.

Should people today name their sons after Mordecai or their daughters after Esther? Of course. Those are names that were held by two individuals who demonstrated courage under fire, who tenaciously maintained their convictions, and who risked their lives for the sake of their people. Other names throughout Scripture, however, might be better used by parents who desire their children to have the same names as biblical characters who were openly committed both to God and to the people of God.

Question 3—What is the structure of the entire book? What does that structure contribute to an understanding of the Book of Esther?

The author designed the Book of Esther according to an overall chiastic structure. He did so in order to highlight the desperate condition of the Jewish people and to show that they, because they exhibit no spiritual commitment to God, had no true hope for success apart from God's providential care of their lives. The chiastic structure of the Book of Esther appears as follows:

- A All is well in a great empire (1:1)
  - B A feast of joy in an empire at peace (1:2–9)
    - C An empire-wide crisis (1:10–22)
      - D The elevation of Jews to power and prominence (2:1–23)
        - E An interpersonal crisis resulting in an empire-wide edict of death (3:1–15)
          - F A time of mourning (4:1–17)
            - G An honor that is tainted by mixed motives (5:1–8)
              - H The peak of Gentile

rule over the people of God (5:9–14)

G′ An honor that is tainted by mixed motives (6:1–11)

F′ A time of mourning (6:12–14)

E′ An interpersonal crisis resulting in an empire-wide edict of death (7:1–8:14)

D′ The elevation of Jews to power and prominence (8:15–17)

C′ An empire-wide crisis (9:1–19)

B′ A feast of joy in an empire at peace (9:20–32)

A′ All is well in a great empire (10:1–3)[1]

By using this chiastic structure, the author implies that the focus of the book is not to be found in the self-preservation activities of the Jews. True, the Jews acted in ways that seemingly secured their release, but the author records those actions as being far less significant than the actions of the hidden God. The Jews merely reacted to the works of the Gentiles; God, however, anticipated those potentially devastating works and brought into existence "coincidences" that effectively thwarted Gentile hopes. Thus, by means of this chiastic structure, the author emphasizes the hopeless, earth-bound condition of God's people as they found themselves at odds with the then greatest superpower of the world. He, therefore, draws attention to God as the great deliverer of his people.

Question 4—What is the overall message of the Book of Esther and what are some of the key points that we can learn from the lives of the people that we encounter in it?

Overall message: God works providentially on behalf of his people despite their spiritual condition. God is actively involved in their lives, even when he is not seen to intervene directly on their behalf, for example, at those times when he is not generating new Scripture, performing miracles, speaking through the spiritual leaders of his people, or manifesting himself personally.

1. As can be seen, the seemingly extraneous chapter 10 plays a vital role in the completion of the literary structure of the Book of Esther. That chapter brings closure to a well-written book that consistently pictures the Jews of Medo-Persia as being less than spiritual.

Important points:

1. Humans do have a hand in shaping their destinies. God, however, can override human action for the benefit or disadvantage of humans.
2. The power of this world (real as it is) is no more than a mere veneer. God lifts up people to positions of power and removes them just as easily.
3. Being a child of God does not guarantee a life of comfort and ease, especially if that person is not serving God faithfully.
4. True and lasting wisdom does not come from human sources.
5. The people of God can work effectively in the midst of a world of nonbelievers.
6. Pride and self-aggrandizement are unstable foundations on which to build an organization.
7. The actions of one individual can have far-reaching effects.
8. The people of God who are out of the will of God do not automatically turn to God in the midst of crises. Often they seek to resolve their problems by themselves.
9. Small irritants can blind one from the major joys and triumphs of life.
10. One's true character shows through during times of crises.
11. Being at odds with those in positions of power can be extremely dangerous. Thus appropriate and meaningful steps need to be taken to develop proper working relations with those who are powerful individuals.
12. Power used wisely can achieve much good; conversely, power used improperly can do much damage.
13. God's people should never quit when pursuing a worthwhile goal since he may transform the situation to their advantage with the next action that they take.
14. God's justice will ultimately be achieved.

Question 5—What comparisons can be made between Haman and Mordecai? If Mordecai is unspiritual, does he act any differently from Haman, who also lacks a spiritual dimension?

Jonathan Magonet argues that "Haman is nothing more than the alternative face of Mordecai, a distorted reflection of the same character. The two are brothers under the skin. . . ."[2] To some extent, Magonet is correct—there are similarities between the two antagonists. There are, however, significant differences in the way the two individuals think and act. The following highlights some of those similarities and differences.

Both Haman and Mordecai

1. were outsiders, that is, non-Persians (2:5; 3:1);
2. rose to prominence, to the second position in the land, yet no reasons were specified as to why either was placed in the role of prime minister (3:1; 8:2);
3. ruled with a strong hand (3:8–15; 8:9–14; 10:2–3);
4. exerted great influence over the king (3:8–11; 10:2–3);
5. interacted extensively with a woman and at times followed the advice of that woman—Haman's wife in Haman's case and Esther in Mordecai's case (4:16; 5:14);
6. despised each other; in fact what brought them together was their hatred for each other (3:2–6; 5:9);
7. did not show compassion for any of their enemies—Haman toward the Jews and Mordecai toward the enemies of the Jews (3:5–15; 8:8–14); and
8. feasted after their respective triumphs—Haman with the king and Mordecai with the Jews (3:15; 8:17; 9:16–23).

Mordecai and Haman, however, part company in the following ways:

1. Haman sought the destruction of the Jews (3:8–15), whereas Mordecai sought their deliverance by means of the destruction of others (8:9–14).
2. Haman brought confusion to the empire by means of an unjust law (3:15), whereas Mordecai brought harmony to much of the empire through the promulgation of a law designed to rectify Haman's unjust law (8:9–17) and through his manner of governing the empire (10:2–3).

2. Jonathan Magonet, "The Liberal and the Lady: Esther Revisited," *Judaism* 29 (spring 1980): 175.

3. Haman was filled with pride and acted in a boastful manner (5:11–12); Mordecai, by contrast, acted with humility (6:12) and did not boast of his great deeds.
4. Haman was humiliated and defeated (6:10–12; 7:6–10); Mordecai received honor and was victorious (6:10–12; 8:15–9:19).

Question 6—In what ways does the Book of Esther parallel or differ from the Book of Ruth—the only other book in Scripture named after a woman?

A comparison between the books of Ruth and Esther reveals a strong spiritual dynamic in the Book of Ruth, but discovers a void of spiritual character in the Book of Esther. What follows are the more significant comparisons between the two books.

Similarities

1. Both stories are presented as being accurate representations of historical events.
2. A mixed nationality wedding plays an important function in each story.
3. The Gentile partner in the marriage has been previously married (Ruth was widowed, King Ahasuerus divorced).
4. Women play prominent roles in each story.
5. The primary female character in each story marries a prominent man who is significantly more well-off than she is.
6. The women are urged by their Jewish relatives (Ruth by Naomi and Esther by Mordecai) to do everything they can to marry the man whom they ultimately marry. Those relatives, moreover, exert a significant influence on the heroine of their respective stories, particularly in the earlier stages of those two stories.
7. The lead women are most closely identified with individuals who are not part of their natural family but who are related by legal ties (Ruth with her mother-in-law, Naomi, and Esther with her adoptive father, Mordecai).
8. The two women are effective communicators who demonstrate a growing level of maturity as the story unfolds.

9. The heroine in each story creatively seeks help from a man (her husband-to-be, in the case of Ruth, and her husband, in the case of Esther) to deal with a problem that seemingly he alone can resolve.
10. Their problems are resolved by resorting to certain prescribed practices (to the cultural traditions of the semi-Levirate activities in the Book of Ruth and to legal procedures of the law of the Medes and Persians in the Book of Esther).
11. The majority of the story takes place within a relatively short period of time in the history of Israel.
12. The primary problems of the two stories occur when the main characters are not living in the land of Israel.
13. Both stories involve times of mourning and times of celebration for the people of God.
14. God is not pictured as taking direct action in either story but is understood to work providentially behind the scenes to accomplish his ends.

Differences

	The Book of Ruth	*The Book of Esther*
1.	Occurs primarily in Israel	Occurs entirely in exile in Medo-Persia
2.	Female Gentile convert to Judaism marries Jew—marries into the faith	Female Jewess marries Gentile—marries out of the faith
3.	Story takes place at the personal level	Story takes place at the political or national level
4.	The author includes much character development in the story	The author spends little time in the development of characters or in the presentation of motives
5.	Tragedy strikes only at the beginning of the story	Tragedy occurs throughout most of the story
6.	Tragedy plays a minor role in the story	Tragedy is central to the story

7.	The story begins with Jews and focuses on those who are of the faith	The story begins with Gentiles and emphasizes Jewish-Gentile relations
8.	The story ends on a spiritual note	The story ends on a political note
9.	God blesses Ruth and Boaz with a child	No child is born to Esther and Ahasuerus
10.	God's name is prominent	God's name is never directly mentioned
11.	People are openly conscious of God's involvement in their lives	No religious concerns are expressed, not even praise to God for deliverance from destruction
12.	The leading Jewish character of the story (Boaz) is seen to exhibit admirable spiritual traits	The leading Jewish characters of the story (Esther and Mordecai) are seen to exhibit no spiritual concerns whatsoever

Question 7—Why is God's name missing from the pages of the Book of Esther?

There is no direct revelation as to why God's name is not mentioned in the Book of Esther. As a result, there has been much speculation regarding that enigma.

Three less-than-satisfying explanations for the lack of any reference to God have found some supporters over the years:

1. the belief that the author feared that, because the Jews were living in exile at the time of the writing of the book, their Persian captors would translate the book into one or more of the languages of the empire and, by so doing, would desecrate the name of God;
2. the belief that the author (who was writing the book to be read during the Purim holiday) was concerned that the Jews who celebrated the days of Purim with much drinking would in their drunken state inadvertently take God's

name in vain when the scroll of Esther was being read; and
3. the belief that the author wanted to picture the one and only time in Jewish history when the Jews, on their own (without God's help), secured their own deliverance from their enemies.

The first suggestion falters because other books of the Scripture which were written while the Jews were in exile contain the name of God.

The second possibility falls short because there is no indication that the Book of Esther, in fact, was written to be read at Purim. Furthermore, if such a view were correct, it would pose a serious challenge to the divine inspiration of the Book of Esther by raising the question as to whether the Holy Spirit could rightly be expected to author a book designed with the specific purpose of being read by those who are inebriated.

The third option, if true, would alter the purpose of the Book of Esther 180 degrees from that which is proposed in this commentary and that which has been held by believers throughout the centuries, namely, that God himself worked providentially to deliver the Jews. The numerous "coincidences" and the timing of those "coincidences" as recorded in the Book of Esther strongly suggest God's handiwork on behalf of the Jews.

The lack of any mention of God's name in the Book of Esther seems to indicate that the people of God did not have a proper relationship with their God. They did not honor, praise, or turn to him at any time in the book. Their actions, moreover, were, at times, suspect and devoid of spiritual consideration. Thus, by intentionally failing to include the name of God in the Book of Esther, the author depicts the people of God as being far removed from their true Deliverer.

Complete Confidence

What should readers derive from a reading of the Book of Esther? If nothing else, they should come to the realization that God cares far more for his people than his people will ever know. He cares about them when they are in trouble; he cares about them even when they do not know that he is there; and he even cares about them when they have little or no interest in him.

The Book of Esther, therefore, should be read during this present age. The book particularly should be read by God's people when they perceive him to be silent or distant, or when they conceive of themselves as being exiles in the midst of a world that shows little or no interest in God or in spiritual things. The book when read under such circumstances would be an encouragement to God's people to know that he is more than capable of providing for them and that he is a God who can and does work wonders.

By reading the Book of Esther, God's people should come to recognize that there truly is a *God behind the seen.* They then should live with complete confidence, knowing that their lives are not at the sole mercy of the whims of the world but are silently and perfectly being directed by the careful choreography of the Creator.

Select Bibliography on Esther

Ackroyd, Peter R. "Two Hebrew Notes." *Annual of the Swedish Theological Institute* 5 (1967): 82–86.

Baldwin, Joyce G. *Esther.* The New Bible Commentary. 3d ed. Edited by D. Guthrie and J. A. Motyer. Grand Rapids: Eerdmans, 1970.

———. *Esther: An Introduction and Commentary.* Tyndale Old Testament Commentaries. Edited by D. J. Wiseman. Downers Grove: InterVarsity, 1984.

Berg, Sandra Beth. "After the Exile: God and History in the Books of Chronicles and Esther." In *The Divine Helmsman: Studies on God's Control of Human Events, Presented to Lou H. Silberman,* edited by James L. Crenshaw and Samuel Sandmel, 107–27. New York: KTAV, 1980.

———. *The Book of Esther: Motifs, Themes and Structure.* Missoula, Mont.: Scholars, 1979.

Bickerman, Elias. *Four Strange Books of the Bible: Jonah / Daniel / Koheleth / Esther.* New York: Schocken, 1967.

Cassel, Paulus. *An Explanatory Commentary on Esther.* Translated by Aaron Bernstein. Edinburgh: T. and T. Clark, 1888.

Clines, David J. A. "The Esther Scroll: The Story of the Story." *Journal for the Study of the Old Testament: Supplement* 30. Sheffield: University of Sheffield, 1984.

Cohen, Abraham D. "'Hu Ha-goral': The Religious Significance of Esther." *Judaism* 23 (winter 1974): 87–94.

Fox, Michael V. *Character and Ideology in the Book of Esther.* Columbia, S.C.: University of South Carolina Press, 1991.

Gordis, Robert. "Religion, Wisdom and History in the Book of Esther—A New Solution to an Ancient Crux." *Journal of Biblical Literature* 100 (September 1981): 359–88.

———. "Studies in the Esther Narrative." *Journal of Biblical Literature* 95 (March 1976): 43–58.

Harris, Monford. "Purim: The Celebration of Dis-Order." *Judaism* 26 (spring 1977): 161–70.

Huey, F. B., Jr. "Esther," in *Expositor's Bible Commentary,* 12 vols., edited by Frank E. Gaebelein. Vol. 4. Grand Rapids: Zondervan, 1988.

Humphreys, W. Lee. "The Story of Esther and Mordecai: An Early Jewish Novella." In *Saga, Legend, Fable, Tale, Novella: Narrative Forms in Old Testament Literature. Journal for the Study of the Old Testament: Supplement* 35, 97–113, 149–50, edited by George W. Coats. Sheffield: University of Sheffield, 1985.

Ironside, H. A. *Notes on the Book of Esther.* New York: Loizeaux, 1921.

Jones, Bruce W. "Two Misconceptions about the Book of Esther." *Catholic Biblical Quarterly* 39 (April 1977): 171–81.

Keil, C. F. *The Books of Ezra, Nehemiah, and Esther.* Biblical Commentary on the Old Testament. Translated by Sophia Taylor. Grand Rapids: Eerdmans, n.d.

Magonet, Jonathan. "The Liberal and the Lady: Esther Revisited." *Judaism* 29 (spring 1980): 167–76.

Moore, Carey A. "Archaeology and the Book of Esther." *Biblical Archaeologist* 38 (1975): 62–79.

_______. "Eight Questions Most Frequently Asked about the Book of Esther." *Bible Review* 3 (spring 1987): 16–31.

_______. *Esther.* The Anchor Bible. Edited by William Foxwell Albright and David Noel Freedman. Garden City, N.Y.: Doubleday, 1971.

Moore, Carey A., ed. *Studies in the Book of Esther.* New York: KTAV, 1982.

Murphy, Roland E. *Wisdom Literature: Job, Proverbs, Ruth, Canticles, Ecclesiastes, and Esther.* In *The Forms of the Old Testament Literature* 13, edited by Rolf Knierim and Gene M. Tucker. Grand Rapids: Eerdmans, 1981.

Paton, Lewis Bayles. *The Book of Esther.* International Critical Commentary. Edited by Samuel Rolles Driver, Alfred Plummer, and Charles Augustus Briggs. Edinburgh: T. and T. Clark, 1908.

Pierce, Ronald W. "The Politics of Esther and Mordecai: Courage or Compromise?" *Bulletin for Biblical Research* 2 (1992): 75–89.

Radday, Yehuda T. "Chiasm in Joshua, Judges and Others." *Linguistica Biblica* 3 (1973): 6–13.

_______. "Esther with Humor." In *On Humor and the Comic in the Hebrew Bible*, edited by Yehuda T. Radday and Athalya Brenner, 295–313. Sheffield: Almond, 1990.

Sabua, Rachel B. K. "The Hidden Hand of God." *Bible Review* 8 (February 1992): 31–33.

Strassfeld, Michael. *The Jewish Holidays: A Guide and Commentary*. New York: Harper and Row, 1985.

Talmon, S[hemaryahu]. "Wisdom in the Book of Esther." *Vetus Testamentum* 13 (1963): 419–55.

Vos, Howard F. *Ezra, Nehemiah, and Esther*. Bible Study Commentary. Grand Rapids: Lamplighter, 1987.

Zadok, Ran. "Notes on Esther." *Zeitschrift für die alttestamentliche Wissenschaft* 98 (1986): 105–10.

Zlotowitz, Meir, trans. and comp. *The Megillah: The Book of Esther: A New Translation with a Commentary Anthologized from Talmudic, Midrashic and Rabbinic Sources*. Brooklyn: Mesorah, 1981.

Joshua

No Falling Words

Dale Ralph Davis

Readable, Reliable, Relevant
– that's the 3 'R's' of Focus on the Bible

'A happy blend of exegetical and historical study on the one hand, and homiletical treatment and application on the other. Ideas pop out everywhere, even in the most unlikely places. New insights abound. No one who reads this book will ever find Joshua dull and tedious again.'
Richard A. Bodey
Formerly Professor of Homiletics
Trinity Evangelical Divinity School

THIS EXPOSITION is rooted first in a thorough analysis of the Hebrew text, employing helpful insights from archaeology and linguistics, and second in the major theological and literary themes discovered in each section. Finally the author brings the fragments together in an expository treatment 'that is not ashamed to stoop to the level of application'.

DALE RALPH DAVIS was formerly Professor of Old Testament at Reformed Theological Seminary, Jackson, MS, and is currently pastor of Woodland Presbyterian Church, Hattiesburg, MS.

ISBN 1 85792 602 1

Judges

Such a Great Salvation

Dale Ralph Davis

Readable, Reliable, Relevant
– that's the 3 'R's' of Focus on the Bible

'an excellent, crisp and lively exposition on Judges' **Bibliotheca Sacra**

'Dr. Davis has a great sense of fun. He must often have his class or his congregation in stitches!' **Christian Arena**

THE CHURCH HAS A PROBLEM WITH JUDGES; it is so earthy, puzzling, primitive and violent - so much so that the Church can barely stomach it. To many it falls under the category of 'embarrassing scripture'. Such an attitude is, of course, wrong - so Ralph Davis here makes Judges digestible by analysing the major literary and theological themes discovered in each section. He provides a 'theocentric' exposition that rings with practical relevance.

About Ralph Davis' other books

'presents historical and theological material in a way that can only excite the expositor.' **Warren Wiersbe**

'a great feast of biblical truth made so digestible, garnished with so many apt illustrations.' **Alec Motyer**

ISBN 1 85792 578 5

1st Samuel

Looking on the Heart

Dale Ralph Davis

Dale Ralph Davis has developed a reputation as someone who is able to communicate the meaning of biblical texts with a freshness that does not compromise the content. That he has managed to do this is an achievement in itself, that he has managed it in a popular commentary is exciting!

'Many preachers are aware of the relative scarcity of reliable commentaries on the Old Testament books. It is therefore a joy to welcome this volume, which is both readable and theologically reliable. It is excellent and highly recommended.'

Evangelical Times

Comments about Ralph Davis' commentaries in this series

'an excellent... crisp, lively... exposition'

Bibliotheca Sacra

'the most practical expository work that this reviewer has ever encountered.'

Southwestern Journal of Theology

ISBN 1 85792 516 5

2 Samuel

Out of Every Adversity

Dale Ralph Davis

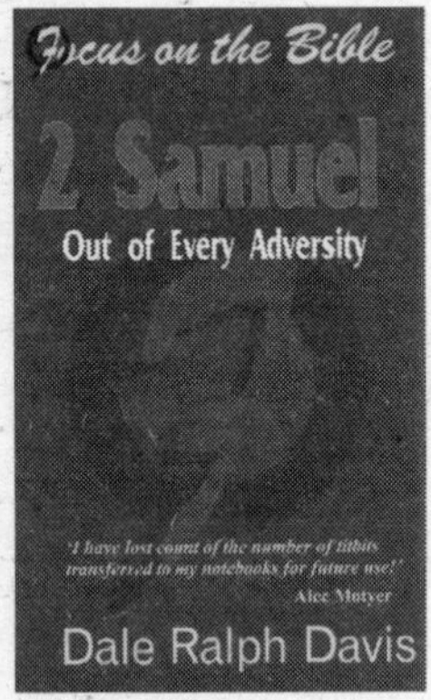

The life of Israel, and David in particular, have obvious modern parallels. Dale Ralph Davis writes with a pastor's heart and the brain of a respected theologian specialising in Old Testament texts.

'I have lost count of the times I stopped reading to pray and praise – and I have certainly lost count of the number of tit-bits transferred to my note-books for future use!'

Alec Motyer

'Dr Ralph Davis' exposition of 2 Samuel has been eagerly awaited and does not disappoint. As with his earlier work this volume stands out first for its excellent Biblical Theology, so that 2 Samuel is seen in the whole sweep of salvation history leading to Christ. Secondly, although the focus is firmly on Jesus, Dr Davis' careful scholarship and examination of the text means that each chapter produces its own fresh message. Thirdly, Dr Davis' lively style and homely illustrations make it a delight to read and a mine for preachers. I cannot recommend it too highly.'

Jonathan Fletcher

'This is no ordinary commentary but an exposure of the very heart and soul of a Biblical book. All this is done with such scholarship, such insight, such verve and with such a unique style that the book is compelling reading.'

Geoffrey Grogan

ISBN 1 85792 335 9

Christian Focus Publications

publishes books for all ages

Our mission statement –

STAYING FAITHFUL
In dependence upon God we seek to help make His infallible word, the Bible, relevant. Our aim is to ensure that the Lord Jesus Christ is presented as the only hope to obtain forgiveness of sin, live a useful life and look forward to heaven with Him.

REACHING OUT
Christ's last command requires us to reach out to our world with His gospel. We seek to help fulfill that by publishing books that point people towards Jesus and help them to develop a Christ-like maturity. We aim to equip all levels of readers for life, work, ministry and mission.

Books in our adult range are published in three imprints.

Christian Focus contains popular works including biographies, commentaries, basic doctrine, and Christian living. Our children's books are also published in this imprint.

Mentor focuses on books written at a level suitable for Bible College and seminary students, pastors, and other serious readers. The imprint includes commentaries, doctrinal studies, examination of current issues, and church history.

Christian Heritage contains classic writings from the past.

The Wisdom and the Folly

An Exposition of the Book of First Kings

Dale Ralph Davis

'The range of scholarship is extraordinary (is there any learned book or paper on First Kings that this writer has not winkled out?), His humour and humanity, plus a priceless American-style turn of phrase, add relish to the dish. Here is a safe and strong pair of hands to guide new, and older, readers through the treasure – and the uninspiring bits – of First Kings.'

Dick Lucas

'Robust – that's the word ...a robust understanding, defence, explanation and application of First Kings as the Word of God. Here is no "First Kings in my own words" – the boring, fruitless fate of most commentaries on Bible History – but a delicious feast of truth, proof that the ancients were right to call the historians "prophets".'

Alec Motyer

'...this exposition enables the contemporary reader to breathe the air of 1 Kings, re-live its challenges, and above all, to encounter the personally the God who speaks and acts throughout its pages. This is a book to unsettle spiritual complacency and challenge us to a deep integrity in our relationship with the living God.'

David Jackman

ISBN 1 85792 703 6